SOUTHEAST ASIAN ANTHROPOLOGIES

SOUTHEAST ASIAN ANTHROPOLOGIES
National Traditions and Transnational Practices

Edited by
Eric C. Thompson and Vineeta Sinha

NUS PRESS
SINGAPORE

Published by:

NUS Press
National University of Singapore
AS3-01-02, 3 Arts Link
Singapore 117569

Fax: (65) 6774-0652
E-mail: nusbooks@nus.edu.sg
Website: http://nuspress.nus.edu.sg

ISBN 978-981-4722-96-4 (paper)

National Library Board, Singapore Cataloguing in Publication Data

Name(s): Thompson, Eric C., editor. | Sinha, Vineeta, editor.
Title: Southeast Asian anthropologies: national traditions and transnational practices / edited by Eric C. Thompson and Vineeta Sinha.
Description: Singapore: NUS Press, [2019] | Includes bibliographical references and index.
Identifier(s): OCN 1079501537 | ISBN 978-981-4722-96-4 (paperback)
Subject(s): LCSH: Anthropology--Southeast Asia. | Anthropology--Southeast Asia--History.
Classification: DDC 301.0959--dc23

Cover Photo: Pattana Kitiarsa, in the field, interviewing his Isan compatriot Srisomporn Sa-nga Sungnern.

Photo Credit: Jaruwat Nonthachai, from the personal collection of Rungnapa Kitiarsa, used with permission.

Printed by: Ho Printing Singapore Pte Ltd

In memory of

Ananda Rajah (1952–2007)

and

Pattana Kitiarsa (1968–2013)

who led the way.

Contents

Preface

The contributions to this volume reflect ongoing endeavors in the making of Southeast Asian anthropologies. The specific project from which this compilation derives was funded by a grant on "Southeast Asian Anthropologies" from the National University of Singapore (R-111-000-134-112). More broadly over several decades, through research, writing and other professional activities, the editors of this volume along with other colleagues in Singapore and from around the region, including the contributors to this volume, have been engaged in ongoing activities to reconfigure and construct anthropologies of and in Southeast Asia. This book takes stock of some, but far from all, of these labors.

In October 2014, it was our pleasure to host more than a dozen scholars from across the region at the National University of Singapore, including amongst them a range of senior to mid career and early career anthropologists. Scholars attending the workshop included Chivoin Peou, Dang Nguyen Anh, Dave Lumenta, Emma Porio, Eric C. Thompson, Jowel Canuday, Nguyen Van Chinh, Noritah Omar, Ratana Tosakul, Roxana Waterson, Vineeta Sinha, Wan Zawawi Ibrahim and Yeoh Seng Guan. In addition, Maria Mangahas and Nico Warouw contributed papers to the workshop for discussion, though they were not able to attend due to scheduling conflicts. We also note that most but not all of these scholars identify primarily as anthropologists; though all are professionally engaged with anthropology and/or social sciences aligned with the rubric of anthropology. Our university hosts many research workshops and meetings, and the editors of this volume attend dozens of workshops and seminars every year and are involved in organizing at least half a dozen or more, in large and small ways. Yet this workshop was special.

It began as the spark of an idea to bring practicing anthropologists from across the Southeast Asia region together and into conversation with each other. The chapters of the book were originally commissioned as papers for the workshop, and ultimately this publication has materialized, with selected practicing anthropologists invited to write about current trends and developments within their own communities of practice. The result, we hoped, would be a productive dialogue on the development of the discipline in various national contexts and discussions on the transnational linkages that exist or could be forged across and amongst these traditions. The outcome has exceeded our highest expectations. Due to the enthusiasm and thoughtfulness of those attending, we were privileged to be a part of two days of intense, often light-hearted, and consistently collegial discussion of anthropology as conceptualized and practiced across the great diversity of Southeast Asian nations. For various reasons, not every paper presented at the workshop could make it into the current volume. But we are happy to be able to include the chapter by Yunita Winarto and Iwan Pirous, not originally a part of our conference, but first presented much earlier in December 2008 at a conference on "The Asia Pacific and the Emerging World System," Ritsumaikan Asia Pacific University, Beppu, Japan.

We hope that the publication of this collection will render increasingly visible the development, trends and paradigms of Southeast Asian anthropologies; first and foremost for scholars working within each of these traditions and second to those working in parallel anthropological traditions across the region. It is not possible for us to reproduce in all their detail the stimulating discussions of the October 2014 workshop. We were impressed by the insightful and sometimes surprising ways in which experiences of practicing anthropologists from the diverse and often very different national perspectives spoke to and aligned with each other. Parallels were drawn and discussed, for example, between the institutional and political landscapes of Malaysia and Vietnam, and between attempts to promote transnational practices by Thai and Indonesian anthropologists, to cite just two examples. While the chapters in this volume cannot replicate those conversations, we hope that their content will be of interest not only to individual anthropologists working in particular countries. Rather, we encourage anthropologists working across the diverse Southeast Asian region—and beyond—to read across these cases, to draw inspiration, parallels, convergences and distinctions that might shed light on their own experience and anthropological practice, both personally and with regard to the disciplinary tradition in which they find themselves working.

In addition to the participants at the workshop and contributors to this volume, many others have played vital roles in bringing this publication to fruition. Ambika Aiyadurai provided crucial support in organizing the initial workshop. Sakunika Wewalaarachchi coordinated our communications with authors. Ben Chua, Junbin Tan, Yvonne Yap and Romit Chowdhury assisted in copyediting the contributions through several rounds of revision and refinement. Julius Bautista, Janet Carsten, Carla Jones, John Marston, Mary Beth Mills and Allen Tran lent their expertise and feedback on various chapters. Two anonymous reviewers for NUS Press played a crucial role, particularly in sharpening the arguments we present in the introduction to the volume. Of course, none of the aforementioned should be blamed for any shortcomings to be found in the chapters to follow. While the process of bringing together this collection has been a long one, it has also been extremely enriching to our own knowledge of anthropological traditions and practices throughout Southeast Asia. We hope that readers will find this product of our endeavors to be equally enriching.

INTRODUCTION

ANTHROPOLOGIES IN SOUTHEAST ASIA

Eric C. Thompson and Vineeta Sinha

The content of this volume lends itself to the paradigm of "world anthropologies" that has emerged particularly since the first decade of this century (Ribeiro and Escobar 2006; van Bremen et al. 2005; Yamashita et al. 2004). The development of the world anthropologies perspective—and the emphasis on "anthropologies" in the plural—can be seen as the formalization of long-standing calls to decolonize anthropological knowledge (Asad 1973; Fabian 1983; Hymes 1972). The "world anthropologies" project foregrounds forcefully the diverse contexts—often but not always framed by nation-state imperatives—in which modern anthropological knowledge has been produced and where the practice of the discipline has flourished in the past half-century or more. The world is far from flat and serious hierarchies of power and knowledge remain. Nevertheless, only the uniformed, with limited and ahistorical understandings of contemporary trends in anthropology, would hold that the discipline is a study of "primitive peoples," filling the "savage slot" within academia through research on "the rest" of the world outside "the West" (Thompson 2008; Trouillot 1991).

Two important trends can be observed in early twenty-first-century anthropology. First is the inward-turning of American anthropology. Second, and of much greater interest to us here, is the flourishing of anthropology outside of the United States, United Kingdom, Australia and other sites in the West where early modern anthropology was first established as an autonomous academic discipline. In the United States, around the mid twentieth century, undertaking a PhD in anthropology generally required field research outside of one's own society—usually by anthropologists of European descent studying non-Western societies. But from the 1990s, the paradigm of "anthropology at home" became increasingly prevalent (Peirano 1998). If one looks to the leading journals of American anthropology today, one is struck by the extent to which contemporary issues of American politics and society receive top billing in many of those journals (e.g. Hurricane Katrina, Occupy Wall Street, Ferguson), in many ways replicating the United States media, in which while all lives may matter, American lives clearly matter more.

But in a contrary, almost contradictory trend, while American anthropology has become more America-focused and parochial, globally anthropology has become more diverse and expansive. The discipline of modern anthropology has evolved and morphed, been adopted in and has adapted to the ecologies of societies outside the United States, United Kingdom and other sites where it spent its infancy. It is this maturation and productive growth that this volume along with others in the world anthropologies paradigm seek to acknowledge and record.

Expansion and inclusion of contributions from beyond "the West," are of course not entirely new in anthropology. Even the earliest modern European and American anthropologists, from the late nineteenth century onward, established serious intellectual collaborations with "native" (non-Euro-American) interlocutors. Franz Boas famously worked and published together with his native Northwest American counterpart George Hunt. Claude Lévi-Strauss made clear that the cultural systems anthropologists sought to study were the work of human intellect and that every society has its own intellectuals, with whom anthropologists should engage and acknowledge as much as they do their own academic colleagues (Lévi-Strauss 1963).

Such collaborations, however, remained in most cases singular, sporadic and marginal well into the mid twentieth century. Only gradually did intellectuals or scholars from beyond the West come to think of themselves, and be recognized by others as "anthropologists" of equal standing with Westerners. Even now, the process is far from complete. And only slowly did the number of such individuals expand to the point of constituting recognizable communities of anthropologists operating outside of the West. In many places, including in parts of Southeast Asia, processes of decolonization and the forging of new, modern nation states, with their own universities, research institutes and similar organizations, provided further material and conceptual support to autonomous communities of anthropologists (Bennagen 1980). Such communities have been key to the gradual—for some painstakingly slow—development of relatively autonomous traditions of anthropology around the world.

Anthropologies and the Production of Knowledge

Anthropology, as a discipline grounded in fieldwork and field sites, has long recognized the important intersection of locally grounded theory with more abstract "global" or "universal" theorization. Periodic review articles written from Southeast Asian or other geographical perspectives highlight the "zones of theory" emerging out of particular localities or regions (Abu-Lughod 1989; Bowen 1995; Kleinen 2013; Steedley 1999). Such discussions are generally heavily weighted toward the contributions of a relatively small number of international scholars and the impact that they have on general theory and thought in the discipline—still largely centered in the West and particularly the United States. In parallel to such analyses of how particular world regions have generated and contributed to "global" (or, if one is less generous, "Western") general theory, since at least the 1970s, mainstream, global anthropology has been consciously self-critical of the colonial, postcolonial and neocolonial conditions of its own production (Asad 1973; Hymes 1972; Fabian 1983; Wakin 1992).

In the 1970s, critiques spawned a tremendous body of literature on anthropology's entrenchment in and, for some, complicity with broader racialized, gendered, linguistic, national, socio-economic and other terrains of privilege and marginalization (Clifford and Marcus 1986; Leonardo 1991; Manganaro 1990; Marcus and Fischer 1986; also see Lewis 1998). These in turn have produced a wide range of suggestions, as well as vigorous debates, on what might be done to decenter the Euro-, andro-, hetero- and other centrisms of the discipline (Alatas 2006; Alatas and Sinha 2017; Werbner 2008). Many of these suggestions and debates have turned on questions of indigenization of anthropology—how that might be accomplished and what "indigenous," "native" or even "local" anthropology might mean (Bennagen 1990; Kuwayama 2004; Morsy 1991; Sausmikat 2012; Sinha 2000; Tan 2004; Wu and Yu 2011; Wu 2004).

Reshaping terrains of privilege and indigenizing anthropology in practice have proceeded at a much slower pace than the outpouring of critical literature and advocacy over the past forty to fifty years.

In 1980, for example, Bennegan wrote cogently of the urgent need for an Asianization of anthropology citing concrete examples of anthropology's institutionalization in Malaysia, the Philippines, Indonesia and elsewhere (1980: 8–18). Nearly 40 years on, however, it is obvious that many of the imbalances of power and representation between—as we commonly gloss it—"the West and the rest" still remain; which several of the contributions to this volume point out (Winarto and Pirous, Ch. 8). This, perhaps, should not be overly surprising. Training new generations of scholars, building institutions, and reorganizing the "invisible colleges" or networks of scholars through which knowledge is produced and disseminated takes more time than writing books or identifying biases.[1] Nevertheless, as Sinha (2000) has previously argued, it is essential that we move beyond mere critique in challenging the biases of our discipline.

It is in this regard that this volume, and world anthropologies literature more generally, plays a crucial role in moving us from a critique to a production of knowledge and towards alternative practices. While remaining critical of disparities of power and representation, the emphasis here is on articulating the development of anthropology and the practices of anthropologists "at home" in Southeast Asia. The contributions to this volume accomplish this in three, often overlapping and intersecting, ways. First, especially in the first three chapters, the contributions detail the making of national anthropological traditions: the intersecting development of anthropology and Filipino national identity in the Philippines (Canuday and Porio, Ch. 1), the struggle for institutionalization in Cambodia (Peou, Ch. 2), and through an ambitious reassessment of colonial, capitalist and Soviet influences in Vietnam (Nguyen, Ch. 3). Second, and particularly in the middle section of the book, the chapters emphasize the practices and practical, everyday challenges of "doing" anthropology: in developing a field of maritime anthropology in the Philippines (Mangahas and Rodriguez-Roldan, Ch. 4), trends and challenges in doing anthropology in Malaysia from colonial times to the present (Yeoh, Ch. 5), and the shifting institutional and intellectual pressures placed on the practice of anthropology in Singapore (Sinha, Ch. 6). And third, the final set of chapters in the volume highlights the increasingly significant and variously configured transnational dimensions of anthropological practice in Southeast Asia: the development of a "Borneo" anthropology cutting across the boundaries of three nation states on one island (King and Zawawi, Ch. 7), how Indonesian anthropologists construct selves and others, both within Indonesia and beyond (Winarto and Pirous, Ch. 8), the opening up and diversification of both theory and practice in Vietnam in relation to increasing internationalization (Dang, Ch. 9), and the role of Thai anthropologists in conceptualizing and carrying out a range of transnational research projects (Tosakul, Ch. 10).

Anthropological Communities

Anthropology, whether conceived in the singular as a global discipline, or anthropologies conceived in the plural, exists only insofar as it is produced by communities of anthropologists, in practice. These are epistemic communities of thought and constituencies of practice made of anthropologists who produce anthropology through teaching, research and writing. Moreover, these plural anthropological communities are not isolates. Rather they are complex networks, through which anthropologists are brought into relationships—based on affinities of theory, subjects of study (e.g. kinship, political economy, religion, ethnicity or gender dynamics) as well as location, configured in terms of both the anthropologists' "field sites" and "homes."

There is no avoiding the tremendous influence and impact of the nation-state framework (emplaced within an international order), and the ways in which this impinges on how anthropological communities too are shaped and typologically organized institutionally, discursively and in practice. We speak and write rather easily of Thai anthropology, Japanese anthropology, Indonesian anthropology, and so on. While we would caution that such nation-state categories of anthropology should not be naturalized, at the same time they do reflect a reality on the ground in which educational and other systems of knowledge production are tied to the hegemony of the nation state as a form of political organization in the world today. Many writings in world anthropologies literature explicitly set out to narrate stories of national anthropologies (Magos 2004; Shamsul 1999; Tan 2004; Sinha 2004, 2012). Several contributions to this volume map fairly closely onto that sort of a narrative. Peou (Ch. 2), for example, provides an account of the difficult path for Cambodian anthropology, given the tragic history of that country through the mid to late twentieth century. Nguyen (Ch. 3) and Dang (Ch. 9) respectively provide a critical reassessment of historical influences on and a programmatic statement for the future of anthropology in Vietnam.

Canuday and Porio (Ch. 1) narrate the role of anthropology in producing constructs of "Filipinos" in the Philippines. With the exception of King and Zawawi (Ch. 7), all of our contributors essentially take the nation-state framework at least as a starting point for thinking about production of anthropological knowledge and communities of practice.

In conceiving the project ourselves, we drew on a nation-state framework in seeking contributors and identifying anthropologists "in the following Southeast Asian countries or subregions: Brunei/Borneo (x1), Cambodia (x1), Indonesia (x2), Laos (x1), Malaysia (x2), Myanmar (x1), Philippines (x2), Thailand (x2), Vietnam (x2)."[2] We originally framed contributions as "a research report about anthropology in each contributor's country or region." As the project evolved through correspondence and dialogue with our collaborators, the range of contributions included both "a broader survey of anthropology in a particular country while others are writing on a more specific domain or subfield within a broader local anthropological tradition [and a few are also writing about emergent 'transnational' anthropological practice from different national perspectives]."[3] Throughout this process, we emphasized that we hoped for authors to conceive and deliver chapters that reflected what they felt was important within and about their own anthropological traditions. In particular, we did not aim to produce a singular "master narrative" of anthropology in each nation.

In this volume, we are particularly pleased to have two contributions each on the state of anthropology in the Philippines and Vietnam. These provide some sense of the internal diversity in national anthropological traditions. For the Philippines, Canuday and Porio (Ch. 1) adopt a broad perspective—historically and nationally—in considering how anthropology has shaped and interacted with notions of a national Filipino subject since at least the nineteenth century. In contrast, Mangahas and Rodriguez-Roldan (Ch. 4) examine the more specific development of a Philippine "maritime anthropology." In the case of Vietnam, Nguyen (Ch. 3) undertakes a critical re-examination of the sources which have influenced contemporary Vietnamese anthropology, arguing that standard accounts overplay the influence of Soviet anthropology while underestimating continuities and influences from colonial and Western "capitalist" anthropology. Dang's (Ch. 9) contribution is more in keeping with the sort of standard account of Vietnamese anthropology critiqued by Nguyen; yet at the same time complementing Nguyen's narrative by focusing on the more recent Doi Moi (renovation) period of anthropological developments and laying out forward-looking recommendations for future development of the discipline.

In addition to these varied perspectives within a community of anthropological practice, the constitution of any such community is likewise influenced but not determined by the singular frame of the nation state. Tosakul (Ch. 10) explores in detail the developments of a "transnational anthropology of Thailand." In practice this involves both research by Thai anthropologists beyond the nation-state borders of Thailand and establishing transnational research collaborations. With regard to research beyond Thailand, as Tosakul points out, this has a long history in Thai anthropology, having largely focused on research among historical and contemporary "Thai diaspora" communities. However, it has also included some investigations of non-Thai communities, within and outside Thailand, by Thai anthropologists. At the same time, Thai anthropologists, supported by Thai state funding, have taken the lead in developing collaborative research projects with counterparts from elsewhere—particularly the Mekong region countries of Cambodia, Laos, Myanmar, Vietnam and also China.

Winarto and Pirous (Ch. 8) also include a discussion of Indonesian anthropologists' transnational research projects. In their narrative of Indonesian anthropology, these are not of an Indonesian diaspora. Rather they sprang from the influence of the "founding father" of Indonesian anthropology Koentjaraningrat. Influenced by his own experiences of working with the Yale University-based Human Relations Area Files, Koentjaraningrat encouraged Indonesian anthropologists towards these twin tasks: one, a cataloging of diversity within Indonesia, and two, undertaking ethnographic investigations of "others" across Asia, in China, Japan, Malaysia, Thailand and elsewhere.

While anthropology and anthropologists have developed distinctive traditions in all of the nation states represented in this volume, their size, scope and diversity vary greatly. In Cambodia, as mentioned, anthropology has at best been only marginally institutionalized, due in large part to the events of the late twentieth century which undermined almost all institutions in the country.[4] But even in those nations where anthropology is more firmly institutionalized, the number of active anthropologists tends to be at most somewhere approaching 100 individuals. Moreover, most institutionalized instances of anthropology exist within universities or research institutes rather than at a national level.

Only two Southeast Asian nations—the Philippines and Indonesia—are represented in the World Council of Anthropological Associations (WCAA).[5] The Philippines association—the Ugnayang Pang-AghamTao (UGAT)—was organized in 1977 and formally incorporated in 1979.[6] As of 2016, its active, dues-paying membership numbers around sixty-five to seventy.[7] The Indonesian affiliate of the WCAA, the Asosiasi Antropologi Indonesia (AAI, Indonesian Anthropological Association) was founded in 1983. As of 2018, the AAI established a formal relationship with the *Jurnal Antropologi Indonesia* [Journal of Indonesian Anthropology]. The *Jurnal Antropologi Indonesia* (JAI), published out of the University of Indonesia, dates to 1969, when it was named *Berita Antropologi* [Anthropology Bulletin]. Both the AAI and JAI have had irregular histories during the past two decades. For example, after hosting five international conferences between 2000 and 2008, the JAI saw a period of inactivity before the tradition was revived for a sixth conference in 2016 and seventh in 2019, along with a revival of the AAI after a period of relatively low activity. The largest formal anthropological association in Southeast Asia is the Vietnam Association of Ethnologists and Anthropologists, established in 1991 as the Vietnam Association of Ethnologists and renamed in 2007 to include "Anthropologists." This association is organized under the Vietnam Museum of Ethnology in Hanoi and claims over 450 members.[8] By comparison, the American Anthropological Association claims a membership of over 10,000 individuals from more than 100 nations.[9]

Malaysia, Singapore and Thailand do not have formal, national-level anthropological associations. In Malaysia, many anthropologists participate in the broader Persatuan Sains Sosial Malaysia (PSSM, Malaysian Social Science Association). In Singapore and Thailand, most interactions among anthropologists beyond the departmental or university level take place informally. A national-level, institutional anchor for Thai anthropology has been the Princess Maha Chakri Sirindhorn Anthropology Centre (SAC) in Bangkok, the annual conference of which many Thai anthropologists consider to be their annual disciplinary conference. But with regard to developing a formal national association—as the Thai contributor to this volume put it—there is little need felt for such an entity, as there are not so many anthropologists in the country and "we all know each other."[10]

Similarly in Singapore, the closest thing to a national-level organization at present is an informal email list, with over fifty members, through which individuals based at the National University of Singapore, and more recently those at the Nanyang Technological University, Singapore University of Technology and Design, and Yale-NUS, have sought to periodically reach out to the broader anthropological community in the country to organize academic and social events. While the number of anthropologists may be numerically small in countries such as Thailand, Singapore and Malaysia, they are research-active, produce important anthropological scholarship, and are plugged into local (national) and international scholarly and disciplinary networks as well as having high profiles as public intellectuals.

Theories in and of Anthropologies

The gold standard of academic anthropology, at least since the early to mid twentieth century, has been contributions to theory. In principle, as a social science, theory should exist in explicit statements—theses or hypotheses—about the world, open in democratic fashion to debate, disputation and revision, based on engagements founded in logic and empirical investigation.[11] In practice, the development and dissemination of theory is extremely hierarchical, dominated over the past century in particular by scholars based in a relatively small number of PhD-granting institutions, whose ideas are disseminated through their ability to eloquently articulate them (especially in English) and the students they train, who in turn overwhelmingly populate and control the global academic ecosystem—within anthropology as much as all other social science disciplines. Since the 1980s or 1990s, hegemonic American anthropology has also been enamored of "critical theory" (and various post-isms), which positions itself as immune to empirical ("scientific") critique and only subject to discursive, narrative disputation—highly dependent on linguistic subtlety and expression. It has been wryly amusing, in Singapore, to encounter more than one PhD student from top anthropology departments in the United States, on their way to or from "the field" in Southeast Asia, who proclaim that their primary interest in anthropology is with "theory." But when asked, "Theory of what?" they are at a loss to explain.

An oft-repeated grievance of anthropologists from various nations and communities of practice across Southeast Asia is the difficulty, both for themselves and their students, in engaging with the sorts of sophisticated yet often linguistically obtuse theoretical texts produced by anthropologists, particularly from the past few decades. Many find it difficult to integrate current work into contemporary syllabi and fall back on teaching more reliable, and easily comprehensible, "classics" (see Yeoh, Ch. 5). Many also feel at a disadvantage not only due to language but also the paradigms of thought and expression they perceive as more easily flowing from the kind of training American and other students receive throughout their schooling, even before the university undergraduate level. The late Pattana Kitiarsa, for example, is hailed in Thailand as a leading "postmodernist" scholar and one of the most innovative thinkers and writers of his generation (Panchadej and Wararak 2013). Yet in private conversation, he frequently expressed the great difficulty he felt in engaging with theory—especially in writing in English. He attributed this, and is supported by many others, in the observation that Thai students are simply never taught the sorts of critical thinking skills that he found commonplace among his American graduate school classmates. Such barriers, unfortunately, not only prevent ideas from Southeast Asian anthropologists being widely disseminated amongst the broader, global anthropological community but discourage many from even trying to find a voice on the global academic stage.

Instead, theoretical developments in Southeast East Asian anthropologies tend to be localized within relatively circumscribed national and domain-specific contexts. Contributions to this volume are weighted more toward descriptive narratives of the histories and practices of anthropology within Southeast Asia, rather than elaborating on specific developments or innovations in substantive theory. But many of the chapters here point to the ways in which anthropologists in the region theorize from their position within local and national traditions and in reference to substantive topics and fieldwork. King and Zawawi (Ch. 7), for example, review the range of topics and angles from which Borneo anthropology has developed a body of work around the framework of negotiated cultural identities, given that the island is both a complexly multi-ethnic and transnational place. Other chapters also highlight the ways in which Southeast Asian contexts have lent themselves to articulating the ways in which anthropologists have been involved in conceptualizing the central subject of anthropology—i.e. people or peoples. Canuday and Porio (Ch. 1) trace the history of anthropology in the Philippines primarily in reference to the ways in which the subject of the "Filipino" has conceptually evolved, from late nineteenth-century efforts at imagining a national Filipino subject, to recent contemporary anthropology's attention to diversity, marginality, representation and minority voices and concerns. Winarto and Pirous (Ch. 8) describe the ways in which anthropologists in Indonesia have positioned themselves and the discipline in reference to a range of "others" both nationally and inter- or transnationally.

Mangahas and Rodriguez-Roldan's (Ch. 4) account of maritime anthropology is a broader consideration of an important subfield within Philippine anthropology. While they focus on the historical development of the field and the role of key scholars such as Cynthia Zayas, the review of the field points to key theoretical developments as well. Among the several strands and themes in Philippine maritime anthropology, for instance, is the articulation between local social relations, technical skills, knowledge, and economic relations of production and distribution with broader national and international political economies. A common theme in the work of many of the anthropologists cited in Chapter 4 is an effort to uncover and explain the ways in which Philippine fisher communities draw on local systems and knowledges while resisting or adapting to challenges of increasingly globalized political economies around fishing and labor. In more recent years, these concerns have intersected with global recognition of the dangers of ecological degradation and climate change. In similar fashion, Tosakul's (Ch. 10) review of Thailand's transnational anthropology illustrates how the field has shifted from theorizing transnational Thai/Tai ethnolinguistic typologies to diaspora, borderland sociocultural processes, and transnational marriage-migration and labor-migration along with other sorts of transnational relationships. These major streams of thought on transnational processes are accompanied by a range of other more specific concerns undertaken by Thai-led but international research teams, particularly in the Mekong Region, who examine (among other things) the social-economics of rice growing, cross-border trade, family and kinship, and religious belief and practice.

As much as the aforementioned chapters and others in this volume highlight various theoretical trends in Southeast Asian anthropologies, they also contribute to our theoretical understanding of anthropology and anthropologies. In this respect, when taken individually, each chapter provides a narrative framework for how and why anthropology has taken the shape it has in each case—from the extreme challenge of institutionalizing the discipline in

Cambodia (Ch. 2) to its centrality in constructing the national-self in the Philippines (Ch. 3) and leadership in promoting a transnational imagination and practice in Thailand (Ch. 10). Reading across the chapters points us in the direction of being able to theorize the conditions under which anthropologies thrive and the ways in which they are configured.

Critiques of anthropology as the "handmaiden of colonialism" or complicity of American anthropology in the mid twentieth century with American Cold War objectives are in fact only two cases of a broader issue (also see Asad 1973; Hymes 1972; Wakins 1992). Anthropology—and in fact all scholarships and disciplines—require some sort of patron-client relationship in order to thrive and develop. This has been true at least since scholars from the Christian and Islamic worlds found patronage under kings and sultans, or Confucian scholars labored under the patronage of Chinese imperial courts. No one, unfortunately, can subsist on words and ideas alone. In most, if not all of the cases described in the chapters to follow, nation states (rather than, for example, colonial or feudal regimes) are crucial to the promotion, institutionalization and, in some cases, impairment of anthropology. Some cases here (Chivoin, Ch. 2) emphasize and illustrate the impediments that the lack of a strong, stable nation-state regime have had on developing local anthropology. Others (Yeoh, Ch. 5; Dang, Ch. 9) point to shifting national regimes and the ways in which they reorient the objectives and environment for anthropological endeavors.

Nation-state regimes, their priorities, and their attitudes toward scholarship influence anthropologists not only within the nation but how they operate transnationally. Thai anthropology (Tosakul, Ch. 10) has taken the lead in developing collaborative, transnational anthropology—particularly in the Mekong region—largely with the financial and ideological backing of the Thai state, which seeks to position itself as a leader among neighboring countries. Singapore (Sinha, Ch. 6) saw an explosion of research activity—not only in anthropology but across social science disciplines—from the late 1990s, when newly affluent Singapore sought to position itself as a leading global city and poured funding into developing the National University of Singapore, Nanyang Technological University and other tertiary institutions as "world class" research institutions. These initiatives have seen Singapore's universities emerge to prominence not only in Asia but on the world stage. Recent popular nationalism, however, is threatening to undo a lot of these achievements. Funding is being pulled from graduate education, in response to complaints that too many research scholarships go to foreign graduate students. And Ministry of Education research grants now have to get special dispensation for any of the money to be spent outside of Singapore—specifically imposing on those who do regional anthropological research.

Beyond shaping a general milieu that to degrees either encourages or discourages the pursuit of good scholarship, national governments and nation states shape research priorities. Philippine anthropology (Canuday and Porio, Ch. 1) has focused increasingly on understanding issues of poverty and marginalization. In Malaysia (Yeoh, Ch. 5), particular attention has been given to theorizing ethnicity and race in a multi-ethnic society. Thai anthropology (Tosakul, Ch. 6) has focused on how groups and individuals navigate borders and terrains of (non)citizenship (also see Sakboon et al. 2017). It is well worth reflecting on how both the focus of anthropology and the ways in which specific issues (e.g. diversity, ethnicity and citizenship) are approached and theorized in light of national discourses and priorities. The chapters here also suggest particular areas—such as migration in Thai transnational anthropology or human-ecological relationships in Philippine maritime anthropology—could and should have a more prominent voice and position in broader "global" anthropological theory and concept formation. While this book does not focus specifically on theory development, we hope that it may be a step in that direction by making the work being done in Southeast Asian anthropologies more accessible within and beyond the communities of practice described in these pages.

Rendering Anthropologies Visible

In sum, the thread connecting all the chapters presented here are deliberations of both practice and theory. While we build upon well-established critiques of anthropological privilege and marginalization, our aim is a constructive and productive one—to render more visible the practices of anthropology and anthropologists in Southeast Asia as well as trends in theorizing and constructing the discipline across the region. Our intention, or at least aspiration, nevertheless is that the book be of greatest value to the ongoing debates with the anthropological traditions mapped and narrated by contributors to this volume. An additional ambition is that the conversations initiated in this volume inspire further dialogue and discussion about the past, present and future of anthropology as well as the networking of scholars and their ideas within the Southeast Asian region.

While the book aims first and foremost to make anthropological traditions within Southeast Asia more visible to anthropologists within these traditions, we certainly also hope for it to be of value to those looking in from beyond. As with other volumes on world anthropologies, the aim is not to document diverse anthropological ideas and practices as a singular master narrative. Rather these are contributions to an ongoing dialogue among anthropologists and more broadly all those interested in empirical, ethnographically grounded understanding of people, in other words of *anthropos*—the object and subject of our *ology*. In that most general sense, anthropology as a social science is a contribution to humanity—whether in Southeast Asia or beyond. Being "locally" situated or even "indigenous" is not to be read as a denial or rejection of our ties to a more universal human endeavor, which, for the editors at least, is a fundamental anthropological tenet.[12]

Moreover, beyond the "local" (often framed as the "national"), our further desire is to make anthropological traditions more transnationally visible across Southeast Asia. While anthropologists everywhere in Southeast Asia have transnational linkages, in the "world system" of academic anthropology these have continued to be much stronger with various metropoles (the West; but in Southeast Asia also Japan and Singapore) than with others situated elsewhere in the periphery, even between immediate neighbors—such as Malaysia and Indonesia or Thailand and Cambodia (Thompson 2006, 2007). Meetings, such as the October 2014 workshop at which much of the work here was first presented and discussed, are one venue for fostering or reworking these networks. This book, we hope, is another—somewhat more durable, less fleeting—venue.

The last among our priorities, though not unimportant, is to make these anthropological traditions visible transnationally beyond Southeast Asia, both within the broader world anthropologies literature and within anthropology—as a diverse yet unified, singular global discipline. We fully understand that busy academic readers are accustomed to dipping into a volume like this to pluck out only the most relevant bits with respect to their own field and endeavors. We would encourage readers to venture beyond their familiar "location" (be it "field" or "home" or both). Reading across, if not the entire set of contributions, then at least selections will lead you—the reader—to engage with anthropological communities living and working elsewhere. Reading, as much as travel or fieldwork, is productively approached as a form of comparative, methodological alterity (also see Thompson 2008: 124–25). The realization of any of the aforementioned aims now lies—quite literally—in the hands of the reader.[13]

Notes

1. On the transnational networks and "invisible colleges" of social scientists in Southeast Asia, see: Thompson 2006, 2007.
2. Project document, c. October 2013. Letter to Collaborators.docx. With regard to the list of contributors sought, after substantial effort, we were able to include contributions from neither Laos nor Myanmar. Similarly, after some discussion among ourselves at NUS, the original list did not include Timor Leste (Southeast Asia's newest independent nation state). These exclusions themselves speak to the uneven terrain and hierarchies of regional "Southeast Asian anthropologies."
3. Project document, May 21, 2014. Letter to SEAsia Anthro RCs 21 May 2014.docx.
4. The same can be said of Laos, Myanmar and Timor Leste; the other nation states in Southeast Asia, which unfortunately are not represented in this volume.
5. http://www.wcaanet.org/about.shtml (accessed February 27, 2016).
6. http://www.ugat.org.ph/index.php?page=general (accessed February 27, 2016).
7. Maria Mangahas, personal communication.
8. http://www.vusta.vn/en/news/Vusta-Head-quarter/The-IVth-Congress-of-the-Vietnam-Association-for-Ethnology-15988.html and http://www.vusta.vn/en/news/Vusta-Head-quarter/The-IVth-Congress-of-the-Vietnam-Association-for-Ethnology-15988.html (accessed February 27, 2016).
9. http://www.americananthro.org/ConnectWithAAA/Content.aspx?ItemNumber=1993 (accessed February 27, 2016).
10. Ratana Tosakul, personal communication.
11. We would stress here that empirical investigation need not be quantitative and numerically expressed. The category error of equating empiricism with quantification has been an albatross around the theoretical neck of anthropology and other social sciences for far too long.
12. We believe this is the general sentiment of all or at least most of the contributors here; but we do not claim to speak for them.
13. *In memoriam*, Umberto Eco (1932–2016); See Eco (1984).

References

Abu-Lughod, Lila (1989) "Zones of Theory in the Anthropology of the Arab World," *Annual Review of Anthropology* 18: pp. 267–306.

Alatas, Syed Farid (2006) *Alternative Discourse in Asian Social Science: Responses to Eurocentrism*. Thousand Oaks: Sage Publications.

Alatas, Syed Farid and Vineeta Sinha (2017) *Sociology Theory Beyond the Canon*. London and New York: Palgrave Macmillan.

Asad, Talal, (ed.) (1973) *Anthropology and the Colonial Encounter*. London: Ithaca Press.

Bennagen, Ponciano L. (1980) "The Asianization of Anthropology," *Asian Studies* 18(1): pp. 1–26.

_____ (1990) "The Indigenization and Asianization of Anthropology." In *Indigenous Psychology*, Enriquez, (ed.), pp. 1–30. Quezon City: Akademya ng Sikolohiyang Pilipino.

Bowen, John R. (1995) "The Forms Culture Takes: A State-of-the-Field Essay on the Anthropology of Southeast Asia," *Journal of Asian Studies* 54(4): pp. 1047–78.

Clifford, James and George E. Marcus (1986) *Writing Culture: The Poetics and Politics of Ethnography*. Berkeley and Los Angeles: University of California Press.

Eco, Umberto (1984) *The Role of The Reader: Explorations in the Semiotics of Texts*. Bloomington: Indiana University Press.

Fabian, Johannes (1983) *Time and the Other: How Anthropology Makes Its Object*. New York: Columbia University Press.

Hymes, Dell H., (ed.) (1972) *Reinventing Anthropology*. Ann Arbor: University of Michigan Press.

King, Victor T. (2013) *Borneo and Beyond: Reflections on Borneo Studies, Anthropology and the Social Sciences*. Working Paper Series 3. Gadong (Brunei): Institute of Asian Studies, Universiti Brunei Darussalam.

Kleinen, John (2013) "New Trends in the Anthropology of Southeast Asia," *TRaNS: Trans-Regional and -National Studies of Southeast Asia* 1(1): pp. 121–35.

Kuwayama, Takami (2004) *Native Anthropology: The Japanese Challenge to Western Academic Hegemony*. Melbourne: Trans Pacific Press.

Lévi-Strauss, Claude (1963) *Structural Anthropology*. New York: Basic Books.

Lewis, Herbert S. (1998) "The Misrepresentations of Anthropology and Its Consequences," *American Anthropologist* 100(3): pp. 716–31.

Leonardo, Micaela di, (ed.) (1991) *Gender at the Crossroads of Knowledge: Feminist Anthropology in the Postmodern Era*. Berkeley, Los Angeles, Oxford: University of California Press.

Magos, Alicia P. (2004) "Towards Indigenization: Responses, Challenges and Experiences in the Philippines." In *The Making of Anthropology in East and Southeast Asia*, Yamashita, Bosco and Eades, (eds.), pp. 307–34. New York: Berghahn Books.

Manganaro, Marc, (ed.) (1990) *Modernist Anthropology: From Fieldwork to Text*. New Jersey: Princeton University Press.

Marcus, George E. and Michael M.J. Fischer (1986) *Anthropology as Cultural Critique: An Experimental Moment in the Human Sciences*. Chicago: University of Chicago Press.

Morsy, Soheir, et al. (1991) "Anthropology and the Call for Indigenization of Social Science in the Arab World." In *The Contemporary Study of the Middle East*, Sullivan and Ismael, (eds.), pp. 81–111. Alberta: The University of Alberta Press.

Panchadej Singtho and Wararak Chaiyathap, (eds.) (2013) สิเก็บเจ้าไว้ในหัวใจตลอดกาล [Dear ... My Postmodernist Friend, You are Posted in My Mind].Co-Kayan Media Team: Chiang Mai.

Peirano, Mariza G.S. (1998) "When Anthropology is at Home: The Different Contexts of a Single Discipline," *Annual Review of Anthropology* 27: pp. 105–28.

Ribeiro, Gustavo Lins, and Arturo Escobar, (eds.) (2006) *World Anthropologies: Disciplinary Transformations within Systems of Power*. Oxford: Berg.

Sakboon, Mukdawan, Prasit Leepreecha, and Panadda Boonyasaranai (2017) "Khon Rai Sanchat: Resident Aliens and the Paradox of National Integration in Thailand." In *Ethnic and Religious Identities and Integration in Southeast Asia*, Ooi Keat Gin and Volker Grabowsky, (eds.), pp. 57–104. Chiang Mai: Silkworm Books.

Sausmikat, Nora. (2012). "Sociology and Anthropology in Twentieth-Century China: Between Universalism and Indigenism by Arif Dirlik, Guannan Li, and Hsiao-pei Yen" (book review), *The Journal of Asian Studies* 71: pp. 1102–04.

Shamsul, A.B. (1999) "Anthropology and the Politics of Identity and Nation-State Formation in Southeast Asia," *Paideuma: Mitteilungen zur Kulturkunde* 45: pp. 103–14.

Sinha, Vineeta (2000) "Moving Beyond Critique: Practicing the Social Sciences in the Context of Globalization," *Southeast Asian Journal of Social Science* 28(1): pp. 67–104.

—— (2004) "Indigenizing Anthropology in India: Problematics of Negotiating an Identity." In *Asian Anthropology*, van Bremen, Ben-Ari and Alatas, (eds.), pp. 139–61. Oxon: Routledge.

—— (2012) "Documenting Anthropological Work in Singapore: The Journey of a Discipline." In *Locating Alternative Anthropological Traditions*, Danda, (ed.), pp. 177–211. Kolkata: Indian Anthropological Society.

Steedly, Mary (1999) "The State of Culture Theory in the Anthropology of Southeast Asia," *Annual Review of Anthropology* 28: pp. 431–54.

Tan Chee-Beng (2004) "Anthropology and Indigenization in a Southeast Asian State: Malaysia." In *The Making of Anthropology in East and Southeast Asia*, Yamashita, Bosco and Eades, (eds.), pp. 307–34. New York: Berghahn Books.

Thompson, Eric C. (2006) "Internet Mediated Networking and Academic Dependency in Indonesia, Malaysia, Singapore and the United States," *Current Sociology* 54(1): pp. 41–51.

—— (2007) "Internet-Mediated Experiences of Underdevelopment: A Four-Country Survey of Academia," *Asian Journal of Social Sciences* 35(6): pp. 554–74.

—— (2008) "A World of Anthropologies: Paradigms and Challenges for the Coming Century (Review Essay)," *Asian Journal of Social Sciences* 36(1): pp. 121–27.

—— (2012) "Anthropology in Southeast Asia: National Traditions and Transnational Practices," *Asian Journal of Social Science* 40(5–6): pp. 664–89.

Trouillot, Michel-Rolph (1991) "Anthropology and the Savage Slot: The Poetics and Politics of Otherness." In *Recapturing Anthropology: Working in the Present*, Richard G. Fox, (ed.), pp. 17–44. Santa Fe: School of American Research Press.

Van Bremen, Jan, Eyal Ben-Ari, and Syed Farid Alatas, (eds.) (2005) *Asian Anthropology*. New York: RoutledgeCurzon.

Wakin, Eric (1992) *Anthropology Goes to War: Professional Ethics and Counterinsurgency in Thailand*. Madison: University of Wisconsin Center for Southeast Asian Studies.

Werbner, Pnina (2008) *Anthropology and the New Cosmopolitanism: Rooted, Feminist and Vernacular Perspectives*. ASA Monograph Series Vol. 45. New York: Berg.

Wu, David Y.H. (2004) "Chinese National Dance and the Discourse of Nativization in Chinese Anthropology." In *The Making of Anthropology in East and Southeast Asia*, Yamashita, Bosco and Eades, (eds.), pp. 198–207. New York: Berghahn Books.

Wu, Zong-jie, and Hua Yu (2011) "Narrative Paradigm of Shiji and Indigenization of Ethnography," *Journal of Guangxi University for Nationalities (Philosophy and Social Science Edition)* 33(1): pp. 70–77.

Yamashita, Shinji, Joseph Bosco, and J.S. Eades, (eds.) (2004) *The Making of Anthropology in East and Southeast Asia*. New York: Berghahn Books.

SECTION 1

THE MAKING OF ANTHROPOLOGICAL TRADITIONS

CHAPTER 1

CONCEPTS OF FILIPINOS Anthropology as Social Science, Politics and Nationhood

Jose Jowel Canuday and Emma Porio

For nearly a century and a half, the crafting of a Filipino anthropological tradition has reflected and resonated with the scholarly works and political engagements of early modern anthropological scholars José Rizal, Isabelo de los Reyes and Pedro Paterno. In making sense of this tradition, we pay attention to a widespread set of practices among generations of Filipino anthropologists that can be described as collectively committed to a project of knowledge production, even while they are not exclusively aligned towards scholastic ends. Under these dynamics, an anthropological practice emerges from circumstances that render the engagement of Philippine anthropology and its practitioners as political acts because it is humanistic and scientific. Philippine nationhood has been at stake throughout this era in which frameworks for conceptualizing Filipinos developed through both indigenous and foreign scholarship.

We see the tug and pull between theory making and practical social action in the work of Filipino anthropologists as they negotiate, question and evaluate differing fields of power while working as researchers and commentators in their home country. Precisely because generations of Filipino anthropologists have worked at home, they have engaged with research subjects who are also their compatriots, and whose travails implicated their own lives as scholars working and living in the larger society crafted by politically engaged intellectuals like Rizal and de los Reyes. Under such circumstances, Filipino anthropologists find themselves and their work unavoidably enmeshed in power relations at play in the country. In this context, we view tradition as a long-standing, consciously shared project of knowledge construction and reconstruction. This tradition simultaneously contributes to scholarship and the making of a national imaginary and its constituent identities. Without claiming an exhaustive examination of these engagements, we see these processes unfolding in the application of anthropological knowledge in key historical events in the Philippines.

Nineteenth-Century Foundations

At the Geographic Society in Berlin in 1887, Rudolf Virchow, a towering figure in German anthropology, met two Southeast Asian gentlemen. Virchow sized up one of the men and asked if he could examine him "ethnographically" (Coates 1962: 103). The man, José Rizal, did not object and politely told Virchow that he would readily submit himself to the "interest of science," but in fashionably quick-witted repartee nudged at his companion and offered him instead as the right "specimen" to work on (ibid.). Virchow burst out laughing and the two men went on conversing between drinks until past midnight, discussing topics of the day including the gathering cloud of racial evolutionary and transcendental human debates sweeping through late nineteenth-century Western anthropology (Guerrero 1974: 161). The encounter endeared Virchow and Rizal to each other, with Virchow and his colleagues inviting Rizal for a fellowship with the Berlin Anthropological Society and the German Geographic Society (ibid.: 180–82). Rizal, who on several occasions underscored the transcendental idea of the equal capacity of races, lectured on Tagalog poetics, language, and other themes before the predominantly European membership of both societies (Palma 1949; San Juan 1974: 35; Rizal [1894] 2002: 15). Implicitly, Rizal had looked up to eighteenth-century German universalist anthropology not only as a science but as a scientific basis supporting his fundamental political critique against the social evolutionist, racist, and ethnocentric underpinnings of Spanish colonial administrative and political philosophy. Rizal would not be alone in mobilizing anthropology to argue for the equal capacity of Philippine society and a Malay "race" to that of white Europeans, an endeavor that would be reflected by others during his time, and practitioners of politically infused anthropology in the Philippines in the following century.

Back in the Philippines, a writer from the province of Ilocos named Isabelo de los Reyes left the Augustinian seminary and started collecting, translating and publishing folklore from Ilocano into Spanish (Bragado 2002). On the basis of his collections, de los Reyes conceptualized folklore as a local form of knowledge and not mere meaningless superstitions (Lopez 2006: 5). De los Reyes' epistemological premise earned him respect and a place in the Spanish Folklore Society, which consequently gathered and published his work for a broader European audience (ibid.: 6). Like Rizal, he engaged European scholars as he wrote on ethnological studies, racial origins, material cultures, government, beliefs and linguistic formations in the Philippines, contributing to the era's broader "growth of science" (Mojares 2006: 291). However, rather than simply collaborating with Western scholars, de los Reyes interrogated their assessment of the origins, racial categories, and accounts of Philippine cultures, peoples and languages. In the dominant era of armchair Victorian science, de los Reyes gained legitimacy by exhibiting an intimate knowledge of Philippine subjects, being one of them himself and an "eyewitness" to their lives (ibid.: 292).

Pedro Paterno, a contemporary and compatriot of Rizal and de los Reyes, attempted to systematically integrate nineteenth-century German anthropological science on the unity of mankind in constructing his own interpretation of the evolution of Philippine culture and civilization. Paterno, a trained lawyer exposed to an Orientalist education at the Universidad de Salamanca, wrote annotated novels and ethnological treatises that tended to conflate European anthropological research of the Philippines, the Malay world, and broader humanity. He anchored his work in evolutionary science, working out distinctive Philippine stages of social evolution to contend that like the Western world, the country's Tagalog and other peoples had already evolved into a civilized constituency long before colonialism (ibid.: 46).

Rizal, de los Reyes, and Paterno were more than men of scholarship. Rizal's German fellowship was a calculated move to acquire analytical knowledge of anthropology for political ends. His ultimate goal was to annotate the *Sucesos de las Islas Filipinas* [*Events in the Philippine Islands*], a 1609 ethnographic portrait of communities extending from the shores of Borneo, through the Philippines, and to the Marianas on the eve of European colonialism (Morga 1971). He would use the annotations to illustrate the vitality and sophistication of the primordial social and cultural life of the "Malay race" to counter condescending European accounts of precolonial native life across the region (Ocampo 1998). Through these annotations, Rizal offered a discursive, if not a remonstrative, assessment against imperialist science and political representation of the Orient as savage and primitive (Guerrero 1974: 210–11). Rizal would later contrast his romantically dynamic view of sophisticated Malayan precolonial societies with a trove of accounts capturing the social malaise created by Spanish colonial rule and Catholic friar oppression. Such claims would eventually lead to his 1896 martyrdom and help inspire the Filipino revolution.

Meanwhile, de los Reyes set up patriotic newspapers in the twilight of Spanish rule and untiringly went on publishing critical accounts of social and political life when the United States took over as colonial master in 1899 (Rosario-Braid and Tuazon 1999). De los Reyes, however, did not settle for merely writing and critiquing colonialism. He was also an active participant in the formation of militant labor unions and a socialist party that served as the precursor to current day labor and Marxist movements in the Philippines (Scaff 1955: 14; Ofreneo 1989, 1998; Bankoff 2004; Sibal 2004). Until today, he is recognized as a working-class hero alongside his academic accolades as an exponent of Philippine folklore and anthropology.

Paterno's intellectual legacy gained mixed evaluation from contemporary historians and writers who regard his writing as pompous and at times brazenly laced with invented facts to support his political argument of an already existing civilized Filipino constituency in the age of the antiquities. Moreover, Paterno's scientific treatises were impertinently infused with self-aggrandizing claims to the point of being regarded as an embarrassment among patriotic Filipino intellectuals (Schumacher 1991 in Mojares 2006). Notwithstanding such reputation, Paterno showed intellectual depth in mobilizing Western theories, covering the works of Virchow, Voltaire, Joseph Montana, A.B. Meyer, Hendrik Kern, Fedor Jagor, and others (Mojares: 69). His goal was to utilize ethnological science to reconstruct the morality, philosophy, and cosmology of Philippine antiquities, reinterpreting it against the social evolutionist European trope that regards non-Western indigenous communities as primitive evolutionary remnants. Through liberal use of fact and fiction from

Filipino mythic and religious narratives that he then tethered to speculative Western social evolutionary thoughts, Paterno asserted the Filipino just like the European had reached a civilized stage in consonance with an evolutionist universal history of humankind. As historian Resil Mojares, who wrote one of the most extensive evaluations of Paterno's work notes, this man's "main interest for us today lies in his position within the discipline and its object. To study the position he took is to learn something about the disciplinary power of Western knowledge as well as the possibilities of testing its limits or opening up autonomous spaces within it" (Mojares: 91).

Rizal's, de los Reyes' and to some extent Paterno's engagement with nineteenth-century anthropology lent credence to their critiques of the most pressing societal problems of their time and resonated with broader Philippine anthropological practice in the succeeding century. Rizal's work on the question of the transcendental capacity of races and de los Reyes' argument on the distinctiveness of local knowledge in the form of folklore, as well as Paterno's deployment of Western evolutionist ethnological theories would set an anthropological tradition mindful of the particularities and plurality of cultural formations in the Philippines. Rizal's, de los Reyes' and Paterno's engagement with anthropology illustrates an anthropological practice that cannot be regarded simply as a "child of colonialism" (also see Asad 1973). Far from simply being born in the pits of colonial imagination, early Filipino anthropological practice thrived within a historical juncture marked by the rise of an intellectual community that dared to question colonial knowledge and politics. Anthropology was primarily deployed as a mobilizing instrument for social involvement and political action, and through it offered contributions to the broader epistemological project of knowing the human condition.

Contested Colonial Constructs

Spanish Catholic missionary chronicles of native life were often credited as the precursor of anthropological works in the Philippines, even though they offer no notable contribution to the epistemological and ontological questions that anthropology has raised as a social science (Abaya, Lucas-Fernan and Noval-Morales 1999; Bautista 2000: 176). While not removed from identity politics, anthropological scholarship was more notable in the dynamic collaboration of Filipino intellectuals and a slew of visiting and less-traveled Western scholars who wrote about the peoples and cultures of the Philippine islands (Jagor [1875] 1916; Blumentritt 1916; Virchow 1916). Filipino intellectuals like Rizal and de los Reyes, collectively referred to as the *ilustrados*, collaborated with these traveling and armchair scholars. In the process, they interjected their own positions in key Western anthropological conceptions of race, linguistic formation, and the transcendence of human capacity, particularly through the construct of the Filipino "Indio."

These engagements show that the Philippine anthropological enterprise was not merely a friar affair under Spanish rule but a cosmopolitan engagement with Filipino and global intellectuals forging scholarly ties while working in or beyond the Philippines. Through these cosmopolitan collaborations, intellectuals like Rizal and de los Reyes established a separate relationship with Ferdinand Blumentritt, a Philippinist scholar from what is today the Czech Republic (Palma 1949: 66–67). Their viewpoints enabled Blumentritt to construct a linguistic taxonomy of the Filipino people, describing them as originally distinctive races of Negrito and Malay that later developed into fifty-one tribes. This formation followed a longer process of population admixture between these races and other peoples of the world (Brinton 1898; Blumentritt [1890] 1980; Padilla 2013). Blumentritt's taxonomy actually privileged Rizal's belief in the constitution of Filipinos as civilized Indios, who emerged from a long process of biological and cultural intermixing with Chinese, Japanese, Arabs, Indians and other peoples (Rizal 1961). On the back of European racial science, Rizal foresaw a broad Indio community with a common history, aspirations and culture that would help set the tone for the imagination of Filipino identity anchored on modern ideas of nationhood (Anderson 1983). That position, however, also influenced European analyses of the ethnic and racial constitution of the peoples of the Philippines (Virchow 1899).

In the adoption of German racial science as a discursive political platform for thinking about the Filipino Indio as a civilized race, the *ilustrados* had inadvertently boxed themselves into one corner of an anthropological debate that was, up to that point, still defined by an evolutionary paradigm. They struggled with responding to social evolutionist representations of Negritos, Moro and other highland dwellers of the Philippine islands as representative of primordially "savage" people during the 1887 Madrid exposition (Aguilar 2005: 622). Rizal and his compatriots purportedly excluded the Moros from the south and highland peoples to the north from their idea of a racially and culturally evolved Indio—an apparent attempt to preserve their carefully constructed narrative of a Filipino race ready to stand among a community of civilized nations (ibid.). Nonetheless, the Filipino and European idea of a racially and culturally evolved Indio—one who emerged from racial and societal transformations occurring across eons—served to complicate the American colonial project of simply invading the Philippines without just cause.

Advocates of the United States' expansion in the Pacific were hard pressed to justify America's ventures in the Philippines without being seen as merely replicating British colonialism and imperialism. Indeed, such an invasion would undermine the ideals of liberty and equality that hallmarked the American revolution of 1776. The Philippine Revolution, partly empowered by erudite university-educated Filipino intellectual elites, had already aligned their organizing principles to the modernizing ideals of the Western enlightenment even before the first American military contingent set foot on the islands. In search of a viable premise to legitimize the American colonial project, a Philippine Commission was organized in US Congress to investigate conditions within the Philippines. It was at this juncture that the Americans turned to, among others, the Victorian and American scientific theories of race and social evolutionism to frame field reports on racial and linguistic variations in the archipelago. Victorian-American social evolutionary and racial science recast the European and Filipino racial anthropological analysis of Philippine peoples in ways that legitimized the agenda of American colonialism.

Though none were formally trained in anthropology, the six-person Philippine Commission crafted separate ethnological sections in its 1899 to 1906 reports to US Congress. The report rejected both Rizal's and the German taxonomic theory of a Filipino constituency formed across time by the gradual mixing of racial and cultural forces (USPC 1901). Instead, the commission took on a French three-wave racial migration theory of subsequent Negrito, Indonesian and Malay settlement patterns, a persuasion conflated with a nineteenth-century American and Victorian social evolutionary paradigm. The goal was to lay down the idea that each of these categories of peoples occupied distinctive stages of physical and cultural development. The report described and designated the island's Negrito and other highland dwellers to the lower rung of the evolutionary ladder, while the Malays (with the exception of the Moros) were regarded as "civilized."

The reports argued that while the majority of the people of the islands "possessed of a considerable degree of civilization," the "head-hunting," polygamous, "human sacrifice-indulging" and "savage" natives occupied broad swaths of the Philippine interior lands (USPC 1901: 16). Although some of these "wild" tribes and races were "physically superior," without American attention they could eventually overrun the civilized peoples of the islands given their "shortcomings and deficiencies" (USPC 1901: 16, 183). Dean C. Worcester, a member of the Philippine Commission, wrote: "Were American control to be withdrawn before the civilization of the wild tribes had been effected, their [Filipinos] future would be dark indeed" (Worcester 1914, 672). Through such an approach, the commission deconstructed the peoples of the Philippine islands as "not a nation" or a "people" but an array of diverse racial, linguistic, tribal and social groups in stark contrast with what Rizal had imagined as the primordial, culturally evolved constituencies of the Filipino nation (ibid.: 12).

Worcester, who would later serve as the colonial Secretary of the Interior, subsequently established a Bureau of Non-Christian Tribes to conduct an expansive ethnological survey across supposedly non-Christianized areas of the archipelago (USPC 1904). The bureau, later renamed the Ethnological Survey of the Philippines, employed American anthropologists who carried out their investigations while embedded in American military formations posted in the northern areas of the Cordilleras and the southern "Moro province" in Mindanao and Sulu. A distinctive military character was thus rendered to the American anthropological project.

The ethnological survey photographed and crafted descriptive accounts of people across highland communities stretching from northern Luzon to the wetlands and islands of the Muslim enclaves in Mindanao and Sulu. Both accounts were then used to construct a Philippine human typology of ethnologically distinctive Christian and non-Christian tribes, each differentiated by languages, material cultures, geographic and topographic locations, religions, and racial features (USPC 1904). Consequently, the typology was used to devise a colonial administrative apparatus that divided the archipelago into two governing bodies—a non-military bureaucracy for the lowland regions, and a military administration in the Cordillera and the Moro province (USPC 1904; Abinales 2003: 162–63). These maneuverings illustrate how colonial administrators turned to ethnology and Victorian-American social evolutionary theories to negate and silence the political and academic construction of the "Filipino race" crafted by the *ilustrados*. With these frames, the Americans subsequently used anthropology's investigatory knowledge as one of the instruments for building a viable and sustainable colonial state.

To be sure, American anthropological readings of the Philippines were hardly monolithic. In the first decade of American colonialism, the cracks between racial and evolutionary conceptualizations of anthropology on the one hand, and of ethnological representations of diverse communities on the other, were evident in published exchanges between colonial agents. This tension would later influence anthropological units of analysis in the postcolonial and ethnographic projects by anthropologists from outside the American academe. It is to these fissures that we shall now turn.

Cracks in Colonial Anthropology and Emergent Typologies

Even the members of the ethnographic survey doubted the validity of the diverse tribal taxonomies they themselves generated. The American anthropologist David P. Barrows, the Chief of the Bureau of Non-Christian Tribes, himself questioned the "superlative" number of tribes in the survey, particularly noting the enumeration of 116 non-Christian groups (Barrows 1905: 467). For Barrows, the problem stemmed from the "errors of nomenclature;" in particular the erroneous application of the scientific terminologies of "tribe" and "race" to the non-Christian communities in the Philippines. Barrows instead proposed that the number of tribal categories in the Philippines be reduced to sixteen, claiming that certain tribes are of "close acquaintance" and that some are actually subgroups or "local branches" of a larger tribe (Barrows 1905: 467, 468).[1] Worcester, a zoologist, disputed Barrows sixteen-tribe typology as "very inconsistent" and considered it a failure in defining the concept of "tribe" (Worcester 1906: 805). Notwithstanding Barrows' rejoinder, Worcester reworked his own taxonomy by defining tribe in a manner that did not exclusively rely on racial and social evolutionary theory. He instead hybridized the nineteenth-century American social and biological evolutionary view of "tribe" with a more cultural approach to documenting and typologizing it. He redefined tribe as a "division of races" whose individual members are aggregated by a shared progenitor and distinguishable by a commonality of:

> physical characteristics, dress, and ornaments; the nature of the communities which they form; peculiarities of house architecture; methods of hunting, fishing and agriculture; character and importance of manufactures; practices relative to war and taking of heads of enemies; arms used in warfare; music and dancing; and marriage and burial customs (Worcester 1906: 803).

On the surface, American colonial anthropological practice in the Philippines exuded a great degree of "malleability" that made it less a scientific taxonomy than a dialogically flexible political project (Goh 2007). These practices were not initiated for the sole purpose of enriching anthropological concepts but instead for marking people, making their location more legible and distinguishable for the purposes of colonial state-building. Nonetheless, the Barrows-Worcester debate on ethnology illustrates the fissures in colonial anthropology that led to a rethinking of the application of ethnological theory and methods in the Philippines from being an inherently political exercise to a conceptual one. This, in several important ways, conditioned the next phase in the way the Philippines was anthropologically conceived.

A new generation of anthropologists began pursuing ethnographic studies in the Philippines by the second decade of American occupation. These scholars were trained amidst the changing milieu of early twentieth-century American-Victorian anthropology, which was undergoing a process of shifting orientations from social evolutionism to a more cultural approach. The shift was instrumental in shaping the anthropological agenda regarding the Philippine colony, coming at the heels of the establishment of the Department of Anthropology at the University of the Philippines (UP) in 1914. Research shifted from typologizing racial difference or physical and evolutionary variations to collecting specimens and photographs of material culture as well as recordings of local customs, social organizations, mythologies, episodes of warfare and peace pacts (Cole 1913; Garvan 1931).

Visiting anthropologists such as Fay-Cooper Cole of the Chicago Field Museum and the University of Chicago, departed from Worcester's claim of racial disparity despite utilizing several of Worcester's photographs in his analysis. Cole contended that there was no indication of any group in the archipelago as having a "pure race" (Cole 1913: 200–203). Alfred Kroeber (1919), a leading proponent of American cultural anthropology, also wrote his analysis of Filipinos by focusing on cultural elements as opposed to the racial records established by Worcester in the *Ethnological Survey*.[2] H. Otley Beyer, curator of the colonial Bureau of Science Museum and the first chair of the UP anthropology department, cast aside the racial and tribal categories formulated by Worcester. Beyer, who trained in America when cultural anthropology gained ground, used the term "ethnographic groups"[3] in typologizing the people of the Philippines. This episode marked the end of the exclusive hold of racial and taxonomical anthropology and the beginning of ethnographic investigations into the cultural diversity of postcolonial Philippine constituencies. Beyer's articulation of the "ethnographic group" serves as an enduring unit of analysis and the basis for the interwoven academic and public constructions of "ethnic" constituencies in the postcolonial Philippines.[4] The ethnographic and linguistic typologies constructed by Beyer would later inform the 1955 survey of "cultural-linguistic groups" in the Human Relations Area Files (HRAF). HRAF would go on to serve as a fundamental resource for post-war Filipino and international anthropology students working on the Philippines.

For all its faults as a highly politicized research agenda, the American colonial ethnological project and its inherent fissures were instrumental in setting the stage for the transition of anthropological practice in the Philippines away from the racial sciences of the nineteenth century. It set the ground for the institutionalization of a postcolonial anthropology and ethnographic research that, while not following Rizal's or de los Reyes' racial politics, reflected the desire for an enhanced knowledge of the local constituencies of the people of the Philippines.

Post-War Rehabilitation and Nation-Building

The end of World War II saw an independent Philippine Republic engaging at a critical historical juncture that had important implications for anthropological practices in the country. A few eminent figures in colonial anthropology decided to remain in the Philippines and worked to establish the discipline from within the larger project of nation-building for the fledging postcolonial state.

Some helped in establishing and carrying out programs that sought to integrate highland populations and Muslim constituencies in Mindanao into the national body politic through state programs such as the Commission on National Integration, the successor of the Bureau of Non-Christian Tribes, and later renamed Ethnographic

Survey of the Philippines. Robert Bradford Fox went on to establish the anthropology department at the National Museum, offering the state a representational apparatus for the constituencies of the nation. In the process, this engagement recast anthropology as an instrument of postcolonial state formation and identity making, especially in the areas of education, museum ethnography, and minority integration. At UP, Cecilio Lopez, recognized as the "father of Philippine linguistics," spearheaded works on linguistic analysis of the typologies, origins, morphemes, and Austronesian connections of Philippine languages. Lopez's scholarship, by implication, established a simultaneous primordial account of Philippine local languages without losing sight of their broader linkages.[5]

Frank Lynch, an American Jesuit educator who later took up Filipino citizenship, earned a master's degree in anthropology at UP in 1949 and was deeply engaged in institutionalizing anthropology, sociology and broader disciplines in the social sciences beyond state supported institutions. Following the end of Western and Japanese colonial ocupation in 1945, Lynch crafted and directed efforts in gathering ethnological accounts and seminal assessments of archeological locations across the Philippines (Lynch 1948, 1962a). In the 1960s and the early 1970s, Lynch played a pivotal part in founding sociology and anthropology departments at the Jesuit Ateneo de Manila and other non-government universities in other parts of the country. He, his students, and his research colleagues at the Ateneo took particular interest in working with fledgling educational institutions in Sulu, resulting in further expansion of ethnographic collections in communities and regions far from the ambit of Manila (Lynch 1962b, 1963; Arce 1963; Stanton 1963). From these engagements, Lynch (1961) came to understand the significance of Islam in the formulation of social analysis and development work in Sulu, as later scholars would also find (Kiefer 1972b; Warren 1981).

In terms of scholarship, Lynch closely engaged with the structural functionalism of Edward Evans-Pritchard and the structural focus of Max Weber, but offered limited theoretical frames in understanding Philippine conditions (Lynch 1952; Cannel 1999: 8). In practice, nonetheless Lynch applied these frames in producing (either by himself or in collaboration with colleagues and former students) nearly 200 accounts of a broad range of ethnographic, archeological and sociological analysis of Philippine communities (Lynch and Hollnsteiner 1961; Porio, Lynch and Hollnsteiner 1978). Lynch also paid attention to the issue of research methodologies, ranging from the significance of surveys to the hermeneutical value of utilizing the expansive collections of Jesuit letters in the conduct of salvaged ethnography (Lynch 1956).

While anthropological tools of investigatory knowledge formed part of the apparatus for postcolonial nation-building, the anthropological department at the state-run University of the Philippines had managed to produce only six students. Merely two of them were Filipinos with master's degrees in the initial years of post-war reconstruction (Zamora 1976: 317; Abaya, Lucas-Fernan and Noval-Morales 1999). Although it may have appeared at first glance that Filipino anthropology was in crisis, the lack of anthropological training inspired universities and intellectuals throughout the country to engage in ethnographic research, folklore collections and related endeavors. This led to the flourishing of anthropological practices and knowledge production outside of greater Manila, the country's center of academic and political affairs.

Some universities in Mindanao linked up with American, French and other European doctoral anthropology students conducting fieldwork closer to their respective localities. Gradually, these universities began forming their own small research outfits and journals that published studies by native and foreign anthropologists and anthropology students. In 1971, for instance, the Notre Dame of Jolo established a Coordinated Investigation of Sulu Culture (CISCU) that brought together native and foreign fieldworkers in Sulu as affiliates. Under the direction of Gerard Rixhon, a Belgian-born Oblates of Mary Immaculate missionary who took Filipino citizenship after leaving the clergy, CISCU set up the *Sulu Studies* journal. The journal published extensive accounts by both native and visiting researchers of the material, performance and visual cultures, folklore, Islamic and customary laws (adat), social and kindred structure, and violence on the Sulu archipelago (Damsani, Alawi and Rixhon 1972; Kiefer 1972; Pellesen 1972; Rixhon 1972a). However, after five issues and amidst the flare-up of secessionist violence in Sulu in 1974, the journal shut operations. But during its run, the journal produced works that form part of the annals of ethnographic and folkloric knowledge of the Philippines and broader Southeast Asia (Eugenio 1982; Tokoro 2003; Sather 2006).

Even when CISCU folded and *Sulu Studies* ceased publication amidst the turbulence of the 1970s, other research institutions and journals surfaced and thrived, publishing ethnographic and anthropological works on Mindanao. The state-run Mindanao State University began publishing the *Mindanao Journal* in 1977, featuring accounts on material culture and social and political affairs in the Muslim communities of the Southern Philippines. The Jesuit-run Xavier University formed the Research Institute on Mindanao Culture (RIMCU) and subsequently issued *Kinaadman: A Journal of the Southern Philippines* in 1979. Ateneo de Davao University, also a Jesuit institution, set up the *Tambara* journal in 1984 with especial focus on the sociocultural affairs of indigenous peoples and other sociological issues in Mindanao.

Collaborations were also established with a new wave of Catholic and Protestant Christian missionaries trained in linguistic anthropology and engaged in the conduct of lexical analysis of the country's diverse linguistic formations in the highlands and the Muslim enclaves of Mindanao. One such organization was the Protestant Summer Institute of Linguistics (SIL). SIL played an instrumental role in establishing a wealth of knowledge on linguistic structures and glotto-chronology, shedding light on many questions including those about the peopling of Mindanao and the common roots of the region's diverse languages (Elkins 1982). Other universities also collaborated with religious missions including the Catholic Society of Divine Word with the University of San Carlos in Cebu, the Oblates of Mary Immaculate with Notre Dame institutions in Jolo and Cotabato, and the Presbyterians with Silliman University in Negros.

In the northern Philippines, a Cordillera Studies Center established by UP investigated and published ethnographic reports as well as studies on indigenous notions of common property and law amidst a national debate on the legal recognition of ancestral domains (Prill-Bret 1992, 1994, 1995). Along similar lines, the University of San Carlos (USC) established the Cebuano Studies Center[6] in 1975 as a response to the "growing demand for research services in local history and vernacular literature." In a sense, this was an implicit response to the English journal, *The Philippine Quarterly of Culture and Society*, founded by German ethnologist and USC president (1960–69) Fr. Rudolf Rahmann. Well loved by locals, Rahmann has had a street named after him by the local city government.

Local universities and foreign ethnographers collaborated and subsequently published monographs and anthologies of ethnographies, folklore, linguistic formations, material culture, ritual processes and cosmology. These collaborations helped inform the production of anthropological knowledge, serving as platforms for later research and instruction. By the late 1960s and early 1970s, a few universities managed to establish joint departments in sociology and anthropology, helping to carry forward anthropological practice in the country. In the 1970s, ethnography and folklore documentation crafted by Filipino anthropologists also started circulating as monographs and anthologies of communities spanning from the northernmost highlands of the Philippines down to southernmost areas of Mindanao (Bruno 1973; Manuel 1973; Kurais 1975; Casino 1976; Burton 1985).

Parallel to the initiatives of local academics and foreign fieldworkers, American overseas development agencies such as the Ford Foundation and Rockefeller Foundation extended support in training emerging Filipino scholars at leading anthropological departments in America. Development groups also offered financial support to investigate other epistemological projects. For instance, the Institute of Philippine Culture (IPC) at the Ateneo de Manila University in the early 1960s started enquiring into the notion of inherent Filipino values and their possible structural functionalist application in the building of a modern nation state. Though the IPC project cultivated deep insights on notions of Filipino kinship connections, pride, hospitality and gratitude, such studies were also viewed by critics as insidious attempts to map out the Filipino psyche under a covert propaganda scheme directed by the American Central Intelligence Agency during the Cold War. The Philippines was viewed as crucial to American foreign interests as it hosted the largest American military installation outside the US. It also dominated America's trade and investment portfolio amidst the spreading influence of Soviet and Chinese communism in Southeast Asia.

Outside the realms of academia and geopolitical affairs, a few anthropologists dedicated their lives to serve highland communities and produce knowledge on managing delicate landscapes. Delbert Rice, an American missionary of the United Church of Christ in the Philippines who later studied anthropology as he adopted Filipino citizenship, spearheaded highland development and environmental work in the mountainous region of northern Luzon. Since the 1960s, Rice worked on non-government initiatives addressing social development, ancestral domains and forest resource management in ways that protected the legal rights and interests of indigenous peoples in highland regions (Rice 1972a, 1972b, 1982, 2007).[7] Rice and others exemplified attempts to reconstruct anthropology and reorient its politics toward nation-building and local community concerns, albeit within the constraints of American Cold War and Marcos-era politics.

Anthropology Under the Dictatorship

The Marcos dictatorship fostered two arenas of public engagement for anthropologists, even while its restrictive political climate left anthropologists with "little option" but to partake in regime-sponsored "developmental research projects" (Magos 2004: 350). The first arena implicated some anthropologists in the regime's vision of building a modern nation through the establishment of institutions, film productions and publication projects that represented Filipino heritage, cultural roots and social history. Anthropologists who decided to continue working with the state during the dictatorship took part in the expansion of the fields of anthropological engagement. This led to the establishment of the National Museum, a presidential office for national minorities, the Cultural Center of the Philippines, Folk Arts Theater, and numerous cultural centers in the Cordillera region to the north and in Muslim regions of Mindanao to the south.

This period enabled the expansion of research on the idea of Filipino heritage, family, and community life (Jocano 1982, 1983) and folk Christianity (Covar 1973) as well as folklore, music and material culture in less studied areas of the country and Southeast Asia (Manuel 1977, 1985; Maceda 1977, Nicolas 1977). Concomitantly, the anthropology of this period manufactured a positive spin on Manila's rapidly expanding slum communities and growing poverty incidences in the rural areas. Drawing insights from ethnographic fieldwork on migrating rural families in a "squalid" Manila slum, F. Landa Jocano would claim that: "attitude toward being poor was set and accepted, and the people took their economic deprivation with ease and comfort" (Jocano 1973: 228). This argument generated a sharp rebuke from some Filipino anthropologists for reinforcing stereotypes of the poor, raising questions on the mobilization of anthropological and sociological knowledge in legitimizing the regime (Hollnsteiner 1976; Magos 2004).

Martial law, however, also paved the way for the revitalization of Mindanao State University (MSU), a state-run higher educational system established at the heartlands of secessionist conflicts to address widespread Muslim discontent with the national government.

MSU initially opened an undergraduate anthropology program and published ethnographic reports and analysis focusing on Muslim communities in the Southern Philippines that in turn helped inform Moro identity assertion (Madale 1977, 1988; Disoma 1990).

The second arena constitutes anthropologists who mobilized anthropological knowledge to check on mounting abuses in the construction of massive infrastructure projects such as hydroelectric dams and commercial crop plantations across peasant and indigenous people's lands in the country. Some anthropologists even laid down their lives as they fought for human rights and social transformation through militant engagement with the dictatorship, living out the spirit of sacrifice that Rizal and de los Reyes exhibited a century earlier (Abaya, Lucas-Fernan and Noval-Morales 1999). Within the social milieu conditioned by the dictatorship, Ponciano Bennagen founded the Ugnayang Pang-AghamTao (UGAT or the Anthropological Association of the Philippines) and helped organize the first of its annual conferences in 1978. These conferences envisioned an anthropological practice that would take a critical view of sociopolitical events unfolding across the country, inadvertently conflating scholarship and advocacy.

The conferences were crafted in a way that pushed the boundaries of anthropological enquiry and theory to think about the pressing social problems of the time. This was done through themes that considered the "power of anthropology" in pursuing dialogue with developers, the interrogation of "power," and the rise of mass movements.[8] These critical themes in a supposedly scholarly conference were pursued against the backdrop of rising tensions, resistance and episodes of counter-resistance towards government plans and programs to build massive infrastructure projects such as dams, irrigation, ports and highways. These programs had displaced indigenous peoples and impoverished both rural communities and urban dwellers. As a testament to the intimate relations between scholarship and advocacy in the anthropological project in martial law Philippines, UGAT suspended the 1986 conference as the nation underwent a tenuous political transition from dictatorship. The conferences resumed the following year, building on the politically relevant themes that marked the critical scholarship in the days of the dictatorship. Moving forward, there was an even stronger emphasis on working with and studying indigenous peoples.[9]

Reclaiming Democratic Spaces

Martial law expanded the role of anthropology beyond taxonomic and ethnographic production towards a discursive and political engagement with state authorities in ways that reflected the critical thinking established by Rizal and de los Reyes a century before. With the dismantling of the Marcos dictatorship in 1986, several democratic spaces opened up for anthropological practice within and beyond the academy. This included historic seats for a handful of delegates tasked to frame a post-martial law Philippine Constitution in 1987. Bennagen mobilized both his state position as constitutional delegate and his identity as an anthropologist to expand the definition of national constituencies to include "indigenous cultural communities." These engagements effectively expanded the meaning and influence of ethnolinguistic taxonomies that nineteenth-century European scholars explored and American colonial agents mobilized for colonial state-building. These taxonomies were transformed from being colonial administrative instruments to fundamental markers of cultural and social plurality in the Philippines. They were the ways through which segments of Philippine society sought recognition, protection and endowment with rights in exercising self-determination.

These engagements established anthropological knowledge as not merely a point for ontological discussion but as a material political resource that helped enshrine indigenous people's rights under the basic law of the state. Bennagen and his colleagues did not stop there. They mobilized themselves and anthropology as a whole to become the knowledge tools for civil society organizations (CSOs) in engaging with state power through legislative and legal advocacy. These engagements eventually resulted in the enactment of the Indigenous Peoples Rights Act (IPRA), one of the world's earliest legal frameworks for protecting the indigenous constituency of a modern state, and in mobilizing more anthropologists in the delineation of ancestral domains in the country.

Meanwhile, drawing on ethnographic perspectives, a few other anthropologists became active in promoting participatory development methodologies in assessing the impact of government programs during and after martial law (Porio 2009, 2012). One of these methodologies, process documentation (PD), became the main tool in assessing the efficiency and effectiveness of government programs (de los Reyes 1984). PD enjoyed high levels of support from multilateral agencies.

Employed in assessing the efficacy of bureaucracies and "beneficiary communities" in huge government projects like irrigation, social forestry, and women in development (WID), this methodology became a popular tool among both government and non-government organizations in the 1980s to the 1990s (Veneracion 1989). Critics, however, have argued that in some cases people-centered methodologies have been utilized by government bureaucracies so as to merely comply with the "community participation" requirement of funders and donors (Porio 1998).

The political-economic recognition of the rights of indigenous peoples and cultural communities seemed to increase with the implementation of IPRA. This was partially because of the continuing pressure and mobilization by local and international non-govermental organizations (NGOs) and grassroots organizations. Still, the state bureaucracy is often slow in responding to demands of local and indigenous peoples. Ironically, the state's promotion of huge "developmental" projects and extractive industries like mining in Mindanao and in the highlands (for example, mining concessions in Mt Province, Surigao, Tampakan, South Cotabato) has intensified political struggles. This has fueled the mobilization of cultural communities, with the support of NGOs and People's Organizations (POs), leading to assertions by critics of the state that such projects are a major source of displacement and oppression of these communities.

Alongside anthropological engagement for direct political action, space was created for ontological discussions of the "indigenization" of knowledge and the problems in applying Western anthropological theories to local realities, albeit with varied trajectories. One framework argues for the grounding of theory in specific cultural contexts, nomenclature, and inherent Filipino psychology. This is seen in Virgilio Enriquez's *Sikolohiyang Filipino*—an epistemological treatise of "indigenous psychology and cultural empowerment" (Enriquez and Marcelino 1984; Enriquez 1994; Pe-Pua and Marcelino 2000). Another path advocates privileging the "native's point of view" an ideology as seen in *Pantayong Pananaw*, initially developed by Zeus Salazar (1997). Yet another view saw the idea of indigenization of anthropology as not necessarily an exclusive Filipino academic affair, but part of a broader process unfolding in the Asian world in the wake of increasing native participation in the enterprise of anthropological enquiry. In his epistemological proposition in the "Asianization of Anthropology" (1980), Bennagen underscores the value of self-awareness and self-assertion of local knowledge toward more democratic and transformative outcomes. Bennagen envisions "non-Western anthropologists finally questioning the premises, uses and directions of anthropology from the perspective of a social scientist striving to understand his own society while actively participating in its transformation" (1980: 6).

A proponent of this vision is Victoria Tauli-Corpuz (2001), a native anthropologist of Igorot ancestry, who moved to occupy a space in the global political and academic discourse on indigenous peoples as a woman, activist and, recently, United Nations Special Rapporteur on the Rights of Indigenous Peoples. Bennagen's resonant influence in indigenizing anthropology is evident in the opening sections of Maria Mangahas and Suzanna Rodriguez-Roldan's survey of Philippine maritime anthropological literature in Chapter 4 of this volume. Both lament "the relative paucity of published ethnographic work on fishing communities in the Philippines written by Filipinos (and implicitly, *for* Filipinos)" and wept "there are more non-Filipino authors than local ones" publishing in this field even while the country is archipelagic." For Mangahas and Rodriguez-Roldan, such a condition indicates the "much needed step toward the indigenization of anthropology in the Philippines, an old but still unrealized call." Attempts to indigenize anthropology, at least at UP, where both Mangahas and Rodriguez-Roldan received their undergraduate and master's anthropological training, by requiring all student papers to be written in Filipino. Both noted that the Filipino-only writing requirement emphasizes "a language our professors considered to be more accessible to the community than English... [and] also a deliberate nationalistic act to avoid using English in communicating knowledge meant for a Filipino audience."

Parallel to preoccupation with indigenizing anthropology at UP, the notion of Philippine highlands and forest cultures rapidly vanishing as a result of Western capitalist developmental ethnocide swept the media, civil society and legal circles in the country (Lynch 1983; Media Mindanao News Service 1993). Along with this view, lowland populations were seen as cultures degraded by colonialism and Westernization, unable to root themselves in a "native 'great tradition'" (Constantino 1969, 1978). From this perspective, the highlands and Muslim regions were seen as the cradle of authentic Filipino culture while "cultural extinction" will be the fate of indigenous tribes as they become integrated into lowland communities subject to the vicissitudes of an exploitative market economy (Eder 1987: 104).

Several Filipino anthropologists, however, stayed clear of the idea of ethnocide as a question for anthropological investigation. Instead, they argued that indigenous anthropological knowledge need not be treated in isolation but as a form of knowing enriched by multiple contexts of knowledge production, including ancestral wisdom and global intellectual flows. From such a standpoint, these anthropologists find value in studying Filipino heritage as a remarkable testimony to the persistence of "indigenous ways" even as it is being transfigured by broader historical, political and cultural forces impinging on the Philippines (Zialcita 2005: 24). As Zialcita notes: "Filipinos have not been merely passive recipients. They, too, transformed influences to conform to their needs in the Philippines…" (ibid.: 181). Through these diverse perspectives, the Filipino anthropological vision of indigenized lifeworlds is not reducible to a pristine and unadulterated native knowledge, nor can it be seen as averse to transformation through engagement with other sociocultural paradigms.

Other anthropologists also paid attention to the tangled relations of power, militancy and intimacy between observers and observed. Precisely because these relations are tangled, it is untenable to disengage despite the hard realities of the political or personal circumstances of the observed. On the other hand, conflating advocacy with scholarship does not always mean an unproblematic alignment of the subject's and the researcher's interests. Albert Alejo (2000), an anthropologist, Jesuit priest, former labor apostolate, and long-standing advocate of indigenous people's rights, has argued to this effect:

> In a very real sense, fieldworkers do all sorts of technical jobs not out of militancy, but because they are in a position to render them. That is how they could go on doing their research especially within a community that has grown more sensitive to politics and ethics of being researched (262–63).

Anthropology in the Philippines has increasingly moved towards diverse undertakings. This includes an investigation of the recasting of global communication and media technology into specific cultural practices and values as opposed to merely precipitating a homogenized global culture (Pertierra 2010). In Mindanao, Karl Gaspar drew on

Frankfurt School theorists such as Habermas in understanding identity formation, land contestation and rights negotiations by Arakan Manobos in North Cotabato (Gaspar 2012). In the Cordillera, Analyn Salvador-Amores (2013) interrogated critical notions of tradition and modernity in examining indigenous tattooing practices and their subsequent circulation in the global enterprise of tattoo artistry. Both ethnographers, however, believed in the broader vision of capturing the attention of those in power towards the difficult socio-economic and political lives of their subjects. This was done by moving outside the parameters of anthropological enquiry and into the realm of advocacy. With anthropology being enriched by individuals with long-standing careers in civil society, journalism, church work and other fields, the trajectory of anthropology in the Philippines has also diversified. But this inclination has almost always been towards a vision of engaging power relations in the likeness of Rizal and de los Reyes.

Entering and Exiting Anthropology

The road to anthropology in the Philippines has numerous starting points. Some practitioners began in anthropology as undergraduates but more than a few joined the discipline convinced of the relevance of anthropological knowledge, not only for its explanatory value but also its capacity to effect the transformation of Filipino communities. Many are activists, social development workers, clergy members and journalists. On the other hand, academy-based anthropologists also ventured into advocacy. Bennagen established an NGO that collaborates with both anthropologists and advocates in advancing indigenous people's rights, even as it publishes papers pertaining to legal and political matters related to ancestral domains. He argues for an anthropological engagement that is not necessarily tied up with the agenda of the academy, but towards that of marginalized local people as "village anthropologists."

Bennagen, a former chair of the UP Department of Anthropology, moved out of the academy and worked with indigenous peoples in the northern and southern Philippines. From that perch, he pursued advocacy work and partnered with communities in researching social policy changes by utilizing the investigatory knowledge of anthropology. As Bennagen notes, "If the aim of the social sciences is both to understand and transform the world then the claim of the others for self-understanding and self-transformation sends to academics a signal for them to rethink their adaptive strategies to help ensure their survival" (Abaya, Lucas-Fernan and Noval-Morales 1999: 6). Bennagen's epistemological position continues to reverberate decades later in scholarly and advocacy works of several anthropologists in the Philippines (Estacio 1996; Gatmaytan 2007; Austria-Young 2012).

In Mindanao, many non-academics have pursued advocacy that resonates with Bennagen's stance, even while they enter into the discipline along contrasting career pathways. These include people who established careers as practitioners in the fields of human rights and other forms of social advocacy, legal work, the media and religious clergy. That pattern received a boost with the establishment of a postgraduate program under the Mindanao Anthropology Consortium of private and state-run universities in 2002. Reflecting the diverse professional roots of anthropologists, the consortium attracted a journalist, value-formation facilitators and information systems managers, as well as philosophy and economics teachers. Although the anthropological consortium lasted for only a brief period, it did manage to produce seven anthropologists with master's and doctorate degrees. This was a considerable achievement for a region that for years has been sending students to universities in Manila or elsewhere for anthropological training.

Notwithstanding its short lifespan, the formation of the consortium led to the establishment of the new anthropology department at the Ateneo de Davao University. It also led to the establishment of courses and programs as well as staffing in various Mindanao universities by locally trained anthropologists. These developments attracted students with life-long engagements with indigenous rights advocacies, Muslim self-determination movements, local governance, journalism, public service, performance arts, and museum curation. In essence, Mindanao anthropologists engendered anthropological knowledge to foster understanding, cultural sensitivity, religious diversity and the idea of shared community amid brewing violence and displacement in some parts of the region (Doro 2007; Torres 2007; Canuday 2009; Husin 2009; Panaguiton 2010).

Conclusion

This chapter has reviewed the institutionalization of anthropological practice in academia, the government, and civil society organizations across the national capital and provincial spaces in the Philippines.

It also located the anthropologies of Rizal, de los Reyes, and that of Paterno to some degree, within the emergent counter-Eurocentric discourses of the early colonial period, which found continuities throughout the 1970s and the period of martial law. Resistance and critiques of state-initiated policies and programs, especially during the twenty-year Marcos regime, have continued. This is reflected in the current mobilization of NGOs/POs and marginalized communities/ sectors (indigenous people's (IP) communities, rural/urban poor, women, etc.) against state and corporate incursions into ancestral domains. The recognition of indigenous people's rights in the 1987 Philippine constitution and the Indigenous Peoples Rights Act a decade later are fruits of these struggles. These successes, now embedded in national laws, are part of the continuing "identities and resource claims" among marginal groups in the Philippine highlands and lowlands.

These community mobilizations have also found resonance in the issues raised within the larger context of social movements for justice (e.g., environment/climate, women, ethnic groups, internally displaced peoples (IDPs), etc). This is poignantly illustrated in the IP communities struggle against state and capital incursions into their ancestral domains and the resulting environmental degradation that have devastating consequences for the marginalized highland, lowland and coastal communities. The proliferation of research and development centers (e.g., Cordillera Studies Center, Mt Kitanglad Development Center) devoted to these critical environmental highland issues illustrate this trend to produce anthropological knowledge that serve vulnerable and marginalized communities. NGOs and community-based organizations (CBOs) have also documented how environmental degradation has led to an increasing number of climate-related disasters (Ondoy 2009; Sendong 2011; Yolanda 2013 to mention a few) that have displaced vulnerable and marginalized people's lives and livelihoods. Ethnographies of displacement, recovery and resilience (Canuday 2009; Torres 2007) have informed the crafting of pro-poor policies and programs in post-conflict and/or post-disaster areas. In the tradition of Rizal and de los Reyes, anthropological knowledge has also been mobilized by CBOs and their partners in civil society, government and academe to craft responsive climate action plans and risk reduction programs (Polack, Luna and Dator-Bercilla 2010; Dator-Bercilla and Porio 2017). These initiatives were embarked upon in the hope that anthropological truths may enhance initiatives to construct power and social justice with and for those in the margins.

The crafting of Philippine anthropology is firmly situated within the unfolding social and political-economic context of Philippine society and culture. Broadly, it resonates with what Bunnel, Kong and Law (2007) asserted as "the situatedness and partiality, the complexity and embeddedness of knowledge" in the production of social and cultural geography in Southeast Asia. Practitioners sought to advance the importance of anthropological knowledge and practice not only for their own sake but also in conjunction with the making, unmaking and remaking of the sociocultural and political tapestry of the peoples of the Philippines and their institutions. This is reflected not only by the efforts of the hegemonic state—be it in the form of its Spanish-American colonial or postcolonial versions—to mobilize the investigatory instruments and instructive knowledge that anthropology (re)produces to support its project of administration and modernity. It defined the substance of counter-hegemonic assertions offered by anthropologists who also serve or have served in various capacities other than as academics, activists, indigenous rights advocates, patriots, civil society leaders, journalists, lawyers, priests, and the like. By virtue of the sociopolitical conditions into which they are embedded, anthropologists in the Philippines, like their counterparts in Latin America, take that "dual position as both researchers and fellow of our subjects of study ... we [are] continually torn between our duty as scientists and our role as citizens" (Jimeno 2008: 72).

Inevitably, Philippine anthropological practice treads the chequered grounds of the country's political history and its contemporaneous politics. Philippine anthropology's subjective practitioners view the subject of their study not only as a fellow human "other" to be understood, but also a person with whom they share a country and must take responsibility for as compatriots. Filipino anthropologists Abaya, Lucas-Fernan and Noval-Morales (1999) view this trajectory of practice as a task and a mission that would make anthropology relevant to the context of its operations, stating that:

> By negotiating the ever-shifting terms of relations with their material, they also finally come to terms with the material conditions under which they remake realities with, for, and against themselves and other people. But the history of anthropology in the Philippines does not only yield lessons in reflexivity. It also makes sure that the discipline in the field where and when it most

> matters, and that is everyday and everytime; in transformative domains of popular culture, gender and sexuality, aesthetics, material culture, ethnicity, diaspora, media technology, cultural rights, political ecology, health, and so forth. The anthropology of this kind will never miss its chance (7–8).

That desire to keep anthropology relevant to the material social and political conditions of the imagined national community shaped the Philippine anthropological practice of the past and of today, and, perhaps, the prospective possibilities of the discipline in this geographic space. Such a view and engagement has been tested and refined by time, eventually emerging as a legacy and tradition of anthropological practice in the Philippines. It is a tradition nurtured by the awareness of the complex issues confronting the country's diversified constituencies and informed by its commitment to construct a reflexive discipline and practice. This tradition mobilizes anthropology as a medium by which it brings its agents and subjects into a dialogue and partnership with an overarching goal of speaking truth to, engaging with, or even struggling against the powers and political forces at play in Philippine society.

Notes

1. Barrows also discarded the Indonesian race theory adopted from the French and argued that the "civilized" Filipino, the Moro and the other non-Christian tribes, except for the Negritos, all belonged to the Malay race. But as Barrows critiqued the "multiplicity" of tribal designation and races (Barrows 1905: 453), he also began looking for the common origins of the Malay race rather than their variegation. In critiquing the earlier ethnological analysis by the Philippine Commission, Barrows by implication criticized the Worcester typology based on the French theory of three racial groups and "diverse migration" (ibid.).
2. Kroeber did not conduct fieldwork in the Philippines but published his 1919 treatise *Peoples of the Philippines*, utilizing photographs and notes produced by ethnographer-officials in the early years of occupation. In explaining the differentiation, Kroeber did not endorse Worcester's three waves of racial migration theory but suggested that "peoples" of the Philippines have been a product of "six to eight separate waves of civilization" that "superimposed" and "interpenetrated one another" across time (Kroeber 1919: 214). He believed that "more than thirty nationalities" should still be apparent in the archipelago with some

nationalities emerging as more dominant than others (Kroeber 1919: 51). For Kroeber, this indicated that the Filipino is "not a single nationality but shares some measure in effects of every one of the cultures" forming "layers of civilization" that have become intricate and "complexly interwoven" (Kroeber 1919: 51). In this sense, Kroeber's theory of differentiation tended to be centripetal, with the interweaving of various origin identities, which he referred as "nationality" into a central or common super-organic identity—the Filipino.

3. Beyer defined an ethnographic group as "any group of people, living in a more or less contiguous geographic area, who have a sufficiently unique economic and social life, language, or physical type to mark them off clearly and distinctly from any other similar group in the Philippine Islands" (Beyer 1917: 36).
4. The taxonomic project of racial, linguistic and ethnic classification a century ago was continued, not with the intention of mapping a colonized people but tracing the diversity of the Filipino nation. For instance, Robert Fox and Elizabeth Flory worked on a compilation of linguistic, ethnographic and ethnological surveys by scholars and Christian missionaries who had worked across the Philippines after World War II. A subscript on the survey's map noted that people had been delineated according to "linguistic, cultural, and racial criteria." Visually, the map appears to be an ecclesiastical presentation with "Christian groups" represented in shades of gray, "Muslim groups" in blue, and "indigenous religion" groups in yellow. The map would later aid the National Commission on Culture and the Arts (NCCA), the official cultural research and development arm of the Philippine state, in categorizing the Philippine population. They were divided into "77 major ethnolinguistic groups" and further split into 224 "subgroups" based on the idea that there are cultural variations among each major ethno-linguistic group or "central culture."
5. Lopez began publishing accounts on linguistic formation in the Philippines during American rule (1941) and carried on with documentation and analysis of various Philippine languages at the time of postcolonial reconstruction. A collection of his writings was compiled by the Archives of Philippine Languages at UP Diliman (1977).
6. The works of the Cebuano Studies Center can be accessed at: www.research.usc.edu.ph/csc.overview.jsp.
7. Rice's work inspired engagement with the ecological systems and peoples of the highlands within and beyond anthropological work. This would help cultivate informed scholarship and assist in facilitating the enactment of state policies, thereby protecting rights of indigenous peoples and upholding the welfare of the forest environment (Olofson 1983; Villamor and Lasco 2006).

8. Critical themes carried out at UGAT conferences during martial law include “The Power of Anthropology: A Dialogue Among Developers” in 1979, “The Anthropology of Power” in 1981, and the “Anthropology of Mass Movements: Peoples Organizations in Social Transformation” in 1983.
9. Post dictatorship, themes of the UGAT conference highlighted issues concerning “Culture Change and National Development” (1987), “Ethnicity and National Unity” (1988), “Anthropology and Resistance” (1989), and “Issues in Cultural Pluralism” (1990), among others.

References

Arce, W.F. (1963) “Social Organization of the Muslim Peoples of Sulu,” *Philippine Studies* 11(2): pp. 242–66.

Abaya, E. (1997) “Territoriality, History, and Identity: An Overview.” Presentation at the 19th UGAT National Conference, Puerto Princesa, Palawan, October 29–31, 1997.

Abaya, E., L. Lucas-Fernan, and D. Noval-Morales (1999) “Shifting Terms of Engagement: A Review of the History of Anthropology in the Philippines.” In *The Philippine Social Science in the Life of the Nation*, V. Miralao, (ed.), pp. 1–10. Quezon City: Philippine Social Science Research Council.

Aguilar, F.V. (2005) “Tracing Origins: ‘Ilustrado’ Nationalism and the Racial Science of Migration,” *The Journal of Asian Studies* 64(3): pp. 605–37.

Alejo, A.E. (2000) *Generating Energies in Mt. Apo: Cultural Politics in a Contested Domain*. Quezon City: Ateneo de Manila University Press.

Anderson, B.O. (1983) *Imagined Community: Reflections on Origin and Spread of Nationalism*. New York: Verso.

Asad, T., (ed.) (1973) *Anthropology and the Colonial Encounter*. London: Ithaca Press.

Austria-Young, J. (2012) “Tungo sa Kultura ng Pakikisangkot: Isang Pagninilay sa Pagpapalakas ng Katutubong Pamayanan Gamit ang Lente ng Antropolohiya” [“Towards a Culture of Involvement: A Reflection on the Strengthening of Indigenous Community Using the Anthropological Lens”], *Agham Tao* 21: pp. 87–110.

Bankoff, G. and K. Weekley (2004) *Celebrating the Centennial of Independence: Post-colonial National Identity in the Philippines*. Manila: De La Salle University Press.

Barrows, D.P. (1905a) *History of the Filipino People*. Indianapolis: The Bobs-Merril Company Publishers.

____ (1905b) “History of the Population: Christian or Civilized Tribes—Non-Christian or Wild Tribes—Chinese and other Foreign Elements in

Filipino Races." In *Census of the Philippine Islands: Vol. 1, Geography, History, and Population*, J.P. Sanger, (dir.), pp. 411–91. Washington: United States Bureau of the Census.

—— (1924) *History of the Philippines, Revised Edition*. London: George Harrap and Company Ltd.

Bautista, M.C.R.B. (2000) "The Social Sciences in the Philippines: Reflections on Trends and Developments," *Philippine Studies* 48(2): pp. 175–208.

Bennagen, P. (1980) "The Asianization of Anthropology," *Asian Studies* 18: pp. 1–26.

Beyer, H.O. (1917) *Population of the Philippine Islands in 1916*. Manila: Philippine Education Co.

Blumentritt, F. (1916) "Philippine Tribes and Languages." In *Philippine Progress Prior to 1898*, vol. 1, A. Craig and C. Benitez, (eds.), pp. 140–62. Manila: Philippine Education Co.

—— (1980[1890]) *An Attempt at Writing a Philippine Ethnography*. M.N. Maceda, trans. Marawi City: University Research Center.

Bragado, E. (2002) "Sukimátem: Isabelo de los Reyes Revisited," *Philippine Studies* 50(1): pp. 50–74.

Brinton, D. (1898) "The Peoples of the Philippines," *American Anthropologist* 11(10): pp. 293–307.

Bruno, J. (1973) *Social World of Tausug: A Study in Culture and Education*. Manila: Centro Escolar University, Research and Development Center.

Bunnell, T., L. Kong, and L. Law (2007) "*Social and Cultural Geographies of South East Asia*." In *Mapping Worlds: International Perspectives on Social and Cultural Geographies*, R. Kitchin, (ed.), pp. 131–45. New York: Routledge.

Burton, E. (1985) "Choice of Curative Resorts: Coping with Illness among the Manobo," *Philippine Sociological Review* 33(1–2): pp. 73–76.

Cannel, F. (1999) *Power and Intimacy in the Christian Philippines*. Quezon City: Ateneo de Manila University Press.

Canuday, J.J. (2009) *Bakwit: The Power of the Displaced*. Quezon City: Ateneo de Manila Press.

Casino, E. (1976) *The Jama Mapun: Changing Samal Society in the Southern Philippines*. Quezon City: Ateneo de Manila University Press.

Coates, A. (1968) *Rizal, Philippine Nationalist and Martyr*. Hong Kong: Oxford University Press.

Cole, F.C. (1913) "The Wild Tribes of Davao District, Mindanao, Field Museum of Natural History," *Publications of the Field Museum of Natural History* 12(2): pp. 49–203.

Constantino, R. (1969) *The Philippines: The Continuing Past*. Quezon City: Foundation for Nationalist Studies.

—— (1978) *The Making of a Filipino: A Story of Filipino Colonial Politics*. Quezon City: Malaya Books.

Covar, P. (1973) *Folk Christianity: A Historic Anthropological Study of Indigenous Religious Movements in the Philippines.* Quezon City: Philippine Social Science Council.

_____ (1995) "Unburdening Philippine Society of Colonialism," *Diliman Review* 34(2): pp. 15–19.

Damsani, M., E. Alawi, and G. Rixhon (1972) "The First People of Sulu," *Sulu Studies* 1: pp. 245–54.

Dator-Bercilla, J. and E. Porio (2017) "Crafting Responsive Local Climate Action Plans through Trust Networks, Social Capital and Community Resilience Initiatives." Presentation, Guian City Local Climate Action Workshop, Philippine Development Research and Resource Center (Visayas), February 5–7, 2017.

De los Reyes, I. (1994[1889]) *El Folklore Filipino* [The Folklore of the Philippines], S.C. Dizon and M. Imson, trans. Quezon City: University of the Philippines Press.

De los Reyes, R. (1984) *Process Documentation: Social Science Research in a Learning Process Approach to Program Development.* Quezon City: Institute of Peoples Culture.

Disoma, E.R. (1990) *The Meranao: A Study of Their Practices and Beliefs.* Marawi City: Department of Sociology, College of Social Sciences and Humanities, Mindanao State University.

Doro, M.E. (2007) "Management and Resolution of Rido Among Meranao in Baloi, Lanao del Norte: Case Studies." In *Rido: Clan Feuding and Conflict Management in Mindanao*, W.M. Torres III, (ed.), pp. 201–53. Makati: The Asia Foundation.

Eder, J.F. (1987) *On the Road to Tribal Extinction: Depopulation, Deculturation, and Adaptive Well-Being Among the Batak of the Philippines.* Berkeley: University of California Press.

Elkins, R. (1982) *Proto-Manobo Kinship System.* Manila: Summer Institute of Linguistics.

Enriquez, V. (1994) *Pagbabangong-dangal: Indigenous Psychology and Cultural Empowerment.* Quezon City: Akademya ng Kultura, Sikolohiyang Pilipino.

Enriquez, V. and E. Protacio-Marcelino (1984) *Neo-colonial Politics and Language Struggle in the Philippines: National Consciousness and Language in Philippine Psychology, 1971–1983.* Quezon City: Akademya ng Sikolohiyang Pilipino, Philippine Psychology Research and Training House.

Eugenio, D.L., (ed.) (1982) *Philippine Folk Literature: An Anthology.* Quezon City: University of the Philippines Press.

Estacio, L.R. Jr. (1996) "Ang Antropolohiya ng Disaster sa Punto de Bista ng mga Ayta (Ang Mga Ayta ng Banawen, Maloma, San Felipe, Zambalaes Bilang Isang Halimbawa)" ["The Anthropology of Disaster from the Point of View of the Aeta (The Case of the Aetas of Banawen, Maloma, San Felipe, and Zambales)"], *Agham Tao* 8: pp. 65–75.

Garvan, J.M. (1931) *The Manobos of Mindanao*. Washington: US Government Printing Office.

Gaspar, K. (2012) *Manobo Dreams in Arakan: A People's Struggle to Keep their Homeland*. Quezon City: Ateneo de Manila University Press.

Gatmaytan, A., (ed.) (2007) *Negotiating Autonomy: Case Study on Philippine Indigenous People's Land Rights*. Quezon City: Legal Rights and Natural Resource Center Kasama sa Kalikasan.

Goh, D. (2007) "States of Ethnography: Colonialism, Resistance, and Cultural Transcription in Malaya and the Philippines, 1890s–1930s," *Comparative Studies in Society and History* 49(1): pp. 109–42.

Guerrero, L. Maria. (1974) *The First Filipino: A Biography of José Rizal*. Manila: National Historical Commission.

Hollnsteiner, M. (1976) "Review of *Slum as a Way of Life in an Urban Environment* by F.L. Jocano," *Philippine Studies* 24: pp. 234–37.

Husin, A. (2009) "Locating Triggers, Reducing Domestic Tensions." In *Conflict Religion and Culture: Domestic and International Implications for Southeast Asia and Australia*, L. Anceschi, J.A. Camilleri, and B. Tolosa Jr., (eds.), pp. 149–58. Quezon City: Ateneo de Manila University Press.

Jagor, F. (1916[1875]) "Feodor Jagor's Travel in the Philippines." In *The Philippines Thru Foreign Eyes*, A. Craig, (ed.), pp. 1–356. Manila: Philippine Education Company.

Jimeno, M. (2008) "Columbia: Citizens and Anthropologists," In *A Companion to Latin American Anthropology*, Deborah Poole, (ed.), pp. 72–89. Oxford: Blackwell Publishing.

Jocano, F.L. (1975) *Slum as a Way of Life*. Quezon City: Punlad Research House.

—— (1982) *A Heritage We Can Be Proud Of*. Quezon City: Punlad Research House.

—— (1983) *Ilocano: An Ethnography of Family and Community Life*. Quezon City: Punlad Research House.

Kiefer, T. (1972a) "The Tausug Polity and the Sultanate of Sulu: A Segmentary State in the Southern Philippines," *Sulu Studies* 1: pp. 19–64.

—— *(1972b) The Tausug, Violence and Law in a Philippine Moslem Society*. New York: Holt, Rinehart and Winston.

Kroeber, A. (1919) *Peoples of the Philippines*. New York: American Museum of Natural History.

Kurais, M. II. (1975) *Boatbuilding of the Sama*. Marawi: University Research Center, Mindanao State University.

Lopez, C. (1941) *A Manual of the Philippine National Language*. Manila: Bureau of Printing.

_____ (1977) *Selected Writings of Cecilio Lopez in Philippine Linguistics*, E. Constantino, (ed.), Quezon City: University of the Philippines Press.

Lynch, F. (1948) "Some Notes on a Brief Field Survey of Hill People of Mt. Iriga, Camarines Sur, Philippines," *Primitive Man* 21: pp. 65–73.

_____ (1952) "Anthropological Interpretation," *Third Science Colloquium* 1: pp. 3–6, 11–13.

_____ (1955) *Evans-Pritchard, Weber, and the Nuer: Discussion*. Unpublished typescript, 6 pages.

_____ (1956) "The Jesuit Letters of Mindanao as a Source of Anthropological Data," *Philippine Studies* 4: pp. 247–72.

_____ (1961) "Islam: The Key to Sulu," Address delivered at the commencement exercises of Notre Dame of Jolo College, Jolo, Sulu, March 19, 1961.

_____ (1962a) "Ateneo Expedition to Sulu," *Philippine Studies* 10: 314–16.

_____ (1962b) "Town Fiesta: An Anthropologist's View," *Philippine International* 6: pp. 4–11, 26–27.

Lynch, F., (ed.) (1963) *Sulu's People and their Art*. Quezon City: Ateneo de Manila University Press.

Lynch, F. and M.R. Hollnsteiner (1961) "Sixty Years of Philippine Ethnology: A First Glance at the Years 1901–1961," *Science Review* 2: pp. 1–5.

Lynch, O.J. (1983) "The Philippine Indigenous Law Collection: An Introduction and Preliminary Bibliography," *Philippine Law Journal* 58: pp. 457–538.

Maceda, J. (1977) "Ang Mga Kaisipan sa Timog Silangang Asya," [Thoughts on Southeast Asia] *Musika Jornal* 1: pp. 5–11.

_____ (1979) "Ang Musika sa Pilipinas sa ika-19 Daangtaon," [Nineteenth-Century Philippine Music], *Musika Jornal* 3: pp. 7–40.

Madale, A.T. (1977) *Aspects of Maranao Taritib and Adat as Reflected in Radia Indarapatra*. Marawi City: University Research Center, Mindanao State University.

_____ (1988) "Muslims: The Misunderstood Filipinos," *Philippine Studies* 46(4): pp. 492–503.

Magos, A.P. (2004) "Towards Indigenisation: Responses, Challenges, and Experiences in the Philippines." In *The Making of Anthropology in East and Southeast Asia*, S. Yamashita, J. Bosco, and J.S. Eades, (eds.), pp. 335–58. Oxford, London: Berghahn Books.

Manuel, E.A. (1973) *Menuvu Social Organization*. Quezon City: University of the Philippines Press.

_____ (1977) *A Review of Oral Literature Scholarship in the Philippine Universities*. Philippines: National Folklore Congress.

_____ (1978) *Toward an Inventory of Philippine Musical Instruments: A Checklist of the Heritage from Twenty-three Ethnolinguistic Groups*. Quezon City: Asian Studies.

——— (1985) *Guide for the Study of Philippine Folklore.* Quezon City: Philippine Folklore Society.

Media Mindanao News Service Investigative Team (1993) *Ethnocide: Is it Real?* Davao City: Media Mindanao News Service.

Mojares, R. (2006) *Brains of the Nation: Pedro Paterno, T.H. Pardo de Tavera, Isabelo de los Reyes, and the Production of Modern Knowledge.* Quezon City: Ateneo de Manila Press.

Morga, A. (1971[1609]) *Sucesos de las Islas Filipinas* [*Events in the Philippines Island*], J.S. Cummins, (trans. and ed.). Cambridge: Cambridge University Press.

Nicolas, A.M. Jr (1977) "Ang Musika ng mga Yakan sa Pulo ng Basilan," ["The Music of the Yakan in Basilan Island"], *Musika Jornal* 1: pp. 79–110.

Ocampo, A. (1998) "Rizal's Morga and Views of Philippine History," *Philippine Studies* 46(2): pp. 184–214.

Olofson, H. (1983) "Indigenous Agroforestry Systems," *Philippine Quarterly of Culture and Society* 11(2–3): pp. 149–74.

Palma, R. (1949). *The Pride of the Malay Race: A Biography of José Rizal,* Roman Ozaeta, (trans.). New York: Prentice-Hall.

Panaguiton, R.V. (2010) "Locating the Sacred in the City: Pilgrimage and Spirituality in Zamboanga City," *Agham Tao* 19: pp. 1–19.

Padilla, S. (2013) "Anthropology and GIS: Temporal and Spatial Distribution of the Philippine Negrito Groups," *Human Biology* 85(1–3): pp. 209–30.

Pellesen, K. (1972) "Reciprocity in Samal Marriage," *Sulu Studies* 1: pp. 123–42.

Pertierra, R. (2010) *The Anthropology of the New Media in the Philippines.* Quezon City: Ateneo de Manila University.

Pe-Pua, R. and E.P. Marcelino (2000) "Sikolohiyang Pilipino (Filipino Psychology): A Legacy of Virgilio G. Enriquez," *Asian Journal of Psychology* 3(1): pp. 49–71.

Polack, E., E. Luna and J. Dator-Bercilla (2010) *Accountability for Disaster Risk Reduction: Lessons from the Philippines.* London: Climate and Disaster Governance.

Porio, E. (2009) "State, Society and the Institution of Sociological Practice in the Philippines." In *Diverse Sociological Traditions around the World,* Sujata Patel, (ed.), pp. 335–45. London: Sage.

——— (2012) "Policy-driven Research, Audit, Culture, and Power: Transforming Sociological Practices in the Philippines." In *The Shape of Sociology for the 21st Century: Tradition and Renewal,* D. Kalekin-Fishman and A. Denis, (eds.), pp. 297–312. London: Sage.

——— (1998) "Participatory/People-Centered Development: A Social Science Discourse in Philippine Politics and Governance." Presentation at the National Social Science Congress IV's Pre-Congress III on Philippine Social Sciences and Public Policy and Practice, Philippine Social Science Center, Quezon City, May 22–23, 1998.

Porio, E., F. Lynch and M.R. Hollnsteiner (1978) *Filipino Family, Community, and Nation*. Quezon City: Ateneo de Manila University Press.

Prill-Brett, J. (1992) *Ibaloy Customary Law on Land Resources*. Working Paper 19. Cordillera Studies Center, University of the Philippines.

____ (1994) "Indigenous Land Rights and Legal Pluralism among Philippine Highlanders," *Law and Society Review* 28(3): pp. 687–97.

____ (1995) "Indigenous Knowledge System on Natural Resource Conflict Management, Cordillera, Northern Philippines," *Diliman Review* 43: pp. 50–84.

Rice, D. (1982) *Development and Ethics: The Kalahan Experience*. Manila: Integrated Research Center, De La Salle University.

____ (2007) *Basic Upland Ecology*. Quezon City: New Day.

Rixhon, G. (1972a) "Ten Years of Research in Sulu: 1961–1971," *Sulu Studies* 1: pp. 1–19.

____ (1972b) "A Cooperative Venture in Folk-Literature Collection Translation," *Sulu Studies* 1: pp. 163–71.

Rizal, J. (2002[1884]) "Homage to Luna and Hidalgo." In *Twenty Speeches that Moved a Nation*, M.L. Quezon III, (ed.), Pasig: Anvil Publishing, Inc.

Tauli-Corpuz, V. (2001) "Diversity, Universality and Democracy: A Perspective of an Indigenous Woman," *Women in Action*, 3: p. 3.

Tokoro, I. (2003). "Transformation of Shamanic Rituals among the Tabawan Island, Sulu Archipelago, Southern Philippines." In *Globalization in Southeast Asia: Local, National and Transnational Perspectives*, S. Yamashita and J.S. Eades, (eds.), pp. 175–78. New York and Oxford: Berghahn Books.

Trimillos, R.D. "The Setting of Vocal Music among the Tausug," *Sulu Studies* 1: pp. 65–80.

Sather, C. (2006) "Sea Nomads and Rainforest Hunter-Gatherers: Foraging Adaptations in the Indo-Malaysian Archipelago." In *Austronesians: Historical and Comparative Perspectives*, P. Bellwood, J.J. Fox, and D. Tryon, (eds.), pp. 235–76. Canberra: Australian National University E-Press.

Salazar, Z. (1997) "Ang Pantayong Pananaw Bilang Diskursong Pangkabihasnan" ["Pantayo Thought as Social Discourse"]. In *Pantayong Pananaw: Ugat at Kabuluhan, Pambungad sa Pag-aaral ng Bagong Kasaysayan* [*Pantayo Thought: Roots and Meanings, an Introduction to the Study of a New History*], A. Navarro, M.J. Rodriguez, and V. Villan, (eds.), pp. 79–121. Philippines: Palimbagang Kalawakan.

Salvador-Amores, A. (2013) *Tapping Ink, Tattooing Identities: Tradition and Modernity in Contemporary Kalinga Society*. Quezon City: University of the Philippines Press.

San Juan, E. (1974) *Introduction to Modern Pilipino Literature*. New York: Twayne Publishers.

Scaff, A. (1955) *The Philippine Answer to Communism*. Stanford: Stanford University Press.

Schumacher, J.N. (1991) *The Making of a Nation: Essays on Nineteenth-Century Filipino Nationalism*. Quezon City: Ateneo de Manila University Press.

Stanton, D. (1963) "Art in Sulu," *Philippine Studies* 11(3): 463–502.

Tamanio-Yraola, M. (1979). "Ang Musika ng mga Bontok Igorot sa Sandanga, Lalawigang Bulubundukin" ["The Music of the Bontok Igorot in Sandanga, Mountain Province"], *Musika Jornal* 3: pp. 41–113.

Torres, W.M., (ed.) (2007) *Rido: Clan Feuding and Conflict Management in Mindanao*. Makati: The Asia Foundation.

United States Philippine Commission (1901) *First Annual Report of the Philippine Commission*, part 1. Washington: Government Printing Office.

——— (1904) *Reports of the Philippine Commission (1900–1903)*. Washington: Government Printing Office.

Veneracion, C.C. (1989) *A Decade of Process Documentation: Synthesis and Reflection*. Quezon City: Institute of Philippine Culture.

Villamor, G.D. and R.D. Lasco (2006) "The Ikalahan Ancestral Domain, the Philippines." In *Community Forest Management as a Carbon Mitigation Option: Case Studies*, D. Murdiyarso and M. Skutsch, (eds.), pp. 43–50. Bogor Barat (Indonesia): Center for International Forestry Research.

Virchow, R. (1916) "The Peopling of the Philippines." In *The Philippines Thru Foreign Eyes*, A. Craig, (ed.), O.T. Mason, (trans.) pp. 536–50. Manila: Philippine Education Company.

Warren, J.F. (1981) *The Sulu Zone, 1768–1898: The Dynamics of External Trade, Slavery, and Ethnicity in the Transformation of a Southeast Asian Maritime State*. Singapore: Singapore University Press.

Worcester, D.C. (1898) *The Philippine Islands and their People*. New York and London: MacMillan and Co.

——— (1906) "The Non-Christian Tribes of Northern Luzon," *The Philippine Journal of Science* 1(8): pp. 791–863.

——— (1914) *The Philippines Past and Present*. New York, London: MacMillan and Co.

Zamora, M. (1976) "Cultural Anthropology in the Philippines 1900–1983: Perspectives, Problems, and Prospects." In *Changing Identities in Modern Southeast Asia*, D.J. Banks, (ed.), pp. 311–40. The Hague: Mouton and Co.

Zialicita, F.N. (2005) *Authentic Though Not Exotic: Essay on Filipino Identity*. Quezon City: Ateneo de Manila University Press.

CHAPTER 2 CAMBODIAN ANTHROPOLOGY Negotiating Identity and Change

Chivoin Peou

Cambodia lacks a distinct national tradition of social-cultural anthropology. The social upheavals from the late 1960s to the end of the 1980s not only made Cambodia inaccessible to researchers for a long period but also left local scholarship in shambles. Early intellectual achievements from the early to mid twentieth century were shattered, and the progress since the 1990s has been fragmentary and slow. Due mainly to historical turmoil in the late twentieth century, social sciences have been poorly developed in the country, let alone any attempt to "indigenize" them, and a lineage of anthropological work—in the sense of there being subsequent generations of local anthropologists whose training or intellectual engagement with certain theoretical perspectives or objects of study can be traced back to a few forebears in colonial times—did not materialize as in the case of some other Southeast Asian countries (see King and Wilder 2003; Yamashita et al. 2004; Ibrahim 2010; Thompson 2012; Kleinen 2013; Fanselow 2014).

The reinvention of Cambodia in the 1990s through massive international aid, imposed democratization and marketization has resulted in impressive economic growth and development as well as social transformation. These transformations have led to ensuing challenges for Cambodia to fit into a new world order, on the one hand, and to reconcile with its past, on the other (see Ollier and Winter 2006; Öjendal and Lilja 2009; Hughes and Un 2011). In this chapter, I demonstrate that these challenges of identity and social change are a central concern of anthropological work by Cambodian intellectuals in the contemporary period as a result of the country's historical developments in the last century.

The focus of this contribution is on "local" scholarship, defined as the works of authors or intellectuals who share a common cultural or national identity with their research subjects—in this case, a sense of being a "Khmer" or of belonging to Cambodia as a political and sociocultural entity.[1] The focus is therefore on the works of Cambodian intellectuals who have been trained in social and cultural anthropology or ethnology, and local institutions engaged with the (re)invention of Cambodia through academic knowledge production. Their contributions are relatively recent, mostly from the last twenty-five years, but are loosely linked to various institutional and intellectual developments throughout the twentieth century. These historical developments were precursors to recent local anthropological works, and will be framed here in two parallel domains. The first domain is that of local knowledge production on Cambodian society and culture, which contributed to a collective imagination and narrative about Cambodia as a unified social entity. The second domain refers to the work of the few foreign anthropologists who were significant in providing "baseline" academic references about Cambodian society or in the training of local anthropologists.[2]

To provide a historically situated account of local anthropology, I begin with a brief description of Cambodia's modern history since the early twentieth century. The main account of both institutional and individual agendas over the century can be organized into three broad periods. The first covers the formative years of a Cambodian national cultural identity from the early twentieth century to 1975, when the Khmer Rouge took control of the country and abolished all intellectual activities through the physical destruction of educational institutions and persecution of intellectuals. The second period refers to the fifteen years of Cambodia's political isolation and physical inaccessibility, including the Khmer Rouge's reign of terror in 1975–79 and the authoritarian People's Republic of Kampuchea in 1979–89. The final period concerns "contemporary Cambodia," beginning with the post-war reconstruction and reopening of the country in the 1990s (Winter and Ollier 2006).

For many who are associated with the Royal University of Fine Arts, a product of the modern nation-building project of the early independence years, the cultural destruction of the tumultuous 1970s and 1980s has driven their anthropological work toward the desire to research and preserve Cambodian cultural identity, including "traditional" rituals, beliefs and arts. For a new but small generation of local scholars who have been trained overseas in anthropology as an applied science, their research agenda has engaged in a broad question of contemporary change in post-conflict Cambodian society, including the issues of local sociopolitical change amidst imposed democratization, rural cultural and organizational responses to international aid, and persisting and changing sociocultural patterns in rural society.

A Brief Modern History of Cambodia

Modernization projects, from the "civilizing mission" of Western colonialists to the opposing visions of modernity in the Cold War era and the post-Cold War democratization and neoliberal globalization, have been powerful in the (re)invention of "Third World" societies in the last century (Chang 2010). Cambodia's historical trajectory into the modern age was typical but more tragic than that of most other countries. French colonial rule started in 1863, but significant changes did not take place until the early twentieth century (Chandler 2008). The French provided a template for a modern nation state through myriad legal, institutional and organizational inventions, including the introduction of land reform, the abolishment of slavery, the creation of (limited) modern public education, industrial production, a bureaucratic administration, and public infrastructure (see Martin 1994: 29–44; Chandler 2008: 167–210).

After independence in 1953, Cambodia briefly prospered economically and culturally under Prince Sihanouk's leadership. The early years of independence, from the early 1950s until the late 1960s, were regarded by many Cambodians as a "golden age" (Ebihara 1993: 150; Chandler 2008: 7). The economic and cultural developments in these years provided a strong basis for configuring a social structure and cultural outlook that came to characterize Cambodian or Khmer society, which includes some continuity of the institutions and values from preceding centuries, including Buddhism, the family, the peasantry and norms that govern social relations.

In the late 1960s, the spillover of the Vietnam War into Cambodia and internal political upheavals brought about civil warfare and utter destruction throughout the 1970s. By 1975, when the Khmer Rouge won the war, up to 300,000 Cambodians are estimated to have died from the war (Heuveline 1998), and half of the population became war refugees (Ablin and Hood 1990). The Khmer Rouge aimed to create a communist utopia by implementing a radical social engineering project through the massive relocation of the population to rural areas and the institutionalization of a new system of values and social relations, which directly or indirectly killed up to 2 million people or one-quarter of the population (Kiernan 1996: 456–63; Chandler 2008: 7).

In 1979, Vietnamese forces defeated the Khmer Rouge and installed a new socialist regime supported by the Vietnamese and the Eastern communist bloc. Throughout the 1980s, the socialist state began rebuilding public infrastructure and services, including roads, hospitals and schools, but poverty, insecurity and political oppression remained rife (see Gottesman 2004). By 1990, a certain degree of social and cultural normalcy was achieved with the flourishing of local markets and trades, the resumption of many cultural practices, an improved educational system, and the return of subsistence-oriented peasantry after the failure of collective farming (Gottesman 2004: 188–204, 271–300; Chandler 2008: 285).

The dissolution of the Eastern bloc and the conclusion of the Cold War spelt an end to "socialist" Cambodia and paved the way for a new Cambodia, engendering a "triple transition" from war, authoritarianism and command economy to peace, democracy and a free market (Peou 2000). The United Nations Transnational Authority in Cambodia (UNTAC), the most expensive United Nations mission to date at the time (Chandler 2008), was established to oversee the political transition in 1991–93 and organized the general election in 1993, although the civil war did not end until 1998. Full-scale liberalization was undertaken throughout the 1990s, starting with the 1994–96 structural adjustment program. Accompanying these political and economic transitions, massive foreign aid began to flow into Cambodia in the early 1990s, transforming Cambodia into one of the world's most aid-dependent countries. The past two decades have seen profound social changes engendered by this reconstruction and reopening of Cambodia. The institutional and individual experiences of knowledge production and (re)inventing anthropology in Cambodia have taken place in this historical context of identity formation through colonial control and postcolonial nation-building, of cataclysmic upheavals, and of reintegration into a new world order.

Pre-1975: Local Anthropological Precursors

In her book *Cambodge: The Cultivation of a Nation, 1860–1945*, Penny Edwards demonstrates how Cambodian "graduates of colonial modernity," referring to local intellectuals who emerged during the French colonial rule through training and working with French administrators and scholars, "helped to weld the fragmented cultural landscape of the precolonial era into a bounded body of culture that would become the focus of nationalist devotion" (2007: 91). The emergence of a national cultural identity in the first half of the twentieth century, therefore, owed much to French colonial legacies and the "colonial graduates," who continued to (re)invent this national identity throughout the postcolonial years (see Peycam 2010, 2011). A few foreign anthropologists also began researching in Cambodia in the mid twentieth century, although little of their work contributed to local scholarship on the Cambodian identity. These studies on nation-building in Cambodia that were initiated by foreigners would become significant in shaping the training and research focus of later generations of Cambodian anthropologists.

Colonial Foundations for Inventing a National Identity

Not only did the French rule between 1863 and 1953 decisively shape the geographical boundary and political character of "modern" Cambodia[3] (see Chandler 2008), but it also played a significant role in bringing about a national cultural identity through colonial knowledge production and political endeavors (for a comprehensive account, see Edwards 2007). As Peycam (2010: 155) remarks, "What we know of the history of Cambodia is largely the result of a colonial era interpretation. Even the name of Cambodia (an English translation of the French *Cambodge*) does not escape this colonial era construction."

The establishment of the École française d'Extrême-Orient (EFEO) in 1902 in Saigon, present-day Ho Chi Minh City, Vietnam, was of particular significance. In Cambodia, the EFEO's main focus was to study, document and represent Cambodia's antiquities through such disciplines as philology and archeology, which contributed enormously to the emergence of a Khmer national narrative and cultural identity in the twentieth century (see Edwards 2007; Peycam 2010, 2011). One of the most significant achievements was the restoration of the Angkor temple complex and discursive construction of the Angkorean era as the glorious past from which present-day

Cambodia descended. The tripartite narrative of a pre-Angkorean origin, Angkorean grandeur, and post-Angkorean decline not only served the political and ideological agenda of the French (Peycam 2010), but also remains an unbreakable identity narrative today among the Cambodian population. Some of the EFEO scholars essential to this legacy included Louis Finot (1864–1935), Goerges Coedès (1886–1969), and Bernard-Philippe Groslier (1926–86), and their works have regularly been referenced in Khmer texts on "Khmer civilization."

The French also helped found other initiatives that were critical to the formation of Cambodia's national cultural character throughout most of the twentieth century. In 1922, the Pali School was brought under the EFEO and renamed École Supérieure de Pali (ESP). In 1925, the Royal Library was founded under the directorship of EFEO scholar Suzanne Karpelès (1890–1968), who started Cambodia's first Khmer language journal *Kambuja Suriya* [*Cambodian Sun*] in 1927, an influential monthly periodical that helped define a national identity for Cambodia (Chigas 2000; Edwards 2007; Peycam 2010). With Karpelès' proposal, the prestigious Buddhist Institute was established in 1930 under her leadership. The Institute was perhaps the single most important institution in invigorating scholarship on Cambodian Buddhism and culture (see Chheat et al. 2005).

French colonial rule was also important in the training of Cambodian intellectuals in France. By the 1960s, several hundred Cambodians had studied in France (Martin 1994), and many became prominent figures in promoting a new modern Cambodia. These included Pou Saveros, the first Cambodian woman with a PhD on Khmer literature; linguist and playwright Keng Vansak; sociologist Man Tay Son; art historian Chea Tay Seng; performing artist Hang Thoun Hak; and architect Vann Molyvann (see Peycam 2011: 118–221).[4] As Edwards (2007) argues, Cambodian individuals working alongside the French and within the colonial and immediate postcolonial milieus were central to the emergence of a national identity of Cambodia in the mid and late twentieth century.

National Identity through Local Knowledge Production

The Buddhist Institute, whose ownership was transferred to Cambodians in 1950, played a critical role in publishing important works by local intellectuals from the 1930s until the early 1970s. Venerable Choun Nath published the first volume of the first Khmer dictionary in 1938, followed by the second volume in 1943. The translation of the holy Theravada scriptures, the *Tripitaka*, began in 1930 (Chheat et al. 2005). At the same time, the journal *Kambuja Suriya* allowed Cambodians to disseminate their scholarly and literary works, including "modern" novels by Kim Hak and Rin Kim, and literary criticisms by Ly Theam Teng, Dik Keam and Leang Hap An (Chigas 2000). The Institute and its Commission of Cambodian Mores and Customs were also active in documenting and publishing on Cambodian cultural values and practices, such as Buddhism, popular dances, music, rituals and norms, written by numerous local intellectuals, including Venerable Huot Tath, Venerable Em Sou, Venerable Pang Khat, Nhok Them, Pich Sal and Chap Pin. Overall, the work of the Buddhist Institute was critical to the (re)invention of a national identity through the (re)discovery and (re)production of a Cambodian national language, national religion and national culture (see also Edwards 2007).

After independence in 1953, an array of secondary school teachers also wrote on Cambodian culture and "civilization" in the form of textbooks and supplementary study texts. Some popular texts survived the destruction of 1975–79 and became widely used again in the 1990s and 2000s for secondary education and university entrance examinations, including *Khmer Civilization* by Ly Theam Teng (1965), *Culture-Civilization: Khmer-India* by Teav Chhay Sok (1971–72), and *Khmer Civilization* by Troeung Ngea (1974). Generally drawing from the works of local intellectuals at the Buddhist Institute and French scholars associated with the EFEO, these texts focused on summarizing the origins and forms of Cambodian culture through religion, art, ethnicity, architecture, customs and literature. They served to consolidate a popular narrative of a Cambodian national identity that was still much shaped by French scholarship. For example, the tripartite narrative of pre-Angkorean, Angkorean and post-Angkorean trajectory and the discursive representation of Cambodia as a "Far Eastern" nation, both of which were constructed through the prism of European colonizers, were taken for granted.

One of the most significant post-independence institutional creations, which had a major impact on the construction of a new modern Cambodian identity, was the establishment of the Royal University of Fine Arts (RUFA) in 1965. Renowned Cambodian architect Vann Molyvann, a graduate from École nationale supérieure des Beaux-Arts in Paris, was appointed the first rector of the university, which had five departments: Architecture and Urban Planning; Plastic Arts; Music; Dramatic and Choreographic Arts; and Archeology. Within these departments, the university's major objectives were to produce indigenous scholars and to reinvent a modern national identity for Cambodia. The latter was to be accomplished through the research and preservation of some classic art forms and the modernization of other Cambodian arts; these art forms included dance, music, theatrical performance, painting, sculpture and architecture (Reyum 2011: 319–36). For instance, in the Department of Dramatic and Choreographic Arts, both classical and folk dance as well as Western ballet instructions were offered. Given Cambodia's colonial past, instructors were mostly French or French-speaking. During the first few years, there were several hundred students at the university, and promising graduates were often given support to pursue further study overseas, especially in France. Given RUFA's presumed role in (re)inventing a national cultural identity in the context of a young independent nation state, first- and next-generation graduates with a strong attachment to the university became preoccupied with the cultural identity agenda.

Anthropological Initiation

Given the EFEO's early focus on Cambodia's antiquities, early French scholar-administrators who documented everyday life and culture, such as Étienne François Aymonier (1844–1929) and Adhémard Leclère (1855–1917), were not associated with the EFEO and were often not given due importance (Peycam 2010). Anthropology and ethnology only became integrated into the school later with the creation of the Institute of Ethnology in Hanoi in 1937 (see Nguyen, this volume), after which ethnographic work was increasingly conducted in Cambodia. This francophone scholarship included Evelyne Porée-Maspéro's work on Khmer customs and George Condominas' on highland peoples on the Cambodian–Vietnamese border. Condominas' work inspired village-based ethnography by other French scholars, including Juliette Baccot, Jean Ellul, Jacqueline Métra and Gabriele Martel (see Peycam 2010: 165–67).

These French anthropologists and ethnologists, however, appeared to have had little impact on local anthropological scholarship, except for the training of an influential, future Cambodian anthropologist: Ang Choulean. Ang Choulean began his undergraduate study at the

Department of Archeology of RUFA in 1965. It was there that he met French anthropologists and ethnologists who came to teach at RUFA. Among them, Jean Ellul, who was conducting research on elephant taming, was particularly influential. Although armed conflicts in Cambodia had begun in the late 1960s, making fieldwork in the country unfeasible, Ellul managed to bring Ang Choulean as a research assistant to study elephant taming among Khmer communities in Surin, a province in Thailand. It was through this initiation process that Ang Choulean became fascinated by ethnography, and in 1974 went to study ethnology at École des Hautes Études en Sciences Sociales, Paris, where he trained under George Condominas and obtained his doctorate in 1982.

Anglophone anthropological work on Cambodia before 1990 was very limited, with only two English-speaking anthropologists known to have conducted fieldwork in pre-war Cambodia. One of them was May Ebihara, who conducted research in a wet rice-growing village in Cambodia in 1959–60 for her doctoral study at Colombia University. Because of armed conflict that broke out in Cambodia in the 1960s, she was not able to revisit the village until 1989. Even though Ebihara never directly trained any Cambodian anthropologists or anthropologists studying Cambodia, she still became important for local anthropology. Her doctoral thesis "Svay, A Khmer Village in Cambodia" (Ebihara 1968; and other later works in 1973, 1990, 1993) became a standard reference text for subsequent generations of scholars—local and foreign—who were trying to understand a pre-war Cambodian village. This is because the study provided a comprehensive description of numerous aspects of a Cambodian village life, including social structure, economic organization, religion, life cycle, political organization, and relations beyond the village—in other words, a holistic ethnographic approach, which was an anthropological tradition that was already losing prominence by the 1970s.

The other English-speaking anthropologist was Milada Kalab of the University of Durham. She conducted fieldwork in a rural village along the Mekong River in 1965–66, but was refused a visa to enter Cambodia for follow-up research in 1967. Her work also covers fundamental aspects of village life in rural Cambodia, including Buddhism, mobility and village structure (see Kalab 1968, 1976, 1990), but is largely unknown among later generations of Cambodian researchers. Kalab is also not known to have trained any anthropologists researching Cambodia.

1975–1989: Detached Observation and Cultural Preservation

What happened to Cambodia between 1975 and 1979 is now well known: the reign of terror by the radical revolutionary Khmer Rouge. All kinds of formal local knowledge production, let alone anthropological scholarship, suffered utter destruction. Institutions such as the Buddhist Institute and the (Royal) University of Fine Arts were closed down.[5] Schools were demolished, textbooks destroyed, and the educated population suffered disproportionately, with just over 10 percent of the country's teachers surviving the Khmer Rouge regime (Russell 1987). Cambodia became completely inaccessible to research. After the Khmer Rouge was defeated by Vietnam in 1979, the authoritarian People's Republic of Kampuchea ran the country throughout the 1980s with military, technical and financial aid from Vietnam and the Eastern bloc. Education was gradually restored to a humble level with technical experts and instructors sent in from the socialist bloc (Russell 1987; Dy 2004). The School of Fine Arts was established in the early 1980s and was only upgraded and renamed the University of Fine Arts in 1989, in an attempt to re-establish the prominence of its pre-war predecessor, RUFA. However, Cambodia remained generally inaccessible to researchers throughout the 1980s. Unlike in Vietnam and Laos, Soviet and Vietnamese ethnology did not appear to have become established due to Cambodia's short-lived socialist rule (see Nguyen, this volume; Dang, this volume; and Evans 2000). In this context, scholarly endeavors concerning Cambodia were limited to three modes: studies of Cambodia by members of the Cambodian diaspora community, the study of the Cambodian diaspora itself, and limited attempts to preserve some aspects of a Cambodian cultural identity.

Given the inaccessibility of Cambodia in the 1970s and 1980s, anthropological work shifted toward studying members of the Cambodian diaspora. Kalab's later, occasional work on Cambodia, for example, was based on observing and interviewing Cambodian refugees in the United States, France, Germany, Australia and Thailand (see Kalab 1990, 1994). Ebihara completed her doctorate in 1968 and went to teach at the City University of New York (CUNY), whose lack of programs on Southeast Asia, such as Southeast Asian history and languages, discouraged her from accepting graduate students who expressed interest in studying Cambodia (see Marston 2011: 203–204).

Regardless, Ebihara continued to write and published several works on Cambodia in the 1970s and 1980s (see Marston 2011: 215–16).

During this period of inaccessibility, the Indochina Studies Program (ISP) based in the United States was critical in sustaining anthropological research on Cambodia. Established in 1983 by the Social Science Research Council and the American Council of Learned Societies, the ISP was aimed at supporting research activities on Cambodia, Laos and Vietnam by scholars and students in North America, Europe and Australia. Given that access to these countries was difficult, the research supported by the ISP was conducted primarily in the Cambodian, Laotian and Vietnamese communities overseas. Ebihara sat on the ISP committee between 1983 and 1988, which allowed her to develop connections with a new generation of anthropologists who were supported by the program and studied Cambodia. One of these was Judy Ledgerwood, who had Ebihara (at CUNY) as an external advisor during her doctoral study at Cornell University. The two would later conduct research and publish several works together, but Ebihara had a greater influence on Ledgerwood in professional and methodological terms rather than theoretical terms. Ledgerwood's doctoral dissertation, completed in 1990, was based on research in the Cambodian diaspora living in the United States. As will be shown, she would later become a vital figure in training local anthropologists in post-war Cambodia. Another ISP recipient was John Marston, whose ISP grant enabled him to complete his MA research on language use during the Khmer Rouge among Cambodian refugees in the United States, and to pursue his doctorate in anthropology and conduct fieldwork in Cambodia in the early 1990s.[6]

The intellectual and cultural destruction by the Khmer Rouge also prompted a group of Cambodian intellectuals based in Paris to establish an association called the Centre de documentation et de recherche sur la civilisation Khmère [Resource and Research Center for Khmer Civilization] (CEDORECK) in 1977. CEDORECK is particularly noteworthy, for it was a "bottom-up" initiative to preserve "Khmer culture" through research and documentation "in exile" (Peycam 2011: 23–28). Given its francophone lineage, CEDORECK's work was predominantly in French. Besides setting up a visitor center and a library, the organization published the annual journal *Seksa Khmer* [*Khmer Studies*] and several books focusing on Cambodian language, literature, arts and customs. Prominent Cambodian contributors to the journal, besides its founding president Nouth Narang, included Pou Saveros, Khing Hoc Dy (both with expertise in Khmer language and literature), and Ang Choulean, whose dissertation "Les êtres surnaturels dans la religión populaire khmère" ["Supernatural Beings in Khmer Popular Religion"], written in French, was also published by CEDORECK in 1986. However, CEDORECK ceased operation in the early 1990s because of disagreements within the group and the departure of some founding members (Peycam 2011).

Post-1990: Inchoate Anthropology

The historical, institutional and intellectual context of twentieth-century Cambodia has had profound impacts on local anthropology in the past twenty-five years. Of particular importance are the cataclysmic events of the 1970s and 1980s, which not only utterly damaged Cambodia's local scholarship but also engendered a sense of loss of traditional cultural order (Ledgerwood et al. 1994).[7] Therefore, the priority among many local intellectuals since the war, some of whom were trained in anthropology, has been to revive the cultural identity of Cambodia. In addition, the post-conflict reconstruction and reopening of Cambodia in the 1990s also increasingly allowed foreign anthropologists to study the country.[8] However, internationally anthropology has shifted from studying the "whole culture," of which Ebihara's work on Cambodia was an exemplary case, toward an applied science of dealing with contemporary issues (see Thompson 2012). In this context, local anthropological work on Cambodia since 1990 has emerged in a twin-track fashion amidst a slow and fragmentary institutional development: as work that is permeated with the culturalist agenda of reviving Cambodia's cultural identity through Khmer studies, and as an applied science of analyzing contemporary change.

Early Institutional Reinvigoration in the 1990s and 2000s

Given the internationally driven agenda of "reconstructing" a post-war Cambodia in the 1990s, several institutional and individual initiatives to (re)generate scholarship on Cambodian culture and society were started, usually with foreign financial and technical support. The Buddhist Institute was re-established in 1992 with support from the Heinrich Böll Foundation and some Japanese agencies and individuals. Among its main tasks was the reprinting of the *Tripitaka* (the holy

Theravada Buddhist scriptures) and other materials, aimed at the "compilation and conservation of Khmer cultural identity in general" (Chheat et al. 2005: 43).

The School of Fine Arts, established in the early 1980s, was upgraded to become the University of Fine Arts in 1989. Its name reverted to the Royal University of Fine Arts (RUFA) in 1993, following the restoration of the constitutional monarchy. It was at RUFA that most of the anthropological work in post-war Cambodia took root, and this was only possible through assistance from some international organizations and a few significant individuals. Ang Choulean returned to help re-establish the Department of Archeology in 1990, and a number of foreign scholars and anthropologists established connections and research activities with the university. Miriam Stark of the University of Hawai'i began archeological research in Cambodia in 1996, and contributed to the training of Cambodian students at RUFA. Judy Ledgerwood, first at the East West Center in Hawai'i and then at Northern Illinois University, established connections with RUFA in the early 1990s and taught anthropology there in 1992 and again from 2002 to 2003.[9] Other foreign scholars researching Cambodian society and culture in the 1990s, including Penny Edwards, John Marston, Kate Frieson, Toni Shapiro, Ashley Thompson, Michael Vickery, Anne Guillou and other French scholars, also became connected with RUFA. This allowed some of RUFA's students to receive fieldwork training under these scholars by working as their research assistants.

Another significant institutional development was the creation of the Department of Sociology at the Royal University of Phnom Penh (RUPP) in 1994. With financial and technical support from the Italian non-governmental organization (NGO) New Humanity and some universities in Italy, graduates from bachelor's programs in philosophy and history at RUPP were supported for further graduate training in social sciences abroad, in countries such as the Philippines and Japan. Among these beneficiaries, Dork Vuthy went on to pursue graduate study in cultural anthropology at Tsukuba University, Japan, in 1996. To continue this capacity-building project at RUPP's sociology department, a master's program in "sociology-anthropology" was established in 2006 with financial support from New Humanity. The combining of anthropology with sociology was understandable given the program's objectives to transcend disciplinary boundaries and focus on training its students in "applied research" (see Sinha, this volume, for parallels in the case of Singapore). Given its attachment to the sociology department, the program has had only a few "part-time" anthropologists in its faculty, including Dork Vuthy himself and Ang Choulean (in addition to his work at RUFA). The master's program in sociology-anthropology has produced about fifty graduates up to 2016, of which only some have conducted ethnographic research of varying standards in Cambodia for their MA theses. Their works discuss a range of issues, such as ethnic minorities, rural livelihoods, socio-economic relations, education and health.

There were also significant initiatives by NGOs in reviving scholarship on Cambodian culture and society, including the Reyum Institute of Arts and Culture (Reyum) and the Center for Khmer Studies (CKS). Ly Daravuth and Ingrid Muan founded Reyum in 1998 with financial support from several international foundations and individuals. Reyum's book publication projects provided support to many Cambodian researchers who wanted to research and publish their works on Cambodian culture and society in Khmer or English. Topics covered include, Khmer silver by Kong Vireak, folk theater by Preap Chanmara, traditional measurements by Chea Narin, Khmer food by Chea Sophary, transportation in Cambodia by Kem Sonine, and narrative mural paintings in pagodas by San Phalla.

The CKS was founded in 1999 as a member organization of the Council of American Overseas Research Centers (COARC) in Southeast Asia with the objective to provide sustained research and training to promote scholarship on Cambodia. Unlike Reyum, the CKS does not only focus on Cambodian culture, and it approaches "Khmer studies" in a broad sense that encompasses not only cultural and archeological but also contemporary socio-economic themes. Besides setting up a library for research, the CKS provides research fellowships and training programs for foreign and local researchers and students. It also organizes academic conferences and publishes the peer-reviewed journal *Siksacakr: Journal of Cambodia Research* (published in Khmer, English and French) although relatively few Cambodian researchers have published in the journal. Some foreign anthropologists working in Cambodia have received CKS funding in its "capacity-building" programs, and CKS has sometimes taught anthropological field methods. For a number of years, anthropologist Chhean Rithy Men administered the CKS capacity-building project.

NGOs dedicated to development such as the Cambodian Development Resource Institute (CDRI) and the Center for Advanced

Study (CAS), were actively engaged in field research and sometimes employed Cambodians like Kim Sedara, Chan Sambath and Hang Chansophea, who were trained in anthropological field methods at RUFA, RUPP or the Buddhist Institute.

Reviving Cultural Identity—Anthropology within Khmer Studies[10]

Within the broader need to revive Cambodian cultural identity through a wide field of Khmer studies described above (see also Peycam 2010, 2011), local anthropology engages with the culturalist agenda of reviving a national cultural identity through an important figure: Ang Choulean. As one of the first students of the Department of Archeology of RUFA in the 1960s, Ang Choulean was insinuated into the university's cultural project of nation-building in the early independence years. After completing his PhD in ethnology on supernatural beings in Cambodian popular religion in 1982 in Paris, he was unable to return to Cambodia due to its socialist isolation. It was not until 1989 that Ang Choulean was able to visit Cambodia, when the new (Royal) University of Fine Arts was being re-established. Partly with his initiative, the Department of Archeology was reinstituted in 1990. Since then, he has prioritized the cultural preservation agenda throughout his institutional initiatives, training of younger researchers, and research and publications.

While teaching anthropology at RUFA, Ang Choulean, together with Vann Molyvann, contributed significantly to the founding of the Authority for the Protection and Management of Angkor and the Region of Siem Reap (APSARA) in 1995. Within APSARA, he led the research activities of the Department of Culture and Research, whereby he brought some of his high-achieving students from RUFA to conduct anthropological research in Siem Reap and other places. In a way, Ang Choulean was able to train a new generation of local anthropologists (although they graduated with bachelor's degrees in archeology) by combining classroom instructions at RUFA and practical research projects. At the same time, he was able to provide them with attractive career prospects at APSARA. Unfortunately, the research group was dissolved in 2004 because of political and institutional change at APSARA.

Ang Choulean also co-founded the peer-reviewed journal *Udaya, Journal of Khmer Studies* (published in Khmer, English and French) in 2000, which has been a major outlet for research output from his students trained in archeology and anthropology. Examples include works on the Khmer version of *Ramayana* epic by Siyonn Sophearith, Angkorean ceramics by Ea Darith and Chhan Chamroeun, palace murals by San Phalla, Cambodian gold and silver craft production by Tho Thon, and various rituals and rites of passage by Sun Chandeb and Preap Chanmara. In addition, Ang Choulean's cultural project also goes beyond the academic realm to include the dissemination of Cambodian cultural information to the popular audience. With financial support from individuals and overseas organizations, such as the Friends of Khmer Culture, Ang Choulean set up an organization called Yosothor, which organizes lectures and publishes books, and has established an online website called "Khmer Renaissance" that is accessible to the public and stores an extensive amount of information on Cambodian culture and customs.

Understanding the linguistic limitations that Cambodian students and researchers face in accessing French scholarship, Ang Choulean has also on several occasions translated French texts on Cambodian culture and published them in *Udaya*. Rather ironically, however, his own work on supernatural beings has not been translated from French into Khmer or English, including "Les êtres surnaturels dans la religión populaire khmère" (1986), "Le Sacré au Féminin" (1987–90), and "La Sol et L'ancêtre. L'amorphe et L'anthropomorphe" (1995). In recent years, his research has apparently shifted from ethnographic work on rituals toward documenting and preserving Cambodian cultural antiquities; such works include "In the Beginning Was the Bayon" (2007) and *Old Khmer Textbook* (2013). Since 2008, he has given up teaching anthropology and has been teaching Khmer epigraphy at RUFA.

Some of the graduates of RUFA's archeology program have been influenced by Ang Choulean and others whose works involved the research and preservation of Cambodia's cultural identity and practices, and employed an anthropological lens or anthropological methods. An example is Hang Chan Sophea's (2004) work, which provides an ethnographic description of present-day practices of worshipping ancient kings and queens. Other examples include students' works that were published in *Siksacakr* and *Udaya* mentioned above, as well as several unpublished BA theses supervised by Ang Choulean and other scholars.

Confronting Contemporary Change: Cultural Anthropology

The training of a new generation of Cambodian social and cultural anthropologists also began to take place in post-war Cambodia. This development has been fragmentary, and American cultural anthropologist Judy Ledgerwood has been a significant figure in this process. In 1990, she completed her doctoral research at Cornell University on Khmer gender conceptions based on folk stories as told in the Cambodian diaspora in the United States, and taught and conducted research frequently in Cambodia between 1989 and 1997. Ledgerwood has been an important figure in supporting and training several Cambodian anthropologists, first through the East West Center program in Hawai'i and then in the MA program in anthropology at Northern Illinois University (NIU), where she has been since 1996. She sees her initiative as "an obligation to give back" to a country upon which she has built her research and career. Ledgerwood also supervised Cambodian students Kim Sedara, Nhean Socheat, Phlong Piseth, and Ann Sovatha[11] for their MA research, and her influence can be observed to varying degrees in their anthropological work.

Due to Ledgerwood's focus on the themes of continuity and change in social organization and relations in post-war Cambodia, issues related to socio-organizational and cultural change in contemporary Cambodia are central to these students' research. Kim Sedara (2001) focused on the resilience of reciprocity in rural Cambodia after the war; Phlong Piseth (2009) on informal rural credit systems; and Nhean Socheat (2010) on the sociopolitical structure of the Khmer Rouge in a rural village. They were graduates of RUFA's Department of Archeology and were mainly introduced to cultural anthropology through Ledgerwood when she taught there. The exception was Ann Sovatha, who earned a degree in English teaching but worked as Kim Sedara's research assistant at a research organization that studied local democratization in Cambodia in the early 2000s. Ann Sovatha went on to complete an MA in cultural anthropology; in 2008, he conducted ethnographic fieldwork on local politics in a coastal village that faced imposed democratization, and was supervised by Ledgerwood.

Despite this connection, the "lineage" of theoretical perspectives and objects of study has not been sustained, as many of these Cambodian scholars have moved on to pursue doctoral study in different disciplines elsewhere. Kim Sedara, affiliated for many years with CDRI, became a prominent researcher of Cambodia's local democratization and completed his PhD in development and politics at the University of Gothenburg, Sweden.[12] Nhean Socheat was working as a researcher at the Documentation Center of Cambodia, documenting the Khmer Rouge history, and he is now beginning his doctoral study on arts and genocide at the University of London; and Phlong Piseth has worked on some research projects with several organizations. Only Ann Sovatha continued in the field of cultural anthropology, and he is now completing his doctoral study on Chinese identity in urban Cambodia at the University of Hawai'i.[13]

Beyond this RUFA-NIU linkage, there are a few other local scholars who conducted research on contemporary social change through the social and cultural anthropology perspective. One of them is Chan Sambath, who graduated from the archeology program at RUFA in the early 1990s, where he also worked as a research assistant for historian Penny Edwards on a project on minority groups in Cambodia. His career began in the NGO sector, and it was when he temporarily moved to Canada that he obtained an MA in anthropology at Concordia University, his thesis a historical study on the Chinese minorities in Cambodia (Chan 2005).

There are three Cambodian anthropologists who were never affiliated with RUFA. One is Dork Vuthy, who finished his bachelor's in philosophy at the Royal University of Phnom Penh (RUPP) and was recruited to teach at RUPP's newly established sociology department in 1994. At the department, he got involved in a research project on a rural community in central Cambodia by Japanese anthropologists at Tsukuba University, Japan. He then received a scholarship to begin his graduate study in cultural anthropology at Tsukuba University in 1996, where he has been conducting research on the survival strategies of highland ethnic minorities in northeastern Cambodia. At present, he teaches cultural anthropology at a number of universities in Phnom Penh while completing his PhD. Another is Chay Navuth, who got his first degree in agriculture and development at Cambodia's University of Agriculture in 1992. He later received a scholarship from the Japanese government for a graduate program in development studies at Waseda University. His supervisors at Waseda happened to be anthropologists, and he ended up completing his PhD in development anthropology in 2006, researching cultural and socio-organizational change in rural Cambodia in response to international aid (see Chay 2006). The third anthropologist, Nguong Kimly, obtained his first degree in English teaching from RUPP in

2003, earned an MA in Southeast Asian Studies at Chulalongkorn University, Thailand, and is currently completing his doctoral research on Cambodian–Thai relations using an anthropological approach at the Australian National University.

As discussed above, these individuals represent the twin-track development of Cambodia's local anthropology. One track is the new but small generation of cultural anthropologists whose research agenda broadly engages with contemporary social and cultural change in Cambodia. The other group is made up of local scholars with some anthropological training and focusing on the documentation and preservation of Khmer cultural identity. Some of the work and individuals cross over in terms of the topical focus of these twin tracks of research and writing.

Current Institutional Lethargy

A climate of urgency to "reconstruct" Cambodia in the 1990s after two tumultuous decades appears to have generated considerable anthropological work on Cambodia (mostly by foreigners), and enabled a new, albeit small, generation of local anthropologists and scholars with some anthropological training to emerge. After nearly two decades of local institutional reinvigoration, however, a sound institutional framework to further support local scholarship generally—let alone anthropology specifically—failed to materialize.

The Buddhist Institute's role in generating scholarship on Cambodian cultural identity has only been partially restored, and failed to reach its pre-war prominence due not only to financial shortage but also a lack of political will. In fact, the future of the Buddhist Institute has recently become uncertain due to ongoing financial and political turmoil. The Reyum Institute offered prospects in knowledge production and cultural preservation in the 2000s for its research and publication activities, and provided support for emerging scholars. However, it has also recently become inactive, with several individuals departing the organization, leaving its future uncertain.

Academic institutions remain slow in developing quality training programs and research capacity due to a lack of financial and political support from the government. RUFA has been re-established since 1989, but its disciplinary and training structures today remain comparable to those of the 1960s, and it does not offer programs beyond the undergraduate level. In addition, the establishment of a degree program in cultural anthropology remains unlikely in the foreseeable future. At RUPP, the master's program in sociology-anthropology has run out of funding from non-governmental partners and is likely to close down soon. Social and cultural anthropology today remains an introductory breadth subject for undergraduate training in a few universities, but most instructors—except those at RUFA—have never received any anthropological training.

Conclusion

Due to Cambodia's historical experiences of the last century, a nascent, twin-track local anthropology has begun to emerge over the past twenty-five years among a small number of Cambodian intellectuals with anthropological training. While modernization processes in the early twentieth century and the nation-building project in the 1950s and 1960s (see Edwards 2007) led to the construction of a national identity based on the (re)invention of a national culture, religion and language, the cataclysmic years in the 1970s and 1980s not only left local scholarship in shambles but also engendered a sense of loss of traditional cultural order (Ledgerwood et al. 1994). In the post-conflict era in the 1990s and 2000s, a climate of urgency to "reconstruct" Cambodia upon the ashes of its past generation increased academic knowledge production on the country and efforts to restore and preserve its cultural identity.

Within this historical unfolding, a number of individuals and institutions, particularly RUFA and people associated with it, have played a significant role in Cambodia's local anthropology. From the beginning RUFA was a product of and a means for nation-building. It suffered from the subsequent social upheaval, through which the important figure of Ang Choulean was introduced to anthropology, and spurred a desire to preserve Cambodia's cultural identity. It is significantly from Ang's research, training of younger scholars, and institutional initiatives in the past twenty-five years, that a local anthropological orientation of reinventing the country's cultural identity is derived.

It is also significantly through RUFA, although sometimes elsewhere, that a new, albeit small, generation of local anthropologists was trained and engaged with a broad question of contemporary change in post-conflict Cambodian society. This applied orientation of local anthropologists often pays attention to the issues of local sociopolitical change amidst imposed democratization, rural cultural and organizational responses to international aid, and persisting and changing sociocultural patterns in the rural society.

Unfortunately, anthropology remains a long way from coming of age in Cambodia. In the current context where higher education is lacking in many respects, especially an absence of academic research and publishing, any prospect of institutional support to promote anthropological training or research is absent. Most Cambodian anthropologists share this pessimism. Many universities offer training programs of doubtful quality that seem to prioritize the generation of quick profit over promoting social science research. Perhaps the biggest problem lies in the lack of governmental support for the development of Cambodia's higher education into research-oriented institutions, which would require funding graduate research programs and providing livable and secure wages for research-oriented academics. Only one Cambodian anthropologist stayed on as a full-time lecturer, and others moved into non-academic careers in NGOs and the government, and only taught anthropology on a part-time basis. While some remain able to use their anthropological perspectives and skills in applied research at their organizations, many are not. The failings of extant structural conditions for the development of social-cultural anthropology in Cambodian universities are nicely encapsulated in a comment by a senior Cambodian anthropologist, "the system has caused a loss of human resources."

Notes

* This chapter is supported by the project Southeast Asian Anthropologies at the National University of Singapore. I wish to thank Eric C. Thompson, Vineeta Sinha, Judy Ledgerwood, Philippe Peycam, and John Marston for commenting on early drafts of this contribution. I also thank Pin Manika and Vorn Sokhan at the Royal University of Phnom Penh for helping collect information and locally published material. Thanks to the following Cambodian and foreign intellectuals for their time in answering my questions: Nguon Kimly, Khing Hoc Dy, Phlong Piseth, Judy Ledgerwood, Philippe Peycam, Ann Sovatha, San Phalla, Ang Choulean, Kim Sedara, Mel Sophana, Dork Vuthy, Chay Navuth, John Marston, Vong Meng, Pou Sovachana, Chan Sambath and Nhean Socheat.

1. "Khmer" firstly refers to an ethnic group that makes up the large majority of Cambodians. The Khmer traditionally make up the rural

peasantry (Steinberg 1959). In a second sense, the term "Khmer" is also used interchangeably with "Cambodian" (an English word generally translated as "Kampuchea") to refer to a national or sociocultural entity. In this chapter, I employ the term "Cambodian" instead of "Khmer" when referring to the national identity or sociocultural realm in general in order to avoid the ethnic exclusiveness of the term "Khmer."

2. As Cambodia was a former French colony, a significant amount of scholarship on Cambodia, including some anthropological work, is in French. Given my linguistic limitations, this francophone scholarship is accessible only through limited secondary accounts available in Khmer and English. It should also be noted that although the reopening of Cambodia since the 1990s has reduced the importance of francophone scholarship in studying Cambodia, the early scholarship on Cambodian society remains largely inaccessible to non-French speaking researchers. There has also been important new scholarship in French in the last twenty years, which includes the works of Anne Guillou, Oliver de Bernon, Fabienne Luco, Soizick Crochet and Alain Forest.
3. During the protectorate, Cambodia was ruled as part of French Indochina, which consisted of present-day Vietnam, Cambodia and Laos.
4. Full names of Cambodian individuals in the text start with their surname; this follows Khmer naming conventions.
5. The Royal University of Fine Arts changed its name to the University of Fine Arts after the establishment of the Khmer Republic in 1970, which resulted from the coup.
6. Other ISP student recipients working on Cambodia I am aware of include Sam Yang, a Cambodian doing his MA on Cambodian Buddhism at Cornell University; Kate Frieson, studying politics at Monash University; and Duong Sotheary, a Cambodian teaching in the public schools in the United States.
7. In the context of the destructive warfare and Khmer Rouge's reign of terror in the 1970s, a debate emerged among foreign anthropologists on the nature of Cambodian rural communities. Some argue that the violent upheaval has destroyed the cohesion and mutual trust in Cambodian rural communities (Frings 1994; Ovesen, Trankell and Öjendal 1996), but others oppose this argument (Ebihara and Ledgerwood 2002; Kim 2011).
8. Foreigners conducting anthropological research in Cambodia in the 1990s included both academic anthropologists (e.g. May Ebihara, Judy Ledgerwood, John Marston, Satoru Kobayashi, Soizick Crochet, Eve Zucker, Alexandra Kent, Ing-Britt Trankell, Jan Ovesen, Toni Shapiro and Alexander Hinton) and professional anthropologists working for NGOs (e.g. William Collins, John Vijghens, Chou Meng Tarr and Fabien Luco).
9. The connection to the East West Center and the University of Hawai'i became critical for the further training in anthropology and archeology

of several graduates of RUFA's archeology program. An exchange program run by Ledgerwood, with funding from the Henry Luce Foundation in the early 1990s took twelve RUFA students for a bridging program. Among them, Bong Savath, currently RUFA's rector, went on the complete his PhD in archeology at the University of Hawai'i in 2003. Others moved on to further anthropological and archeological study elsewhere, including Kim Sedara at NIU. Among the next generation of RUFA's graduates, Heng Piphal is now pursuing his PhD in archeology at the University of Hawai'i.

10. "Khmer studies" has a loosely defined agenda for the study of Cambodian society. It was originally concerned with researching and documenting local cultural identity and practices, especially in postcolonial and post-conflict contexts, but in recent years it has also engaged with the questions of contemporary cultural, economic and political change. Besides the institutional initiatives and programs mentioned above, there are other academic and NGO projects that have contributed to the general field of Khmer studies, such as Bophana, DC-Cam, and RUPP's graduate program in linguistics. Several Cambodian intellectuals overseas have also contributed to scholarship on Khmer studies beyond anthropology, including Ly Daravuth, Nut Suppya, Um Khatharya, Au Sokhieng and Leakthina Ollier.
11. There was also Cambodian-American Chhean Rithy Men, who was supervised by Ledgerwood for his MA research on the Cambodian diaspora.
12. Kim Sedara's work after his MA in cultural anthropology has mostly been applied research on Cambodia's local politics and development, for example, Kim et al. (2002), Hughes and Kim (2004), and Rusten et al. (2004). His more recent academic work has been focused on local democratization process, including Öjendal and Kim (2006) and Kim (2012).
13. His recent work based on his doctoral study is on the Chinese ritual practice of paper money in Phnom Penh, Cambodia (Ann 2011).

References

Ablin, David A., and Marlowe Hood (1990) "The Path to Cambodia's Present." In *The Cambodian Agony*, David A. Ablin and Marlowe Hood, (eds.), pp. xv–lxi. London: M.E. Sharpe.

Ang, Choulean (1986) *Les êtres surnaturels dans la religión populaire khmère* [*Supernatural Beings in Khmer Popular Religion*]. Paris: Cedoreck.

____ (1987–90) "Le Sacré au Féminin" ["The Sacred in the Feminine"]. *Seksa Khmer* 10–13: pp. 3–30.

____ (1995) "La Sol et L'ancêtre. L'amorphe et L'anthropomorphe" ["The Soil and the Ancestor: The Amorphous and the Anthropomorphic"]. *Journal Asiatique* 283: pp. 213–38.

_____ (2007) "In the Beginning Was the Bayon." In *Bayon: New Perspectives*, J. Clark, (ed.), pp. 368–72. Bangkok: River Books.

_____ (2013) *Old Khmer Textbook*. Phnom Penh: Yosothor.

Ann, Sovatha (2008) *Patron-Clientelism and Decentralization: An Emerging Local Political Culture in Rural Cambodia*. Unpublished Master's thesis, Northern Illinois University, United States.

_____ (2011) "Paper Money in Phnom Penh: Beyond the Sino-Khmer Tradition," *EXPLORATIONS: A Graduate Student Journal of Southeast Asian Studies* 11(1): pp. 93–104.

Chandler, David (2008) *A History of Cambodia*, 4th edition. Boulder: Westview Press.

Chang, Kyung-Sup (2010) "The Second Modern Condition? Compressed Modernity as Internalized Reflexive Cosmopolitization," *The British Journal of Sociology* 61(3): pp. 444–64.

Chan, Sambath (2005) *The Chinese Minority in Cambodia: Identity Construction and Contestation*. Unpublished Master's thesis, Concordia University.

Chay, Navuth (2006) *Toward an Effective International Development Assistance: Grassroots Level Community in Cambodia*. PhD dissertation, Waseda University, Japan.

Chheat, Sreang, Yin Sombo, Seng Hokmeng, Pong Pheakdeyboramy and Soam Sokreasey (2005) *The Buddhist Institute: A Short History*. Phnom Penh: Buddhist Institute.

Chigas, George (2000) "The Emergence of Twentieth Century Cambodian Literary Institutions: The Case of *Kambujasuriya*." In *The Canon in Southeast Asian Literatures: Literatures of Burma, Cambodia, Indonesia, Laos, Malaysia, the Philippines, Thailand and Vietnam*, David Smyth, (ed.), pp. 135–46. Surrey: Curzon.

Dy, Sideth S. (2004) "Strategies and Policies for Basic Education in Cambodia: Historical Perspectives," *International Education Journal* (5)1: pp. 90–97.

Ebihara, May (1968) *Svay, A Khmer Village in Cambodia*. PhD dissertation, Columbia University, United States.

_____ (1973) "Intervillage, Intertown, and Village-City Relations in Cambodia," *Annals of the New York Academy of Sciences* 220: pp. 358–75.

_____ (1990) "Return to a Khmer Village," *Cultural Survival Quarterly* 14(3): pp. 67–70.

_____ (1993) "'Beyond Suffering': The Recent History of a Cambodian Village." In *The Challenge of Reform in Indochina*, Borje Ljunggren, (ed.), pp. 149–66. Cambridge: Harvard Institute for International Development.

Ebihara, May and Judy Ledgerwood (2002) "Aftermaths of Genocide: Cambodian Villagers." In *Annihilating Difference: The Anthropology of Genocide*, Alexander L. Hinton, (ed.), pp. 272–91. Berkeley: University of California Press.

Edwards, Penny (2007) *Cambodge: The Cultivation of a Nation, 1860–1945*. Honolulu: University of Hawai'i Press.

Evans, Grant (2000) "Apprentice Ethnographers: Vietnam and the Study of Lao Minorities." In *Laos: Culture and Society*, Grant Evans, (ed.), pp. 161–90. Singapore: Institute of Southeast Asian Studies.

Fanselow, Frank (2014) "The Anthropology of the State and the State of Anthropology in Brunei," *Journal of Southeast Asian Studies* 45(1): pp. 90–112.

Frings, Viviane (1994) "Cambodia after Decollectivization 1989–1992," *Journal of Contemporary Asia* 24(1): pp. 49–66.

Gottesman, Evan R. (2004) *Cambodia after the Khmer Rouge: Inside the Politics of Nation Building*. London: Yale University Press.

Hang, Chan Sophea (2004) "*Stec Gamlan* and *Yay Deb*: Worshiping Kings and Queens in Cambodia Today." In *History, Buddhism, and New Religious Movements in Cambodia*, John Marston and Elizabeth Guthrie, (eds.), pp. 113–26. Honolulu: University of Hawai'i Press.

Heuveline, Patrick (1998) "'Between One and Three Million': Towards the Demographic Reconstruction of a Decade of Cambodian History (1970–79)," *Population Studies* 52: pp. 49–65.

Hughes, Caroline and Kim Sedara (2004) "The Evolution of Democratic Process and Conflict Management in Cambodia: A Comparative Study of Three Cambodian Elections." Working Paper 30. Phnom Penh: CDRI.

Hughes, Caroline and Kheang Un (2011) "Cambodia's Economic Transformation: Historical and Theoretical Frameworks." In *Cambodia's Economic Transformation*, Caroline Hughes and Kheang Un, (eds.), pp. 1–26. Copenhagen: NIAS Press.

Ibrahim, Zawawi (2010) "The Anthropology of the Malay Peasantry: Critical Reflections on Colonial and Indigenous Scholarship," *Asian Journal of Social Science* 38: pp. 5–36.

Kalab, Milada (1968) "Study of a Cambodian Village," *The Geographical Journal* 134(4): pp. 521–37.

——— (1976) "Monastic Education, Social Mobility, and Village Structure in Cambodia." In *The Anthropological Study of Education*, Craig J. Calhoun and Francis A. Janni, (eds.), pp. 61–74. Chicago: Aldine.

——— (1990) "Buddhism and Emotional Support for Elderly People," *Journal of Cross-Cultural Gerontology* 5(1): pp. 7–19.

——— (1994) "Cambodian Buddhist Monasteries in Paris: Continuing Tradition and Changing Patterns." In *Cambodian Culture: Homeland and Exile*, May M. Ebihara, Judy Ledgerwood, and Carol A. Mortland, (eds.), pp. 57–71. New York: Cornell University Press.

Kiernan, Ben (1996) *The Pol Pot Regime: Race, Power, and Genocide in Cambodia under the Khmer Rouge, 1975–79*. New Haven: Yale University Press.

Kim, Sedara (2001) *Reciprocity: Informal Patterns of Social Interactions in a Cambodian Village Near Angkor Park*. Unpublished Master's thesis, Northern Illinois University, United States.

——— (2011) "Reciprocity: Informal Patterns of Social Interaction in a Cambodian Village." In *Anthropology and Community in Cambodia: Reflections on the Work of May Ebihara*, John A. Marston, (ed.), pp. 153–70. Caulfield: Monash University Press.

——— (2012) *Democracy in Action: Decentralisation in Post-conflict Cambodia*. PhD dissertation, University of Gothenburg, Sweden.

Kim, Sedara, Chan Sophal and Sarthi Acharya (2002) "Land, Rural Livelihoods and Food Security in Cambodia: A Perspective from Field Reconnaissance." Working Paper 24. Phnom Penh: CDRI.

King, Victor T. and William D. Wilder (2003) *The Modern Anthropology of South-East Asia*. London: Routledge.

Kleinen, John (2013) "New Trends in the Anthropology of Southeast Asia," *TRaNS: Trans-Regional and -National Studies of Southeast Asia* 1(1): pp. 121–35.

Ledgerwood, Judy, May Ebihara and Carol A. Mortland (1994) "Introduction." In *Cambodian Culture: Homeland and Exile*, May M. Ebihara, Judy Ledgerwood, and Carol A. Mortland, (eds.), pp. 1–26. New York: Cornell University Press.

Ly, Theam T. (1965) *Ariyathor Khmer* [*Khmer Civilization*]. Phnom Penh: Ly Theam Teng.

Marston, John, (ed.) (2011) *Anthropology and Community in Cambodia: Reflections on the Work of May Ebihara*. Caulfield: Monash University Press.

Martin, Marie A. (1994) *Cambodia: A Shattered Society*. Berkeley: University of California Press.

Nhean, Socheat (2010) *Democratic Kampuchea: Chain of Command and Sociopolitical Structure of the Southwest Zone*. Unpublished Master's thesis, Northern Illinois University, United States.

Öjendal, Joakim and Sedara Kim (2006) "*Korob, Kaud, Klach*: In Search of Agency in Rural Cambodia," *Journal of Southeast Asian Studies* 37(3): pp. 507–26.

Öjendal, Joakim and Mona Lilja (2009) *Beyond Democracy in Cambodia: Political Reconstruction in a Post-Conflict Society*. Copenhagen: NIAS Press.

Ollier, Leakthina C. and Tim Winter, (eds.) (2006) *Expressions of Cambodia: The Politics of Tradition, Identity, and Change*. New York: Routledge.

Ovesen, Jan, Ing-Britt Trankell, and Joakim Öjendal (1996) *When Every Household is an Island: Social Organization and Power Structures in Rural Cambodia*. Uppsala Research Reports in Cultural Anthropology, No. 15. Uppsala: Uppsala University.

Peou, Sorpong (2000) *Intervention and Change in Cambodia: Towards Democracy?* Singapore: Institute of Southeast Asian Studies.

Peycam, Philippe M.F. (2010) "Sketching an Institutional History of Academic Knowledge Production in Cambodia (1863–2009) – Part 1," *Sojourn: Journal of Social Issues in Southeast Asia* 25(2): pp. 153–77.

—— (2011) "Sketching an Institutional History of Academic Knowledge Production in Cambodia (1863–2009) – Part 2," *Sojourn: Journal of Social Issues in Southeast Asia* 26(1): pp. 16–35.

Phlong, Piseth (2009) *Informal Credit Systems in Cambodia*. Unpublished Master's thesis, Northern Illinois University, United States.

Reyum Institute of Arts and Culture (2011) *Cultures of Independence: An Introduction to Cambodian Arts and Culture in the 1950s and 1960s*. Phnom Penh: Reyum Institute of Arts and Culture.

Russell, Ross R. (1987) *Cambodia: A Country Study*. Washington: Library of Congress.

Rusten, Caroline, Kim Sedara, Eng Netra, and Pak Kimchoeun (2004) *The Challenges of Decentralisation Design in Cambodia*. Phnom Penh: Cambodia Development Resource Institute.

Steinberg, David J. (1959) *Cambodia: Its People, Its Society, Its Culture*. New Haven: Human Relations Area Files Press.

Su, Christine M. (2003) *Tradition and Change: Khmer Identity and Democracy in the 20th Century and Beyond*. PhD dissertation, University of Hawai'i, United States.

Teav, Chhay Sok (1971–72) *Wabbathor-Ariya: Khmer-India* [*Culture-Civilization: Khmer-India*]. Phnom Penh: Teav Chhay Sok.

Thompson, Eric C. (2012) "Anthropology in Southeast Asia: National Traditions and Transnational Practices," *Asian Journal of Social Science* 40: pp. 664–89.

Troeung, Ngea (1974) *Ariyathor Khmer* [*Khmer Civilization*]. Phnom Penh: Troeung Ngea.

Winter, Tim and Leakthina C. Ollier (2006) "Introduction: Cambodia and the Politics of Tradition, Identity and Change." In *Expressions of Cambodia: The Politics of Tradition, Identity, and Change*, Leakthina C. Ollier and Tim Winter, (eds.), pp. 1–19. New York: Routledge.

Yamashita, Shinji, Joseph Bosco, and Jeremy S. Eades (2004) "Asian Anthropologies: Foreign, Native, and Indigenous." In *The Making of Anthropology in East and Southeast Asia*, Shinji Yamashita, Joseph Bosco, and Jeremy S. Eades, (eds.), pp. 1–34. New York: Berghahn Books.

CHAPTER 3

VIETNAMESE ANTHROPOLOGY AT THE CROSSROADS OF CHANGE

Nguyen Van Chinh

This chapter examines the development of cultural anthropology in Vietnam, specifically the influence of French colonialism and the Soviet school of ethnology on contemporary Vietnamese anthropology, and the challenges it faces with regards to integration into the global academic world. Its primary foci are anthropology within academia, anthropology in practice and the role of cultural anthropology in government policymaking. I argue for a reassessment of the roles of both French and Soviet anthropology in the making of contemporary Vietnamese anthropology, specifically that the role of the former was greater and the role of the latter less than standard accounts within Vietnam suggest.

While anthropological knowledge in Vietnam possibly dates as far back as the fourteenth and fifteenth centuries, Vietnamese anthropologists tend to emphasize that cultural anthropology as a discipline only emerged in the 1960s (Khổng Diễn 1998: 277, 2003: 16; Phan Hữu Dật 2004: 50). In doing so, these scholars emphasize Vietnamese anthropology's Marxist background in an attempt to reject the legacy of colonial anthropology and its influences on communist anthropology (i.e. anthropology conceived as being practiced according to a communist model) and to distinguish today's Vietnamese cultural anthropology from that of the West. In contrast, I move away from viewing Vietnamese anthropology today as a break from colonial or even contemporary Western anthropology (Luong Van Hy 2001: 7) and instead emphasize the continuity between colonial and postcolonial (i.e., communist and Doi Moi) anthropology.

Upon the demise of colonial anthropology in Vietnam, the Soviet school had a profound impact on the development of Vietnamese communist anthropology. However, I argue that the Soviet influence has generally been overstated and oversimplified. Without a doubt, the Vietnamese anthropology was shaped by the Soviet ethnography discipline, while most key Vietnamese anthropologists were trained in the Soviet Union and socialist Eastern European countries, the process of "sovietization" of ethnography in Vietnam did not take place as expected. The influence of the Soviet school at the beginning of the 1950s was not total and ubiquitous, and gradually declined when the world socialist bloc collapsed in the 1980s and 1990s and Vietnam entered the era of globalization. Bearing the imprint of both colonial and communist anthropology, Vietnamese anthropologists today find themselves at the crossroads of socialism, nationalism and globalization.

The Legacy of Colonial Ethnology

The discipline of cultural anthropology was introduced into Vietnam more than 100 years ago by missionaries, explorers and army officers of the French administration who collected ethnographic information to serve their practical policies. After the army pacification campaign was carried out to establish colonial rule, French researchers produced a series of ethnographies on the history, culture, religion and society of indigenous peoples in Indochina, which itself was an important contribution to world ethnology generally (Bayly 2000). During this time, French anthropology, also known as *ethnologie*, paid much attention to the monographs of language, folklore, customary laws, forms of local government, religions and local cultures. Knowledge of indigenous peoples in colonial Indochina was produced by two groups of researchers: non-professional researchers (including explorers, missionaries, army officers and colonial administrators) and professional researchers who were trained at research institutions and universities. It was the non-professional researchers who were responsible for conjuring images of cultures in Indochina, aimed at expanding their colonial empire in Indochina, and spreading the

French civilization to "inferior" native peoples, therefore promoting anthropological research as an instrument of colonial administration.[1]

Despite the popularity of this non-professional research, a system of professional research in French Indochina was institutionalized very early in the colonial period with the 1902 establishment of École française d'Extrême-Orient (EFEO) in Hanoi. This research institution operated for nearly sixty years until its Vietnamese offices closed in 1959. Researchers working in this school were appointed, paid and assigned by the colonial government. The *Bulletin of École française d'Extrême-Orient* (*BEFEO*) published hundreds of research papers, including books and articles that largely focused on aspects of religion, lifestyle and local traditions.[2] Two other colonial journals that are often cited by Vietnamese anthropologists are the *Bulletin des Amis du Vieux Hué* (*BAVH*) and *Indochina* (*RI*).[3] Together with these initiatives, the French established a new research institute named Institut Indochinois pour l'Etude de l'Homme (IIEH) in 1938. IIEH was placed under the framework of EFEO, and was aimed at "strengthening the understanding of human beings in Indochina, physically and culturally" (Trịnh Kim Ngọc 2006).[4] The establishment of IIEH created the foundation for Vietnamese anthropology with a combination of archeology, cultural anthropology, physical anthropology and linguistics, similar to the "four fields" approach still popular in the West, especially the United States.

By reviewing the establishment of research institutions and initiatives in colonial Vietnam, it is clear that Vietnamese anthropology has developed significantly since the early 1900s and has produced significant knowledge of Vietnam in particular and Indochina in general. Many French researchers straddled a divide between working for the colonial power and maintaining close involvement with native populations, and their research did not always represent colonial interests.[5] Furthermore, anthropological knowledge produced by French researchers not only impacted cultural anthropology outside Indochina but also affected Vietnamese ethnology after the colonial regime left. Their research was an important source for references, often cited by leading Vietnamese communist anthropologists eager to distance themselves from colonial projects. Recent translations and publications of work by colonial scholars such as M. Mauss, L. Cadier, P. Gourou, G. Condominas, H. Maitre, J. Dournes, and J. Cuisenier attest to the valued contribution of colonial anthropology in shaping ethnology research in modern Vietnam.[6]

Besides the research institutions that produced and disseminated knowledge on the cultures and societies in Indochina, the establishment of universities and colleges in Vietnam to train a new generation of local scientists was another important contribution in the development of the field of anthropology after independence. At the University of Indochina, which was officially established in Hanoi in 1906, anthropology was for the first time taught in different departments through courses by well-known researchers from EFEO. In 1917, the university set up the Department of Anthropology with August Bonifacy appointed as its first chair. Bonifacy was a military officer who arrived in North Vietnam in 1894 and collaborated with EFEO between 1901 and 1902. In 1906 he obtained a position at EFEO as press correspondent. Well known for his research on the Yao, Bonifacy was also a member of the Paris Anthropology Association under its Asian Studies Association, as well as part of the International Ethnology Association in Paris.[7] When the Communist Party of Vietnam (CPV) set up a section on ethnic minority studies, textbooks written by Bonifacy were used as the initial source of reference for students.[8] Furthermore, other researchers and faculty from EFEO and École des Supérieure Lettres (founded in 1923), including Victor Goloubev and Louis Bezacier, were invited to give lectures on anthropology and the history of art and Oriental civilizations at the University of Indochina (Université Indochinoise) in Hanoi. Thus, with the establishment of EFEO (1901), IIHS (1938), and the Department of Anthropology at Hanoi University (1917), the discipline was firmly embedded in the research and training system in Vietnam. Well-known Vietnamese scholars in the field such as Nguyễn Văn Tố, Nguyễn Văn Huyên, Nguyễn Văn Khoan, Trần Văn Giáp, Nguyễn Thiệu Lâu and Đỗ Quang Hợp can all be seen as the fruit of the colonial training system. They were the first generation to lay the foundation for the anthropological sciences in Vietnam. Although having received a French education, these scholars tended to use their knowledge to contribute to the cause of national salvation, saving the country from colonial domination and backwardness, and promoted modern culture (Nguyễn Phương Ngọc 2012).

It was upon this foundation that present-day Vietnamese anthropology and ethnology developed.[9] Although the Soviet model led by Marxist–Leninist views became increasingly influential in Vietnamese social sciences from the 1960s onwards, colonial anthropology in the country was well developed long before. I therefore consider the establishment of state institutes and departments of ethnology during the 1960s as just another developmental period in Vietnamese anthropology.

The Influences of Soviet Ethnology

Researchers who study the development of ethnology in Vietnam strongly believe that the discipline developed directly under the tutelage of Soviet scholars. However, there has been almost no serious study on how and to what extent the Soviet school affected the practices of Vietnamese ethnology. The available literature on the emergence of ethnology as a discipline in postcolonial Vietnam seems to point towards the Russians, as opposed to the French, as being responsible for bringing the discipline into Vietnamese universities and research institutions. Trần Văn Giầu, the first chair of the University of Hanoi's history department (established in 1956) recalled that upon obtaining his position as chair, he wished to develop a branch of ethnology and archeology in the Department of History but was unable to find staff with adequate knowledge of these disciplines. To him, the French had intensively studied indigenous peoples in Indochina and published considerable work, but left a vacuum when they left Hanoi as there were no local scholars who were able to create curricula and teaching programs in ethnology and archeology.

The first steps towards a new ethnology in Vietnam were made when Trần invited Soviet experts to prepare textbooks and give lectures on these fields, and chose young faculty members to study with Soviet mentors (Trần Văn Giầu 1999: 172–73). In pursuing this, the University of Hanoi sponsored the fieldwork of two young Soviet ethnographers so that they could take advantage of this opportunity to learn more techniques and skills in doing field research in 1960. S.A. Ariuchinov and A.I. Mukhonilov arrived in Hanoi in 1960 as merely postgraduates in ethnology but were treated as firmly established scholars.[10] The University of Hanoi sent a team of six faculty members to escort them into the field.[11] Đinh Xuân Lâm (1999: 176–82), a member of that team, recalled that their group was provided with three jeeps filled to the brim with food and water as they went straight to the northwestern highlands, somewhere between Sơn La and Lai Châu. After roughly two weeks of fieldwork among the Thai and Muong ethnic groups, they returned to Hanoi because the food and water had run out. Đặng Nghiêm Vạn and Đinh Xuân

Lâm, who later became well-known Vietnamese professors, reported that they had learnt a lot from the two-week field trip.

The Soviets were sent not only to guide young Vietnamese researchers on ethnography in the field, anthropological experts such as E.P. Buxughin (ethnology) and P.I. Boricopski (archeology) were invited to Hanoi to directly lecture and help prepare textbooks in the early 1960s. They brought with them textbooks introducing basic ethnology and archeology that were also used in universities in the Soviet Union. These teaching materials were then translated into Vietnamese and published in 1961 (Đinh Xuân Lâm 1999: 180). The textbook *General Introduction to Ethnology*, compiled by E.P. Buxughin, served as the first conduit in transferring the Soviet school of ethnology into Vietnamese universities. Although the textbook was rather sketchy and limited, it became a seminal book for many ethnology students. Many years later, it was still used as a reading reference for history and ethnology majors at the University of Hanoi. Even today, newer Vietnamese ethnology textbooks do not seem to move beyond the content produced by these early texts.[12] Furthermore, translated and then published under the title *What is Ethnology?* in Hanoi in 1960, key articles from the *Journal of Soviet Ethnography* were later used as a guideline for the practice of ethnography in Vietnam.

What is surprising is that beyond the often-quoted translated textbook and essays mentioned above, there were few ethnographic works by Soviet scholars that were translated or brought into use within Vietnamese universities and libraries. Among that set of rare Soviet literature that was translated and used for internal circulation within the universities was the work by S.A. Tocarev on primitive forms of religion. It was only recently, however, in 1994 that this work was officially published in Vietnamese, indicating that Soviet ethnology did not flood into bookshops and university libraries to the extent that is commonly assumed. Indeed, the reading references for Vietnamese ethnology students were very poor. An examination of university libraries found that imported Soviet ethnology books were few and far between. Moreover, Russian books are difficult to find in bookshops.

While it can be inferred that the influence of Soviet ethnology in Vietnam was limited due to the small number of works circulated in the country over the past forty years, it is important to note that many Vietnamese ethnologists were sent for training in the former Soviet Union and Eastern European socialist countries. We studied profiles of ethnologists working at the Institute of Ethnology & Anthropology (Vietnam Academy of Social Sciences) and two ethnology departments at the Vietnam national universities in Hanoi and Ho Chi Minh City and found that from 1955 to 1995, roughly thirty-three Vietnamese ethnologists working in these research institutes and universities received their degrees in ethnology from Soviet Union and Eastern European universities. Among them, twenty-two received graduate and postgraduate degrees, seven received bachelor degrees and four were exchange scholars. Upon returning home, these Soviet-trained ethnologists were nominated for leading positions in academic management. Some can be referred to as the leading professors of Vietnam's ethnology including Phan Hữu Dật, Đặng Nghiêm Vạn, Mạc Đường and Bế Viết Đẳng. Their presence at the research institutes and universities however does not necessarily speak much to the influence of Soviet ethnology in Vietnam. A careful examination of how these Vietnamese students were actually trained in the social sciences and ethnology while in the Soviet Union may shed more light.

In the first place, most students who were sent for a higher degree in ethnology in the Soviet Union obtained their first degree from local Vietnamese universities. They were then selected and sent abroad, mainly to the Soviet Union for postgraduate studies. The postgraduate program normally took three to four years, with the first year focused on language training, the second on studying Marxist–Leninist philosophy and political theory, and the last two years dedicated to coursework and writing a thesis. My interviews with these students indicate that most Vietnamese who did a postgraduate degree in ethnology wrote their graduate thesis on local Vietnamese themes. However, only a small percentage actually returned to Vietnam to conduct fieldwork. Rather, many wrote their ethnographies without actual field research. It is difficult to understand how one can write an ethnography for a PhD without the opportunity to develop field research skills and actually apply them in research. This may explain why, despite a fairly large number of PhD theses being completed at Soviet Union universities by Vietnamese students, few were actually published, even as a single chapter or part of a thesis.[13] While this observation certainly does not warrant a conclusion on the quality of ethnological training in Soviet universities, it still raises the question of the actual influence of Soviet schools on Vietnamese ethnology as a field.

What we have seen seems to suggest that although Vietnamese communist anthropology received direct training from the Soviets, the extent of the latter's influence is questionable. In order to test this hypothesis, I have conducted a small survey examining a total of 1,078 articles that were published by the *Journal of Ethnology* run by the Institute of Ethnology from its establishment in 1974 up to 1994. I found twenty-nine articles written by Soviet scholars such as I.V. Bromley, M.V. Kriukov, S.A. Tocarev, N.N. Tseboxrov and S.A. Aritiunov that were translated and published in the journal. Articles by the Western ethnologists including G. Condominas, F. Proschan, A.G Haudricourt and S. Thierry were also published in the journal. What surprised me was that almost all of the articles written by Vietnamese ethnologists did not use Russian literature as their source of references. In order to have more details on this trend, I examined references quoted in books written by influential Vietnamese ethnologists, focusing on works by Lã Văn Lô (the first director of the Ethnology Institute), Vương Hoàng Tuyên (professor and head of ethnology department), Nguyễn Từ Chi (the professor and the State Prize winner for his scholarly works), Phan Hữu Dật (Hanoi University president and head of ethnology department), and Mạc Đường (professor and director of the Ethnology Institute in Ho Chi Minh City). Surprisingly, the most often-quoted references were mainly from French colonial works while Russian sources only made up a small percentage of citations. This finding, compounded with the earlier evidence regarding training processes received by Vietnamese ethnologists at Soviet universities, suggests that Soviet ethnology was but one of multiple factors influencing the making of cultural anthropology in Vietnam, and perhaps not even the most influential.

In response to my question of sources of academic references, a leading professor, the former head of the Department of Anthropology in Ho Chi Minh City said:

> It is not correct to say that we did not use the source of Russian literature in our reference. We did use them, even a lot more than you can think of, but we don't indicate the source of reference. I can tell you that most of our works were reproduced in a form of compilation, and in that case, we did not quote directly (Interviews with professor NVT, 2009).

My interviews with those anthropologists who were trained in the Soviet Union revealed that the proficiency in Russian language could have been the major problem for Vietnamese students. Some of the graduate students did not have good command of Russian, and could not write graduate theses on their own. I brought this finding to discussion with the group of Russian-trained anthropologists, and one of them told his story as follows:

> My points could be partial, but I should frankly say that the quality of Vietnamese graduate students in [the] Soviet Union was problematic. Many PhD students I knew could not read and write Russian very well, how [could] they understand sophisticated matters of sciences? We cannot deny the fact that our Vietnamese students received great influences in Marxism–Leninism's points of view, but [they] had a lot of limits in receiving the knowledge of academic disciplines because of their weakness in language skills.

One of the other major differences between colonial anthropology and Soviet-style ethnology in Vietnam is their different goals with regard to both ethnology and theory. Key papers in the *Journal of Ethnology* that discussed the functions and tasks of communist ethnology focused on distinguishing colonial-bourgeois and Marxist ethnology. These works of political rhetoric seek to convince the reader that colonial ethnology is merely an administrative instrument of the ruling class. It is "extremely idealistic and reactionary" because "its purpose is to serve the ruling class while its theory and methodology are based on subjective idealism" (Phan Hữu Dật 1973: 1). The common criticism is that Western "bourgeois anthropology," developed after the colonial era, is even more "reactionary" as it is closely linked with imperialism, the utmost period of capitalism, and is therefore unacceptable to communist ideals. While emphasizing a break from a Western anthropology believed to be deeply attached to colonialism and capitalism, the leading figures of Vietnamese ethnology also claimed that the task of Marxist ethnology is to actively serve the political work and ethnic policies of the Party, fighting against both the old colonial ethnology and present-day capitalism (Phan Hữu Dật 1973: 3).

Vietnamese Ethnology in Practice

However, research outcomes for communist ethnology in Vietnam did not meet expected requirements, particularly in the sense of developing theoretical frameworks and applying them to the development of the mountainous regions and ethnic minorities. While the government budget for ethnological studies has recently been on the rise, the quality of research is relatively incomparable to the standards set by publications in the early days of the new ethnology. One of the reasons for this situation, as indicated by ethnologists themselves, is the absence of applying new social theories to academic research, making ethnology merely a kind of descriptive endeavor that does not significantly aid in producing knowledge about ethnic minorities. In the view of ethnologist Nguyễn Văn Huy, the low quality of recent ethnological works is caused by the fact that "long-term field research was not applied as before, instead the short tour visits became more popular with quick interviews conducted on a large scale." Nguyễn Văn Huy added that Vietnamese ethnologists are likely underestimating the importance of anthropological theories and research experience from around the world.

> Everyone is aware of this [lack of theory in social–cultural research], and they talk about filling this gap as a necessity for any academic research. Yet it is usually ignored, and that is why our research results in such low quality, and therefore [can] not fulfill the potential impact of ethnological research (Nguyễn Văn Huy 2000: 3–4).

Nguyễn Văn Huy raises a controversial issue that is almost impossible to solve. Vietnamese ethnologists clearly understand that their research can only be further developed and serve the country better when they become more integrated with worldwide trends necessarily led by renovated theories (see Đặng Nguyên Anh, this volume). In the meantime, the common principles of field research and data collection must be applied carefully in analysis. However, the obstacles that prevent achieving such a state are rooted in the theoretical approach and cultural interpretation. As long as Vietnamese researchers still consider Western anthropological theories as "extremely idealistic and reactionary," dichotomizing the two systems of anthropology as "right" and "wrong," they will not see the need to understand, develop, introduce and apply academic theories novel to Vietnam into their research. If such a view continues, it will be difficult for Vietnamese ethnology to move beyond political posturing, and it will continue to merely move through the rut of uninspired topics and atheoretical description.

Here, I further discuss research trends in cultural anthropology in Vietnam. I focus on two interrelated issues that have been raised in discussions with other anthropologists in Vietnam: first, ethnology in Vietnam is built on theoretical principles and political orientations that are distinctly different from those in Western anthropology; and second, ethnological works produced by Vietnamese researchers tend to concentrate on aspects of tradition, describing cultures from a static point of view instead of seeing them as dynamic and fluid.

Vietnamese anthropological research tends to concentrate on describing the cultural features of ethnic groups located within the political borders of the country. Cross-border ethnic groups living in neighboring countries are rarely given attention (also see Tosakul, this volume). By focusing on ethnicity and ethnic boundaries, anthropologists aim to discover long-lasting, immutable values. Anthropological works of this sort usually cover almost every aspect of social life, from social and family relations to material and spiritual life. These are then placed within a preconceived analytical framework linked with a certain period of national history, often the mythical period of the Hung kings. Doing so implies that ethnic minorities and the ethnic Kinh majority originated from the same source. This historical fact purportedly unites them against foreign invaders, and today they have the same responsibility to build a common nation state. Because of such a narrative, the historian David Marr observed that most ethnographies by Vietnamese scholars share a similar pattern where "much of the presentation has a timeless, museum-like character, as if most of these people had not undergone incredible trials and transformations during the past half-century" (1992: 169).

Interviews with a leading professor in ethnology confirm the above comment. In his view, when he studied an ethnic group in the Central Highlands of Vietnam, its traditional culture was no longer observable. He came to this conclusion through collecting the stories told by elders in different villages and then reconstructing this "shattered culture" into an imagined culture. It was through this imagination that he could describe the traditional culture of any ethnic group he studied. The question then becomes why are our ethnologists merely focusing on "typical" and "long-lasting" features of culture even when they are no longer observable, while overlooking issues in modern societies? Why are they gazing at traditional values, searching for them in remote, isolated communities, while continuing to ignore other topics regarding the changing patterns in society and the dynamic diversity of culture? In their practice, Vietnamese ethnologists rarely question themselves as to why they are pursuing the static features of culture as opposed to adopting a different approach.

In my view, this practice is influenced by Marxist theory as much as colonial anthropology. Global anthropological traditions in general, and in Indochina in particular, were closely linked with the social evolutionist approach of the colonial era. They explored "alien societies" outside of Europe and viewed indigenous peoples as belonging to a lower level in social development. Salemink (1999: 54–55) points out that evolutionary discourse was clearly seen in French ethnographic descriptions that depicted the aboriginal population of Indochina as savage and "primitive" tribes with the implication that they needed support from civilized races. According to Salemink, the evolutionary discourse that had disappeared with the colonial regime has re-emerged as an important ingredient for nation-building and modernization because evolutionism was a constituent element of the Marxist state–ideology. Thus, the evolutionary framework of colonial anthropology was extended into postcolonial anthropology due to the evolutionist assumptions of Marxism. Salemink's critique of the evolutionist perspective helps explain why Vietnamese anthropology today struggles to go beyond colonial ethnographical practice. While social evolutionism is merely seen as a historical relic in present-day international anthropology (Lương Văn Hy 2001: 7), leading anthropologists in Vietnam still call for the "rightness" of evolutionism "because it acknowledges the unity of human beings and maintains the standpoint of social development from the lower to higher levels" (Phan Hữu Dật 1973: 1).

Besides such problematic theories, the recent calls for a renovation of ethnology in Vietnam tend to emphasize the applicability of the discipline in development and social policy (also see Đặng Nguyên Anh, this volume). Hoàng Lương (2000: 7), for instance, argued that application should be given more attention so that ethnology can better serve socio-economic development policies and not remain as merely descriptive ethnography in search of bygone traditions. Such a statement says nothing new. Three decades ago, Evans (1985: 120) argued that the central aim of ethnological research in Vietnam is in serving the communist party and state policy. The discipline of ethnology, fueled by strong nationalism, has turned itself into a political instrument. It has therefore lost its academic character, especially when researchers become involved in activities to develop the economy and culture of supposedly "backward" peoples. Indeed, for the past few decades, Vietnamese ethnologists have been deeply involved in designing ethnic policies and development programs in the mountainous regions. Among these are socio-economic development programs in the Central Highlands; the abolition of ethnic autonomous regions; facilitating the massive migration from lowlands to uplands for economic development; and the changing of religious policies.[14] While there have been calls for more applied ethnology to better serve the government's development programs, universities and research institutes are not yet ready. In discussing the major tasks of ethnology in the coming decades, Khổng Diễn suggests that "anthropology in the twenty-first century, on the one hand, has to enhance the capacity of basic studies and regards this as the core task, and in the meantime, pay more attention to applied research. These two tasks have to go hand in hand together" (Khổng Diễn 2003: 28). The question that remains is then what to study and how to apply ethnographical knowledge to the country's development agenda.

Moving Forward: Ethnology or Anthropology

In the early 1990s, the Department of Ethnology at Hanoi National University initiated a call for renovation (reform) because ethnology in Vietnam was regarded as a part of history, and its curriculum and training programs were part of the history department (also see Đặng Nguyên Anh, this volume). The call of renovation aimed to create a new curriculum for training in which four fields in anthropology—linguistics, archeology, social-cultural anthropology (i.e. ethnology), and physical anthropology—should be combined. Furthermore, ethnology and cultural anthropology should be separated from the historical sciences to become an independent discipline. However, such a call did not receive any support from academic authorities at universities and research institutes. Authorities argued that so-called anthropology was inapplicable in Vietnam due to the fact that the country has fifty-four ethnic groups and ethnology is meant to serve the Party's ethnic policies. Such a response reveals that anthropology as a discipline in Vietnam is understood differently than global anthropology. Still, this call did raise questions among academic authorities who began to question their understanding of anthropology and the possible need for change (Interviews with Prof. Hoàng Lương, December 2006).

During the late 1990s and the early 2000s, the Ford Foundation in Hanoi funded a few billion-dong projects in departments of ethnology in universities and the state institutes of ethnology to facilitate further discussion and exchange in the discipline in Vietnam. Scholarships for training abroad in anthropology and sociology were also provided to encourage young researchers and students to advance their academic careers. National conferences were organized in Hanoi, Hue and Ho Chi Minh City with the purpose of strengthening the exchange of training and research activities among staff working in the fields of ethnology and cultural studies. Although these conferences did not lead to any concrete common agreement with discernable impact, the Ford Foundation continued to fund separate projects aimed at supporting universities and research institutes to renovate their training programs at all levels. Still, these projects were unable to change the view of academic authorities on the position of ethnology and the necessity for renovation. However, the negative response from the academic management did not hinder change. In 2000, the Ministry of Education and Training (MOET) agreed to provide a separate training code for a discipline that was for the first time officially named "anthropology," code number 523146 (Ngô Văn Lệ and Nguyễn Văn Tiệp 2000: 7). This landmark decision opened the way for changes to take place in anthropological research training at universities and institutes.

In 2003, the Vietnam National University in Ho Chi Minh City established the Faculty of Anthropology. In 2004, Hanoi University of Social Sciences and Humanities renamed the Department of Ethnology the Department of Ethnology and Anthropology. In the wake of such change, the Vietnam Association of Ethnology and the Institute of Ethnology petitioned the government to add "and Anthropology" after the term "Ethnology." Although this request was not officially accepted by the government, the Institute of Ethnology used the new name "Institute of Anthropology" for their international transactions with the aim of being pioneers with respect to international integration. In 2005, the PhD training curriculum submitted by the Institute of Human Studies at the Vietnam Academy of Social Sciences was accepted by MOET as the first institution with a PhD program in cultural anthropology in Vietnam.

I have briefly reviewed several changes in research and training in ethnology/cultural anthropology in Vietnam during the last decade. Such changes have occurred in parallel with economic reform and with the country undergoing integration into the world economy. As I see it, the process of intellectual and academic change is not as easy and fruitful as that observed in the economic sector. This raises the question, why has change in the former been so slow and difficult? In search of answers, I conducted a series of interviews with colleagues and other prominent persons in the field and found that their responses were significantly diverse. The general impression I received was that the majority of our established scholars and academic authorities lack information regarding research and training in the field of ethnology and anthropology outside of Vietnam. Their responses can be divided into four categories:

1) It is necessary to separate ethnology from the historical sciences and it needs a comprehensive curriculum of training. Whether it is called ethnology or anthropology is not important because they are effectively identical.
2) It is impossible to move from ethnology to anthropology because they are two different disciplines altogether. Furthermore, "Vietnam is a multi-ethnic country. Ethnological studies are to contribute to ethnic policies in Vietnam."
3) We should not change the training curriculum since we do not really understand what anthropology is. Cultural anthropology is a Western science with the purpose of serving capitalist interests. We should also be especially careful when we receive funds from foreign sources that may alter our research and training.[15]
4) Research and training in ethnology should be renovated to make the discipline more internationally integrated so that research and training in ethnology can receive more funding from foreign foundations.

The above opinions reflect the struggle of Vietnamese anthropologists in search of change and renovation. On the one hand, they are bound by attitudes of nationalism and nation-building. On the other hand, they face the reality of rapid globalization that calls for alternatives in training and new human sources for development. However, responses from academic authorities to this process have been slow. Consequently, while a new name has been added to the field of ethnology, old practices remain unchanged. This indicates that all the ground-up efforts seeking change have been partial, moderate, anxious and incomplete.

Moreover, the new trend of the "renovation" of ethnology in Vietnam is influenced by parallel changes in the former Soviet Union, the Eastern European socialist bloc and China. A study of the changes in the field of ethnology in these countries may help explain the recent trend of ethnology in Vietnam. Available literature (Guldin 1990, 1994; Tong 1996) reports that after economic reforms in China were launched during the late 1970s, many southern Chinese universities started to voice a need to change the ethnological approach to anthropology with its separation into four fields as seen in European and American universities (Smart 2005). Actually, even before the socialist regime was established in China, four-field anthropology had already been introduced in various universities in the country. As early as 1923, the Nakai University of Tianjin offered anthropology courses in their curriculum. Since 1928, the Department of Anthropology was set up at Beijing's Academia Sinica where the fields of paleo-anthropology and archeology were taught together with ethnology (*minzuxue*). Like in Vietnam, this discipline was changed into ethnology as China adopted Soviet approaches in social science after independence in 1949.

After recent economic reforms, a number of universities in China started to teach anthropology (*releixue*) instead of ethnology. Zhongshan University in Guangzhou province was a pioneer in this when they established the Department of Anthropology in 1980. This was soon followed by Xiamen University in Fujian province in 1984 and Yunnan University in 1994. At present, almost all universities and research institutes in China have moved from ethnology to anthropology. In 2000, Beijing University set up the Institute of Sociology and Anthropology even though Beijing's Central University of Nationalities had already built the Research Centre for Social-Cultural Anthropology in 1994. To explain the reasons for the establishment of anthropology in universities and research institutes, Liang Zhaotao of Zhongshan University, Guangzhou, points this out:

> All other countries have this discipline (*releixue*); why not us? We have such a glorious culture and large population. Why not us? We Chinese must study our 1 billion Chinese! We must study our bountiful material—if not us, who will? We can't leave this science only to the foreigners! Let anthropology make its contribution to the Four Modernizations! (Guldin 1994: 12).

Beside nationalistic rhetoric, the move towards favoring anthropology in China is also explained by the belief that the discipline is necessary for exploring and understanding the changing world. Tong Enzheng argues:

> Another characteristic of cultural anthropology is its recognition of the necessity for social change. This means that in this world, nothing is static and absolute. We must recognize reforms and evolution as a universal principle. It also means one should renounce all static doctrines which [are] no longer suitable in the current changing situation (Tong 1996: 4).

The establishment of anthropology in replacing ethnology also occurred in Russia and the former Eastern European socialist bloc. Recent surveys by Vesna Godina in Ljublian University (Slovenia) report that although the term "social-cultural anthropology" was broadly used in Middle and Eastern Europe before 1990, it was not taught as an independent discipline in universities. According to her, social and cultural anthropology spread in these countries after 1990 through various ways: first, by setting up new institutions (department or institute) of anthropology; second, by renaming the former departments and institutes of ethnology into social-cultural anthropology departments and institutes; and third, by retaining the old name "ethnology" and merely adding "anthropology" after it (e.g. Institute of Ethnology and Anthropology).

The reasons for this change are explained in various ways, but mainly focus on the need for international integration and the requirement of academic renovation to meet the fast changing needs of the socio-economic system. Another reason is the desire to break away from dated Marxist traditions that ruled the social sciences in these countries for decades.

Conclusion

The history of modern anthropology in Vietnam can typically be divided into three distinct periods: first, the emergence of cultural anthropology under French colonial rule from the beginning of twentieth century up to 1954; second, the introduction of the Soviet school of ethnology under the socialist construction from 1954 to the collapse of the Soviet bloc in the early 1990s; and third, the new trends of globalizing cultural anthropology in the era of integration from the 1990s up to the present.

Global anthropological traditions are not immune to the social forces that shape their objects of study. Cultural anthropology in former socialist countries experienced significant change after the worldwide collapse of communism in the 1990s. The renovation movement in cultural anthropology taking place in Vietnam, China and other places from the 1990s till today indicates that the discipline is closely associated with and influenced by social change. That the demand for change occurred right after economic reforms in these countries can be interpreted as a positive response aimed not only at taking part in global academic integration but also at meeting the increasing need for new knowledge to propel change.

In the case of Vietnam, we can see that the process of the academic integration of ethnology has come at a relatively slower pace in comparison to economic integration. For decades under socialism, ethnology did not seem to relate to the socio-economic system as a means for knowledge production but instead stood aside, contributing little to the demand for reform and social development. Until recently, ethnology was still considered to be a sub-discipline in the historical sciences and did not enjoy a position deserving of its role but instead appeared as a sort of "illustrative science."[16] Meanwhile, a "closed policy" has been applied to the social sciences for too long. Vietnamese anthropologists were not updated about new developments in the international field for decades. Integration and international cooperation is therefore becoming an inevitable, necessary path for development. Nevertheless, it seems that even at present, state agencies in social sciences as well as researchers themselves are not yet ready to face the challenges of innovation. Public research and training institutions in cultural anthropology in Vietnam are still being ignored, leaving this field at the crossroads of change and integration as individual anthropologists find themselves akin to confused pedestrians who have lost their sense of direction.

I would like to stress that the social sciences and humanities are themselves social constructions. While Vietnamese society has been on the road towards intensive integration into the world economic system, the social sciences cannot remain on the sidelines. The call for renovation in anthropology in Vietnam by individual scholars and researchers, though hindered by a slow response, reflects the strong demand from within to renovate academic research and training to produce new knowledge for development.

At a regional conference held at Chiang Mai University in 2007, I met many young Vietnamese researchers and graduate students who were sent abroad for training in anthropology. They were pursuing degrees at different universities in Europe, Australia and the United States. Coincidentally, they met in Chiang Mai as they participated in various sessions at the conference. Looking at them, I can see the future of Vietnamese anthropology. There is no doubt that it is these young people who will bring anthropology into a bright new future.

Notes

* This piece of work was completed with the support of the Vietnam National Foundation for Science and Technology (NAFOSTED). I would like to express my deep gratitude to Dr Eric Thompson (Department of Sociology, the National University of Singapore), for his efforts in editing the text.

1. Singaravélou, Pierre (1999), *L'École française d' Extrême-Orient ou l'institution des marges (1898–1956). Essai d'histoire sociale et politique de la science colonial.* Paris: L'Harmattan, 1999. Vietnamese version *Trường Viễn đông Bác cổ (EFEO) trong bão táp thuộc địa*, (École française d'Extrême-Orient (EFEO) in Colonial Storm; EFEO Hanoi). I sincerely thank Dr Andrew Hardy, Director of EFEO in Hanoi, for providing the document.
2. According to Kleinen (1997, 353–94), BEFEO published eighty-eight research papers from 1901–45, of which more than one third focused on religion, morality and Vietnamese customs.
3. *Bulletin des Amis du Vieux Hué* (*BAVH*) has been recently published by EFEO in the form of a CD-Rom. All papers published by *BAVH* were recently translated into Vietnamese by the publisher, Thuan Hoa.
4. On March 20, 1943, the French Governor J. Decoux signed a decree to accept the regulation on IIEH's research activities. George Coedes was nominated as the director of the institute with two vice directors—Pierre Huard (Medical College of Hanoi University) and Paul Levy (Ethnology section at EFEO). The technical advisors included Riou, Lanessan Hospital in Hanoi, Nguyen Van Huyen (EFEO), Nguyen Xuan Nguyen (Hanoi Optical Hospital), Nguyen Van To (administrator at EFEO). Among the researchers at this institute, Do Xuan Hop later became well known in the field of paleoanthropology in postcolonial Vietnam.
5. Even some EFEO staff did not hide their anti-colonialism and were friendly with Vietnamese communists. Among them are Paul Mus, Jacques Gernet, Paul Levy, Roger Billard, Louis Gernet, and Andre-George Haudricourt. (See *École française d'Extrême-Orient (EFEO) in Colonial Storm*, Vietnamese version.)

6. See, for instance, G. Condominas, *Chúng tôi ăn rừng* (Nous avons mange la foret, Hà Nội: Thế Giới, 2003; P. Gourou, *Người nông dân châu thổ Bắc Kỳ (Les paysans du delta tonkinois. Etudes de geographie humaine).* Hà Nội: Nhà Xuất bản Trẻ, 2003; J. Dournes, *Rừng, đàn bà, điên loạn (Foret, Femme, Folie).* Hà Nội: Hội Nhà văn, 2002. Do Trinh Hue recently reviewed entire works by L. Cadier and came to the conclusion that it was Cadiere who laid the foundations for Vietnamese studies. See Do Trinh Hue, *Van hoa, Ton giao, Tin nguong Vietnam duoi nhan quan hoc gia L. Cadiere* [Culture, Religion, Beliefs of the Vietnamese Through the Eyes of L. Cadiere]. Hue: Thuan Hoa, 2006.
7. Information used in this paragraph is based on the translated version of *École française d'Extrême-Orient (EFEO) in Colonial Storm*, provided by Hanoi EFEO.
8. Professor Mạc Đường recalled in his memoir: "Comrade Lã Văn Lô often used an ethnology textbook by Bonifacy and works by De la Jonquiere on northern highlands to teach us. Comrade Nguyễn Hữu Thấu carefully studied ethnographic works by Henri Maitre, Jacque Dournes, Sabatier on central highlands and he did use these literatures for his teaching to our young generation" (Mạc Đường 1997, 386–87).
9. Most of the Vietnamese researchers who worked at EFEO later became well-known scholars and high-ranking officials serving the revolutionary government of Vietnam. Among them, Nguyễn Văn Tố became the first Vice President of Vietnam's National Assembly; Nguyễn Văn Huyên served as the Minister of Education; Vũ Đình Tụng was the Minister of Health and Red Cross; Nguyễn Thiệu Lâu was appointed to be the General Director of the Statistical Office in the Cabinet.
10. Indeed, these two researchers later became well-known Soviet scholars in the field of cultural anthropology.
11. Those who took part in the first trip to the northwestern highlands and escorted the two Russian researchers included Nguyễn Khắc Đạm, Lã Văn Lô, Nguyễn Đổng Chi, Đặng Nghiêm Vạn, Nguyễn Văn Chi, Đinh Xuân Lâm, and Vương Hoàng Tuyên (Đặng Nghiêm Vạn 1999, 183–84).
12. For instance, ethnological textbooks compiled by Phan Hữu Dật (1973); Lê Sỹ Giáo (1997); Hoàng Nam (1997); Đặng Nghiêm Vạn (2000).
13. Phan Hữu Dật was among the few cases of ethnology graduates from Moscow University who later became influential figures in Vietnamese ethnology. He was sent to Russia for training in ethnology in 1955, received his PhD from Moscow (Lomonosov) University in 1963, and became a lecturer of ethnology at Hanoi University in 1964. He then served as the head of the Faculty of History from 1971–75 as well as the Rector of Hanoi University and head of the Ethnology Department from 1985–88 (Lâm Bá Nam 2012).
14. Nguyễn Hồng Dương (2000, 9–34) praised two outstanding contributions from Professor Đặng Nghiêm Vạn, a leading ethnologist, on government

policies of the abolishment of ethnic autonomies in Vietnam, and changes in recent religious policies. The idea of national worship of Hung kings and the ritual ceremony held in the Hung Temple as a national ceremony is said to come from Đặng Nghiêm Vạn.

15. This information was obtained from the minutes of discussions held at the Department of Ethnology, Hanoi National University in 2000 and 2005.
16. There is a strong trend towards the homogenization of sciences and politics in Vietnam and other socialist countries. Science has often been used to legitimize political will. For further information and to hear the voices of scientists with regards to this matter, please see Nguyễn Sỹ Phương (2010); Vietnam Net (2014).

References

Barfield, Thomas (1997) *The Dictionary of Anthropology*. Oxford: Blackwell Publisher.

Bayly, Susan (2000) "French Anthropology and the Durkheimenians in Colonial Indochina," *Modern Asian Studies* 34(3): pp. 581–622.

Bế Viết Đẳng (2006) *Dân tộc học Việt Nam: Định hướng và thành tựu nghiên cứu (1973–1998)* [*Vietnamese Ethnology: Orientation and Research Achievement (1973–1998)*]. Hà Nội: Khoa học Xã hội.

Bloch, Maurice (1983) *Marxism and Anthropology: The History of a Relationship*. Oxford: Clarendon Press.

Buxưghin, E.P. (1961) *Dân tộc học đại cương* [*An Introduction to Ethnology*], translated into Vietnamese by Đặng Công Lý and Lê Thế Thép. Hà Nội: Trường Đại học Tổng hợp.

Đặng Nghiêm Vạn (1999) "Anh Tuyên, một người bạn." ["Mr Tuyen, a Friend."] In *Vương Hoàng Tuyên, Nhà giáo, Nhà dân tộc học* [*Vương Hoàng Tuyên, A Teacher and Ethnographer*], Khoa Sử, (ed.), pp. 183–93. Hồ Chí Minh: Nhà Xuất bản Trẻ.

Đặng Nghiêm Vạn, (ed.) (2000) *Dân tộc học đại cương* [*An Introduction to Ethnology*]. Hà Nội: Giáo dục.

Đinh Xuân Lâm (1999) "Chuyến đi định hướng cho một sự nghiệp" ["A Field Trip that Opens to a Life Career"]. In *Vương Hoàng Tuyên, Nhà giáo, Nhà dân tộc học* [*Vương Hoàng Tuyên, A Teacher and Ethnographer*], Khoa Sử (ed.), pp. 176–82. Hồ Chí Minh: Nhà Xuất bản Trẻ.

Evans, Grant (1985) "Vietnamese Communist Anthropology," *Canberra Anthropology* 8(1–2): pp. 116–47.

——— (2000) "Apprentice Ethnographers: Vietnam and the Study of Lao Minorities." In *Laos Culture and Society*, Grant Evans, (ed.), pp. 161–90. Singapore: Institute of Southeast Asian Studies.

Guldin, Gregory Eliyu, (eds.) (1992) *Anthropology in China*. Armond: M.E. Sharpe.

Guldin, Gregory Eliyu (1994) *The Saga of Anthropology in China: From Malinowski to Moscow to Mao*. Armond: M.E. Sharpe.

Harms, Erik Lind (2000) "Vietnam, Anthropology, and Ethnographic Authority through Time and War." Unpublished conference paper, Cornell University, United States.

Khổng Diễn (1998) "Công tác nghiên cứu dân tộc học trong những năm qua" ["Ethnological Studies in the Last Years."] In *Khoa học Xã hội và Nhân văn: Mười năm đổi mới và phát triển*, Tập 2 [*Social Sciences and Humanities: Ten Years of Renovation and Development*, vol. 2], Phạm Tất Dong, (ed.), pp. 277–90. Hà Nội: Khoa học Xã hội.

_____ (2003) "Tổng quan về dân tộc học Việt Nam trong một thế kỷ qua" ["An Overview on the Vietnamese Ethnology in a Past Century."] In *Dân tộc học Việt Nam thế kỷ XX và những năm đầu thế kỷ XXI* [*The Vietnamese Ethnology in the 20th and Early 21st Centuries*], Khổng Diễn and Bùi Minh Đạo, (eds.), pp. 15–54. Hà Nôi: Khoa học Xã hội.

Kleinen, J. (1997) "The Village as Pretext: Ethnographic Praxis and the Colonial State in Vietnam." In *The Village in Asia Revisited*, J. Breman, P. Kloss and A. Saith, (eds.), pp. 353–94. Delhi: Oxford University Press.

Koh, Priscilla (2004) "Vietnamese Ethnology in the Doi Moi Period (1986–2001)," *Southeast Asian Studies* 5(1): pp. 1–21.

Hoàng Lương (2000) "Một số gợi ý về sự kết hợp công tác đào tạo và nghiên cứu dân tộc học trong thời kỳ công nghiệp hoá, hiện đại hoá đất nước" ["Some Suggestions on the Combination Between Training and Research in Ethnology for the Period of Industrialization and Modernization of the Country"]. Presentation at the Conference Proceedings on Research and Teaching Ethnology, Hanoi, August 2000.

_____ (2003) "Vài suy nghĩ về việc đổi mới chương trình và phương pháp đào tạo dân tộc học" ["Some Thoughts of Renovation in Teaching Program and Training Methods of Ethnology"]. In *Dân tộc học Việt Nam thế kỷ XX và những năm đầu thế kỷ XXI* [*The Vietnamese Ethnology in the 20th and Early 21st Centuries*], Khổng Diễn and Bùi Minh Đạo, (eds.), pp. 122–31. Hà Nôi: Khoa học Xã hội.

Hoàng Nam (1997) *Dân tộc học đại cương* [*An Introduction to Ethnology*]. Hà Nội: Văn hoá – Thôngtin.

Lâm Bá Nam (2012) "GS. TS. Phan Hữu Dật, người trọn đời vì sự nghiệp giáo dục và phát triển ngành Nhân học" ["Prof. Dr. Phan Huu Dat, Who Spent his Whole Life for Development of Vietnamese Anthropology"]. In *100 Chân dung – Một thế kỷ Đại học Quốc gia Hà Nội* [*100 Portraits – A Century of Hanoi National University*]. Hà Nội: Đại học Quốc gia.

Lê Sỹ Giáo, (ed.) (1997) *Dân tộc học đại cương* [*An Introduction to Ethnology*]. Hà Nội: Giáodục.

Lê Văn Hảo (1965) *Hành trình vào dân tộc học* [*A Journey into Ethnology*]. Nam Sơn: Sài Gòn.

Lương Văn Hy (2001) "Lời Giới thiệu" ["Introduction"]. In *Nhân học: Một quan điểm về tình trạng nhân sinh* [*Anthropology: A Perspective on the Human Condition*], E.A. Schultz and R.H. Lavenda, (eds.), pp. 7–8. (Vietnamese version by Phan Ngọc Chiến and Hồ Liên Biện), Hà Nội: Chính trị Quốc gia.

Mạc Đường (1997) *Dân tộc học và vấn đề xác định thành phần dân tộc, Lý thuyết–Nghiên cứu–Tư liệu* [*Ethnology and the Question of Ethnic Classification, Theory-Studies-Data*]. Hà Nội: Khoa học Xã hội.

Marr, David (1978) "The State of the Social Sciences in Vietnam," *Bulletin of Concerned Asian Scholars* 10(4): p. 73.

_____ (1992) *World Bibliographical Series: Vietnam*. Oxford: Clio Press.

Ngô Văn Lệ và Nguyễn Văn Tiệp (2000) "Kết hợp nghiên cứu và giảng dạy dân tộc học: Thực trạng và giải pháp" ["Research and Training in Ethnology: Current State and Solutions"]. Presentation at the Conference Proceedings on Research and Teaching Ethnology, Hanoi, August 2000.

Nguyễn Hồng Dương (2000) "Giáo sư Đặng Nghiêm Vạn, vài nét về thân thế và sự nghiệp" ["Professor Đặng Nghiêm Vạn: A Sketch of Life and Works"]. In *Giáo sư Đặng Nghiêm Vạn: nhà giáo, nhà nghiên cứu,* [*Professor Đặng Nghiêm Vạn: A Teacher and Researcher*], pp. 9–34. Hà Nội: Viện Nghiên cứu Tôn Giáo & Viện Dân tộc học.

Nguyễn Phương Ngọc (2012) *À l'origine de l'anthropologie au Vietnam* [*The origin of anthropology in Vietnam*]. Aix-en-Provence: Presses universitaires de Provence.

Nguyễn Sỹ Phương (2010) "Hãy đọc lời ai điếu cho khoa học minh họa." ["Let's Say Goodbye to Illustrative Sciences"]. In *Tuần Việt Nam*, accessed September 30, 2010. http://tuanvietnam.net/2010-09-29-hay-doc-loi-ai-dieu-cho-nghien-cuu-khoa-hoc-minh-hoa.

Nguyễn Văn Chính (2006) "Một thế kỷ dân tộc học Việt Nam, và những thách thức trên con đường đổi mới và hội nhập" ["A Century of Vietnamese Ethnology and Challenges on the Road to Renovation and Integration"]. Paper presented at the conference "A Hundred Years of Research and Training in Social Sciences and Humanities in Vietnam." Đại học Quốc gia Hà Nội.

Nguyễn Văn Huy (2000) "Một số vấn đề đổi mới, nâng cao chất lượng nghiên cứu dân tộc học hiện nay" ["The Questions of Renovation and Enhancing the Quality of Today's Ethnological Research"]. Presentation at the Conference Proceedings on Research and Teaching Ethnology, Hanoi, August 2000.

Nhà XB Sử học (1960) *Dân tộc học là gì* [*What is Ethnology?*]. Hà Nội: Sử học.

Pelley, Patricia (1998) "'Barbarians' and 'Younger Brothers': The Remaking of Race in Postcolonial Vietnam," *Journal of Southeast Asian Studies* 29(2): pp. 374–91.

Phan Hữu Dật (1973) *Cơ sở dân tộc học* [*Basic Ethnology*]. Hà Nội: Đại học and Trung học chuyên nghiệp.

_____ (2003) "Về mối quan hệ giữa dân tộc học và nhân học." ["On the Relation Between Ethnology and Anthropology."] In *Dân tộc học Việt Nam thế kỷ XX và những năm đầu thế kỷ XXI* [*Vietnamese Ethnology in the 20th and Early 21st Centuries*], Khổng Diễn and Bùi Minh Đạo, (eds.), pp. 73–79. Hà Nôi: Khoa học Xã hội.

_____ (2004) "Quá trình hình thành và phát triển dân tộc học Việt Nam" ["The Establishment and Development of Vietnamese Ethnology"]. In *Góp phần nghiên cứu dân tộc học Việt Nam* [*Contribution to Vietnam's Ethnology*], Phan Hữu Dật, (ed.), pp. 49–73. Hà Nội: Chính trị Quốc gia.

_____ (2006) "Từ dân tộc học đến nhân học" ["From Ethnology to Anthropology"]. In *100 năm nghiêncứu và đào tạo các ngành khoa học xã hội và nhân văn ở Việt nam* [*A Hundred Years of Research and Training in Social Sciences and Humanities in Vietnam*], Đại học Quốc gia Hà Nội, (eds.), pp. 217–23. Hà Nội: Đại học Quốc gia Hà Nội.

Phan Lạc Tuyên (2003) "Nghiên cứu và giảng dạy dân tộc học ở miền Nam trước 1975" ["Ethnological Research and Training in the South Before 1975"]. In *Dân tộc học Việt Nam thế kỷ XX và những năm đầu thế kỷ XXI* [*Vietnamese Ethnology in the 20th and Early 21st Centuries*], Khổng Diễn and Bùi Minh Đạo, (eds.), pp. 196–213. Hà Nôi: Khoa học Xã hội.

Salemink, Oscar (1999a) "Ethnography as Martial Art: Ethnicizing Vietnam's Montagnards, 1930–1954." In *Colonial Subjects: Essays on the Practical History of Anthropology*, Peter Pell and Oscar Salemink, (eds.), pp. 282–325. Ann Arbor: University Of Michigan Press.

_____ (1999b) *Beyond Complicity and Naiveté: Contextualizing the Ethnography of Vietnam's Central Highlanders*. PhD dissertation, University of Amsterdam, Netherlands.

Sarkany, Mihaly (2002) *Cultural and Social Anthropology in Central and Eastern Europe*. http://www.cee-socialsciences.net; accessed September 23, 2013.

Singaravélou, Pierre (1999), *L'École française d'Extrême-Orient ou l'institution des marges (1898–1956). Essai d'histoire sociale et politique de la science colonial*. Paris: L'Harmattan.

_____ (1999), *Trường Viễn đông Bác cổ trong bão táp thuộc địa* [*Far East School of Uncle Ho in the Colonial Storm*]. Vietnamese translation by EFEO Hanoi, unpublished.

Smart, Josephine (2005) "In Search of Anthropology in China: A Discipline Caught in the Web of Nation Building Agenda, Socialist Capitalism, and Globalisation," Wane-Journal news; http://www.ram-wan.org/html/documents.htm.; accessed October 9, 2009.

Tocarev, X.A. (1994) *Các hình thái tôn giáo sơ khai và sự phát triển của chúng* [*The Earlier Forms of Religions and their Development*], translated into Vietnamese by Lê Thế Thép. Hà Nội: Chính trị Quốc gia.

Tong Enzheng (1996) "Cultural Anthropology and the Social Reforms in China." Presentation at Wesleyan University, February 15, 1996.

Trần Văn Giầu (1999) "Họ chỉ "nhờ" tôi ở một chỗ duy nhất là …" ["The Only Thing They Asked for Help Was …"]. In *Vương Hoàng Tuyên: Nhà giáo, Nhà dân tộc học* [*Vuong Hoang Tuyen: A Teacher and Ethnograper*], Khoa Sử, (eds.), pp. 172–73. Hồ Chí Minh: Nhà Xuất bản Trẻ.

Trịnh Kim Ngọc (2006) "Viện Nghiên cứu con người Đông Dương, quá trình thành lập và nhữnghoạt động nghiên cứu" ["Indochinese Institute for Human Studies: Establishment and Research Activities"]. Unpublished paper, the Institute for Human Studies, Hanoi.

Vietnam Net (2014) "Đừng dùng chuyên gia như hình thức minh họa" ["Don't Make Use of Experts as a Way of Illustration"]. http://vietnamnet.vn/vn/khoa-hoc/184081/dung--dung--chuyen-gia-nhu-hinh-thuc-minh-hoa.html; accessed April 13, 2014.

Vũ Minh Chi (2004) *Nhân học văn hoá: Con người với thiên nhiên, xã hội và thế giới siêu nhiên* [*Cultural Anthropology: People, Nature, Society and the Supernatural World*]. Hà Nội: Chính trị Quốc gia.

SECTION 2

CHALLENGES IN ANTHROPOLOGICAL PRACTICE

CHAPTER 4 RECOVERING FILIPINO PRODUCTION OF A MARITIME ANTHROPOLOGY

Maria F. Mangahas and
Suzanna Rodriguez-Roldan

> Despite the prevalence of fisheries in the Philippine archipelago, the dearth of anthropological studies focusing on this aspect of national life is a yawning gap in Philippine social science. Philippine anthropologist Ponciano Bennagen notes: "Maritime anthropology in the Philippines is young and poor relative to upland and even lowland ethnographies, which is ironic for an archipelagic country" (*UP Arcoast E-NEWS* Issue No. 2. 1998).

The Philippines is an archipelagic nation of more than 7,000 islands with marine resources under intense pressure from market-driven extraction, numerous maritime interests to protect, and pressing issues including pollution, overfishing and degradation of resources, ineffective regulation of coastal and marine resources, population growth, urbanization and poverty. Over 60 percent of the Philippines' more than 100 million population live in coastal areas. From the perspective of demography alone, the significance of the fisheries sector for the Philippine population is considerable. Yet, ethnographic work written by Filipinos on coastal fishing communities in the Philippines is surprisingly sparse. In terms of published books and academic journals, there are more non-Filipino authors than local ones. Given the Philippines' archipelagic character and reliance on aquatic resources, an important question looms: Why hasn't the surrounding sea played a larger role in the rise of Philippine anthropology?

The Philippines is also a leader in biodiversity conservation initiatives such as setting up marine protected area networks. In these efforts, far more is known about fish stocks and behavior of marine species than about the humans that dwell there—their social identities, subsistence strategies, exchange networks and the cultural knowledge that enables sea-oriented livelihoods. Intensification and decline in Philippine fisheries was observed as early as the 1930s (Butcher 2004: 114). Fishers routinely remark on how they must go farther out to sea to bring back greatly diminished catches. Today, in fact, an urgent issue for research is: Why does fishing continue as a livelihood option in the face of uneconomic returns? Recently, foreign scholars have called for ethnography to understand the social complexity of Philippine coastal settings (Eder 2009; Fabinyi, Knudsen and Segi 2010).

We show in this chapter that a substantial amount of well-written, theoretically framed, and sensitively nuanced ethnographies based on extended periods of fieldwork already exists. However, these are mostly unpublished works in the form of MA theses, PhD dissertations and research reports produced in the course of long-term projects on coastal resource management (CRM). Examples of significant ethnographic content that can be gleaned from these resources include insights into sharing behavior among fishers; fisher mobility, sociality and access to marine resources; cultures of resource use and abuse; local knowledge related to fishing gear; and insights into changing seascapes.

This "gray literature"[1] from the unpublished margins constitutes a significant body of research on fisherfolk and their communities. This literature spans more than a century, yet remains relatively inaccessible and unknown. To understand why this is so, we begin by reflecting on our own experiences as researchers in coastal communities and our trajectories as students of anthropology from the 1980s. We then examine practices of preserving student anthropology papers in the early years of the Department of Anthropology at the University of the Philippines (UP) from 1914 until the 1960s and 1970s, and interest in indigenous resource management and customary tenure aspects of fisheries from the 1980s. From the mid 1990s to the present, we highlight in particular the contributions of Cynthia Neri Zayas in establishing a sea-oriented anthropology, and we outline the proliferation of recent research as well as further sources of gray literature that have yet to be fully explored. Along the way, we note intersections of maritime anthropology literature with prominent individuals and concurrent discourses or debates in Filipino anthropology and social science in the Philippines in general.[2] This slightly personal exploration of maritime anthropology touches on broader themes in the history of Filipino anthropology, also exposing something of how anthropology has been practiced in the Philippine context—from socializing students into the discipline, to research, teaching and its application.

"Gray Literature" from the 1980s

We initially made a contribution to this ethnographic gray literature on fishing when we first trained in anthropological field methods. Our first exposure to long-term fieldwork was in the same fishing community on an island off southern Luzon. We picked up the vernacular in situ and spent an entire semester of roughly four months in 1984–85 on the island. This extended period of lengthy research training was pioneering in the curriculum for senior anthropology majors at the time.

For the field school we were enlisted in field methods courses in social anthropology, archeology and physical anthropology, as well as folklore and traditional and peasant communities. We were required to write all our research papers in Filipino—a language our professors considered to be more accessible to the community than English. It was also a deliberate nationalistic act to avoid using English in communicating knowledge meant for a Filipino audience, and possibly it may have also been a condition imposed by the funding that supported our field schools. Among the library materials brought to the field school was a guide on reporting research in the social sciences in Filipino (*Ang Ulat ng Pagsisiyasat sa Agham-Panlipunan* 1978), authored by social psychologist Virgilio Enriquez and anthropologist Ponciano Bennagen, two pioneers who had worked for social science indigenization during the martial law period, leading to the establishment of the Pambansang Samahan para sa Sikolohiyang Pilipino [National Organization of Filipino Psychology] by Enriquez in 1975 and the Ugnayang Pang-AghamTao [The Anthropological Association of the Philippines] (UGAT) by Bennagen in 1978.

As BA anthropology graduates who had already done fieldwork, we and five others with the same training found employment as research assistants at the UP Institute for Social Work and Community Development for the first Coastal Resource Management Project (CRMP) in Lingayen Gulf, Pangasinan. This was a United States Agency for International Development (USAID) and Association of Southeast Asian Nations (ASEAN) funded research project from 1987–88, jointly conducted by three units focused on fisheries, marine biology and community development from UP-Diliman. Our key references were James Acheson's "Anthropology of Fishing" (1981) and David Szanton's *Estancia in Transition* (1971). More recent and relevant materials written by anthropologists may have been available, such as Alexander Spoehr's *Protein from the Sea: Technological Change in Philippine Capture Fisheries* (1980), but this was not accessible to us at the time. This reflected the "Third World" conditions of scholarship in the Philippines at the time, wherein many reference works about the Philippines were not readily available because they were published abroad. Hence pirating by photocopying and developing personal collections were and still remain necessary for research and education in the Philippines (Mangahas 2014: 117).

Before we began fieldwork, which involved ten to twenty days work every month from 1987 to 1988, we attended a lecture by a fisheries professor on the principles of "stock assessment." and Virgilio Enriquez gave us a talk on research methods. Enriquez specifically lectured on the art of gradually entering into a community and the consequent intersubjective process of transformation of the researcher from an outsider or "other" (*ibang tao*) into a "non-other" (*hindi ibang tao*) in the eyes of the community. "Establishing rapport" would be the common equivalent in most English textbooks. But the latter has a utilitarian connotation that does not capture "loss of inner anxiety" or gaining intersubjective trust (*pakikipagpalagayang-loob*) nor the relational end state of solidarity with a community as demanded by the Sikolohiyang Pilipino methodology. Enriquez also emphasized alertness to linguistic and cultural systems of classification.

During our fieldwork, we observed local practices of sharing of fish. We drafted a paper discussing diverse forms of "sharing and related social norms." For example, *pakikisida* ("asking for a few fish") and *pakikikamel* (taking a "handful of fish") were among everyday forms of redistribution or sharing encountered in all the fishing communities along the Lingayen Gulf. Such practices resulted in a significant proportion of the catch being diverted from market transaction to community sharing or reciprocal exchanges. These informal sharing behaviors observed in CRMP field reports have been largely unnoticed by foreign fieldworkers. Sharing practices have rarely been highlighted in the maritime anthropology literature outside of tradition-based or formal sharing arrangements.

Papers were written after our fieldwork period (1987–88) on themes such as leadership, women's roles, specific methods of illegal fishing, and sharing and related social norms. Papers with senior-ranked co-authors were read at conferences. Abridged versions were eventually published in conference proceedings (Galvez 1989; Tungpalan et al. 1991; Rodriguez 1991; Hingco and Rivera 1991). However, the proceedings demanded brevity, resulting in much descriptive ethnography being edited out. Overall, these publications did not do justice to the energy devoted to long-term fieldwork. Since then, without a repository archive and 1990s digital technology rendered obsolete, many of the original field reports and academic papers became inaccessible and lost even to their authors.

On the key issue of illegal fishing with explosives, the CRMP produced a research paper by Roberto Galvez which made it into a published volume albeit in a highly abridged form, merged with other research reports on illegal fishing (Galvez et al. 1989). Galvez, based in an enclave of blast-fishers from May 1987 to April 1988, was one of the senior researchers of the CRMP. Drawing on his training in psychology and as an advocate of the Sikolohiyang Pilipino (Filipino Psychology) movement, his paper's notable features included observations on children's socialization into blast-fishing, the sharing of a successful catch among community and kin, the paradox of "fiesta atmosphere" surrounding illegal fishing, and the absorption of government agents through interpersonal relationships. The case studies demonstrated an atmosphere of shared social values amidst poverty as a significant factor undermining state efforts at coastal regulation. However, we have been unable to locate the full original paper as the author himself did not save a copy. Needless to say, the full paper has not been referenced in later research on blast-fishing.

Meanwhile, the CRMP brought to light growing interest in coastal resource management from the mid 1980s. Funding made available by institutions such as USAID, and later the International Development Research Center based in Canada for purposes of conservation also provided external stimulus for such research. The first CRMP was meant to be part of a concerted effort to formulate local policy recommendations based on research findings. These findings were summarized into profiles and used as the basis for the Lingayen Gulf Coastal Area Management Plan (McManus and Chua 1990). However, our field reports did not play a role in the formulation of that plan; and for the most part, they never reached an audience that would have been interested in ethnographic viewpoints. Many are unpublished and some remain as personal copies, old loose notes and unarticulated memories.

Marginalization of Filipino Maritime Anthropology

The dearth of Filipino studies on maritime anthropology results not only from the inaccessibility of unpublished materials and under-appreciation of past ethnographic studies. From our experiences, other reasons include contingencies of personal priorities, scholarly interest being inclined toward land-based topics and hierarchical practices that have inhibited knowledge production.

As alumni of the CRMP, we went on from graduate studies to teaching anthropology subjects to undergraduates and subsequently completed MA degrees in anthropology. Given our commitments, we took some time to finish master's theses that were ethnographies of distinct fishing technologies and the knowledge and social organization linked to them. While some parts of these works have been published, a significant portion still remains unpublished.

Embarking on academic careers without a solid publication profile was often due to a lack of early career mentoring, guidance and encouragement, or possibly because of a lack of self-promotion. Publications were not regarded as essential for university hires at that time. Completion of a thesis or dissertation was already a sufficient accomplishment and researchers did not perceive publication as the end goal of research. Moreover we felt that with rapid changes in the field, the output was at once "preliminary" and at the same time "dated," or having historical rather than ethnographic significance. Some scholars were kept busy with their efforts to contribute to society through non-academic engagements, preferring to forego the scholastic channels in which much of their work remained untapped or undervalued. In this vein, the publications that were actually produced were aimed at socially practical, rather than purely academic utility or intellectual, engagement. Consequently, less time was devoted towards contributing to the theoretical development of anthropology as a discipline.

Another reason for the marginalization of maritime-related literature was Philippine anthropology's initial focus on "non-Christian peoples." With the exception of the Bajau, in the ethnographic works of H. Arlo Nimmo (1972, 1994, 2001), lowland groups and coastal people's histories of assimilation have tended to be subsumed by studies that were more oriented toward understanding the conditions of rural folk as peasant farmers. Moreover, as will be seen below, Filipino anthropology of fishing communities has been more inclined to focus on "indigenous" aspects of fisheries.

Previous ethnographic knowledge production on fishing communities by non-Filipino authors (Hart 1956; Mednick 1965; Szanton 1971; Spoehr 1980) had observed the minimal work done in this area despite its significance for Filipino livelihoods, and the increasing vulnerability, depletion and degradation of marine resources. *The Psychology of Modernization in the Rural Philippines* (Guthrie 1970) made a quiet nod to this prominent reality with a frontispiece photograph of a generic fisherman holding up a net even though that was the only allusion to fishers in the entire volume. From the 1950s to 1970s, there was much transdisciplinary engagement, anthropologists published in the journals of other disciplines such as the *Philippine Sociological Review* and the *Philippine Journal of Psychology*. Articles attempted to delineate a "Philippine social structure" and explored themes such as reciprocity (*utang na loob*), "smooth interpersonal relationships" and "patron-client" relations, as well as social change or "modernization." Academics based at UP engaged in vehement exchanges with proponents of "lowland Philippine values" based at the Ateneo de Manila University Institute of Philippine Culture regarding reproduction of negative portrayals of the Filipino fostered from the colonial past (also see Tan 1997; Canuday and Porio this volume). The intense debate over modernization theory and Filipino values as hindrances to Philippine development was also related to the focus on lowland farming or peasant communities.

The first fishing-related ethnography to be published by Filipino authors was F. Landa Jocano and Carmelita Veloro's (1976) "ethnoecological study" of the lakeside community of San Antonio in Bay, Laguna. Jocano belonged to the first generation of Filipinos who pursued PhDs abroad (he received his doctorate at the University of Chicago in 1963). His student Veloro would pursue her degree at the State University of New York in Buffalo (Veloro 1995). From her field research in a Palawan coastal frontier settlement she later published a paper in the first volume of the Visayan Maritime Anthropological Studies (VMAS) publications.

Meanwhile, other reasons for the lack of anthropological publications by Filipinos have more to do with the practice of research. Firstly, funds for conservation-oriented research during the 1980s were mostly controlled by non-anthropologists (e.g. biologists) or by social scientists not primarily inclined to qualitative methodology. Secondly, a frequent condition of research projects is that research assistants (RAs) are not acknowledged as authors. RAs, in fact, draft papers but may or may not receive intellectual credit. In some cases, this is even written into the research contract and RA-produced ethnographic descriptions and analysis may have to accommodate senior co-authors who never undertook fieldwork. Thirdly, in the context of large research projects with multiple publication prospects, only a few papers would be selected for distribution among other participants belonging to the different disciplinary prongs of the research. Later on, in the course of editing for brevity, ethnographic descriptions tend to be cropped from papers. Descriptive ethnographic material simply was not valued in scientific research dissemination systems aimed at brief technical statements of results and findings.

Recovering Maritime Anthropology

Valuing original fieldwork, the earliest generation of formally trained anthropologists in the Philippines had sought to carefully select, compile and preserve student papers. H. Otley Beyer, the man who initiated teaching anthropology in UP in 1914 and established the Department of Anthropology in 1917, compiled a "Philippine ethnography" collection that includes 195 volumes spanning from 1912 to 1930. According to E. Arsenio Manuel, only one complete set of these volumes survived World War II (Manuel 1990). Maritime themes abound in these papers, which span a diversity of topics such as folklore, customary laws, "superstitious beliefs," marriage practices and social customs. The collection was acquired by the Australian National Library shortly after Beyer's death in 1966 (Gosling 1997). The ethnographic series is available in the UP Main Library and at the National Library microfiche and digital collections, albeit with varying degrees of legibility.

Many of these were short papers authored by students for the General Anthropology course. They most likely did fieldwork in their own provinces, and one can sense that they keenly engaged in documenting technologies, customary laws and folklore. We discovered that Federico Mangahas, the grandfather of the first author of this chapter, had written a paper on "St John's Day and Santa Cruz de Mayo in Hagonoy," his hometown, a coastal barangay (the smallest unit of local government in the Philippines) in Bulacan in 1930. Browsing the list turns up the familiar names of many individuals who went on to prominent careers in Philippine administration and politics. These student materials still constitute a valuable well of ethnographic information.

In a similar vein, a few good student papers may be discovered in the library of the Museum of Anthropology at UP. These are materials that were typically reproduced by mimeograph for limited circulation in the 1960s up to the early 1980s. Before the age of photocopying, mimeographing was the standard method of reproducing multiple copies of a typescript to be distributed as a reference for students and researchers. After extended runs, demand for such materials could sometimes provide justification for their eventual publication (Carroll [1963] 1968: iii; Cruz and Valera 1979: 247).

One such paper is "Blast-Fishing in Lucap," originally submitted by Jerome B. Bailen (1978) as an academic requirement for an economic anthropology course. Bailen joined blast-fishing trips in his hometown and conversed with buyers and sellers. His informants were his own relatives and their acquaintances. Guided by Raymond Firth's classic *Malay Fishermen* ([1946] 1975), and by his own professor's unpublished overview of fishing for the University of Chicago's Philippine Studies Program (Mednick 1956, cited in Bailen 1978), he compared blast-fishing with other local fishing techniques. These ranged from fish corrals to hooks and lines, fish traps and nets and were compared in a well thought out matrix of the costs and risks of using each method. Bailen's paper documented three kinds of homemade explosive technology: *suman* (ammonia gelatin from mining operations), *klorato* (potassium chlorate obtained from drugstores or grocery stores mixed with sulfur and almaciga resin, and sugar, alcohol or gasoline), and *bugi* (retrieved by specialist divers from unexploded bombs in sunken World War II vessels in the Lingayen Gulf). It included observations on relative exposure to the blast, fishing knowledge, the more dangerous variations of blast-fishing, interactions and sharing with other fishers at sea, as well as the shares system and marketing by women. It concludes by discussing the local valuation and perceptions of blast-fishing, or how it "makes sense" to the locals (Bailen 1978).

Bailen went on to become a faculty member at the Department of Anthropology. In 1987, his native familiarity with the language made him a logical choice to head the ethnographic research component of the "Legal and Institutional" study for the first CRMP in the Lingayen Gulf led by fellow Pangasinense Elmer Ferrer, of the UP Institute of Social Work and Community Development (ISWCD). The project hired anthropology graduates from the first three pioneering batches of the one-semester UP anthropology field school (including the authors of this chapter) as research assistants for the project. Each research assistant was assigned to be the sole fieldworker to a barangay, in different municipalities located along the Lingayen Gulf. Each research site had a distinct ecological context.

Together with archeologist Israel Cabanilla, Bailen simultaneously directed the UP Anthropology Field School in Sual, Pangasinan. As part of their academic activities, the students were tasked to help administer surveys to communities along the Lingayen Gulf in which the research assistants were based. The assistants thus informally served as teaching assistants and the students as "junior research assistants" who were trained to be enumerators. The survey was administered to a stratified random sample (based on household head occupation) of the populations in the eight barangay locations along the gulf. The survey provided valuable training and experience for the student enumerators. However, its findings were consigned to the dustbin when Bailen dropped out of the research project immediately after the field school. Only the profile of respondents served as input for devising the CRM plan by the National Economic Development Authority.

Indigenous Coastal Resource Management

Two years after the first CRMP, a sequel research program called the Participatory Action Research for Community-Based Coastal Resource Management (PAR-CBCRM) was established, implemented by three institutional partners in UP. Reflecting the shift towards more applied research practices, the study focused on just one municipality along the Lingayen Gulf (Bolinao, Pangasinan) and emphasized the "participatory approach" in its implementation. Two former researchers from the original CRMP joined this team with the understanding that the data collected could be used for their MA theses. Meanwhile, one other "alumnus" of the CRMP obtained research funding from the UP Center for Integrative and Development Studies (a policy think tank) to explore a new field area: traditional fishing as "indigenous coastal resource management" in the northernmost province of Batanes.

As RAs-turned-faculty-members-and-graduate-students the authors of this chapter decided to stay focused on the anthropology of fishing. For thesis fieldwork we turned to documenting long-thriving "traditional" fisheries that could also be described as systems of "customary marine tenure" or "indigenous coastal resource management": the fish corral (*baklad*) concession for siganid (*barangen*), in Bolinao, Pangasinan overseen by the local government (Rodriguez 1997), and the hook-and-line fishers of migratory dorado and flying fish in Batanes (*mataw*) (Mangahas 1994). The *baklad* or fish corral is an old technology, currently listed among the *sagisag kultura* or national "cultural icons" compiled by the National Commission for Culture and the Arts (NCCA n.d.). *Mataw* hook-and-line fishing for dorado or dolphinfish in Batanes entailed the performance of rituals for the collective good fortune of fishers belonging to the same landing site or "port" (*vanua*).

Apart from appreciating their continuing adaptive significance as fishing technologies and forms of social organization, the authors were struck by the complexity of the "shares systems" in these long-standing technologies. Shares systems are routinely documented by ethnographers of fishing technologies. However, what has not been documented is the potential of these systems to evolve with changes to environmental, economic and personal subsistence patterns. Often, these systems express within themselves contradictory moral principles of social hierarchy and egalitarianism. The shares systems for these two deeply traditional methods were found to be surprisingly elaborate and constantly evolving, encompassing a large number of participants and implicated networks. As the second author of this chapter, Rodriguez, observes in her MA thesis:

> The elaborate rules and interactions on sharing schemes represented social distance or proximity to the concessionaire. Such internally defined informal character of fishers' regulations rendered the system flexible to shifts in the environment, social, economic, and political conditions that impact fishing operations until the leasing of this specific fishery lot was finally discontinued in the mid-90s (Rodriguez 1997).

Mangahas described the use of dried catch as a form of local currency, and shares arrangements that amounted to barter exchange for labor, cash, and even land in Mahatao, Batanes (Mangahas 2004).

By the 1990s, there was growing anthropological and environmental interest in biodiversity conservation and "indigenous resource management" in the Philippines. This was spurred by a number of factors such as the promulgation of Agenda 21 of the United Nations Conference on Environment and Development held in Rio de Janeiro in 1992, the Philippines' ratification of the ensuing Convention on Biodiversity, and the availability of funds for research and conservation efforts. The overview publication entitled *Consulting the Spirits, Working with Nature, Sharing with Others: Indigenous Resource Management in the Philippines*, edited by Ponciano Bennagen and Maria Luisa Lucas-Fernan (1996), cited studies across the Philippines, in which only three ethnographic cases for coastal resources were mentioned. These were Eric Casino's (1967) study on the ethno-ecology of the Jama Mapun, National Museum researcher Nicolas Cuadra's article on fishing rituals in a Visayan community (1992) published in a Japanese journal not readily accessible in the Philippines, and Maria Mangahas' unpublished MA thesis at the UP on the *mataw* fishers of Batanes (Mangahas 1994).

Cynthia Zayas and "Archipelagic Studies"

By this time, returning to UP with her doctorate earned at the University of Tsukuba in Japan, Cynthia Neri Zayas initiated the Visayan Maritime Anthropological Studies (VMAS) project. With Japanese government funds, she involved Japanese scholars and Filipino anthropologists in fieldwork in the Visayas (islands in central Philippines). With her Japanese mentor, Zayas eventually co-edited three VMAS volumes (Ushijima and Zayas 1994, 1996, 1998). The authors also published articles in *Yakara: Studies in Ethnology*, a journal of the University of Tsukuba. A fourth VMAS volume has just recently been published (Zayas, Kawada and de la Peña 2014).

The VMAS project brought together an earlier generation of Filipino anthropologists, most of whom had already distinguished themselves in academia, with an equal number of Japanese scholars, who by contrast were PhD candidates at the time. The Filipino anthropologists included Carmelita E. Veloro and Carolyn I. Sobritchea, both faculty members at the UP Asian Center, who had once been students of F. Landa Jocano. Sobritchea had previously done her MA on a fishing community (Israel 1973), and her PhD dissertation is cited as a groundbreaking study of gender. Sobritchea (2002) reflects on how in her career as an anthropologist, she had at first internalized the structural-functionalist tendency to portray normative or "typical culture," avoiding issues of change and inequality. Along the way, especially when she began her PhD work at the State University of New York in Buffalo (which she finished at UP), she struggled against her previous training and eventually became a feminist anthropologist. She went on to head the Center for Women's Studies and later was Dean of the Asian Center, retiring from UP in 2014. When she participated in the VMAS project, she collected women's stories of abuse in relation to ecological deterioration and economic change, and chose to write on women's resistance (Sobritchea 1992, 1993, 1994). Aside from Sobritchea, another prominent personality among the Filipino scholars was Alicia Magos of UP in the Visayas. Magos had already authored a well-regarded ethnographic monograph on the *maaram* healer/medium of Panay (Magos 1992). Interestingly, the majority of maritime ethnographic research by Filipinos has been conducted by women.

Filipino-authored research papers published in the three VMAS volumes touched on notions of fishing success and social relations (Veloro 1995); gender and economic change (Sobritchea 1994); the notion of "dangerous" (*mari-it*) sea-oriented practices, folklore, and worldview (Magos 1994, 1996); fishing gear innovation (Cañete 2000); images of the Bisaya migrant (Abaya 2000); and changes in pottery production and trade on an island (Paz 1996). These scholars are prominent figures in Filipino anthropology, although not specifically for "maritime anthropology." Victor Paz established the Archeological Studies Program at UP upon his return from PhD studies at the University of Cambridge in 2002. Eufracio Abaya had previously been associated with research in medical anthropology and psychological anthropology, and has recently shifted focus to the anthropology of education.

On the other hand, Zayas' name is synonymous with "maritime anthropology" in the Philippines. Her very important contribution lies in illuminating the dynamic phenomenon of continuing fisher mobility and migration. This is expressed in the status relationships between sojourners engaged in *pangayaw* "raiding" or temporarily migrating to other islands in pursuit of income opportunities, and their hosts, the *tumandok* or "original" settlers (Zayas 1994). The prominence of fisher mobility and migration in the Visayas also connects to a previously established theme for impoverished and marginalized sectors that have no secure claim to land, such that coastal areas and fisheries tend to be the "last recourse" for settlement and livelihood opportunities in the Philippines (Illo and Polo 1990; Padilla 1996).

Zayas also participated in developing an interdisciplinary policy research agenda for UP, whose Board of Regents created the ARCOAST network on August 27, 1998, to integrate "archipelagic studies and oceans policy" in the university. Zayas argued that there is an innate "maritime orientation" to be found in Philippine culture and society, specifically evidenced in a few areas: the symbolism of the boat as a vessel for human remains as preserved in certain iconic prehistoric artifacts; the historical rise of "port-polities" as centers of commerce and power; her own ethnography of the *pangayaw-tumandok* network and pattern of seasonal migration; and the linguistic reconstruction of the proto-Filipino word *isda* signifying both "fish" and "viand" (viand in this case encompassing meat). According to Zayas, an "archipelagic studies" approach must both uncover and use the underlying maritime worldview in Filipino culture.

Zayas and Magos established a course on "Coastal Anthropology" at the UP Visayas. Zayas expressed frustration at the lack of a sustainable curricular landscape in which to teach novel maritime anthropology courses and in the difficulty of finding other faculty and students interested in maritime culture. Her vision of a UP system-wide graduate program in "Marine Social Science," modeled on similar existing degree programs in universities in Sulawesi and Japan, was perhaps ahead of its time for the university.

Zayas' book *The Ethnographies of Two Japanese Maritime Communities* based on her dissertation, published by the Third World Studies Center at the UP Diliman (1999), is also significant as a Filipino contribution to the wider field of Asian area studies. Fieldwork beyond the Philippine archipelago by Filipinos is relatively rare, unless related to Filipino diaspora communities. Generally, this is because it is cheaper to do anthropology closer to home than abroad, and because there is locally available research funding and employment opportunities to go to the field.

Filipino anthropology has generally been "Philippine Studies" given numerous extant populations of "exotic" people within the

Philippines requiring attention as anthropological subjects. Such populations often have their own set of social problems connected to cultural difference and development or other intense experiences relating to acculturation and social change in the Philippine context. There is also a certain inward-looking bias towards a "nation-building" agenda for the social sciences in Philippine academia, a nationalism conceived from anti-neocolonial struggles and heightened by the student activism before and during the martial law period. This was a justification for the founding of the anthropological association Ugnayang Pang-AghamTao (UGAT) which Cynthia Zayas also actively participated in founding when she was still an undergraduate.

Trained as a practicing anthropologist during this period, Zayas has made herself equally at home in the Japanese academic tradition. According to Zayas, unlike Philippine anthropology, the Japanese have a long tradition of studying sea-oriented lore and customs. Moreover, many Japanese anthropologists have come to the Philippines for fieldwork. Over the years, a substantial amount of ethnographic descriptions of fishing and coastal communities in the Philippines have actually been produced in Japan, by Japanese scholars and written in Japanese (and are therefore generally inaccessible to Filipino scholars). There are grounds to suspect that there have been more journal articles describing small-scale fishing in the Philippines published in Japan than in the Philippines.

Given that it was only during the 1950s and 1960s that social anthropology in the Philippines turned sharply to lowland groups (also see Davis and Hollnsteiner 1969), it is not surprising that Zayas observed that Philippine anthropology is "mountain anthropology," a comment Zayas made after we encountered each other at a conference. She shared that she herself had followed this tradition but experiences during fieldwork in the 1970s made her turn to the sea. She was divested of her films by the New People's Army in the Cordillera in northern Philippines, after which she decided to discontinue research in the mountains.

VMAS's intellectual offspring in the Philippines however are relatively few in number. Possibly the project had a stronger impact on the career trajectories of young Japanese scholars than on Filipino anthropologists. Nevertheless, this research initiative continues. One junior Filipino VMAS author is Lilian de la Peña, who continues to collaborate with Zayas (Zayas and de la Peña 2012) and with whom she has co-edited the fourth VMAS volume. From our own cohorts,

Ma. Paz Palis is an alumni of the first CRMP who completed her graduate studies at the Ateneo de Manila University. This was after working as an assistant for Zayas and being mentored by Eufracio Abaya, who had also published in VMAS. Palis wrote her thesis on the nuances of identity and social relations between *pangayaw* (seasonal migrants) and *tumandok* (natives or settlers) (Palis 2001).

Zayas, meanwhile, continues to conduct research in the Philippines and Japan, most recently inquiring into material culture of sea-oriented peoples. She has been inquiring into structural and kinship connections in "water villages" and boat caravans, particularly among the Bajau, and into the extant stone tidal weirs in Japan and the Philippines, a research significant in bridging ethnography, archeology and heritage conservation (Zayas 2004, 2009).

Expansion Beyond the Visayas

With very few exceptions, Visayan fishers have generally represented "maritime anthropology" in the Philippines. Practically all published ethnographies of fishing in the Philippines are on Visayan/Bisaya peoples, including those who migrated and settled in proximate regions. In recent times, however, research by Filipino graduate students of anthropology on maritime themes has expanded beyond Visayas and Luzon to explore distinct ethnic dynamics elsewhere. These include studies among fishers in Mindanao and Palawan looking into the politico-ecological dynamics of fisher knowledge systems, as well as the processes and relationships underlying changing seascapes.

Research among the Tagbanua of Coron, Palawan, has provided insight into an indigenous sea-oriented people with extensive knowledge and conservation practices (Guieb 1999, 2000, 2010; Sampang 2005, 2007, 2010). Eulalio Guieb III wrote his thesis on Tangdol Tagbanua oral histories that tell of the renaming and altering of maps along with the histories of many places due to misunderstandings caused by language barriers between local people and American colonizers. Other obstacles and challenges mentioned in the texts refer to greedy businessmen, Tausug slave-raiders, and migrant fish workers from Cavite who "steal" local men's wives. Arlene Sampang who did fieldwork among the Calamian Tagbanua toward a master's degree in environmental science, documented ethno-icthylogical knowledge, technologies of fishing, and conservation practices. The Calamian

Tagbanua became the first Philippine indigenous group to successfully claim land and marine waters as part of their "ancestral domain" under the Indigenous Peoples Rights Act (IPRA) of 1997. However, enforcement of this entitlement has led to run-ins with politically dominant in-migrating Visayan fishers, reiterating the pattern discussed earlier (Mangahas 2010).

Wilfredo Torres, meanwhile, has produced historical and socially nuanced ethnographies of the Bajau in Sulu. He has examined changes in sea tenure brought about by the introduction of seaweed farming—by which the dominant group Tausug appropriated the customary use rights of the sea-going Bajau—while also examining gender relations (Torres 2004).

Maria Mangahas went on to conduct fieldwork in Samal Island, Davao (Mangahas 2000). Her findings reiterate the migration pattern involving Visayan and also Muslim fishers from other parts of Mindanao, stimulating innovation in the local fishing technology and leading to diminishing catches and rapid turnover in methods used. The fishers frame this in terms of the fish "getting smarter" such that fisher knowledge has to adapt to fish learning (Mangahas 2003, 2008).

Rosa Castillo, inspired by her research experience at the UP Anthropology Field School (Castillo and Ragragio 2001), explored fisher knowledge and the distinct perceptions of compressor divers in a community on an outer reef of Danajon Bank in Bohol for her MA thesis at the UP Diliman (Castillo 2009). These fishers' knowledge and bodily "enskillment" were derived from diving and engaging with the depths of the sea, rather than fishing from the surface, using the risky compressor technology. She later returned to her informants to follow up on their experiences of climate change, discovering that due to poverty, they had "no other choice" but to migrate and then come back (Castillo 2011).

Eulalio Guieb III went on to do fieldwork in Bohol for his PhD dissertation (2008). He recently published on "Competing Narratives of Place in Malampaya Sound," (2014) tracing historical conflicts between differently situated groups claiming rights over space and resources within the Malampaya Sound, particularly as seen in filed legal cases.

Nelson Turgo is also interested in "place" and on how there may be multiple "spaces" within, such as in fish-trading houses in a coastal town located at the fringes of Quezon, a place associated with "structural economic marginality" (Turgo 2012a). Fishmongers visited museums, watched plays, and attended seminars to compensate for their lack of formal education. They also joined socio-civic groups. Still, contestation between their own people and those from the town center are inevitable when unspoken desires are unmet. Coming from a place associated with deprivation, obstacles to attaining middle-class status persist (Turgo n.d.).

These insights on class and occupation add nuance to what we know of actors and agency in markets, apart from transactions (Davis 1973; Blanc-Szanton 1972; Kawada 1994). In his unpublished paper, Guieb further explores the geography of rights across fisheries trade networks, he writes that the fishing community

> is, by and large, a site of exchange of resources (natural resources and people). It is also a circulation site of cash and rights. The village is inextricably linked with inter-village, intra-regional and global networks of trade and discourses on marine resource practices. This space of flows also encompasses a geography of rights that provides the borders and frames within the resource access, use, management and alienation rights are distributed, awarded, "trafficked" or denied (Guieb III n.d.).

Both Guieb and Turgo are well known in the field of Filipino creative writing as prize-winning writers and mass media practitioners. Turgo describes his research as doing "homework" in his hometown as his father was a fisherman. He has published several articles on "fieldwork at home," reflecting on the benefits along with the limits of such positionality (Turgo 2012b, 2012c).

Most of the persons discussed above have connections to UP. They pursued their PhDs abroad and are currently publishing academics. Still, we expect there is relevant knowledge production especially where seaside universities offer anthropology and social science programs, or where there may be CRM or conservation projects such materials would be found in the records of government agencies and non-governmental organizations. It is clear that the scope of our search should be much wider. A colleague from the University of San Carlos enjoins us to look into the unpublished papers and monographs written by their students and faculty (Zona Amper, personal communication, 2015). We have not explored knowledge production by graduate students of Silliman, a university that has strong programs in marine biology and anthropology and at least one prominent maritime anthropologist in Enrique Oracion (2005). Neither have we ventured into the University of the Philippines

Visayas (also see Cichon n.d.), which offers degrees in fisheries and marine affairs and where Zayas was based during the VMAS project in the 1990s, much less colleges and universities in other coastal areas where research may tend to the production of ethnographic knowledge.

Meanwhile, there are anthropological materials produced by students and professors identifying with other disciplines such as archeology (Bolunia 2013), history (Lorenzo-Abrera 2002; Ango 2014), geography (Saguin 2008), sociology (Lamug 2005), folklore (Rola 1980), linguistics, and psychology, many of which are also unpublished. There are also other maritime themes that we have not looked into in this paper such as seafaring and boatbuilding, which should also be drawn into the domain of Filipino maritime anthropology.

Developments within Philippine maritime anthropology continue to expand and proceed apace. A new professional master's program in Tropical Marine Ecosystem Management has run three cycles at UP since 2015; initially for practitioners with specialization in Marine Protected Areas, it incorporates courses with anthropological perspectives (Mangahas 2017; also see PM TMEM 2014, UP 2014). In October 2015, UGAT held its 37th annual conference on the theme "Dagat ug Kinabuhi: Maritime Cultures, Spaces, and Networks" with Cynthia Neri Zayas as convenor, at Silliman University, Dumaguete City. The conference, jointly organized by UGAT and the Philippine Geographical Society, has surfaced more maritime-oriented research (also see UGAT/PGS Conference 2017 Book of Abstracts). Some of the papers mentioned in this chapter are no longer in the "gray" zone, having since been published in UGAT's official journal *Aghamtao* (Roldan 2016; Mangahas 2016; Turgo 2017).

Conclusion

Delayed attention to ways of living with the sea in Philippine ethnographies can perhaps be attributed to coastal communities occupying an "unexotic" space associated with assimilated lowlanders. Nevertheless, formative experiences like the anthropology field school thrust some students in the direction of coastal resource management and maritime anthropology by way of serendipitous encounters with funding opportunities or professional appointments.

Some of the structural reasons for why anthropological observations and ethnographic material remained in a gray zone have to do with change in the relative prominence of anthropology vis-à-vis other disciplines, compartmentalization between the sciences, and the priorities within anthropology subject matter and advocacy. Time-consuming and hierarchical practices and intermittent access to project funding often lead to a shift of attention from one sphere of knowledge to interest in others on the part of researchers. Unfortunately, the output from fieldwork for academic requirements and applied research projects like the CRMP and PAR-CBCRM remain as underutilized ethnographic material that contributed little to published literature and theorizing on maritime anthropology. Undoubtedly, there are many CRM initiatives nationwide that produce hidden ethnographic literature and a significant amount of "gray" material that deserves closer inspection. Until Philippine universities embark on digitization of such materials for open online reference, theses and dissertations will tend to remain unpublished and out of sight.

"Archipelagically oriented" ethnographic research has received belated appreciation in the Philippines because, as Zayas notes, our American and European anthropology orientation is largely terrestrial-oriented as compared to other academic spaces such as Japan, which by contrast has a longstanding tradition of folklore research on the sea. Zayas is one of few Filipinos who received a graduate education in an Asian context. It is interesting that a link with another Asian country was the impetus to initiate academic and publication-oriented "maritime anthropological studies," though it seems that interest in this topic may have been greater from the Japanese, at least initially. The research in marine contexts for our (the authors') fieldwork on the other hand is consistent with the government and international emphasis on biodiversity conservation since the 1990s.

The maritime anthropological knowledge that we have surfaced reveals conscious intention to indigenize ideas, privilege local knowledge, and craft and claim one's own grounded practice. In this, our chapter echoes the insights of Canuday and Porio (this volume) that there has been a recurrent theme of counter-hegemonic discourse simultaneously stimulated by outside scholarship, which dates back to the time of Isabelo de los Reyes and José Rizal. Our experiences in the 1980s of being honed to do fieldwork in coastal communities, asked to read studies by Filipinos, trained to be sensitive and respectful of the knowledge gained from people we encounter, and even compelled to express thoughts using Filipino, are consistent with the deliberate efforts by local scholars to assert a separate "Filipino-ness" and to actively engage and negotiate with the representations of external discourses that Canuday and Porio also discuss. However we are also aware that our particular experiences may not be identical to those of the current generation of Filipino students of anthropology.

Engagements in addressing marine resource conservation and livelihood sustainability as well as in documenting practices from diminishing heritage traditions has been instrumental in the gradual "maturation" of maritime scholarship. Current maritime issues such as climate change and sustainability combined with geopolitical tensions in the West Philippine Sea are bound to add impetus to developing interest on the anthropology of the sea.

As our survey of maritime anthropology in the Philippines suggests, despite its marginalization, this literature has important theoretical and empirical contributions to scholarship. Student papers archived from the second decade of the twentieth century, for example, provide an important record of indigenous maritime practices. Later work in this field of studies contributed to theorizing indigenous coastal resource management and addressing issues such as cultures of illegal fishing or resource abuse; the dynamics of fisher mobility; and even what is now termed "multi-species ethnography" (e.g. incorporating interactions and relationships between humans and fish). From the 1990s onward, there have been attempts at promoting systematic thinking about maritime or archipelagic anthropology in the face of anthropology's otherwise "inland bias" in the Philippines.

By tracing ethnographic material produced by local authors, along with our own personal experiences, we hope to have heeded the call to fill the yawning gap in maritime anthropology observed by Ponciano Bennagen decades ago. We also hope to have responded to the renewed recognition of the merits of ethnography in addressing marine "resource management" issues. We take this as a much needed step toward the indigenization of anthropology in the Philippines, an old but still unrealized call (Bennagen 1980). Anthropology students in the Philippines are not usually guided by overview and reassessment of their Filipino intellectual heritage, and sometimes have no access to the original material such as in the area of maritime anthropology.

It is our hope to make ethnographies from the late 1980s to the present accessible for wider public appreciation. In fact, we found it difficult to end this paper as we have continued to unearth more material in the process of writing, and knowing that there are still numerous places to scour for seemingly voluminous gray literature. This, then, is not the end, but merely the beginning of an endeavor to bring to light historical and contemporary Philippine maritime anthropology.

Notes

1. "Gray literature" is defined as: "produced on all levels of government, academics, business and industry in print and electronic formats, but which is not controlled by commercial publishers." For this reason it is relatively difficult to access. [Grey Literature Report, *The New York Academy of Medicine*; http://www.greylit.org/about].
2. Several histories and overviews of "Philippine Anthropology" have already been written over the years. For the field of social and cultural anthropology in particular, the reader is directed to Lynch and Hollnsteiner 1961; Davis and Hollnsteiner 1969; Zamora and Arcellana 1971; Zamora 1976; Panopio and Bennagen 1985; Abaya, Fernan and Noval-Morales 1999; Tan 2010; Tatel (2010, 2014). The University of the Philippines, University of San Carlos, and Silliman University are the three universities that have long-standing academic programs (of at least 50 years) in anthropology as a "four-field" discipline.

References

Abaya, Eufracio (2000) "Affinity and Estrangement: Bisaya Republic Along Balayan Bay." In *Bisayan Knowledge, Movement, and Identity*, Iwao Ushijima and Cynthia Neri Zayas, (eds.), pp. 319–38. Quezon City: Third World Studies Center.

Abaya, Eufracio, Luisa Lucas-Fernan, and Daisy Noval-Morales (1999) "Shifting Terms of Engagement: A Review of the History of Anthropology in the Philippines." In *The Philippine Social Science in the Life of the Nation*, Virginia Miralao, (ed.), pp. 1–10. Quezon City: Philippine Social Science Research Council.

Acheson, James M. (1981) "Anthropology of Fishing," *Annual Reviews in Anthropology* 10: pp. 275–316.

Ango, Junald Dawa (2014) *Kaagi Sang Kubkob: History of an Indigenous Fishing Technology in Bantayan, c. 1900 to 2011*. Unpublished Master's thesis, University of the Philippines.

Bailen, Jerome B. (1978) "Blast-Fishing in Lucap." Unpublished term paper, University of the Philippines Diliman.

Bennagen, Ponciano (1980) "The Asianization of Anthropology," *Asian Studies*, 18: pp. 1–26.

Bennagen, Ponciano and Maria Luisa Lucas-Fernan, (eds.) (1996) *Consulting the Spirits, Working with Nature, Sharing with Others: Indigenous Resource Management in the Philippines.* Quezon City: Sentro para sa Ganap ng Pamayanan.

Blanc-Szanton, Maria Cristina (1972) *A Right to Survive: Subsistence Marketing in a Lowland Philippine Town.* Manila: Institute of Philippine Culture.

Bolunia, Mary Jane Louise (2013) *Linking Butuan to the Southeast Asian Emporium of the 10th–13th Century C.E.* PhD dissertation, University of the Philippines Diliman.

Butcher, John G. (2004) *The Closing of the Frontier: A History of the Marine Fisheries of Southeast Asia c. 1850–2000.* Singapore: Institute of Southeast Asian Studies

Cañete, Aloysius M. (2000) "Innovations in Baling Sa Higad and Sapyaw Fisheries in Bantayan." In *Bisayan Knowledge, Movement, and Identity,* Iwao Ushijima and Cynthia Neri Zayas, (eds.), pp. 179–201. Quezon City: Third World Studies Center, University of the Philippines Diliman.

Carroll, John Joseph (1963) *Provisional Paper on Changing Patterns of Social Structure in the Philippines, 1896–1963.* Quezon City: Ateneo De Manila University Press.

——— (1968) *Changing Patterns of Social Structure in the Philippines, 1896–1963.* Quezon City: Ateneo De Manila University Press.

Casino, Eric S. (1967) "Jama Mapun Ethnoecology: Economic and Symbolic (of Grains, Winds and Stars)," *Asian Studies* 5(1): pp. 1–32.

Castillo, Rosa Cordillera (2009) *Way Laing Panginabuhi (There Is No Other Livelihood). Negotiating Danger and Survival in the Life World of a Community of Compressor Fishers.* Unpublished Master's thesis, University of the Philippines.

——— (2011) "When Fishing Is No Longer Viable: Environmental Change, Unfair Market Relations, and Livelihood in a Small Fishing Community in the Philippines." Working Paper 105. Bad Salzuflen, Germany: Center on Migration, Citizenship and Development.

Castillo, Rosa Cordillera and Andrea Ragragio (2001) "Parabuso: Isang Silip sa Mapanganib na Trabaho ng Kompresor Diving sa Behia" ["Parabuso: A Peek at the Risky Occupation of Compresor-diving in Behia"]. Unpublished term paper, Department of Anthropology Field School, University of the Philippines Diliman.

Cichon, Melchor (n.d.) "Fisheries Bibliography". http://www.fisheriesbibliography.blogspot.com/; accessed September 2015.

Cruz, Teresa, and Rafelita S. Valera (1979) "A Bibliography of Frank Lynch, S.J.," *Philippine Studies* 27: pp. 247–63.

Cuadra, Nicolas C. (1992) "Fishing Ritual in a Visayan Community," *Yakara* 17(5): pp. 1–23.

Davis, William G. (1973) *Social Relations in a Philippine Market: Self-Interest and Subjectivity*. Berkeley: University of California Press.

Davis, William G. and Mary R. Hollnsteiner (1969) "Some Recent Trends in Philippine Social Anthropology," *Anthropologica* 11(1): pp. 59–84.

Eder, James F. (2009) *Migrants to the Coasts: Livelihood, Resource Management and Global Change in the Philippines*. Belmont, CA: Wadsworth.

Enriquez, Virgilio G. and Ponciano L. Bennagen (1978) *Ang Ulat ng Pagsisiyasat sa Agham Panlipunan* [*The Report of Research in the Social Sciences*]. Quezon City: Pambansang Samahan sa Sikolohiyang Pilipino.

Fabinyi, Michael, Magne Knudsen, and Shio Segi (2010) "Social Complexity, Ethnography and Coastal Resource Management in the Philippines," *Coastal Management* 38(6): pp. 617–32.

Fabinyi, Michael (2010) "The Intensification of Fishing and the Rise of Tourism: Competing Coastal Livelihoods in the Calamianes Islands, Philippines," *Human Ecology* 38: pp. 415–27.

Firth, Raymond William (1975) *Malay Fishermen: Their Peasant Economy*. New York: Norton.

Galvez, Robert E. (1989) "Blast Fishing and Government Response in Lingayen Gulf." In *Coastal Zone '89*, Orville Magoon, Hugh Converse, Dallas Miner, L. Thomas Tobin, Jr, and Delores Clark, (eds.), pp. 2286–99. New York: American Society of Civil Engineers.

Galvez, R.E., T.G. Hingco, C. Bautista, and M.T. Tungpalan (1989) "Sociocultural Dynamics of Blast Fishing and Sodium Cyanide Fishing in Two Fishing Villages in the Lingayen Gulf Area." In *Towards Sustainable Development of the Coastal Resources of Lingayen Gulf, Philippines*, G.T. Silvestre, E. Miclat, and C. Thia-Eng, (eds.). Makati: International Center for Living Aquatic Resources Management.

Gosling, Andrew (1997) "An American in Manila: Otley Beyer and His Collection at the National Library of Australia," *National Library of Australia News* 7(10): pp. 6–8.

Guieb, Eulalio R. III. (n.d.) "Not by Fish Alone: Local Resource Utilization, Global Trade and the Rationality of Livelihood Options by Jandayan Norte Villagers in Bohol." Unpublished paper, McGill University, Canada.

——— (1999) "Reasserting Indigenous Spaces in a Tagbanua Text," *Lundayan Journal* Special Issue: pp. 23–33.

——— (2000) *Anin, Laud, Beltay, Pandaw, Dagoy: Lunan, Kaakuhan at Kapangyarihan Sa Texto Ng Mga Komunidad Kostal Sa Hilagang Palawan* [*Anin, Laud, Beltay, Pandaw, Dagoy: Place, Self and Power in the Texts of Coastal Communities in Northern Palawan.*] Unpublished Master's thesis, University of the Philippines.

——— (2008) *Community, Marine Rights, and Sea Tenure: A Political Ecology of Marine Conservation in Two Bohol Villages in Central Philippines*. Unpublished PhD dissertation, McGill University, Canada.

——— (2010) "Tablay and Banua of Young Tagbanua Calamianen in Northern Palawan: Narrating the Tablay of the Banua, Mapping the Banua of the Tablay," *Plaridel* 7(2): pp. 147–76.

——— (2014) "Competing Narratives of Place in Malampaya Sound." In *Palawan and Its Global Connections*, James Eder and Oscar Evangelista, (eds.), pp. 306–45. Manila: Ateneo de Manila University Press.

Hart, Donn Vorhis (1956) *Securing Aquatic Products in Siaton Municipality, Negros Oriental Province, Philippines*. Manila: Bureau of Print.

Hingco, Therese Gladys and Rebecca Rivera (1991) "Aquarium Fish Industry in the Philippines: Toward Development or Destruction?" In *Towards an Integrated Management of Tropical Coastal Resources*, L.M. Chou, T.E. Chua, H.W. Khoo, P.E. Lim, J.N. Paw, G.T. Silvestre, M.J. Valencia, A.T. White, and P.K. Wong, (eds.), pp. 249–53. Singapore: National University of Singapore; National Science and Technology Board, Singapore; International Center for Living Aquatic Resources Management.

Illo, Jeanne Frances I. and Jaime B. Polo (1990) *Fishers, Traders, Farmers, Wives: The Life Stories of Ten Women in a Fishing Village*. Quezon City: Institute of Philippine Culture, Ateneo de Manila University.

Israel, Carolyn Crispino (1973) *A Life-Cycle Study of a Tagalog Fishing Community*. Unpublished Master's thesis, University of the Philippines.

Jocano, Felipe Landa and Carmelita E. Veloro (1976) *San Antonio: A Case Study of Adaptation and Folk Life in a Fishing Community*. Quezon City: UP-NSDB Integrated Research Program.

Kawada, Makito (1994) "Public Market in Bantayan: Social Tie in Local Economic Activities." In *Fishers of the Visayas*, Iwao Ushijima and Cynthia Neri Zayas, (eds.). Quezon City: CSSP Publications, University of the Philippines.

Lamug, Corazon B. (2005) "The Accomplishment of Community among Small-Scale Fishers in Mercedes, Camarines Norte," *Philippine Sociological Review* 53: pp. 75–87.

Lorenzo-Abrera, Ma. Bernadette G. (2002) *Bangka: Isang Paglalayag Tungo sa Pagunawa ng Kasaysayan at Kalinangan*. [*Bangka: A Voyage Toward Understanding History and Culture*]. Unpublished PhD thesis, University of the Philippines Diliman.

Lynch, Frank and Mary Hollnsteiner (1961) "Sixty Years of Philippine Ethnology: A First Glance at the Years 1901–1961," *Science Review* 2: pp. 1–5.

Magos, Alicia P. (1992) *The Enduring Ma-Aram Tradition: An Ethnography of a Kinaraya Village in Antique*. Quezon City: New Day.

——— (1994) "The Concept of Mari-It in Panaynon Maritime Worldview." In *Fishers of the Visayas: Visayas Maritime Anthropological Studies 1: 1991–1993*, Iwao Ushijima and Cynthia Neri Zayas, (eds.), pp. 305–55. Quezon City: University of the Philippines Press.

Mangahas, Maria (1994) *Mataw, Amung Nu Rayon, Anitu/Man, the "Fish of Summer", and the Spirits: An Ethnography of Mataw Fishing in Batanes.* Unpublished Master's thesis, University of the Philippines.

____ (2000) *Managing Luck and Negotiating Change: Ethnographies of Fishing and Sharing in the Philippines.* Unpublished PhD dissertation, University of Cambridge, United Kingdom.

____ (2003) "Two Fishers' Knowledge Systems and Frontier Strategies in the Philippines." In *Putting Fishers' Knowledge to Work*, N. Haggan, C. Brignall, and L. Wood, (eds.), pp. 340–46. Vancouver: University of British Columbia.

____ (2008) "Making the Vanua: Collective Fishing Technology in Batanes and an Austronesian Archetype of Society," *Philippine Studies* 56(4): pp. 379–412.

____ (2010) "Seasonal Ritual and the Regulation of Fishing in Batanes Province, Philippines." In *Managing Coastal and Inland Waters Pre-Existing Aquatic Management Systems in Southeast Asia*, Kenneth Ruddle and Arif Satria, (eds.), pp. 77–98. New York: Springer.

____ (2014) "DVD Piracy as Alternative Media: The Scandal of Piracy, and the Piracy of 'Scandal' in the Philippines, 2005–2009," *Kasarinlan (Philippine Journal of Third World Studies)* 29(1): pp. 109–39.

____ (2016) "'Gear conflicts' and changing seascapes in Batanes," *AghamTao*, 25: pp. 174–200.

____ (2017) "On 'Intercultural Understanding', 'Communities of Practice', and the Value of 'Anecdote': Issues and Narratives in and Around Environmental Work in Coastal Contexts," Unpublished paper presented at the "H. Otley Beyer Museum Talks," H. Otley Beyer Museum, February 21, 2017.

Manuel, E. Arsenio (1990) "The Philippine Ethnographic Series." In *Guide to H. Otley Beyer Philippine Ethnographic Collection on Microfiche*, Maria Luisa C. Moral, (ed.), pp. iv–viii. Manila: National Library.

McManus, Liana T. and Chua Thia-Eng (1990) *The Coastal Environmental Profile of Lingayen Gulf, Philippines.* Manila: International Center for Living Aquatic Resources Management.

Mednick, Melvin (1956) "Fishing." In *The Philippines (Subcontractors' Monograph HRAF-16 Chicago-5)*, Fred Eggan, (ed.), New Haven: The Human Relations Area File.

____ (1965) *Encampment of the Lake: The Social Organization of a Moslem-Philippine (Moro) People.* Unpublished PhD dissertation, University of Chicago, United States.

National Commission for Culture and the Arts (n.d.) "Baklad." http://ncca.gov.ph/philippine-cultural-education-program-pcep/sagisag-kultura/9127-2/; accessed October 20, 2018.

Nimmo, H. Arlo (1972) *The Sea People of Sulu: A Study of Social Change in the Philippines*. San Francisco: Chandler Publishing Company.

——— (1994) *The Songs of Salanda and Other Stories of Sulu*. Quezon City: Ateneo de Manila University Press.

——— (2001) *Magosaha: An Ethnography of the Tawi-Tawi Sama Dilaut*. Quezon City: Ateneo de Manila University Press.

Oracion, Enrique G. (2005) *Beyond Physical Space, the Human and Cultural Complexities in Marine Protected Area Management*. Dumaguete City: Silliman University.

Padilla, Jose E. (1996) "Water Quality and Fisheries Issues Accompanying Population Growth in the Philippines," *Journal of Philippine Development* 23(2): pp. 315–37.

Palis, Maria Paz E. (2001) *Tumandok/Pangayaw: Identity, Power and Resource Utilization in a Visayan Island*. Unpublished Master's thesis, Ateneo de Manila University.

Panopio, Isabel, and Ponciano Bennagen (1985) "The Status of Sociology and Anthropology in the Philippines." In *Sociology and Social Anthropology in Asia and the Pacific*. New Delhi: Wiley Eastern.

PM TMEM (2014) "Professional Masters in Tropical Marine Ecosystem Management [Initial Area of Specialization: Marine Protected Areas]." University of the Philippines. Brochure, http://intranet.upv.edu.ph/docs/PM_TMEM_Announcements.pdf; accessed September, 2015.

Rodriguez, Suzanna F. (1991) "Small-Scale Fishermen's Participation in the Salt Industry: An Alternative Source of Income?" In *Towards an Integrated Management of Tropical Coastal Resources*, L.M. Chou, T.E. Chua, H.W. Khoo, P.E. Lim, J.N. Paw, G.T. Silvestre, M.J. Valencia, A.T. White, and P.K. Wong, (eds.), pp. 245–47. Singapore: National University of Singapore; National Science and Technology Board, Singapore; International Center for Living Aquatic Resources Management.

——— (1997) *The Barangen Fishing Concession in Bolinao: An Ethnographic Study of a Customary Marine Tenure System*. Unpublished Master's thesis, University of the Philippines.

——— (2016) "Resource Sharing Amid Limited Access: The Case of the Barangen Concession in Bolinao, Pangasinan," *AghamTao* 25: pp. 135–73.

Rola, Dionisia A. (1980) *Fishlore of Western Visayas*. Iloilo City: University of the Philippines Visayas.

Saguin, Kristian Karlo (2008) *Fisherfolk Livelihoods and the Transformations of Philippine Coasts: Tourism Development, Industrial Growth and Municipal Fishing in Mabini, Batangas*. Unpublished Master's thesis, University of the Philippines.

Sampang, Arlene G. (2005) *Ethnoicthyology and Conservation Practices of the Calamian Tagbanwa in Coron Island, Palawan, Philippines*. Unpublished Master's thesis, University of the Philippines.

_____ (2007) *The Calamian Tagbanwa Ancestral Domain (Coron Island, Palawan, Philippines): Evaluation of Traditional Fishing Practices towards Biodiversity Conservation and Sustainability*. The World Fish Center. https://www.academia.edu/7247170/The_Calamian_Tagbanwa_Ancestral_Domain_Coron_Island_Palawan_Philippines_Evaluation_of_traditional_fishing_practices_towards_biodiversity_conservation_and_sustainability; accessed October 20, 2018.

_____ (2010) "Towards a Sustainable Management and Enchanted Protection of Sacred Marine Areas at Palawan's Coron Island Ancestral Domain." In *Sacred Natural Sites: Conserving Nature and Culture*, Bas Verschuuren, Robert Wild, Jeffrey McNeely, and Gonzalo Oviedo, (eds.), pp. 254–62. London: Earthscan.

Sobritchea, Carolyn I. (1992) "Women's Production and Domestic Roles in a Sea Fishing Community in Central Visayas, Philippines," *Yakara: Studies in Ethnology* 17: pp. 89–115.

_____ (1993) "An Anthropological Study of Economic Change, Gender and Power in a Visayan Fishing Community," *Review of Women's Studies* 3(2): pp. 27–41.

_____ (1994) "Gender Roles and Economic Change in a Fishing Community." In *Fishers of the Visayas*, Iwao Ushijima and Cynthia Zayas, (eds.). Quezon City: College of Social Science and Philosophy, University of the Philippines.

_____ (2002) "Revisiting Fieldwork: On Becoming a Feminist Ethnographer." In *Selected Readings on Health and Feminist Research: A Sourcebook*, Sylvia Guerrero, (ed.) Quezon City: UP Center for Women's Studies. http://anthro.upd.edu.ph/centennial/contributions-in-phil-anthropology/195-revisiting-fieldwork-on-becoming-a-feminist-ethnographer?fbclid=IwAR1LO3Fe72GADH8A-b3M-ngLGPudsLiJrMSUdtjxaqmUgnE335UMXi-6M4U.

Spoehr, A. (1980) *Protein from the Sea: Technological Change in Philippine Capture Fisheries*. Pittsburgh: University of Pittsburgh.

Szanton, David (1971) *Estancia in Transition: Economic Growth in a Rural Philippine Community*. Quezon City: Institute of Philippine Culture, Ateneo de Manila.

Tan, Allen (1997) "Values Research in the Philippines," *Philippine Studies* 45(4): pp. 560–69.

Tan, Michael L. (2010) "Philippine Anthropology in a Post-Anthropology Age." In *Philippine Social Science Discourses*, Jorge V. Tigno, (ed.), pp. 7–24. Quezon City: University of Philippines Diliman.

Tatel, Carlos P., Jr. (2010) "Anthropology at the University of the Philippines: Examining Institutional History and Academic Dependency in a South-East Asian University." In *Academic Dependency in the Social Sciences: Structural Reality and Intellectual Challenges*, Kathinka Sinha-Kerkhoff and Syed Farid Alatas, (eds.), pp. 213–66. New Delhi: Manohar.

——— (2014) "Anthropology and Sociology at UP: Lessons from an Academic Union, 1914–1951," *Philippine Sociological Review* 62: pp. 109–37.

Torres, Wilfredo Magno III. (2004) "Kalluman Ma Tahik: Household Strategies, Gender, and Sea Tenure in a Sama Dilaut (Bajau) Community in Kabuukan Island, Sulu." *AghamTao* 10: pp. 82–98.

Tungpalan, M.T.V., Maria Mangahas, and Maria Paz Palis (1991) "Women in Fishing Villages: Roles and Potentials for Coastal Resources Management." In *Towards an Integrated Management of Tropical Coastal Resources*, L.M. Chou, T.E. Chua, H.W. Khoo, P.E. Lim, J.N. Paw, G.T. Silvestre, M.J. Valencia, A.T. White, and P.K. Wong, (eds.), pp. 237–43. Singapore: National University of Singapore; National Science and Technology Board, Singapore; International Center for Living Aquatic Resources Management.

Turgo, Nelson Nava (2017) "'Amoy Isda': The Middle Class Life of Fishmongers," *AghamTao* 25(2): pp. 201–29.

——— (2012a) "'Bugabug Ang Dagat' ['Rough Seas']: Experiencing Foucault's Heterotopia in Fish Trading Houses," *Social Science Diliman* 8(1): pp. 31–62.

——— (2012b) "'I Know Him So Well': Contracting/tual 'Insiderness', and Maintaining Access and Rapport in a Philippine Fishing Community," *Sociological Research Online*, 31 August. http://www.socresonline.org.uk/17/3/18.html; accessed September 2016.

——— (2012c) "A 'Balikbayan' in the Field: Scaling and (Re)producing Insider's Identity in a Philippine Fishing Community," *Qualitative Research* 12: pp. 66–85.

University of the Philippines (2014) "Professional Masters in Tropical Marine Ecosystems Management with Area of Specialization in Marine Protected Areas". Briefer, http://ifpds.weebly.com/uploads/8/1/7/4/8174629/briefer_pm_tmem_14may.pdf; accessed September 2016.

Ushijima, Iwao and Cynthia Neri Zayas (1994) *Fishers of the Visayas.* Quezon City: College of Social Science and Philosophy, University of the Philippines.

Veloro, Carmelita E. (1995) *Pioneering, Livelihood, and Everyday Success in Palawan.* Unpublished PhD dissertation, State University of New York, United States.

——— (1996) "Frontier Colonization and Legitimation in a Palawan Coastal Settlement." In *Binisaya Nga Kinabuhi* [*Visayan Life*], Iwao Ushijima and Cynthia Zayas, (eds.), pp. 11–41. Quezon City: CSSP Publications.

Zamora, Mario D. (1976) "Cultural Anthropology in the Philippines, 1900–1983: Perspectives, Problems, and Prospects." In *Changing Identities in Modern Southeast Asia*, David J. Banks, (ed.), pp. 311–39. The Hague: Mouton.

Zamora, Mario D. and Jose Y. Arcellana, (eds.) (1971) *A Bibliography of Philippine Anthropology.* Baguio City: University of the Philippines Press.

Zayas, Cynthia Neri (1994) "Pangayaw and Tumandok in the Maritime World of the Visayan Islanders." In *Fishers of the Visayas*, Iwao Ushijima and Cynthia Neri Zayas, (eds.) Quezon City: CSSP Publications and University of the Philippines Press.

——— (1998) "Tungo Sa Maritimong Oryentasyon Sa Pag-Aaral Ng Lipunan at Kulturang Pilipino." In *Archipelagic Studies: Charting New Waters*, Jay L. Batongbacal, (ed.). Quezon City: University of the Philippines.

——— (1999) *The Ethnographies of Two Japanese Maritime Communities*. Quezon City: Third World Studies Center.

——— (2004) "Atob and Bato: Two Sides of Philippine Lithic Heritage," *Pilipinas*, 43: pp. 55–70.

——— (2009) "'Bato Nga Tinumpok': Stone Tidal Weirs as Representations of 'Kabilin', Knowledge Heritage and Cultural Landscapes," *AghamTao* 18: pp. 124–33.

Zayas, Cynthia Neri and Lilian de la Peña (2012) "The Promise of the Southwest Wind: Visayan Fish/Migrant Wives in the Shifting Fishery of Central Philippines," *SIGNS: Feminist Journal on Culture and Society* 37(3): pp. 573–80.

Zayas, Cynthia Neri, Makito Kawada, and Lilian de la Peña, (eds.) (2014) *Visayas and Beyond: Remainder of Continuing Studies on Subsistence and Belief in the Islands*. Quezon City: UPCIS Publications.

CHAPTER 5

DOMESTICATING SOCIAL ANTHROPOLOGY IN WEST MALAYSIA

Yeoh Seng-Guan

Although anthropology has been taught in universities in Malaysia for around four decades, ethnographic studies of Malaysia (formerly British Malaya) have been conducted for much longer, some authored more than a century ago. Reading these "classics" from the standpoint of the present is valuable for tracing not only the kinds of social transformations that have taken place but also the durability of social beliefs and cultural practices. These works are, in effect, ciphers of how subject matter, methodological concerns and theoretical frameworks have both shifted and persisted over the decades. Thus, despite substantially changed historical conditions, doing anthropology in contemporary West Malaysia shows much continuity with research enquiries and ethical dilemmas spawned decades earlier, albeit still embedded within a metropolitan-periphery political economy of anthropological scholarship.

This chapter, structured generally in chronological order, has three parts. In the first section, I provide a brief history of anthropology in West (or Peninsular) Malaysia from the colonial past up to the postcolonial present in order to track the broader contexts under which anthropology and social science have evolved and continue to change. In the second section, I draw out and weave together some of the salient insights of previous reviews of the state of anthropology in Malaysia to illuminate how the discipline has evolved across a span of four decades. The recurring characteristics highlight some of the persistent impediments perceived to beset the discipline—notably, the recalcitrant ethnicization of anthropology in/of Malaysia. The third and final section returns to the present and discusses the reflections of local anthropologists who teach or have taught in public universities, on the challenges and opportunities that beset the discipline today.

Emerging from Colonial Social Anthropology

As elsewhere, the genesis of anthropology in Malaysia is often retrospectively viewed with some ambivalence. Criticisms of the discipline as a "child of imperialism" (Gough 1968) or as complicit in legitimating colonial knowledge as a particular kind of "epistemological space" vis-á-vis local knowledge (Cohn 1996; Shamsul 1998) are now commonplace in academic and popular discourses. Pioneering anthropological entrepreneurship was made possible because of the intense period of colonial capitalist global expansion that entangled metropolitan scholars with the "other" as found in the far-flung overseas colonies of British, European and American empires from roughly the late eighteenth century onwards (Eriksen and Nielsen 2001).

As an emerging academic discipline in the metropolitan center, proponents of anthropology faced an uphill battle that was also manifested in the periphery. Nevertheless, over time, "anthropological ideas began to be adopted and used actively in the analysis and organisation of data, when the notion of anthropology's usefulness to colonial administration was promoted, and when anthropology or ethnology as a separately defined field of scholarly enquiry had managed to begin to gain a firm presence in the institutions of higher education in the West and Southeast Asia" (King and Wilder 2002: 25–26). In British Malaya, ethnological and philological details on the "Malay race" and aboriginal peoples[1] penned by colonial administrator-scholars and ethnographers (like Hugh Clifford, Frank A. Swettenham, Richard O. Winstedt, Richard J. Wilkinson and Walter W. Skeat) were infused with an array of Orientalist, diffusionist and evolutionist assumptions even as they also overtly served "practical" administrative needs (Tham 1980).

By the early decades of the twentieth century, the intellectual underpinnings of these earlier works were being progressively undermined by metropolitan anthropologists. Viewing these notions as "unscientific," the two major doyens of "new anthropology," Bronislaw Malinowski (1884–1942) and A.R. Radcliffe-Brown (1881–1955), advocated a more robust perspective (Eriksen and Nielsen 2001: 51). Malinowski's self-proclaimed "functionalist" framework for interpreting the beliefs and practices of "primitive" and stateless groups as essentially mechanisms for social order began to hold more sway among the anthropological fraternity. From the 1930s, a formidable rival perspective promoted by Radcliffe-Brown and his colleagues (such as Meyer Fortes and Evans-Pritchard) and emphasizing analysis of social facts and social structures synchronically ("structural functionalism"), became the dominant perspective in British social anthropology. Prevalent in the study of small-scale political organization, kinship and descent in Africa, structural functionalism was less commonly applied in Southeast Asia. King and Wilder believe this was because "many of the non-unilineal or cognatic societies in Southeast Asia presented a different set of problems for those anthropologists interested in principles of social structure" (King and Wilder 2002: 59).

Strands of the "new anthropology" were embodied by a number of seminal figures who conducted research in post-war British Malaya and trained the first generation of local anthropologists from 1957 onward in newly independent Malaysia. Raymond Firth, Edmund Leach and Michael Swift were all closely associated with the London School of Economics and Political Science. Firth had been a student of Malinowski and continued his mentor's intellectual legacy. After early research on Polynesia, Firth turned his attention to British Malaya, conducting fieldwork on small-scale Malay peasant fishing communities in the late 1930s and 1940s in Kelantan and Terengganu. Essentially working within economic anthropology and following Malinowski's "methodological individualism," Firth argued for the primacy of individual interests, action and choices vis-á-vis the pervasive force of structures. His view of fishermen as peasant-like was novel, and revealed Marxist influences on his work.

Firth was a key member of the Colonial Social Science Research Council (CSSRC), a branch of the Colonial Research Committee, established in 1944. As the secretary of CSSRC, Firth commissioned Edmund Leach—a former student of both Malinowski and Firth—to prepare a general survey of the Crown Colony of Sarawak in order "to suggest projects for sociological research" and "to provide Government with data for gauging the probable local response to the various schemes of development under consideration" (King and Wilder 2002: 32). Together with his wife Rosemary, also an anthropologist, Firth conducted a similar survey of British Malaya. Subsequently, based on their respective recommendations, a number of pioneering anthropological case studies were conducted on locality-specific indigenous and ethnic groups (Iban, Bidayuh, Melanau, Malay and Chinese) by non-local scholars. Now considered as classics in the functionalist genre, these publications provided theoretically informed interpretations of ethnographic data gathered on kinship, descent, marriage, religious beliefs, village life and organization, and social stratification. Rosemary Firth's work, along with that of Judith Djamour, pioneered the study of women in Malaysia—a trend that was influential on later work on gender. In the mid 1950s, another gifted PhD student of Raymond Firth, Michael Swift, embarked on researching peasant economy in the matrilineal Malay state of Negri Sembilan. Later, Swift published several essays on various aspects of Malay peasant society which subsequently became important texts for the Malay intelligentsia advocating for economic reforms in the country (Shamsul 2002: 22). After teaching stints in the Malay Studies Department at the Universiti Malaya (UM, 1957–61) and the Department of Anthropology at the University of Sydney (founded by Radcliffe-Brown in 1925), Swift went on to lead the anthropology department at Monash University (1968–84) before his death in 1985.

In 1959, nearing the end of the undeclared civil war with the communist insurgency (The Emergency, 1948–60), Swift assessed the state of sociological studies on Malaysia in the following terms:

> From a sociological point of view, Malaya is not a well-documented country. Its British administrators concentrated their intellectual interests on the Malays, but despite their labours they produced nothing comparable in scope to the scholarship of the Dutch in Indonesia. The gaps in sociological knowledge pointed out in Firth's *Report on Social Science Research in Malaya (1948)* are for the most part yet to be filled. Only a handful of British scholars have carried out sociological research in Malaya in recent years (and some of these have been concerned mainly with urban questions), while Malaya has been largely ignored, so far as field research is concerned, by the various American "projects" in Asia which had added greatly to our knowledge of neighbouring countries. Sociology, in any guise, is not widely taught in Malaya. There are no professional Malayan sociologists. The literature is, in consequence, thin, and can throw light only on a few of the questions which naturally fall within the scope of rural sociology ...

> Much has been written on the political aspects of the Chinese, some of it with a bearing on rural matters. Family and kinship studies have been made of both Malays and Chinese, stressing the responses to modern changes in society. The Indians have unfortunately been largely ignored, but something fresh has been produced on the Aborigines since they came to prominence as a result of being disturbed by the fighting which has been going on in the jungle (Swift 2001[1959]: 67–68).

To redress the research lacuna, both Firth and Swift were instrumental in providing PhD opportunities for the pioneering generation of local Malay anthropologists (Dahlan 2006[1974]; Shamsul 2001; Zawawi 2010). Subsequently, while the spectrum of choices for overseas anthropology postgraduate studies has since widened and theoretical paradigms or fashions shifted over time, the London School of Economics (LSE) and Monash University would nevertheless retain a significant place in the academic kinship chart. In the mid 1960s, the "LSE trio"[2] consisted of Abdul Kahar Bador, Mokhzani Abdul Rahim and Syed Husin Ali, all recruited from the Malay Studies Department at UM.[3] All of them later took up key leadership positions in UM, which was still a relatively young university (established 1949) and at the time was the only public university in the country. All three were involved in training the subsequent generation of local anthropologists. In the 1970s, Wazir Jahan Karim (1981) pursued her PhD at LSE and researched on the Ma'Betisek of Carey Island. This bucked the dominant trend of local anthropologists studying their own ethnic group (see below).

The LSE brand of social anthropology faced formidable rivals from other national social science traditions in terms of their strategic relevance and practicality to new nation states. "Modernization theory," especially the perspectives of liberal economists such as W. Arthur Lewis and W.W. Rostow, enjoyed much currency in framing nation-building priorities in several Southeast Asian countries. Post-war Malayan planning was thus mainly preoccupied with:

> Effecting the evolutionary, gradual, balanced transition from "traditional" to "modern" social formation by promoting economic growth and industrialisation. In particular, this entailed encouraging individuals and groups, typically the Malay peasantry, away from traditional ways of thinking, behaving, and organising economic life to rational, individualistic, risk-taking, innovative behaviour (King 1999: 54).

The National Context

The *First Malayan Plan* (1956–60) was the outcome of a World Bank mission visit to the country in 1954. The plan advocated the need for rapid economic growth and the shift from overdependence on primary export commodities of rubber and tin to a broad-based economy more oriented towards manufacturing and a diversified productive agriculture. In 1965, at the request of Deputy Prime Minister Tun Razak, who was also the Minister for Rural Development, two American consultants Milton Esmen (Department of Government, Cornell University) and John D. Montgomery (Harvard Kennedy School of Government) were invited to draft guidelines for a Development Administrative Unit (DAU) in the Prime Minister's Department. A vital component of *The Montgomery-Esmen Report* (1966) called for the creation and support of undergraduate and graduate programs in development administration at UM for the training of civil service officers. Esmen later became senior adviser when the DAU was established, and devised an American-inspired curriculum for the program.[4] Several American social scientists were involved in streamlining various research activities in several government departments (such as the Statistics and Census Department). Moreover, key civil servants were identified for graduate studies in the social sciences in the United States. The penchant in American social science for quantitative empirical data was mainstreamed in UM largely through expatriate American lecturers. A number of them also guided the first generation of "area studies" specialists.[5] Not surprisingly, it was in the discipline of economics that the methodological impact of "Americanization" was felt most strongly (Rustam and Noraini 1991: 4). Writing in the mid 1990s, Shamsul (1995) observed retrospectively that *The Montgomery-Esmen Report* "almost single-handedly nationalised social science in Malaysia" (104) and institutionalized "non-university social science concentrated on policy-oriented matters or profit-motivated business issues" (ibid.: 100; also see Provencher 1979: 441).

Upon his return from LSE, Syed Husin Ali advocated the creation of a separate anthropology department at UM. Hitherto, anthropology was only taught as a subject under the "culture" stream of Malay studies. The other streams comprised "Malay literature" and "linguistics."[6] Although the department was eventually established in 1971, permission was not immediately forthcoming from the

University Senate (also see Zainal 1995a). Ironically, the push to set up social science disciplines and departments in public universities was given more urgency after the Kuala Lumpur "race riots" of May 1969 (also see Kua 2007). In 1970, a report prepared for the Prime Minister's Department by the Harvard Advisory Group recommended this course of action to help better manage agonistic interethnic relations in the country (Glazier et al. 1970; Abdul Rahman 2010: 64–65).

In the same year, Universiti Kebangsaan Malaysia (UKM) was created in response to long-standing pressure for the Malay language to be the medium of instruction at the apex of education in the country.[7] It had included a Jabatan Kajimanusia dan Kajimasyarakat (Department of Human Studies and Social Studies), subsequently renamed Jabatan Antropologi dan Sosiologi (Department of Anthropology and Sociology) in 1974, thus earning the distinction of being the first Malaysian public university to have a full-fledged anthropology and sociology department, ahead of UM (Rahimah 2005: 53). Several junior lecturers in the Department of Malay Studies at UM crossed over to take up positions at UKM. Up north in Penang, at Universiti Sains Malaysia (USM), which was created in 1969 as the second public university in the country, the discipline was already taught, but as part of "an integrated approach" involving rural and urban studies for a Bachelor of Social Sciences degree. Recruitment of teaching staff in the "anthropology and sociology division" (which also included psychology) within the School of Comparative Social Science had drawn in several foreign anthropologists with newly acquired PhDs.[8]

These innovations were made within a milieu of global ferment and social upheaval. In particular, anti-imperialist/colonial movements, the Middle East conflicts, and, closer to Malaysia, the American–Vietnam war provided fuel for renewed debates on the ethical role and responsibility of universities in troubled times. Metropolitan anthropologists and their discipline were not exempt from criticisms and self-critique (Gough 1968; Asad 1973). For many Malaysian postgraduate students, studying abroad at Western universities through the late 1960s and early 1970s, witnessing these events first-hand left a deep impression. Later, as academics back in Malaysia, they conveyed and translated these formative experiences to their students. Empowered local university student groups pressed for intervention and remedial action to perceived injustices inside and outside of the country. Their mobilization efforts were supplemented by progressive academics, several of them social scientists, who were invited to share their expert knowledge on these pressing issues in various public forums. The most noteworthy was in December 1974 when several thousand university and college students converged in central Kuala Lumpur to show their support for the aggrieved peasants in Baling, Kedah. Clashes with the police ensued, and a sizeable number of student leaders and academics were arrested in the aftermath. A smaller targeted group, including student activist leader Anwar Ibrahim and anthropologist Syed Husin Ali, were further detained under the Internal Security Act (ISA), a colonial-era anti-terrorist legislation which allows for detention without trial.[9]

In 1976, under the watch of Education Minister Mahathir Mohamad, the University and University Colleges Act (UUCA) was amended to criminalize the involvement of students and staff in societies, trade unions and political groups outside the university. The content of lectures and the conduct of lecturers were closely monitored. Individuals charged under this Act were suspended or expelled from universities. Besides crippling university autonomy, academic freedoms and the right to freedom of association, the UUCA has also continued to influence the types of topics considered suitable for academic research undertaken by local scholars. Similarly, foreign scholars were required to apply for official research permits from the Prime Minister's Department, and quickly became familiar with the range of research topics considered "sensitive." For critical social commentators, the wide-reaching policing and censoring powers of this Act have been largely responsible for fostering decades of weak and mimetic scholarship, and intellectual stagnation in the Malaysian academe, especially in the social sciences (Rustam 2008; Ali 2012).

The 1970s was a watershed in terms of the development of wide-ranging social engineering policies that subsequently influenced the range of topics for anthropological research. In addition to recommendations from the Harvard Advisory Group to set up university social science departments, there were also proposals that the fragile plural structure of Malaysian society needed closer governmental policing and management. As the root cause of the May 1969 riots was diagnosed to be widespread endemic Malay poverty as a consequence of several decades of laissez-faire economic policies, a "redistribution with growth" affirmative action strategy was adopted. The Department of National Unity was created to devise a national ideology, the Rukun Negara, to frame all other development planning policies.

In particular, the New Economic Policy (in 1971), the National Education Act (in 1970), and the National Cultural Policy (in 1972), and their subsequent incarnations, are premised on positive discrimination in favor of ethnic Malays (with other indigenous groups now collectively known as bumiputeras) and Islam as the sine qua non for national unity and harmony.

Another major shift two decades later also attracted a fair amount of anthropological attention (Ong 2006). Although the New Economic Policy formally ended in 1991, the ethos of this and other related policies persisted. Additional policies were set in place in view of the impact of neo-liberal economic and cultural globalization. With the catchphrase of *Wawasan 2020* (Vision 2020), Prime Minister Mahathir Mohamad outlined a grand narrative of arriving, by the year 2020, at the status of a "fully developed" and self-sufficient industrialized nation. This ambitious project paralleled a global Islamic revivalism inspiring a range of local innovations in Islamic piety, not all of them perceived to be theologically orthodox by the state religious authorities. Many of these sects and movements essentially seek to alleviate, if not provide alternatives to, the perceived contradictions of the secularist developmental path promoted by the government.

Over the years, both repression and various assimilation countermeasures have been adopted with regard to Islamization. In particular, during the long first tenure of Prime Minister Mahathir Mohamad (1981–2003), a number of interlocking policy initiatives were developed to "Islamize" both government and society through the establishment of an integrated network of judicial, financial and educational institutions operating in towns and cities throughout the country. Mahathir essentially believed that a modern Islamic society in the mould of Sunni orthodoxy was possible, and that returning to a "correctly understood Islam," devoid of superstition and fatalism, would help Malay Muslims address poverty and political subjugation (Sloane 1999; Peletz 2002; Schottmann 2013).

In the post-Mahathir era, as the telos of *Wawasan 2020* approaches, subsequent prime ministers have essentially maintained this key trajectory. As evident in the Tenth Malaysia Plan (10MP, 2011–15), the administration of Najib Abdul Razak underscored an entrepreneurial thrust to all government policymaking. In comparison to previous Malaysia Plans, the neo-liberal, globalist and urbanist aura of the 10MP is quite distinctive. The trope of "transformation" is given prominence in the New Economic Model (NEM), which warns that Malaysia is at risk of being "caught in the middle-income trap" and overtaken by other countries because of increased international, regional or global competition (10MP, 5). To move to a high-income status, it proposes that the structure of the country's economy be substantially altered. This translates into developing far more investor-friendly policies and shifting away from ethnic-based to merit-based affirmative action policies. In this brave new world, the private sector has been identified as a major engine of growth for the national economy.

Past Reviews of Anthropology

In this section, I draw out salient observations made in past reviews on the state of Malaysian anthropology and Malaysian social sciences generally, authored by both local and foreign scholars. They are revealing for what they show both in terms of the development of the discipline, and the changing social and political conditions of Malaysia under which the discipline has operated.

In August 1974, the Department of Anthropology and Sociology at UKM organized a pioneering two-day national conference to critically reflect on the state of the social sciences in Malaysia.[10] The position paper on anthropology was presented by H.M. Dahlan of UKM (2006[1974]).[11] In his overview, Dahlan highlighted several salient features of the existing corpus of studies. First, except for singular monographs on urban Chinese (Freedman 1957) and South Indians working in the plantations (Jain 1970), Dahlan noted that these studies had thus far been largely "Malay-centric" at the expense of scholarship on many other ethnic communities living in Malaysia. Moreover, these studies assume that Malays are a homogeneous group living in clearly demarcated villages, mukims and districts. Second, the "pribumis" (indigenous peoples), especially those living in Sabah and Sarawak, had been generally overlooked. Finally, Dahlan discerned that these studies posited sharp discontinuities between the ethnic groups researched and other ethnic communities living in Malaysia, giving the impression of hermetically sealed worlds.

Dahlan further argued that local anthropologists should abandon "structural functionalist" frameworks as they are not only unable to deal with social and economic changes in the country but they also promote a sense of "complacency" (Dahlan 2006[1974]: 61–62). Indeed, in contrast to foreign anthropologists, the challenge for local Third World anthropologists studying their own societies is to orientate their research priorities to be more relevant to problems of their research subjects while remaining cognizant of being part of an international community of anthropologists. Moreover, Dahlan counselled a move away from a "particularizing anthropology" to a more "generalizing anthropology," the latter necessitating an interdisciplinary framework while still maintaining the humanist hallmark of anthropology—an empathy with research subjects.

Not long afterwards, Tham Seong-Chee (1980), based in Singapore, published a much longer piece reviewing the state of social science in Malaysia throughout the 1970s. The research was commissioned by the Institute of Developing Economies based in Tokyo. In his chapter on sociology and anthropology, Tham remarked that as a consequence of the communal upheavals of May 1969, "research interest on the Malays in particular, took on a new meaning and intensity ... [and] Malaysian academics in general have become preoccupied with research on the Malays" (Tham 1980: 73). By comparison, research on the "other Malaysian communities [like the non-indigenous Chinese and Indians] was comparatively much less significant" (ibid.). Moreover, the plural situation of Malaysia has attracted a "disproportionate attention from scholars" on interethnic relations, particularly from political scientists (ibid.: 84). But despite the volume of research, he opined that:

> Research done on race relations up till now [has] not contributed to a better understanding between the various Malays ethnic communities simply because of the tendency of researchers and scholars in general to over-emphasize the centrifugal forces undergirding the race situation. Indeed, in a sense, it might be said that such studies have made the situation more acute (ibid.: 84).

As a corrective, Tham suggested a need to change the tendency of Malaysian social scientists to "look at problems as being specifically Malay or specifically Chinese (a tendency inherited from the past perhaps) with no attempt in any conscious or consistent way at unification" (ibid.: 102). Tham was, however, cautiously optimistic that this state of affairs might change as "more Chinese and Indian Malaysians becoming competent in Bahasa Malaysia (Malay) there might be more efforts shown in cross-cultural research but in the context of current political conditions, research on the Malays will continue to be given higher priority" (ibid.: 105).

In 1979, another review of *Malaysian Studies* edited by John Lent was published by the Center for Southeast Asian Studies, Northern Illinois University. In the chapter on anthropology, Vinson Sutlive Jr reiterated his observations on the ethnicized features of anthropological research in Malaysia:

> In addition to foreign researchers and lecturers, there are 20 Malaysian anthropologists ... Little research is done by members of one ethnic community among others in West Malaysia. Malays study the Malays, Chinese study the Chinese, and Indians study the Indians. Given the administration's policies on "sensitive issues", particularly ethnicity and inter-ethnic relations, this limitation on ethnographic research is regrettable but understandable (Sutlive Jr 1979: 61–62).

He also noted that while some West Malaysian anthropologists had now begun researching ethnic (indigenous) communities in East Malaysia, they had not yet explored other Southeast Asian countries or other areas in the world. In his opinion: "Since doing an ethnography of a foreign society is the traditional rite of passage for cultural anthropologists, efforts should be made to encourage Malaysian graduate students in anthropology to do fieldwork outside their nation" (ibid.: 62).

On whether anthropological theory had been "localized," Sutlive Jr lamented that: "Anthropology theory used in Malaysia is still Eurocentric in orientation and tradition. There is a need for Malaysian anthropologists to study non-Malaysian societies. They will achieve a deeper understanding of their own culture *only* by studying non-Malaysian cultures" (Ibid., 85, original emphasis).

Writing in the epilogue of the same volume, Ronald Provencher articulated a similar critique of the contemporary state of Malaysian studies:

> Necessary improvements include greater and more sophisticated use of documents and records, use of quantitative and computational analytical methods where these are applicable, more thoughtful application of theoretical models to avoid Western-centric misinterpretations, more systematic elicitation and analysis of data on culturally defined perceptions and cognition, and more conscious development of testable hypotheses. Another means of developing greater methodological sophistication among Malaysian scholars would be to encourage their participation in research on cultures and societies other than their own (Provencher 1979: 457).

Nearly two decades later, not much progress appeared to have been made in the push for the "indigenization" of anthropological theory in the observations of Zainal Kling, the head of the anthropology and sociology department in UM, written for a publication marking the department's twentieth anniversary:

> The department, however, remained conservative as most of its academics were trained in functionalism in spite of the advocacy of Syed Husin Ali for a dialectical sociology. By the 1980s, the theoretical orientation was somewhat influenced by the rise of interest in Islamic sociology. This, however, has only a few followers. In the 1990s, the younger academics seemed to have been influenced largely by the rise of a critical sociology which was the outcome of recent European movements (Zainal 1995b: xiv).

Tan Chee-Beng, one of the co-editors of the above publication, addressed the indigenization of anthropology in Malaysia a decade later in more substantive terms (Tan 2004).[12] In place of the ambivalent phrases "native anthropology" or "indigenous anthropology" as intellectual counterpoints to Western anthropology, Tan prefers "local anthropologist" which he defined as:

> An anthropologist who participates continuously in a national society, such as living in that society permanently and following local events. Thus, an anthropologist of Malaysian origin who has migrated permanently to another country and who does not participate in Malaysian academic circles regularly cannot be considered as a Malaysian local anthropologist (Tan 2004: 308).

Despite an increase in the number of trained "local anthropologists" researching a variety of topics and ethnic and indigenous communities since the 1970s, Tan observed that: "The development of anthropology has paralleled ethnic divisions, with Malay anthropologists generally studying Malay and aboriginal communities only, while the anthropology of the Chinese and Indian communities is poorly developed as there are few anthropologists of Chinese or Indian origins" (Tan 2004: 309).

Moreover, the key reason why there continues to be small numbers of Malaysian anthropologists of Chinese and Indian origins is not primarily because of linguistic reasons as earlier observed by Tham Seong-Chee. Instead, "it is difficult for them to get a job in academic institutions in Malaysia, and this does not encourage non-Malay Malaysians to become professional anthropologists in the country" (ibid.: 317). Even if postgraduate anthropology students were to aspire towards studying non-Malaysian societies, they are fearful of not being able to find employment in Malaysian public universities where the emphasis is on producing human capital for nation-building priorities. Moreover, because of the small number of professional anthropologists (less than thirty by his reckoning) and the absence of a national anthropological association to bring together anthropologists across ethnic boundaries, there is "still no clearly defined local tradition of anthropology to speak of" (ibid.: 319).

For Tan, the kind of "indigenization" project promoted in Malaysia has been premised on the "questionable rhetoric" that only local anthropologists can produce scholarship that is deemed to be relevant and has more practical application than that of foreign anthropologists (also see Wazir 1996). This nativist standpoint has become so embedded in public universities that scholarship has been dominated by "criticizing colonial practices and discussing Western [United States] dominance in the region and the world" (ibid.: 320). By contrast, for Tan: "The issue is really the commitment of anthropologists to the local, irrespective of whether they are local or foreign scholars. In fact, in Malaysia, there are many local scholars who have contributed to the construction of Malay-dominated nationalist ideology" (ibid., 322).

A consequence of the "Malay-dominated nationalist ideology" has been the declining fluency in English language:

> In Malaysia, part of the problem is that some younger local scholars, who are products of Malay nationalism, are weak in English, and this does not encourage them to read international publications. The implementation of nationalist policies has also eroded professional standards based on merit, and this has affected the quality of scholarship (Tan 2004: 325).

More than a decade earlier, Rustam Sani and Noraini Othman had similarly bemoaned the poor quality of Malaysian social science scholarship in broader terms. They diagnosed that:

> Despite increasing use of the National Language as the language of discourse in social science in universities in Malaysia, the indigenisation process has been slow and has failed to cultivate in the various social science disciplines any novel content or critical stance ... Instead, it has created a parallel imitative version of the

> heaps of sawdust already piled up elsewhere (Rustam and Noraini 1991: 2).

For these scholars, the quantitative improvement in the social science discipline both in terms of departments created and scholarly output in journal articles and books since the 1970s is characterized by its "overwhelmingly pragmatic and instrumental orientation" that takes its lead from the "methodological, technical and utilitarian dimensions of Western social science, especially their dominant United States versions" (ibid.: 8). This state of affairs has further contributed to: "The lack of intellectual depth in our society, the narrow and under-developed character of our modern intellectual culture and our consistent failure to engender a rational, scientific and critical outlook as the common culture among our community of scholars, the intelligentsia and the so-called intellectuals" (ibid.: 11).[13]

In summary, a number of salient points can be drawn from these past reviews of anthropology in Malaysia. First, over the past few decades, anthropology has been facing strong competition from its more positivist-oriented cousins in the social sciences. This can be attributed to the historical circumstances of the entry of social sciences into Malaysia and the subsequent bias towards "applied" social science research instruments, perceived to be better equipped in helping to inform and manage social change in the country. Second, the ethical dilemmas of "race" and interethnic relations inherited from the colonial period but reconfigured in the postcolonial present have continued to frame how local anthropological studies have been conducted among the different ethno-religious communities in the country (also see Lim et al. 2009; Holst 2014[2012]). Not only has there been a research bias towards the dominant Malay Muslim group as key research subjects, deepening militant ethno-nationalist trends in the past two or three decades have also promoted parochial kinds of scholarship that eschew going beyond the notions of hermetically sealed and often antagonistic wholes. This leads to the final third point. While local anthropologists (and other social scientists) might be prodigious in collecting empirical and ethnographic data, there is still heavy reliance on scholarship emanating from the metropolitan centers of Europe and America for anthropological theorizing. Moreover, because of the current lack of fluency in academic English language among younger scholars, the theories that are favored are comparatively dated and often mimetically appropriated to local contexts without much critical interrogation (also see Alatas 2005).

Anthropological Landscapes in Malaysia

This section provides a synopsis and discussion of key findings based on interviews with self-identified anthropologists who are (or were) based at three premier public universities in West Malaysia—Universiti Malaya (UM), Universiti Kebangsaan Malaysia (UKM), and Universiti Sains Malaysia (USM). Additionally, I scanned through four major local social science journals, in which writings by local anthropologists are most likely to be found, in order to have a sense of the changing intellectual and academic concerns over the last four or five decades. These journals are *Manusia dan Masyarakat* (Man and Society), *Jurnal Antropologi dan Sosiologi* (Journal of Anthropology and Sociology), *Akademika* (Academia), and *Ilmu Masyarakat* (Knowledge of Society).

I begin with summary observations about the local social science publications. *Manusia dan Masyarakat* has been published by the Department of Anthropology and Sociology at UM since 1972. Before it ceased publication in 1995, *Jurnal Antropologi dan Sosiologi*, started in 1971, was the annual publication vehicle of the Department of Anthropology and Sociology, UKM. *Akademika* is the journal of Humanities and Social Sciences at UKM and has been published since 1972. *Ilmu Masyarakat* is an occasional journal publication of the Malaysian Social Science Association (MSSA). In terms of content, although containing fewer articles, earlier journal publications were much longer and allowed space for ethnographic reports as well as substantive book reviews of ethnographies in other regions. Later publications tended to have shorter pieces, more articles and perspectives that were more sociological and quantitative in orientation. There is also more focus on macro issues or trends perceived to be affecting the country. While all the journal publications have had a bilingual (English and Malay) editorial policy from their inception, there are notable differences in how these publishing aspirations have played out between them and across time. *Manusia dan Masyarakat* has generally maintained a large proportion of articles in English over the years with some Malay articles appearing only in recent years. In contrast, while the early years of *Jurnal Antropologi dan Sosiologi* saw a large proportion of the articles published in English, the journal progressively changed to being almost entirely a Malay-language journal except for rare contributions by established foreign scholars. In general, both *Akademika* and *Ilmu Masyarakat* have maintained a balance in the use of both languages and included numerous contributions from foreign scholars working on Malaysia.

As already noted by previous reviewers, the global hegemony of the English language in academic research continues to be the key reason for the comparative invisibility of local Malaysian scholars who are fluent only in the Malay language. But, in recent years, there has been the compounding factor of technological advancement that has fine-tuned the metrics for assessing academic excellence in terms of productivity and citations. None of the journals discussed presently have a professional online presence, thus making it difficult for their scholarly work to be easily disseminated. Nevertheless, ever since local public universities were drawn into the various annual global university ranking regimes, there has been pressure for local scholars to publish in Scopus or Institute for Scientific Information (ISI) cited international English language journals as part of their academic key performance indicators (KPIs). Many of my interviewees, particularly young academics, admitted to feeling a sense of linguistic inadequacy given that they have been immersed in a Malay-medium milieu since the beginning of their careers. Senior scholars hailing from the 1970s generation, by comparison, are less perturbed since they are equally proficient in both languages. But many of them have retired from academia or are approaching retirement age.

Despite these linguistic and non-linguistic obstacles, various corrective measures have been attempted in the past. Besides various incentive schemes provided by universities to publish internationally, the most pertinent are those initiated or organized by the MSSA. Most, if not all, of their activities have an international slant, providing local and aspiring scholars with opportunities to engage with a wider academic network. The biennial international conferences, in particular, attract significant numbers of foreign scholars (including anthropologists) working on Malaysia to share their findings and to build networks for research collaboration. Moreover, since the mid 2000s, MSSA has initiated a Malaysian Studies book series under the auspices of Routledge, a major global player in academic publishing. To date, fifteen volumes have been published with much of the material drawn from papers presented at the Malaysian Studies conferences. More recently, since 2012, due to prohibitive prices of Routledge for Malaysian purchasers and to encourage local scholarship, MSSA has also collaborated with an established local publishing house, Strategic Information and Research Development Centre (SIRD), to produce the "MSSA Social Science Series" under the general editorship of Abdul Rahman Embong, Zawawi Ibrahim and Mohd. Hazim Shah. Two volumes have been published to date.

Besides attending to research matters, an important pedagogical role of professional anthropologists is to replenish the disciplinary fold through the induction of students into their respective university departments. All interviewees felt that undergraduate enrolment numbers in anthropology units in their departments have been consistently high over the years, and anthropology appears to be "quite popular" with the students (also see Shamsul 1993). This is notwithstanding the handicap that enrolling students are usually not familiar with the discipline in comparison to better known secondary school subjects such as geography and history, and subjects popularized in mainstream media like psychology. A common early misconception among university students is that anthropology is primarily confined to the study of "primitive societies" like the Orang Asli in Malaysia, and thus has no practical relevance for their urban, modern and future working lives. Through word of mouth and trial and error, however, many eventually choose to take up anthropology units as electives or opt for anthropology clusters as majors/minors. Common feedback in university exit surveys is that students would have liked to take more anthropology units if they were to start their tertiary studies all over again. In particular, many students have enjoyed reading ethnographies of unfamiliar communities and societies around the region and world, and have seen ethnographic fieldwork as the most appealing dimension of anthropology.

In terms of theoretical orientation, students have found it particularly challenging to understand assigned readings influenced by a mix of "post-structuralist" and "postcolonial" theoretical standpoints. Their lack of command of academic English and the sophisticated prose of these works act as formidable communication barriers. Similarly, some of my interviewees also admitted that they too find this particular genre of anthropological writing to be difficult. Moreover, they are not averse to selecting "functionalist" and "structuralist functionalist" informed ethnographies as the bulk of their teaching material. Some reasoned that it is important for their students to engage with the anthropological classics, however dated they might be, rather than follow the theoretical fashion of the day. A couple of interviewees, however, contended that it is because of choices like these, that students unnecessarily end up "getting stuck in the 1960s." This theoretical time warp is further exacerbated by the lack of university funds to support undergraduate and postgraduate anthropology students eager to conduct fieldwork beyond the Malaysian nation-state borders. Thus, despite their datedness, the observations made by scholars like Vinson Sutlive Jr and Ronald Provencher some three decades ago have a contemporary ring to them. Nevertheless, with the renewed emphasis on English as a medium of instruction at all educational levels and further shifts of the discipline with the passage of time, this current malaise might possibly become a footnote of history.

The appeal of anthropology is not confined to young full-time on-campus students. For instance, at the School of Distance Learning (USM) enrolment numbers for off-campus cohorts in the social sciences (anthropology and sociology) are usually high with a majority of them being working married or single women, for whom acquiring a university qualification is a pathway to promotion in their workplaces or to other careers. Students have found the units on offer to be relevant and useful, especially if they are employed in occupations that involve a great deal of human interaction, for example, social workers and the police force. Unable to conduct conventional fieldwork because of the constraints of work and family commitments, many of my interviewees' students were nevertheless described as "highly motivated," and learned to improvise and produce credible academic work. A small number have gone on to postgraduate studies and subsequently pursued new careers as researchers and academics.

Contrary to bureaucratic doubts about the marketability of anthropology graduates in Malaysia, my interviewees pointed out that based on alumni surveys and anecdotal evidence over the years, this was not the case. In fact, many employers have the perception that social science graduates have good analytical and cross-cultural skills in understanding complex human behavior and conceptualizing culturally impactful communication in a country like Malaysia. Besides being employed in an array of occupations in the private sector, a number of high-ranking and senior administrators in the civil service and in civil service training institutes such as the National Institute of Public Administration (INTAN) are known to be anthropology graduates of public universities (also see Shamsul 1993, 2004).

Shifts in government policies, including those noted above, have a bearing on the research priorities of local public universities. To better serve industries and support the country's entrepreneurial push towards the "developed" country status, various premier public universities such as UM, UKM and USM have been promoted to become "research universities," with academics required to increase their publication output and conduct "high-impact" research with readily available university and government funds. Enrolment numbers at undergraduate levels are expected to drop significantly in research universities and, conversely, postgraduate intakes are set to increase in line with the aspiration to generate higher skilled human capital. Together with other social science disciplines, anthropology has been caught in this radically recalibrated research orbit. However, whether the reduction in enrolment numbers will readily translate into improving the quality of "local" or "indigenous" anthropological theorizing in Malaysia is as yet too early to predict. Nevertheless, one of the early outcomes of efforts to elevate the global standing of local public universities has been the increase of foreign postgraduate students from Southeast Asia, South Asia, East Asia and the Middle East. This has led to the diversification and internationalization of research topics beyond the usual fare, concomitantly requiring their supervisors to acquire broader theoretical frameworks and geographical perspectives.

In the recent past, a number of local anthropologists have been proactive in conceptualizing and setting up new research initiatives to address important national issues, harnessing the benefits of multidisciplinary perspectives, and keeping up with changing global research trends. Subsequently, their expertise has been redeployed to these "centers" or "institutes" clustered around a range of themes, local and international. At UKM, these initiatives have resulted in research institutes such as the Institute for Malaysian and International Studies (IKMAS), the Institute for Occidental Studies (IKON), and the Institute for Ethnic Studies (KITA).[14] Similarly, at UM, women anthropologists have been instrumental in founding the pioneering Gender Studies Programme (created in 1995). Unlike earlier initiatives in other public universities, for example, the Centre for Research on Women and Gender (KANITA) based at USM, which placed more emphasis on research, the Gender Studies Programme has undergraduate teaching, research and advocacy components (Tambiah et al. 2011).[15] The program has been particularly fruitful in helping students become more aware of the importance of gender and other social justice dimensions in social analysis and policymaking, and in making sense of their personal lives.

As before, local anthropologists also try to keep abreast of recent foreign scholarship on Malaysia despite the linguistic constraints noted earlier. Moreover, the scholarship of both senior and younger generations of foreign-based anthropologists researching on Malaysia has not abated in the last decade or so. Indeed, their innovative anthropological theories interwoven with lucid and reflexive ethnographies have continued to put the country on the global anthropological map. Among others, they have covered topics as diverse as urbanism in Kuala Lumpur (Baxstrom 2008; Yeoh 2014) and Penang (Goh 2002), kinship practices in a Malay fishing village (Carsten 1997), Chinese popular religion and identity politics in Penang (DeBernardi 2004, 2006), urban Muslim consumption habits and entrepreneurship (Sloane 1999; Fischer 2008), urban Muslim women's piety (Frisk 2009), Malay cosmopolitanism (Kahn 2006), modern Muslim identities and the Islamic modern (Peletz 2002; Hoffstaedter 2011), working class Chinese identities (Nonini 2015), the internet and urban governance (Postill 2011), urbanism in a rural Malay setting (Thompson 2007), a neo-Hindu movement (Kent 2004), and Tamil-Hindu identity politics (Willford 2006, 2014). The long-standing interest in the Orang Asli also continues to have research currency among both foreign (Gomes 2004, 2007; Nobuta 2006; Endicott and Endicott 2007; Dentan 2008; Benjamin 2014) and local (Lye 2004) anthropologists.[16] It is notable that Juli Edo, the first Orang Asli anthropologist who was based in UM until his recent retirement, earned a PhD from the Australian National University. No doubt, in time, some of these works will join the growing canon of anthropological classics on Malaysia. To be sure, not all of these classics will necessarily be authored by anthropologists or have a strictly anthropological slant.[17] Nor will the range of objects and subjects of anthropological research in Malaysia remain static or theoretically framed in predictable ways. These kinds of intellectual challenges and changes are already reflected in the metropolitan centers of anthropology and, as before, will also find favor among some local anthropologists in Malaysia in terms of theoretical and methodological orientations.

Conclusion

The contexts for social anthropology in West Malaysia have morphed much since its genesis and early development. New vistas for anthropological research have been opened up as the country transforms from being primarily agricultural based to a mixed and globalist economy with significant inputs from manufacturing, property investment, banking and tourism in order to "move up the value chain." Among others, new communication technologies, the migration of peoples from near and far in search of better livelihoods, the competition for limited resources manifesting in ethno-religiously inflected identity politics, the democratic push for recognition and legitimacy by an array of minorities, and the remaking of places, territories and natural environments all present themselves as prime topics not only for anthropologists but also other social scientists (also see Zawawi 1998).

Nevertheless, because of the particular colonialist legacies of the discipline and contemporary political contestations in the postcolonial milieu, local anthropologists have often been put in subject positions that are arguably discordant with the broad humanist ethos of anthropology. The contours of a "transethnic," let alone "transnational" (also see Ratana Tosakul, this volume), scholarship among local anthropologists in Malaysia are, at the moment, not discernible on the horizon given the social history of the discipline and the kinds of self-inflicted inhibitions discussed earlier. Moreover, local anthropologists have also to contend with the instrumentalist manner in which anthropological (and other disciplinary) knowledge continues to be produced and consumed globally under the regime of technologically driven academic excellence discourse. Nevertheless, despite these many challenges, local anthropologists and anthropology in/of Malaysia are not in danger of drowning in the fast-flowing river of social science. The country's polyglot and culturally variegated communities continue to invite anthropological intrigue both local and foreign. In Malaysia, as elsewhere, its multidisciplinary stance and long-term fieldwork methodology are trademarks that set anthropology and anthropologists apart from other academic disciplines and scholars. As resilient and flexible scholars, some, however, might well find themselves having to work outside the confines of departmental walls of public universities in Malaysia, and possibly thrive in the process.

Notes

* I would like to thank my colleagues for generously sharing their reflections on anthropology in Malaysia. In particular, I would like to thank Professor Abdul Rahman Embong for bringing to my attention various important publications pertaining to the early years of the discipline.

1. Aboriginal peoples were renamed "Orang Asli" (original peoples) by the British Administration during The Emergency (1948–60) as part of a counter-propaganda strategy.
2. As characterized by Abdul Rahman Embong (interview on June 11, 2014), President of the Malaysian Social Science Association (MSSA, or Persatuan Sains Sosial Malaysia) from 2000–10.
3. The Malay Studies Department was established in 1953, five years after it was first proposed by the Carr-Saunders Commission in the University of Malaya (Singapore).
4. For a personal account of the project, see Esmen 1972.
5. "Area studies" developed out of World War II strategic intelligence research and the Cold War geopolitics. The American–Vietnam war, in particular, solidified a "North American style of social sciences," curtailing discipline switching that was hitherto common (Goh 2012: 86–87).
6. Then, the Arts Faculty at UM at the time comprised five departments, viz. Malay studies, Chinese studies, Indian studies, history and geography.
7. Syed Husin Ali also played a significant role in promoting the idea of setting up a national university with the Malay language as the main medium of instruction (Ali 2012: 55).
8. Mohd. Razha Abdul Rashid (interviewed on April 23, 2014) recounted an impressive mix of academic mentors at USM, including Shuichi Nagata from University of Illinois, Anthony Walker from Oxford, and Clifford Sather from Harvard.
9. See Ali (2008) for a memoir of these events.
10. Following a proposal from this conference, the Malaysian Social Science Association (MSSA, or Persatuan Sains Sosial Malaysia) was formed in September 1978. For an overview of the work of MSSA, see Abdul Rahman (2010).
11. H.M. Dahlan obtained his master's from Monash University under the supervision of Michael Swift in 1973.
12. Tan Chee-Beng obtained a Bachelor of Social Science (Hons) from USM before earning an MA and then a PhD (1979) from the Department of Anthropology, Cornell University. After working at the University of Malaya, he left Malaysia to join the anthropology department at the Chinese University of Hong Kong. He has researched various ethnic and indigenous groups in East and West Malaysia as well as the Chinese diaspora generally.
13. See also Khoo Kay Jin (1995) who argues that the pedagogical challenge is to equip social science students with the habits of critical intellectual inquiry.
14. Professor Dr Shamsul was instrumental in the formation of IKON and KITA.

15. Professor Dr Wazir Jahan Karim led KANITA for many years after its establishment.
16. For a fuller review of the current state of Orang Asli studies in Malaysia, see Lye 2011.
17. A case in point, James Scott's *Weapons of the Weak* (1985), over thirty years old, was the single recurring piece of work cited by my interviewees as required reading for their students.

References

Abdul Rahman Embong (2010) *Malaysian Studies: Looking Back, Moving Forward.* Kajang: Persatuan Sains Sosial Malaysia.

Alatas, Syed Farid (2005) "Indigenization: Features and Problems." In *Asian Anthropology*, Jan van Bremen, Eyal Ben-Ari, and Syed Farid Alatas, (eds.), pp. 227–44. London & New York: Routledge.

Ali, Syed Husin (2012) *Memoirs of a Political Struggle.* Petaling Jaya: SIRD.

Asad, Talal, (ed.) (1973) *Anthropology and the Colonial Encounter.* Atlantic Highlands, NJ: Humanities Press.

Baxstrom, Richard (2008) *Houses in Motion: The Experience of Place and the Problem of Belief in Urban Malaysia.* Stanford: Stanford University Press.

Benjamin, Geoffrey (2014) *Temiar Religion 1964–2012: Enchantment, Disenchantment and Re-enchantment in Malaysia Uplands.* Singapore: NUS Press.

Carsten, Janet (1997) *The Heat of the Hearth: The Process of Kinship in a Malay Fishing Community*. Oxford: Oxford University Press.

Cohn, Bernard (1996) *Colonialism and its Form of Knowledge: The British in India.* Princeton: Princeton University Press.

Dahlan H.M. (2006 [1974]) "Peranan dan orientasi antropologi dan ahli-ahli antropologi di Malaysia" ["Role and Orientation of Anthropology and Anthropologists in Malaysia"]. In *Peranan dan orientasi sains sosial Malaysia* [*Role and Orientation of Malaysian Social Science*], Abdul Rahman Embong, (ed.), pp. 39–69. Bangi: Universiti Kebangsaan Malaysia.

DeBernardi, Jean (2004) *Rites of Belonging: Memory, Modernity and Identity in a Malaysian Chinese Community*. Stanford: Stanford University Press.

_____ (2006) *The Way that Lives in the Heart: Chinese Popular Religion and Spirit Mediums in Penang.* Stanford: Stanford University Press.

Dentan, Robert Knox (2008) *Overwhelming Terror: Love, Fear, Peace and Violence among Semai of Malaysia.* Lanham: Rowman and Littlefield Publishers.

Easmen, Milton (1972) *Administration and Development in Malaysia.* Ithaca: Cornell University Press.

Endicott, Kirk and Karen Endicott (2007) *The Headman was a Woman.* Long Grove: Waveland Press.

Eriksen, Thomas Hylland and Finn Sivert Nielsen (2001) *A History of Anthropology*. London: Pluto Press.

Fisher, Johan (2008) *Proper Islamic Consumption: Shopping Among the Malays in Modern Malaysia*. Copenhagen: Nordic Institute of Asian Studies.

Freedman, Maurice (1957) *Chinese Family and Marriage in Singapore*. London: HMSO.

Frisk, Sylva (2009) *Submitting to God: Women and Islam in Urban Malaysia*. Seattle: University of Washington Press.

Glazier, Nathan, Samuel Huntington, Manning Nash, and Myron Werner (1970) *Social Science Research for National Unity: A Confidential Report to the Government of Malaysia*. New York: Ford Foundation.

Goh, Beng-Lan (2002) *Modern Dreams: An Enquiry into Power, Cultural Production and the Cityscape in Contemporary Urban Penang*. Ithaca: SEAP Cornell.

——— (2012) "Southeast Asian Perspectives on Disciplines and Afterlives of Areas: Studies in a Global Age." In *Social Science and Knowledge in a Globalising World*, Zawawi Ibrahim, (ed.), pp. 79–102. Kajang & Petaling Jaya: Malaysian Social Science Association & SIRD.

Gomes, Alberto G. (2004) *Looking for Money: Capitalism and Modernity in an Orang Asli Village*. Petaling Jaya: Centre for Orang Asli Concerns.

——— (2007) *Modernity and Malaysia: Settling the Menraq Nomads*. New York & London: Routledge.

Gough, Kathleen (1968) "Anthropology: Child of Imperialism," *Monthly Review* 19(5): pp. 12–27.

Hoffstaedter, Gerhard (2011) *Modern Muslim Identities: Negotiating Religion and Ethnicity in Malaysia*. Copenhagen: NIAS Press.

Holst, Frederick (2014 [2012]) *Ethnicization and Identity Construction in Malaysia*. London & New York: Routledge.

Jain, Ravindra K. (1970) *South Indians on the Plantation Frontier in Malaya*. New Haven: Yale University Press.

Kahn, Joel (2006) *Other Malays: Nationalism and Cosmopolitanism in the Modern Malay World*. Hawai'i: University of Hawai'i Press.

Kent, Alexandra (2007 [2004]) *Divinity and Diversity: A Hindu Revitalization Movement in Malaysia*. Singapore: Institute of Southeast Asian Studies.

Khoo, Khay-Jin (1995) "Antropologi dan sosiologi dalam era baru" ["Anthropology and Sociology in the New Era"]. In *Antropologi dan Sosiologi Menggaris Arah Baru* [*Anthropology and Sociology, Outlining a New Direction*], Abdul Rahman Embong, (ed.), pp. 79–90. Bangi: Universiti Kebangsaan Malaysia.

King, Victor (1999) *Anthropology and Development in Southeast Asia*. Oxford: Oxford University Press.

King, Victor and William Wilder (2002) *The Modern Anthropology of Southeast Asia*. London & New York: Routledge.

Kua, Kia-Soong (2007) *May 13: Declassified Documents on the Malaysian Riots of 1969*. Petaling Jaya: Suaram Kommunikasi.

Lim, Teck-Ghee, Alberto Gomez, and Azly Rahman, (eds.) (2009) *Multiethnic Malaysia: Past, Present and Future*. Petaling Jaya: SIRD.

Lye, Tuck-Po (2004) *Changing Pathways: Forest Degradation and the Batek of Pahang*. Petaling Jaya: SIRD.

____ (2011) "A History of Orang Asli Studies: Landmarks and Generations," *Kajian Malaysia* 29(1): pp. 23–52.

Nobuta, Toshihiro (2006) *Living on the Periphery: Development and Islamization among the Orang Asli in Malaysia*. Subang Jaya: Center for Orang Asli Concerns.

Nonini, Donald (2015) *"Getting By": Class and State Formation among Chinese in Malaysia*. New York: Cornell University Press.

Ong, Aihwa (2006) *Neoliberalism as Exception: Mutations in Citizenship and Sovereignty*. Durham: Duke University Press.

Peletz, Michael (2002) *Islamic Modern: Religious Courts and Cultural Politics in Malaysia*. Princeton: Princeton University Press.

Postill, John (2011) *Localising the Internet: An Anthropological Account*. New York & Oxford: Berghahn Books.

Provencher, Ronald (1979) "An Overview of Malaysian Studies." In *Malaysian Studies: Present Knowledge and Research Trends*, John Lent, (ed.), pp. 437–61. Urbana: Center for Southeast Asian Studies, Northern Illinois University.

Rahimah Abdul Aziz (2005) "Pengajian Ilmu Antropologi dan Sosiologi di Universiti Kebangsaan Malaysia: Menoleh ke Belakang, Melangkah ke Hadapan" ["The Study of Anthropological and Sociological Knowledge at the National University of Malaysia: Looking Back, Stepping Forward"], *Akademika* 66: pp. 51–80.

Rustam Sani (2008) *Failed Nation? Concerns of a Malaysian Nationalist*. Petaling Jaya: SIRD.

Rustam Sani and Noraini Othman (1991) "The Social Sciences in Malaysia: A Critical Scenario," *Ilmu Masyarakat* 19 (April/June): pp. 1–20.

Scott, James (1985) *Weapons of the Weak: Everyday Forms of Peasant Resistance*. New Haven: Yale University Press.

Schottmann, Sven Alexander (2013) "God Helps Those Who Help Themselves: Islam According to Mahathir Mohamad," *Islam and Christian-Muslim Relations* 24(1): pp. 57–69.

Shamsul, A.B. (1993) "Consuming Anthropology: The Social Sciences." In *Consuming Ethnicity and Nationalism: Asian Experiences*, Kosaku Yoshino, (ed.), pp. 133–57. London: Routledge Curzon.

____ (1995) "Malaysia: The Kratonization of Social Science." In *Social Science in Southeast Asia*, Nico Schulte Nordholt and Leontine Visser, (eds.), pp. 87–109. Amsterdam: VU University Press.

——— (1998) "Ethnicity, Class, Culture or Identity? Competing Paradigms in Malaysian Studies," *Akademika* 53: pp. 33–59.

——— (ed.) (2001) "Reputation lives on: On Michael Swift remembered." In *Social Anthropology of the Malays: Collected Essays of M.G. Swift*. Bangi: Universiti Kebangsaan Malaysia.

——— (2004) "Anthropology, Identity and Nation Formation in Malaysia." In *The Making of Anthropology in East and Southeast Asia*, Shinji Yamashita, Joseph Bosco, and J.S. Eades, (eds.), pp. 286–306. New York & Oxford: Berghahn Books.

Sloane, Patricia (1999) *Islam, Modernity and Entrepreneurship among the Malays*. Houndmills, Hampshire: Macmillan Press.

Sutlive Jr, Vinson H. (1979) "Anthropology." In *Malaysian Studies: Present Knowledge and Research Trends*, John Lent, (ed.), pp. 59–134. Urbana: Center for Southeast Asian Studies, Northern Illinois University.

Swift, Michael G. (2001 [1959]) "Rural Sociology in Malaya." In *Social Anthropology of the Malays: Collected Essays of M.G. Swift*, A.B. Shamsul, (ed.). Bangi: Universiti Kebangsaan Malaysia.

Tambiah, Shanthi, Maimuna Hamid Merican, and Ruhan Padzil (2011) "Teaching Gender and Social Justice at the University of Malaya, Malaysia." Unpublished paper.

Tan, Chee-Beng (2004) "Anthropology and Indigenization in a Southeast Asian Setting: Malaysia." In *The Making of Anthropology in East and Southeast Asia*, Shinji Yamashita, Joseph Bosco, and J.S. Eades, (eds.), pp. 307–34. New York & Oxford: Berghahn Books.

Tham, Seong-Chee (1980) "Research Trends in Sociology and Anthropology in the 1970s." In *Social Science Research in Malaysia*. Tokyo: Institute of Development Economics.

Thompson, Eric C. (2007) *Unsettling Absences: Urbanism in Rural Malaysia*. Singapore: NUS Press.

Wazir Jahan Karim (1996) "Anthropology without Tears: How a 'Local' Sees the 'Local' and the 'Global'." In *The Future of Anthropological Knowledge*, Henrietta Moore, (ed.), pp. 115–38. London & New York: Routledge.

——— (1981) *Ma' Betisék Concepts of Living Things*. LSE Monographs in Social Anthropology. London: Athlone Press.

Willford, Andrew (2006) *Cage of Freedom: Tamil Identity and the Ethnic Fetish in Malaysia*. Ann Arbor: Michigan University Press.

——— (2014) *Tamils and the Haunting of Justice: History and Recognition in Malaysia*. Honolulu: University of Hawai'i Press.

Yeoh, Seng-Guan, (eds.) (2014) *The Other Kuala Lumpur: Living in the Shadows of a Globalizing Southeast Asian City*. London & New York: Routledge.

Zainal Kling (1995a) "Pengajian Antropologi dan Sosiologi di Universiti Malaya" ["The Study of Anthropology and Sociology at the University of Malaya"]. In *Antropologi dan Sosiologi Menggaris Arah Baru* [*Anthropology and Sociology, Outlining a New Direction*], Abdul Rahman Embong, (ed.), pp. 53–68. Bangi: Universiti Kebangsaan Malaysia.

_____ (1995b) "Foreword." In *Dimensions of Tradition and Development in Malaysia*, Rokiah Talib and Tan Chee-Beng, (eds.), pp. vi–xv. Petaling Jaya: Pelanduk Publications & Department of Anthropology and Sociology, Universiti Malaya.

Zawawi Ibrahim, (ed.) (1998) *Cultural Contestations: Mediating Identities in a Changing Malaysian Society*. London: Asean Academic Press.

_____ (2010) "The Anthropology of the Malay Peasantry: Critical Reflections on Colonial and Indigenous Scholarship," *Asian Journal of Social Science* 38: pp. 5–36.

CHAPTER 6

DOCUMENTING "ANTHROPOLOGICAL WORK" IN SINGAPORE
The Journey of a Discipline

Vineeta Sinha

Reconstructing the history of anthropology in Singapore has proven to be challenging for a number of reasons, intellectual and practical. Assuming a historical perspective, this chapter has three interrelated aims. First, to detail the institutional structures within which the discipline of anthropology has found a presence in Singapore. The second objective is to document the kind of "anthropological work" that has been done in/from/about Singapore from 1965 to date. A third intention is to articulate the nature of this shared experience across anthropology and sociology over the last fifty-two years, with a view to unpacking their relationship in more substantive terms. Presently, the disciplines of sociology and anthropology coexist at the Department of Sociology at the National University of Singapore (NUS). This disciplinary "joint-ness" and their institutional co-location goes back to the year 1965 when the first Department of Sociology was founded at the then University of Singapore.

The historical material I present, including interview data from founding members of the department and secondary sources, reveals the politics of this coexistence and the high and low points of anthropology's journey in Singapore in an institutional setting. Methodologically, I draw on my own experiential knowledge starting in 1981 as an undergraduate student through to my graduate years and then as a member of the faculty; an intimate association and experience that has framed my own institutional memory of the department and the university. Today, anthropology has a firm, formal, institutional presence within the Department of Sociology. In addition, the discipline also has a pervasive and expansive visibility across the larger Faculty of Arts and Social Sciences (FASS) at NUS. Anthropologists who conduct research in different parts of Asia are located in several other departments in FASS. Collectively their teaching efforts reveal a strong anthropology-based curriculum in five "area studies" departments but also in the Department of English Language and Literature. Undergraduates and graduate students have myriad opportunities for exposure to anthropological methods and theoretical frames and indeed a great deal of student research is inspired by the ethnographic lens.

Apart from NUS, key anthropologists are also on the teaching faculty at Nanyang Technological University (NTU), Singapore Management University (SMU), Singapore University of Technology and Design (SUTD), not to mention a handful at the newly set up Yale-NUS outfit which offers an anthropology major. A comprehensive portrayal or representation of anthropological work in Singapore needs to attend to this much wider presence of the discipline's practitioners on the academic landscape but that is a much larger project. The remit of this chapter is rather more circumscribed, that is to portray how anthropology as a discipline has been conceptualized and sustained within departmental and faculty frames at NUS. The intention is to map and specify the impact of institutional structures over a span of more than fifty years, which have both facilitated and challenged anthropology's very existence. But first, a turn to colonial British Malaya to map how colonial encounters focused an anthropological, ethnographic and natural history lens on the region and the anthropological knowledge(s) thus produced. The latter inevitably constitutes the historical backdrop against which subsequent anthropological work in the region must be theorized.

Colonialism, Anthropology and Knowledge Production

The relationship between anthropology and colonialism has been subjected to considerable critical scrutiny (Asad 1973). The multiplicity of colonial encounters and the historical specificities of these complex processes make it impossible to render any universally generalizable statement about the impact of colonialism of knowledge production (see especially Canuday and Porio; Peou; Nguyen, this volume). The relationship between colonialism and anthropology is an idiom for engaging in a discussion about the ethical and political underpinnings of the discipline. The notice of crises within Euro-American anthropology and questions about its future, articulated in postcolonial, postmodernist, post-Orientalist and feminist scholarships are plentiful by now. In Britain the challenge to functionalist anthropology occurred in the post-World War II era with the end of formal colonial rule and the rise of nationalist movements (Asad 1973; Banaji 1970; Greg and Williams 1948; Hooker 1963; Jarvie 1964; Lewis 1973; Maquet 1964; Worsley 1968). In the USA, the challenge to cultural anthropology came in the wake of revelations about the US government's use of anthropologists to undertake research surreptitiously for strategic, political reasons—in Southeast Asia, South Asia and Latin America (Berreman 1968; Gough 1968a; Gjessing 1968; Hymes, Huizer and Mannheim 1970; Wolf and Jorgensen 1970).

In 1973, Asad observed that "there is a strange reluctance on the part of most professional anthropologists to consider seriously the power structure within which the discipline has taken shape" (1973: 15), a critique that was challenged by practitioners who cited counter-examples including the work of Victor Turner (1971) and Raymond Firth (1972). At the same time it would be simplistic to accept that anthropology was merely a "child" or "handmaiden" of colonialism (Gough 1968a, 1968b). James (1973) offers a useful reminder that this was a vexed relationship and far from one of complete collegiality and complementarity between colonial administrators and anthropologists. These two parties (when they could be clearly separated) did sometimes have an oppositional relationship and neither the discipline nor its practitioners had a direct role in "building empire." The links, liaisons, connections and influences were much more nuanced and indirect. Undeniably, early generations of ethnographers working in the colonies successfully engaged in their "trade" and professional activities due to these existing hegemonic relations between the colonizer and the colonized. The work that anthropologists performed in the name of generating scholarly knowledge not only had the potential of being utilized but was in fact invoked to further colonial interests and agendas.

Anthropological narratives from former colonies like India, Sri Lanka, the Philippines and Indonesia have noted the discipline's links with the complex and multifaceted experience of colonialism and how anthropology and anthropologists have (though not necessarily intentionally) participated in imperialist projects (Asad 1973). These associations between anthropological knowledge production and colonial rule have been problematized through a series of questions: Were anthropologists as colonial administrators complicit with the colonial process or was the link more subtle and indirect? How did a colonial context facilitate anthropological research? Which features of native life were accorded visibility and which remained unnoticed in the act of knowledge production? How did relations of domination and subordination affect access to natives as informants and the collection of data, as well as the interpretations that were subsequently offered? There has been much scholarly activity in this field and complex responses to these critical questions. The role of "administrator-anthropologist" in colonial governance and knowledge production has been noted in many colonies.

In the case of India, the work of this category of social actors has marked the world of tribes and castes "and its administration" (King 2007: 97). Although Indian anthropologists have tried to expand their repertoire by carrying their research to other areas such as education, housing, population studies, rural planning, structures in the workplace and urban contexts, tribal welfare and the concern with scheduled castes and tribes have remained their expertise. The administrator-anthropologist's preoccupation with "primitives" and "tribes" and the early engagement of Indian scholars with the same issues continue to haunt Indian anthropologists today.

The detailed mapping of "tribes" and "castes" through categories of colonial administration led to their reification and ossification in India. Verrier Elwin, an English missionary turned anthropologist, served as an advisor on tribal affairs to Jawaharlal Nehru, the first prime minister of independent India. Upon the advice of the former, Nehru devised a plan for the appropriate administration of tribes in India. Elwin's contributions have taken on the proportion of a myth/legend in Indian anthropological circles, but were at the time vehemently opposed by some Indian anthropologists. Amongst them was G.S. Ghurye who argued that the best solution to the tribal "problem" was to assimilate them into mainstream Hindu society. Keeping them in isolated "national parks," he elaborated, would lead to accusations that anthropologists were trying to keep the tribes "primitive" to facilitate their discipline's interests.

In comparison to the nuanced African and Indian material on the subject, one struggles to find similar works for British Malaya. This lacuna can partly be explained by the rather different terms on which British colonialism was translated into practice in the region and the mode in which it affected colonized peoples. While there was clear resistance to colonial forces in British Malaya, by and large, the impact of colonialism in places like Singapore and parts of Malaysia has been interpreted in rather more benign terms using the language of non-violence and non-confrontation. Certainly in the Straits Settlements, British input from the nineteenth century is perceived to have had a modernizing effect, engendering economic progress and commercial success, revealing the biases of colonial historiography.[1] Turning to the impact of colonial rule in British Malaya in general, the scholarship is thin, although some crucial works are available. Generally speaking, the more insidious and destructive impact of colonial rule in British Malaya has received less scholarly attention, a rare exception being Syed Hussein Alatas' *The Myth of the Lazy Native* (1977). In this book, Alatas documents not just the structure and tone of imperial rule but how colonialist narratives were internalized and normalized by colonized populations, leading to their failure to either recognize the pitfalls of such ideological manipulation or to act on it.

Thompson (2012) has rightly noted that the history of anthropology in Singapore is yet to be fully narrated. Indeed, a comprehensive account demands a deeper historical perspective in documenting anthropological research in Singapore as part of British Malaya. With respect to the Malayan context, the story of anthropology's intersection with colonial encounters is yet to be told comprehensively (also see Yeoh; King and Zawawi, this volume). What kind of "anthropological" presence in Malaya existed during the period of colonial rule? What was the motivation of colonial administrators for collecting and commissioning various kinds of data about the physical and natural landscape of the colony, together with sociocultural and linguistic details of native life and how was such information relevant (or utilized) in the task of administration and governance? Most crucially, how does one write and reconstruct the history of anthropology in the context of Malayan society with a rather atypical experience of British colonialism? These are fascinating but testing questions that demand considered responses.

At least part of the challenge has to do with access to particular kinds of data that will allow a historically informed narrative. An obvious place to begin is the Straits Branch of the Royal Asiatic Society (SBRAS)[2] which was established in 1877 by a group of colonial administrators in Singapore and reflected interest in the life of the "natives" in the Malay Peninsula and the archipelago. In the same year, this body established an important publication, the *Journal of the Straits Branch of the Royal Asiatic Society*, which carried scholarship about the physical and natural landscape of the region, including its botany and zoology together with an interest in history, culture and archeology of these territories. There were concerns that resonated with mid nineteenth-century conceptions of anthropology in Britain, with its strong roots in the discipline of natural history and its emphasis on documenting flora and fauna of regions—including its human populations. An institutional history of this society and others like this, together with a review of the works published in journals and periodicals would reveal how anthropology was practiced in the region during the colonial period and with what effects. Information about the folklore, language, magic, mystical and healing practices of its inhabitants is embedded in these pages, primarily through contributions and input of colonial administrators who were additionally fascinated by the cultural life of the "natives" and doubled as anthropologists, sometimes unintentionally.

Another strategy for documenting anthropological work in the colonial period would be a biographical approach and would require scrutiny of their works and engagements, including those of such luminaries as William Farquhar, Stamford Raffles, but also W.W. Skeat, R.O. Winstedt, W.E. Maxwell, R.J. Wilkinson, R. Braddell and H.N. Ridley, all of whom, in rather different modes, contributed to an early "colonial anthropology" of these regions. Collectively they contributed to crystallizing both a regional and intellectual space for anthropological enquiries and constructing an object of inquiry for the discipline. Such construction was accomplished by naming specific sociocultural elements (magic, mysticism, supernatural beliefs, etc.) as constitutive of native identities and by ignoring other aspects, for example the presence of religion as a rational system of beliefs, scientific knowledge or theories of land tenure or systems of political governance.

Daniel Goh's incisive work (2007), is a rare example of theorizing colonial state input in the production of multiculturalism in British

Malaya—and the firm persistence of its discursive practices in nation-state and postcolonial contexts. Goh explores these themes in his comparative work on the Philippines and Malaya in scrutinizing the relationship between colonialism and ethnography. Sandra Khor Manickam's exciting book, *Taming the Wild* (2015) is another excellent illustration of the kind of detailed historical work that needs to be done. Manickam follows the careers, preoccupations and contributions of "administrator-anthropologists" in museums, census and other government departments in British Malaya—William Marsden and John Leyden (and their concern with the originality question), Stamford Raffles and John Crawfurd (highlighting for these two men the relationship between slavery and scholarship), John Andersen and T.J. Newbold (and their framing the "aborigines-Malay" encounter), Ivor, H.N Evans and H.D. Noone—to demonstrate the "changing relationship between anthropology and Malaya's colonial government" (ibid.: 183). H.D. Noone, the local correspondent for the Royal Anthropological Institute for the East Indies, for instance, wrote about the Senoi of Perak and Kelantan. Manickam notes that he was "commissioned as an anthropologist studying aboriginal peoples and to make government recommendations about what action the government should take in that regard" (ibid.: 183). Mapping the contours of "colonial anthropology," she concludes that "official government work was an enabling factor for anthropological research into indigenous peoples" (ibid.: 170).[3]

Notably then it is possible to identify a body of naturalist history and ethnographic work and thus speak of anthropology's visibility in the region during the colonial period. Figures like Skeat, Ridley and Winstedt have been viewed as forerunners of future ethnographic research in the Malay Peninsula, but I suggest in the sections to follow that while some elements and emphases have persisted, there have also been crucial discontinuities and a disconnect both in the institutionalization of the discipline across these periods and the anthropological work carried out within in the contemporary moment.

A related challenge concerns the issue of how to conceptualize and theorize the relationship between anthropological research and specific regions. Is defining anthropology according to boundaries of nation states (a post-World War II phenomenon for many former colonies) the most meaningful mode of recognizing and representing configurations of the discipline? For example, does it make sense to speak of "Singapore's" anthropological tradition given that this nation state has come into existence officially in 1965, prior to which it was part of several other regional configurations? Historically, Singapore has been a constituent part of several other geographical descriptions—the Straits Settlements, British Malaya and Malaya—during a period of British colonial rule, starting in 1819 through to partial self-government in 1959 and moving to independent nationhood in 1965. Through these periods of political transition and governance, the British retained interest and control in the region first through the involvement of the English East India Company and then as a Crown Colony. Would different territorial descriptors, such as the Straits Settlements, British Malaya and Malaya, be more meaningful given the island's historical embeddedness?[4] These queries demand responses and are constitutive of the story of anthropology's presence in Singapore, but such a comprehensive historical project is clearly beyond the scope of the remainder of this chapter, which speaks specifically to the more recent presence of anthropology in Singapore since the mid 1960s.

Relevance of Anthropology in Singapore

The introduction of anthropology to the university system in Asian contexts is a post-World War II phenomenon (Shamsul 2004). A survey of the scholarship unearths no more than a handful of historical accounts about the founding of social science disciplines in Singapore and Malaysia. In the noted absence of sustained historical research about the kindred disciplines of sociology and anthropology in a postcolonial, nationalist moment, a search for their origins and importation into Singapore leads to but a few scattered references (Benjamin 1991; Chen 1976; Quah 1999). In these accounts, institutionalized traces of social science disciplines (including sociology, psychology and anthropology) in Singapore have been noted to be fairly recent, taking us no further back than the 1950s and 1960s. The Department of Sociology was formally established at the University of Singapore in 1965 but Benjamin observes that "some sociology and social anthropology had already been taught at the University for fifteen years" (1989: 1). These traces appeared in a "special unit" housed within the Department of Economics, an entity that subsequently morphed into independent departments named "Social Studies" and then "Applied Social Studies" (ibid.).[5]

The institutionalization of the social sciences in the University of Singapore was far from a unique event. It was instead part of the formalization of its fields of study globally and certainly within decolonized parts of the world.[6] However, already in Singapore in the early 1960s, there were discussions about how to "widen the scope of teaching and research in the social sciences" (ibid.), and a committee was set up to debate these issues. Under the auspices of the then Dean, this committee recommended that "the University should set up a Research Centre, and Departments of Psychology, of Social Work, and of Sociology and Anthropology. The suggestion to allocate a separate department to the latter two subjects was rejected as likely to weaken both disciplines" (ibid.). It would seem from Benjamin's narrative that this early formal conjoining of the two disciplines in a single department was in the first instance a practical decision designed to ensure a consolidation of social science teaching and research, a resolution which nonetheless carried consequences for the intellectual directions the disciplines would traverse.

Given the rather tenuous positioning of anthropology in NUS through the 1970s and 1980s, it is perhaps ironic that the newly formed Department of Sociology was first headed by an Australian social anthropologist, Murray Groves, who had done fieldwork in Papua New Guinea and who also "instilled a concern for methodological rigour that marks much of Singaporean sociology" (Benjamin 1996: 1). Social and cultural anthropology thus already had an early presence in the department in the form of this leadership. A colleague of Groves recalls that he "was a strong-willed character, always at odds with the university administration" (personal communication). Groves remained in this leadership position till 1968, when he "had gone on long leave and declined to return" (Benjamin 1989: 2).[7] The American sociologist, Joseph Tamney who had an interest in Chinese society was appointed as Acting Head from 1969 to 1970 and Riaz Hassan, an American-trained sociologist from Pakistan who had joined the department in 1968, held fort till 1971. H.D. Evers, a German sociologist with American training and considerable fieldwork experience in Southeast Asia, was appointed Head of Department in 1971, a post he held until 1974. He recalls his coming to Singapore as follows:

> I first visited the Sociology Department in 1969, while returning from field research in Padang, West Sumatra ... In 1970 I met then PM Lee Kuan Yew at Yale University, while I was there as Associate Prof of Sociology and Director of Southeast Asian Studies. The event set a process in motion that eventually brought me to Singapore as Head of the Sociology Department [until 1974] (personal e-mail communication).

Colleagues who worked alongside H.D. Evers have noted the critical role he played in shaping research, teaching and administrative practices at the department in these formative years; he was also instrumental in stimulating empirical, local research and expanding the scope and range of topics taught and researched in the department. Benjamin (1989: 4) notes:

> Hans Evers was a strong influence on the Department's attempts to indigenize the sociological and anthropological materials being used, and he took an active interest in the quality and overall structuring of the teaching. He democratized decision-making processes in the Department by instituting regular meetings at which problems were openly discussed; in some cases this involved elected student representatives. He put the weekly Research Seminars—which had been started some years earlier by Chiew Seen Kong when he was a Master's student—on a formal basis, at a time when such activities were rare elsewhere in the University. Postgraduate research was given a boost at this time; several Master's degrees had already been awarded, but now the department had doctoral candidates too. Most importantly Professor Evers instituted the Working Papers, largely to encourage members of the Department to aim for international publication of their research by circulating draft versions in semi-published format.

It is not insignificant that while sociology and anthropology streams coexisted in the department from the outset, they were marked as "distinct" and did not produce an amalgamated "social anthropology" as in other Asian contexts like India, the Philippines and Indonesia. Interestingly, a 1967 advertisement for lecturers at the Singapore department, specified different teaching fields without asking for the disciplinary background of candidates:

> **University of Singapore**: Lecturer or assistant lecturer; teach undergraduate courses in one or more of the following fields: sociological statistics, demography, urban sociology, industrial sociology, race relations, political sociology, sociology of religion, kinship and family, social stratification, social change; contract 3–5 years with gratuity; every opportunity and encouragement for research in Southeast Asia (*The American Sociologist* 1967: 44).

The first full-time social anthropologist, Geoffrey Benjamin, who was Cambridge-trained and worked with the Temiars in Malaysia, was appointed to the department in 1967. The first Singaporean to join the department was Peter Chen, an American-trained sociologist who arrived in 1970. Despite being embedded within a British system of tertiary education, there was an overall gradual shift in the department in terms of an American emphasis, seen in the hiring of American-trained faculty members. This early period saw the co-location of "American-style sociology with British-style social anthropology" (Benjamin 1989: 2) and a faculty largely made up of non-Singaporeans. Singaporean and Asian scholars gradually began to be appointed in the 1970s. With respect to anthropology, although the model of British anthropology prevailed, the presence of and input from American-trained anthropologists gradually increased at the department.

In the 1970s, the Singapore government had a keen interest in the kind of research that was being produced at the department. Already there was the view that the social sciences should be undertaking "relevant" research, reflecting the concerns, priorities and direction of a newly emerging nation state managing the dynamics of a multi-ethnic, multi-religious population. Evers notes that in the 1970s:

> The government, represented by PAP VC Toh Chin Chye kept a close watch on our research efforts. Work on HDB housing and on hawkers was welcome, work on industrial workers for NTUC was stopped. I myself did what I called "Saturday afternoon anthropology" by collecting data on Kuburan keramat and other holy places. I never wrote up my field notes, but turned them over to ISEAS (personal communication).

The department started teaching in 1966, with an offering of three courses (Benjamin 1989; Quah 1995) and with only three faculty members. Within a decade, thirteen full-time and seven part-time teaching staff existed (together with five visiting lecturers) and an impressive total of twenty-eight courses were offered. These emphasized "social aspects of economic, political, ecological, demographic and cultural change in Singapore and Southeast Asia" (*Department of Sociology, Prospectus*, 1974/5, 1). According to the department's prospectus for 1974/75, undergraduates were expected to take two compulsory modules—one in sociology and one in anthropology—a situation that continued uninterrupted till 1998 or so. In 1975, social anthropology courses (with a focus on Singapore and Southeast Asia) were offered in the second, third and fourth years, and examinations were set on established anthropological curricula. An honors level thesis—the "Academic Exercise"—which emphasized primary research through fieldwork in the generation of original data was introduced. The department thus embarked on a tradition of student research by instituting the honors thesis and postgraduate research and was also successful in drawing students at these levels. As noted in the 1974/75 Department Prospectus: "The department also offers opportunities for postgraduate work in sociology and social anthropology. At present there are ten graduate students working on their master's or doctoral degree [*sic*] in the department (ibid.)."

In fact, it was a requirement that at the honors level, thesis work undertaken by students must be grounded in primary fieldwork—this indeed has been a hallmark of the anthropological tradition in Singapore and links these efforts with similar endeavors elsewhere. Since these early days, the honors and graduate student research that has been generated at the department is expected to prioritize attention to empirical and ethnographic detail. While students through the years have requested to pursue non-fieldwork based topics (either in the use of secondary data or in considering theoretical subjects) for their thesis, these topics have not generally been encouraged.

Funding for social science research was provided largely by the Singapore government, a situation that persists. In addition, social science research was supported by global and local foundations, which had a general interest in stimulating local social science research. There was a felt need to generate important information about the kinds of sociocultural, economic and political changes that were occurring in a rapidly industrializing and urbanizing Singapore. In a promotional tone, the Department Prospectus of 1974/75 noted:

> Singapore offers excellent opportunities for Sociological and Social Anthropological research and there has been considerable interest in expanding such research. Several international and local organizations such as the Ford Foundation, the Asia Foundation, the IDRC [International Development Research Centre], the Population Council, the Wenner-Gren Foundation, the Royal Anthropological Institute, AMIC [Asian Media Information and Communication Centre], the Friedrich-Eibert Foundation and the Lee Foundation have financed research projects carried out in Singapore and elsewhere in Southeast Asia by members of the sociology department (p. 1).

These funding opportunities for research served to stimulate a strong empirical interest amongst practitioners but also increasingly a concern with producing "local" knowledge, often about Singapore. This empirical bent, some have noted, was at the expense of developing a theoretical stance in Singapore sociology (Benjamin 1989: 3). As far as anthropological research was concerned, it was not confined to Singapore, as anthropologists did venture into Southeast Asian and South Asian terrains and researched a variety of topics.

Anthropological Work in/from/about Singapore

The emphasis in post-independence Singapore was on economic development and planned social change. This reflected the context of a newly independent Third World country where economic development and the restructuring of societal domains were urgent priorities. The expectation that social science research output should feed into the nation-building project demanded that this research should be "relevant," if not contribute directly to the modernizing process. In such a context, what contributions could the discipline of anthropology in Singapore make, especially as it was stereotypically portrayed as being concerned with "tribes," "primitives" and "backward communities"? The discipline of anthropology in Singapore was seen to be largely "irrelevant" to this modernization and nation-building project and marginalized in at least two ways: first, through its focus on research beyond Singapore and, second, in the fact that it could not claim an "anthropological other" in the Singapore context to legitimize its existence. In any case, there is little evidence that anthropologists in Singapore tried to break out of the discipline's inherited "savage slot" in order to build an alternative identity or play the "culture card."

Negative, stereotypical perceptions about anthropology as being defined by its association with the tribal, rural world and with primitive peoples denied it the potential/capacity to contribute to the nation-building project or to speak to a society "in transition." How could such a discipline be relevant to, or contribute to the construction of a modern, developed nation state? While anthropological research was not deemed relevant for making sense of an industrializing, modernizing urban society, from about the mid 1970s, several anthropologists based at the department did undertake research about sociocultural details of Singapore society, particularly within the context of a rapidly urbanizing and changing society (Babb 1974a,

1974b, 1976, 1978; Benjamin 1976; Hassan 1976). One enduring feature of anthropological work in Singapore over time has been precisely its contribution to urban anthropology in the production of urban ethnographies since the mid 1970s. A collection of essays carried in the volume, *Singapore: Society in Transition* (1976) edited by Riaz Hassan illustrates this well.

The research efforts of sociologists and anthropologists in the first decade of the department's founding were concentrated on generating empirical data about Singapore and the Southeast Asian region. The substantive focus of the emergent body of anthropological knowledge straddled the following domains: kinship, religious practices, health, language, urban life, race, ethnicity and multiculturalism. In 1974, the department described its research focus as follows: "Research in the department can be categorised under four broad areas: (1) social problems of rapid industrialisation (2) social problems of rapid urbanization (3) changing occupational structures and (4) changing sociocultural patterns" (*Department of Sociology, Prospectus* 1974/75: 2).

Interestingly it was in the last category that a great deal of anthropological work was slotted, including: "Studies on national identity, ethnic relations, attitudes towards Western medicine and ethnographic research" (ibid.).

Without being articulated explicitly as such, we see here the association of anthropological research with research on the "self," contrary to the classic definition of anthropology's concern with understanding the "other." This was hardly surprising given the greater numbers of Singaporean students enrolling for graduate studies at the Department of Sociology. This was far from a unique trend, with ready examples from the Indian context, popularized and legitimized by M.N. Srinivas, who promoted "self-study" by "native anthropologists." Thus Singaporean social anthropologists (and certainly sociologists) conducted research in their own backyard. In this context, where the anthropological "other" could not be readily identified and appropriated by anthropologists for scrutiny. It was the ethnic and religious minorities who moved into and "occupied" this slot and thus became the focus of anthropologists—both local and foreign. Additionally, anthropological research did concern itself with tribal groups in Malaysia and Orang Asli communities in Singapore and its offshore islands, in addition to undertaking some comparative research in the broader Southeast Asian region, especially Indonesia.

This regional focus, and especially on Singapore, was with a view to generating data about the sociocultural and religious life on the island, and led to a prioritizing of empirical research but also plugged a crucial gap in social science scholarship. Strikingly, in the early decades of the department, there was a larger, comparative interest amongst sociologists and anthropologists in other regions, like India, Fiji, Hong Kong and China, either through the efforts of full-time staff or visitors. There was a narrowing of research interests to Singapore and to certain regions in Southeast Asia, with negligible cross-cultural interest beyond, even in East Asia or South Asia, for example. However, recently there have been important shifts in reaching out towards these regions.

In the mid 1970s, the department's research agenda made explicit connections with the issues of practical importance and social development and rather unreflexively specified its regional interest, describing its research orientation thus:

> Studies are generally related to practical problems of social development in Singapore and other Southeast Asian societies. Though every effort is made to utilise sociological and anthropological theories to explain the social processes studied, the research programme generally takes its focus from pressing day-to-day problems of rapidly changing societies rather than from problems posed by current sociological theory. Research in the Department tends therefore to be problem-oriented rather than theory-oriented (*Department of Sociology, Prospectus* 1974/75: 11).

An assessment of the tenor of anthropological research through the 1990s, 2000s and into the present suggests that there has been a significant shift away from these early emphases. Certainly, far greater attention to conceptual and theoretical issues is evident in ethnographic, empirical work of recent years, a positive move for the discipline's maturity in Singapore.

After five decades of existence, is it possible to speak of an "anthropological tradition"—Singapore style? Is anthropological work produced in Singapore typified by particular features? One important thing to note is that anthropological work produced by Singapore-trained students is defined by methodological rigor, emphasizes empirical grounding and the methodologies of fieldwork and participant observation. Adequate evidence for this is available in the goldmine of mostly unpublished student research about Singapore that is produced in honors year "Academic Exercises" and master's and PhD theses at the Department of Sociology at NUS.[8] A great deal of original, primary qualitative data and theorizing about sociocultural and political features of life in Singapore lies buried in these efforts. Another feature is the documentation of sociocultural, religious and political practices and their embeddedness within an urban context, by the sustained production of urban ethnographies, of a society in transformation.

Among the many substantive topics addressed by anthropologists, the study of Singapore's religious landscape has engaged students over several generations. Students of religion have researched a variety of religious traditions and their intersection with social, economic and political forces in Singapore—and especially religious practice in urban, bureaucratic and modernist frames. Singapore-based sociologists and anthropologists have produced nuanced accounts of Chinese religion, Islam, Buddhism and Hinduism (Mariam Mohd Ali 1986; Nilavu Mohd Ali 1985; Rajah 1975; Sinha 1985, 1988; Stephens 1982; Tong 1980; Wee 1977). This body of work is not only ethnographically rich but also engages important theoretical questions, starting with the very critique of the category "religion." For example, Geoffrey Benjamin and Syed Farid Alatas have both problematized this category in their work (Alatas 1993; Benjamin 1987). Despite being defined as a highly sensitive subject, "religion" has been a popular field of study both amongst faculty and graduate students. At the level of teaching, "religion modules" continue to be popular and have consistently attracted large student enrollments, with the teaching of religion-specific courses having been enhanced by primary research on religions in Singapore. Although, interestingly, in the last 5–6 years student interest in this topic seems to be waning. Similar benefits derived from primary research and its relationship to teaching have been seen with regard to the study of race and ethnicity, transnationalism and migration, food and food-ways, family and kinship, as well as numerous other topics.

Unpacking a "Joint" Relationship

In many ways, the full formalization of anthropology as an autonomous discipline in Singapore remains an unfinished project. To date there has been no separate Department of Anthropology, although individual anthropologists have found a home in several departments in FASS at NUS. Neither have strong calls for a separate department been made by practitioners. From the outset in 1965, anthropology in an institutional setting existed in an entity named and recognized as a "Department of Sociology." In this shared existence, the two disciplines were weighted differently. The Singapore situation was one where a joint department carried two separate disciplines, with differing interests and strengths and there was little intellectual convergence. Although practitioners of the discipline invoked the description, "social anthropology," sociologists and anthropologists did not attempt to bridge the theoretical or methodological divide between sociology and anthropology or seek to build a common discursive space.

Members of the department have observed that despite the institutional "joint-ness" of the department, anthropology has been the "poorer cousin" and has not always enjoyed "equal" status with sociology. However, it must be remembered that sociology, too, struggled to demonstrate its competence and relevance in the early decades of the department's establishment. Sociology has been prioritized in terms of numbers of faculty appointments, funding for research, and the bent of the undergraduate curriculum, especially the nature and number of courses offered. The subsidiary status of anthropology was reflected in the fewer number of anthropologists that were hired and the number of courses that were dedicated to anthropology. Yet, cultural anthropology did have a presence in this early institutional social science configuration. Through the 1970s, several prominent anthropologists visited the department for varying periods, including M.N. Srinivas, Clifford Geertz, Lawrence Babb, Peter Metcalf and Mark Hobart. The years between 1982 and 1988 were probably the most exciting, in terms of the range of anthropology courses taught by enthusiastic and internationally recognized anthropologists.

With the expansion of the tertiary education scene in Singapore in the 1980s, there were greater opportunities for "increased recruitment of sociologists and social anthropologists" (Benjamin 1996: 2) but "in a ratio of roughly 3:1 as faculty" (ibid.).[9] In her 1995 survey of sociology in Singapore, Stella Quah (1995: 89) acknowledges that sociology and anthropology have coexisted here, but notes the dominance of sociology on the basis of courses offered and number of faculty members. By the mid 1980s, the report card on sociology was a highly positive one, as seen in the faculty strength of the department at NUS, its research output and publications and its capacity to attract undergraduate and graduate students (Chen 1986). Yet, it is important to remember that sociology did not always enjoy tthis status. In the 1970s, sociology had to legitimize itself and justify its existence. Benjamin notes a widely held perception even within the university that "sociologists were simply reporting, at great length, what they already knew to be the case" (1989: 2).

While it is critical to map the institutional scene vis-á-vis relations between sociology and the anthropology in Singapore, it is further crucial to "unpack" the relationship in more substantive terms, by drawing on the narratives of practitioners in the field. My further comments in this section draw on discussions and interviews with such practitioners, who have been both students and faculty members in the department.[10] Deconstructing this relationship also requires access to specific kinds of data, of "articulated/official" and "implicit/unofficial" varieties. While some published, official data about anthropological research and teaching are available in the department's archives, it is far more challenging, if not impossible, to access the everyday attitudes and decisions embodied in the thoughts and practices of individuals who were "in charge" at the department and faculty levels for example. The latter's actions and judgments would have had an impact on the experiences of individual anthropologists (and sociologists) at the level of teaching and research and certainly recruitment and retention of faculty.

Another challenge has been to access information about the everyday politics of the department, given that some who were involved in managing and leading the department and faculty in its formative periods still remain connected in various ways to the department, faculty and university. In trying to elicit experiential knowledge from colleagues at the department, expectedly a further obstacle was that individuals were hesitant to articulate controversial views, in acknowledging past departmental politics. However, I did have some success in this endeavor as some parties were surprisingly forthcoming.

An important caveat is that in accessing these individual narratives, I did not simply capture subjective experiences but also tapped into institutional memories carried and embedded in individual recollections. By a stroke of good fortune I was able to access (by e-mail communication and through face to face interviews) recollections, remembrances, anecdotes and experiences from a group of anthropologists who were in the department from the mid 1970s—both those who stayed for long periods and those who were visitors. I was also able to access narratives from some students of anthropology who pursued honors and graduate research at the department in the 1980s and 1990s. Within the ambit of these constraints, the following account presents a construction of what it was like to be in a joint "Soci-Anthro" department at the level of practice, from the perspective of former and current faculty and students.

A social anthropologist in the department from the mid 1970s remembers the relationship between anthropology and sociology at the department thus:

> This was in 1976. Anthropology was then the poor relation of sociology and I think there were only three or four of us. But we were all very productive and were a good counter-weight to the very quantitative, methodology-oriented stuff going on amongst the sociologists. Our students went on to some first-class graduate schools so we must have done something right. Anthropology had a rather ambiguous status—considered a bit marginal on the one hand but also somehow "deeper" than the local sociology (personal e-mail communication).

The same former colleague noted that one significant difference between the two disciplines came down to the question of methodology. However, on other practical everyday matters of teaching and research supervision, he perceives a common ground across the two disciplines, a situation that he contrasts with his experience in the UK:

> But in Singapore I found that despite the slightly marginal status that anthropology had in the department this was not for serious intellectual reasons, but because we did not much use numbers and were not fixated on methodology, which then meant quantitative methodology. In terms of our ideas I think there was a grudging feeling that we were ahead and that the anthropologists' work was more universal, better grounded in theory and interesting. We were certainly left alone to do our thing and at the level of the actual daily running of the department (academic exercises, exams, etc.) there was no distinction at all. We also had better international links, and I think that the department valued that although the university was always grudging with conference leave (personal e-mail communication).

Lawrence Babb, a visiting research fellow at the Department in 1973–74, who did pioneering and widely cited work on popular Hinduism in Singapore, recalls the department scene thus:

> It was a department of sociology housing both sociologists and anthropologists. It seemed to me to be a comfortable arrangement, and of course sociology and social anthropology grade into each other in a fairly seamless way. I learnt much from my colleagues in the department, and thoroughly enjoyed the departmental seminars in which I was encouraged to take part. I was but a temporary sojourner, but my association with the department was a true stepping stone in my growth as a social anthropologist (personal e-mail communication).

This view of a natural comfort zone between qualitative sociology and cultural anthropology would no doubt resonate with practitioners in a place like India where the two disciplines were institutionalized in many places with ease. Antagonism across the two fields, typical in American and UK academic landscapes, seems not to have been replicated in Singapore—certainly not through the 1970s and into the early 1980s. Anthropologists who were in the department in these periods also report that there was little interference and meddling from either the department or university leadership or from sociologists in their work, although they are highly critical of the broader bureaucratic and what they deemed to be authoritarian university structures.

During this period, anthropologists report some level of indifference on the part of their sociology colleagues but also note that there was no expressed hostility. Certainly there seems to have been no consolidated effort to eject anthropologists from the department or to eliminate the discipline. Despite feeling somewhat marginalized, anthropologists did not call for a separate institutional location and identity for themselves. In fact it would appear that to some extent this marginality "freed" anthropologists from having to be concerned with solving problems of an emergent developing society, or be forced to do research on Singapore, and it also facilitated basic anthropological research liberated from applied considerations and beyond Singapore.

In several locations including Singapore, declining student interest in anthropology courses and reduced student enrollments have often been cited as justifications for reducing emphasis on anthropology or for removing institutional support (Shamsul 2004). Admittedly, the overall numbers who enrolled in undergraduate anthropology courses in Singapore were smaller than those in the sociology courses. Certainly, a category of students found anthropology courses "more interesting" and opted to not only enrol in them but also pursue dedicated research at honors and graduate levels. Speaking from personal experience and from conversations with some of these students in the mid to late 1980s, those who came to anthropology liked its comparative, cross-cultural reach, its focus on a universal human condition, its scrutiny of diverse human cultures and its comparative lens; they appreciated its concern with long-term human history, garnered from discussions of physical and biological anthropology; some were indeed fascinated with the discussion on tribes and primitive groups, which to them appeared exotic, but many were also attracted to studying minorities and marginalized communities; the ethnographic method and doing fieldwork with "real people" were additional appeals. Not surprisingly, over the years, at honors and postgraduate levels, students have opted to undertake qualitative and ethnographic research under the supervision of anthropologists and sociologists.

The main perceived difference between sociology and anthropology amongst students and some faculty seemed to rest on the choice of methodology—represented by the polarities of "qualitative" and "quantitative" methods. Already in the 1970s, sociologists at the department aspired to undertake survey research using quantitative methodologies and data analysis techniques that Benjamin notes "came to be recognized by others as Singapore style of sociology" (1989: 2). In contrast, anthropologists prioritized qualitative research methodologies, using participant observation, in-depth interviews, life histories and case studies.[11] In Singapore, fieldwork and the ethnographic approach were associated exclusively with the discipline of anthropology and not sociology. This is ironic given the centrality of qualitative research techniques and, in particular, ethnographic approaches in the history of sociology elsewhere, especially urban sociology.

At an institutional level, sociology and anthropology seemed to have begun more or less on an equal footing, even though anthropology was invisible in the overt naming of the department. Over time, however, sociology was perceived to be more relevant to the needs of a developing, modern, urban society. Despite this logic, anthropology continued to be conspicuous in the department's undergraduate curriculum and research undertakings. Indeed, from the outset two first-year courses, Introduction to Anthropology (SC102) and Introduction to Sociology (SC101) were compulsory for all students majoring in sociology. But in 1998, with a reorganizing of the degree structure and curriculum, students majoring in a subject could be asked to do only one essential module. SC102 was made optional, and SC101 was the preferred departmental choice on the basis of higher enrollments, which were interpreted as registering greater popularity. Even then, the optional module continued to attract significant numbers of students, not all of whom would go on to major in sociology.

Starting in the mid 1990s, anthropology experienced a low point with a large number of anthropologists leaving the department. Amongst these were pioneering members of the department who were crucial in shaping and institutionalizing the teaching of social anthropology. This has undoubtedly reconfigured the kind of presence anthropology has subsequently had in the department. With the departure of five key social anthropologists (four British trained and one American trained) through the late 1980s and into the 1990s, the influence of British-style social anthropology waned, and was gradually replaced by American-trained anthropologists—both Singaporean and non-Singaporean. This exodus was due to a combination of structural factors and personal career choices, but also reflects disciplinary politics within the department at the time.

Beginning around the year 2000, largely American-trained anthropologists (many of whom are non-Singaporeans) have been gradually hired. On the basis of the cumulative evidence presented thus far and despite the absence of a separate institutional entity dedicated to anthropology, we see that anthropological research and anthropologists have had a sustained visibility in Singapore for more than fifty years. The future of anthropology as a discipline in Singapore is linked to the structural frameworks within which it is located and operates. Today, anthropological research has a vigorous presence in Singapore largely through individual research and publication initiatives and teaching endeavors.[12]

Currently, the "unequal" relationship (in terms of faculty strength and curriculum) between sociology and anthropology at NUS persists, although in the present institutional configuration there is no antipathy to anthropology. At the level of individual research, anthropologists and sociologists are marked by their disciplinary commitments, especially at the level of methodology. Some disciplinary-specific modules (many of them essential) continue to exist and are taught by respective practitioners. However, significant shifts in a positive direction are discernible. For instance, in recent curriculum review exercises, several courses were renamed to enable both anthropologists and sociologists to teach them, while in the supervision of student research and examination of theses (honors and graduate), a similar fluidity and flexibility prevails. As a result of changes implemented at the faculty level, graduate studies in the department have been reshaped to move from exclusively thesis-based degrees to the introduction of a coursework component to supplement research achievements—yet further evidence of the Americanization of the university system.

While graduate studies in sociology and anthropology have been possible at the department since the early 1970s, until recently no separate track for either discipline had been recognized in terms of graduate training. In 2012, the department successfully applied to the faculty to have a "PhD program in anthropology" explicitly named and recognized. This reflects an institutional commitment to anthropology and the first intake of PhD students arrived in the 2012/13 academic year. This recognition means that the disciplinary grounding of graduate students is now registered formally. These graduates, in order to compete effectively in the job market, must be identified as trained anthropologists, and the overt marking of their graduate training in anthropology lends institutional credence to their professional identity. Since 2006, graduate students have had to take a set number of courses—essential and optional—in addition to completing a thesis based on primary research. A comprehensive and qualifying examination system has also been instituted recently. Consequently, the number of course offerings in anthropology has had to be increased, with new anthropological methods and theory courses being added to the curriculum.

This is both a recognition of graduate student interest in anthropology and of the fact that doctoral students in the Department of Anthropology (and Sociology) have been largely non-Singaporean. They came primarily from countries in Southeast, South and East Asia, but also Australia, New Zealand, North America, Europe and elsewhere. Upon graduation, most returned to their home countries and found jobs in universities there, often in leading departments of sociology and anthropology.[13] The department had to position itself as a center of anthropological training in Asia and boost interest in its graduate program. However, in the midst of changes in the graduate landscape at NUS, the balance of Singaporean and international doctoral students could change.

This trend is in contrast to the situation in the 1970s, when the graduate program in the department attracted and trained

Singaporeans, many of whom were then recruited as faculty. In comparison, since the 1990s, Singaporean students have been trained in anthropology departments in UK, North American and Australian universities, and may not necessarily return to work in Singapore. Many in this group also opt not to work on "Singapore-related" topics as these might be seen as "too local and narrow" and "not marketable" for a job in Europe or America, thus pursuing more "global, universal" subjects for research. In any case, while the local academic market is highly competitive, there are now also many more tertiary institutions to absorb the number of Singaporean PhDs being produced annually.

For a variety of reasons, through the 1990s and 2000s, NUS did not encourage the hiring of its own PhDs, and recruitment typically tapped the pool of PhDs trained overseas, including its Singaporean hires. However, there was a recent moment of greater openness to hiring NUS PhDs as faculty members provided they could compete effectively. But it would seem that this moment may also have passed. In the last few years there has been a turn toward more dedicated graduate funding for Singaporeans wishing to pursue a master's or a PhD degree within Singapore with reduced funding for training non-Singaporean graduate students. There has been considerable funding support earmarked for training Singaporean PhDs in Singapore and for bringing back those with international PhDs to fill a perceived vacuum of Singaporean social science PhD holders. These developments have already hugely reconfigured the landscape of graduate training and the composition of the graduate student community in NUS and the other universities in Singapore. But the scene is far from settled and even more changes to graduate education can be anticipated.

Looking Ahead: Naming Anthropology

Singapore anthropologists, until very recently, did not have non-academic platforms where their research could find expression. Sociologists, in contrast, have been called upon by government agencies to apply their sociological knowledge and expertise in analyzing and explaining particular sociocultural trends. Quah has argued that "Singapore provides positive structures of opportunity for the growth of Sociology" (Quah 1995: 99). What about anthropology? Have similar "structures of opportunity" existed for anthropological research? Given the institutional co-location of the two disciplines, did anthropology also benefit from the same positive structures Quah has noted for sociology? Or were the two disciplines evaluated differently at the level of practice? Offering adequate responses to these questions requires particular kinds of data from university administrators and policymakers who make decisions about research and conference funding, faculty hiring and curriculum review committees—information that would be a challenge to access.

Critically, in the absence of the institutionalization of anthropology as a distinct department and profession in Singapore, a number of critical gaps can be identified in the anthropological scholarship. It has been noted that early research efforts that lasted well into the 1990s and anthropological scholarship emerging from the department at NUS, have had a strong empirical flavor. However, it is important to highlight that while conceptual and methodological discussions have not been overtly articulated or prioritized, they have not been non-existent. Over the last two decades, NUS-based anthropologists have made a call for rethinking the limited view of ethnography merely as "description" and "data collection." The association of anthropologists with the ethnographic method narrowly defined (and interestingly the distancing of sociology from ethnography) has also served to stigmatize anthropology as lacking a theoretical component. In their research and teaching, NUS anthropologists have argued that "ethnography" is both a methodological tool and a theoretical strategy that enables nuanced sense-making. Additionally, through the production of sophisticated ethnographies (about Singapore, Malaysia and Indonesia for example), they have demonstrated that ethnography can be the basis for generating concepts and theories and for re-conceptualizing existing theoretical formulations.

A second discernible gap in the local scholarship is that the calls to "nationalize," "nativize," "localize," "decolonize" and "indigenize" anthropology in Singapore have not been made—as compared to the vibrancy of these discourses found in other Asian contexts such as India, Japan and Taiwan. Neither does one hear of the need to re-conceptualize anthropology to address its Eurocentric biases or generate "alternative" anthropological discourses. The lively discussions one encounters amongst anthropologists in India and Japan, for example, about the need to reconstruct a discipline "relevant" for the local context, freed from mindless imitation of Western anthropological models has yet to be collectively registered by Singapore-based practitioners. The varied attempts to indigenize social sciences in Taiwan (Chan 1993; Sun 1993; Yeh 1994), Japan

(Kuwayama 2003, 2004) and China (Guldin 1995) reveal interesting comparative material and show contrasting trends in these places. Amongst these indigenization attempts, some conceptions are reactionary in glorifying "native" perspectives and tradition, while others are more critical and progressive.

However, amongst anthropologists at NUS, individual research and teaching endeavors do historicize the colonial roots of their discipline and engage the problematics this recognition generates. There are also perceptible efforts to rethink existing unequal relations within the global academic and intellectual arenas. For example, anthropologists are critical of the view that scholars from the West are largely perceived as generators of concepts and theory (of universal and comparative value), while their non-Western counterparts are viewed largely as providers of empirical material and local knowledge. Given this stance, what is to be the nature of the relationship between the kind of anthropological research that is done by "Western" scholars and their "non-Western" counterparts? This also alludes to the kinds of links, associations and interactions that exist (or not) amongst anthropologists in Southeast Asia and Asia (Thompson 2012) and their engagements (or lack of) with anthropological enterprises in North America and Europe, beyond the regional interest in a focus on area studies.

But it would be fair to say that there has been no notion of developing an "alternative" (Alatas 1993) voice or a search for identity in Singapore sociology or anthropology, some but not all of which remains conventional, especially at the level of teaching, and connected to Euro-American disciplinary norms and practices. A contributory factor is possibly the lack of a critical mass of Singaporean sociologists and anthropologists trained and practicing in Singapore. Perhaps a weak sense of an indigenous Singaporean identity as academics has also worked against developing a collective vision of challenging a hegemonic Western social science tradition. While some of these critical ideas have been debated amongst clusters of social scientists in NUS and in other universities, they certainly merit greater intellectual and political scrutiny—and now need to be acted upon.

It is possible that supporting institutional mechanisms might create opportunities for more formalized, systematic, enthusiastic and spirited debates about the identity and status of Singapore and Southeast Asian anthropology. There is as yet no association for anthropology or sociology in Singapore. Given the large number of individual anthropologists who are based in Singapore, in the universities and as independent scholars and consultants, as well as practitioners in the private sector, the time is ripe for an association of social scientists (including sociologists and anthropologists) to be formed and registered. Practitioners from NTU and NUS have been in conversations about this and do undertake collaborative work (like workshops, conferences, research projects and publications) and are indeed collaborating to register greater impact and presence of a larger and more effective social science community on the island.

The academic landscape and social science scene in Singapore have changed significantly since the 1960s and 1970s, as has the city state itself. The Department of Sociology currently consists of thirty-eight staff members, sixteen hold a PhD in anthropology although several of the remaining faculty members conduct research and teaching that combine both sociology and anthropology. In August 2017, NUS sociology department staff voted overwhelmingly to introduce a new undergraduate major in anthropology to be offered by the department. This proposal has been submitted to the authorities with a concurrent proposal to officially add "Anthropology" to the name of the department, recognizing a rebranded "Department of Sociology and Anthropology." Both these proposals have been overwhelmingly supported by the sociology department as a collective, the university leadership and members of Sociology's Visiting Committee (made up of international scholars) whom the department hosted in March 2017. The proposed new major, if passed, will continue to reflect the department's long and firm disciplinary "joint-ness" and their institutional co-location. There are already firm indications that there is a market for this major amongst the NUS undergraduate population, and good reason to anticipate that undergraduates will find the proposed anthropology major an exciting option at FASS. The proposed new name "Department of Sociology and Anthropology" better represents the range of research and teaching expertise of existing and future faculty members, which will enhance visibility of anthropological research, teaching and consultancy and further augment the recognition and awareness of the department in the global social science circuit and beyond. It will further represent an institutional commitment and recognition of the department's curriculum both for the PhD in anthropology program that was implemented in 2012, as well as the undergraduate major in anthropology that has been proposed. These processes are on-going and there is a welcome convergence of views and optimism that the desired results will materialize.

The current situation for anthropology in Singapore thus looks highly promising. Practitioners of the discipline at NUS and the other autonomous universities have been engaged in fashioning anthropology curricula to reflect core foci within the discipline and to translate these into a set of course offerings for undergraduates and graduates. The current faculty and university leadership at NUS as well as Singapore's political leaders recognize anthropology's presence as a distinct and valuable discipline of key contemporary relevance. The reproduction of disciplinary knowledge, the training of students, the institutionalization of discipline-specific norms and practices are not possible without institutional support, which the discipline has received at NUS. Material and economic considerations, compounded by ideological and political factors, profoundly influence how any discipline can be conceptualized and practised.

The current intellectual and political leadership seems to agree that anthropology and especially ethnography wield important industry relevance in public culture through the application of applied anthropology and an engagement with contemporary social issues and problems. As a discipline, major subfields of anthropology have been developed over the years, including formative work in urban, nutritional, political, legal, agricultural, maritime, environmental and educational anthropology. This moment also signals an altered landscape in Singapore that recognizes the importance of social science and humanities research in general, with greater opportunities for accessing research funding through the newly set up Social Science Research Council, Singapore.[14] These are long overdue but very welcome initiatives. The current enhanced availability of resources (including crucial funding) and institutional support will positively impact not only the growth of anthropology in Singapore but also recognize the distinct value of an anthropological perspective for theorizing the complexities of everyday lives in rapidly changing socio-economic, cultural and political landscapes.

Notes

* An earlier version of this chapter was published in Ajit K. Danda and Rajat K. Das' edited volume, *Alternative Voices of Anthropology* (2012). I am grateful to the editors for their permission to use parts of the published chapter. The current piece is a more elaborated and updated version of the 2012 piece.

1. King 2007: 97.
2. In 1923 the SBRAS was renamed the "Malayan Branch of the Royal Asiatic Society" (MBRAS), and consequently the publication was renamed the *Journal of the Malayan Branch of the Royal Asiatic Society* (*JMBRAS*). With the formation of Malaysia in 1964, the society was marked with the identity of a new nation state "Malaysian" and the journal re-named a third time as the *Journal of the Malaysian Branch of the Royal Asiatic Society.*
3. Also see Matthew J. Schauer. *Custodians of Malay Heritage: Anthropology, Education, and Imperialism in British Malaya and the Netherlands Indies 1890–1939*, Department of History, Oklahoma State University 2012.
4. As an alternative to mapping nationalist traditions of anthropology, and recognizing the distinction of "regions within nation states" Sutlive Jr et al. speak of archeology and anthropology in "East Malaysia and Brunei" (1987) rather than the more encapsulating and homogenizing notion of "Malaysia."
5. A narrative of anthropology's presence in Singapore cannot be disentangled from the development of sociology, especially the attention to institutional structures that enabled both disciplines to grow in Singapore.
6. Comparatively speaking, sociology and anthropology were formalized in Singapore rather later than in India and Indonesia, for example.
7. Groves later established the Department of Sociology in Hong Kong (Benjamin 1998; Thompson 2012).
8. Occasionally such work is published (Walker 1994).
9. Chen notes that in 1986, of a total of 27 faculty members, 6 were anthropologists (1986: 34).
10. To date, these include only anthropologists. A more comprehensive narrative in progress seeks to interview and include the voices of sociologists as well.
11. Even though sociologists have self-defined themselves as being concerned with quantitative methodologies, the reality is that in practice, as Quah (1995) rightly notes, sociologists in Singapore have relied on a combination of methodologies in their research. Quah encapsulates the latter as "a combination of historical, quantitative and qualitative approaches" (1995: 94).
12. Apart from NUS, anthropologists are also on the teaching faculty at Nanyang Technological University (NTU), Singapore Management University (SMU), Singapore University of Technology and Design (SUTD), not to mention the presence of anthropologists that the newly set up Yale-NUS outfit which offers an anthropology major.
13. NUS PhDs from India, for example, have been recruited at the Indian Institute of Technology in Delhi and Gandhinagar as well as at the Institute of Management in Kolkata. Those from the Philippines have been recruited at the departments of sociology and anthropology at the Ateneo de Manila University and the University of Philippines.

14. Amelia Teng, "MOE to put in $350 million for social sciences and humanities research over next five years." *The Straits Times*, Singapore. Accessed September 29, 2018.

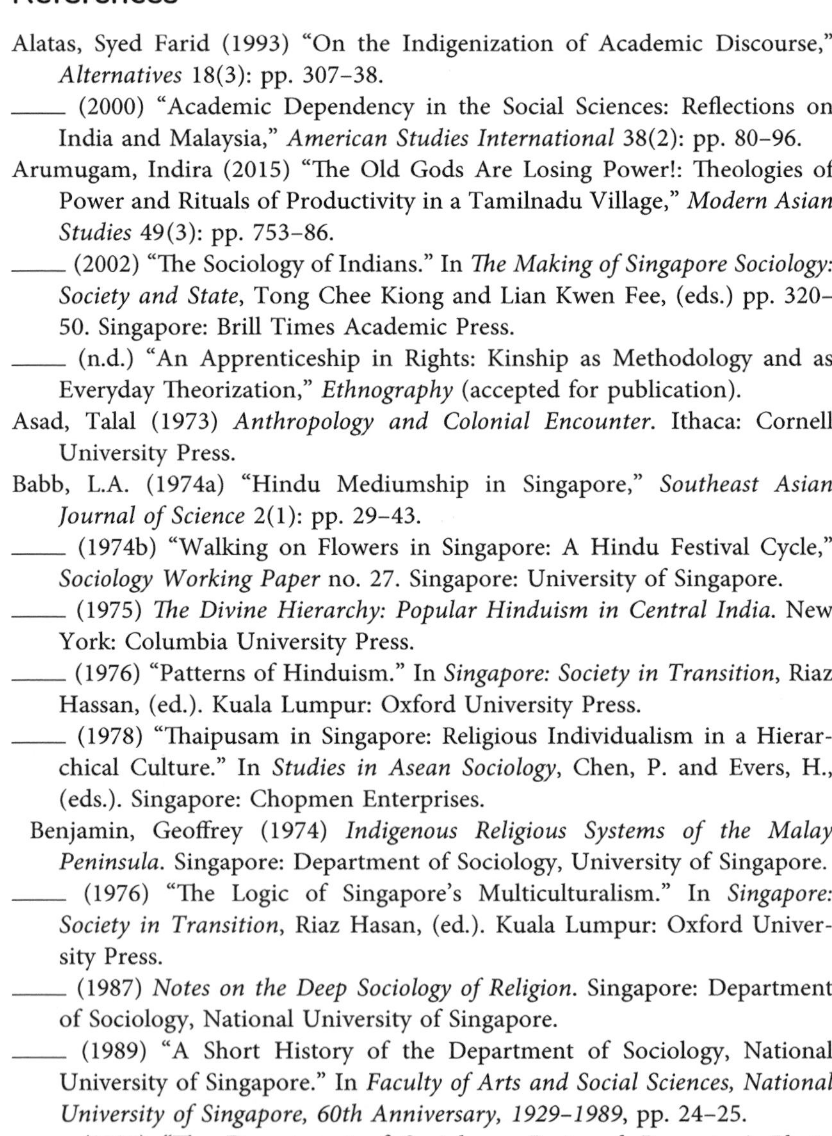

References

Alatas, Syed Farid (1993) "On the Indigenization of Academic Discourse," *Alternatives* 18(3): pp. 307–38.

——— (2000) "Academic Dependency in the Social Sciences: Reflections on India and Malaysia," *American Studies International* 38(2): pp. 80–96.

Arumugam, Indira (2015) "The Old Gods Are Losing Power!: Theologies of Power and Rituals of Productivity in a Tamilnadu Village," *Modern Asian Studies* 49(3): pp. 753–86.

——— (2002) "The Sociology of Indians." In *The Making of Singapore Sociology: Society and State*, Tong Chee Kiong and Lian Kwen Fee, (eds.) pp. 320–50. Singapore: Brill Times Academic Press.

——— (n.d.) "An Apprenticeship in Rights: Kinship as Methodology and as Everyday Theorization," *Ethnography* (accepted for publication).

Asad, Talal (1973) *Anthropology and Colonial Encounter*. Ithaca: Cornell University Press.

Babb, L.A. (1974a) "Hindu Mediumship in Singapore," *Southeast Asian Journal of Science* 2(1): pp. 29–43.

——— (1974b) "Walking on Flowers in Singapore: A Hindu Festival Cycle," *Sociology Working Paper* no. 27. Singapore: University of Singapore.

——— (1975) *The Divine Hierarchy: Popular Hinduism in Central India*. New York: Columbia University Press.

——— (1976) "Patterns of Hinduism." In *Singapore: Society in Transition*, Riaz Hassan, (ed.). Kuala Lumpur: Oxford University Press.

——— (1978) "Thaipusam in Singapore: Religious Individualism in a Hierarchical Culture." In *Studies in Asean Sociology*, Chen, P. and Evers, H., (eds.). Singapore: Chopmen Enterprises.

Benjamin, Geoffrey (1974) *Indigenous Religious Systems of the Malay Peninsula*. Singapore: Department of Sociology, University of Singapore.

——— (1976) "The Logic of Singapore's Multiculturalism." In *Singapore: Society in Transition*, Riaz Hasan, (ed.). Kuala Lumpur: Oxford University Press.

——— (1987) *Notes on the Deep Sociology of Religion*. Singapore: Department of Sociology, National University of Singapore.

——— (1989) "A Short History of the Department of Sociology, National University of Singapore." In *Faculty of Arts and Social Sciences, National University of Singapore, 60th Anniversary, 1929–1989*, pp. 24–25.

——— (1991) "The Department of Sociology - Past and Present: A Photo Essay." In *Explorations in Asian Sociology*, Chan Kwok Bun and Ho Kong Chong, (eds), pp. 7–14.

____ (1996) "Singapore Sociology." In *Velky Sociologicky Slovnik*, H. Marikova, M. Petrusek and A. Vodakova, (eds.), pp. 1140–42. Charles University, Prague: Karolinum, (Original in Czech, English translation by the author).

____ (2014) *Temiar Religion, 1964–2012: Enchantment, Disenchantment and Re-enchantment in Malaysia's Uplands*. Singapore: NUS Press.

Chan, Hoiman (1993) "Some Metasociological Notes on the Sinicisation of Sociology," *International Sociology* 8(1): pp. 113–19.

Chen, Peter S.J. (1986) "Sociological Studies in Singapore Society." In *Singapore Studies: Surveys of Humanities and Social Sciences*, Basant K. Kapur, (ed.), pp. 33–64. Singapore: Singapore University Press.

Clammer, John (1973) "Colonialism and the Perception of Tradition in Fiji." In *Anthropology and the Colonial Encounter*, Talal Asad, (ed.), pp. 199–220. Ithaca: Cornell University Press.

____ (1976). *Literacy and Social Change: A Case Study of Fiji* (vol. 11). Brill Archive.

____ (1986) *Singapore, Ideology, Society, Culture*. Singapore: Stosius Inc/ Advent Books Division.

____ (1998) *Race and State in Independent Singapore, 1965–1990: The Cultural Politics of Pluralism in a Multiethnic Society*. Farnham: Ashgate Pub Limited.

____ (2011) *Contemporary Urban Japan: A Sociology of Consumption*. New Jersey: John Wiley & Sons.

Danda, Ajit (1981) "On the Future for Anthropology in India," *Journal of Indian Anthropological Society* 16: pp. 221–30.

Danda, Ajit and Rajat K. Das, (eds.) (2012) *Alternative Voices of Anthropology*. Kolkata: Indian Anthropological Society.

Dang, B.S. (1982) "Future of Applied Anthropology in India," *Indian Anthropologist* 2: pp. 31–37.

Erb, Maribeth (1988) "Flores: Cosmology, Art and Ritual." In *Islands and Ancestors: Indigenous Styles of Southeast Asia*, Jean Paul Barbier-Mueller and Douglas Newton, (eds.). Monaco: Prestel.

____ (1994) "Becoming Complete Among the Rembong: This Life and the Next," *Southeast Asian Journal of Social Science* 21: pp. 10–33.

____ (1997) "Negotiating History: Myth, Power and Ethnicity in Manggarai (Flores, Eastern Indonesia)." In *ASEAN in the Global System*, H.M. Dahlan, J. Hamzah, J.H. Ong and A.Y. Hing, (eds.). Kuala Lumpur: Penerbit UKM.

____ (1999) *The Manggaraians: Guide to Traditional Life Styles*. Singapore: Times Editions.

____ (2001) "Eco-tourism and Environmental Conservation in Western Flores: Who Benefits?" *Antropologi Indonesia* 66: pp. 72–88.

Evers, Hans Dieter (1973) *Modernization in Southeast Asia*. Kuala Lumpur: Oxford University Press.

_____ (2011) *Beyond the Knowledge Trap: Developing Asia's Knowledge-Based Economies*. Singapore: World Scientific.

Evers, Hans Dieter and Heiko Schrader (1994) *The Moral Economy of Trade, Ethnicity and Developing Markets*. London: Routledge.

Evers, Hans Dieter and Rudiger Korff (2000) *Southeast Asian Urbanism: The Meaning and Power of Social Space*. New York: Palgrave Macmillan.

Fahim, Hussein, (ed.) (1982) *Indigenous Anthropology in Non-Western Countries*. Durham: Carolina Academic Press.

Fox, Richard G., (ed.) (1991) *Recapturing Anthropology*. New Mexico: School of American Research Press.

Groves, Murray (1954) "Dancing in Poreporena," *The Journal of the Royal Anthropological Institute of Great Britain and Ireland* 84(1/2): pp. 75–90.

_____ (1960) "Motu Pottery," *The Journal of the Polynesian Society* 69(1): pp. 2–22.

_____ (1963) "Western Motu Descent Groups," *Ethnology* 2(1): pp. 15–30.

Guldin, Gregory Eliyu (1995) *The Saga of Anthropology in China*. Armonk: Sharpe.

Hassan, Riaz (1976a) *Singapore: Society in Transition*. Kuala Lumpur: Oxford University Press.

_____ (1976b) *Families in Flats*. Singapore: Singapore University Press.

_____ (1983) *A Way of Dying: Suicide in Singapore*. Kuala Lumpur: Oxford University Press.

Kelly, William W (1991) "Directions in the Anthropology of Contemporary Japan," *Annual Review of Anthropology* 20: pp. 395–431.

Kuwayama, Takami (2003) "'Natives' as Dialogic Partners: Some Thoughts on Native Anthropology," *Anthropology Today* 19(1).

_____ (2004) *Native Anthropology*. Melbourne: Trans Pacific Press.

Pathy, Jaganath (1988) "In Pursuit of Indigenization: Trends and Issues on Building Sociology for India," *The Journal of Sociological Studies* 7: pp. 70–84.

Quah, Stella (1995) "Beyond the Known Terrain: Sociology in Singapore," *The American Sociologist* 26(4): pp. 88–106.

Rajah, Ananda (1975) *The Ecological Study of Shrines*. Unpublished academic exercise, Department of Sociology, National University of Singapore.

_____ (2004a) "A 'Nation of Intent' in Burma: Karen Ethno-nationalism, Nationalism and Narrations of Nation." In *Political Fragmentation in Southeast Asia: Alternative Nations in the Making*, Kevin Hewison and Vivienne Wee, (eds.). London: RoutledgeCurzon.

_____ (2004b) "Burma: A State in Name and Not in Fact – Movements for Ethnic Autonomy, Centres, Peripheries and Resource Control." In *Political Fragmentation in Southeast Asia: Alternative Nations in the Making*. Keven Hewison and Vivienne Wee, (eds.). London: RoutledgeCurzon.

____ (2008 [1986]) *Remaining Karen: A Study of Cultural Reproduction and Maintenance of Identity*. Canberra: ANU E-Press.

Rudolph, Jurgen and Indira Arumugam (2000) "More Than Meets the Eye: The Political Causes of the Asian Economic Crisis," *The Copenhagen Journal of Asian Studies* 14: pp. 42–73.

Saloni, Mathur (2000) "History and Anthropology in South Asia: Rethinking the Archive," *Annual Review of Anthropology* 29: pp. 89–106.

Sather, Clifford (1997) *The Bajau Laut: Adaptation, History, and Fate in a Maritime Fishing Society of Southeastern Sabah*. Oxford: Oxford University Press.

____ (1990) "Trees and Tree Tenure in Paku Iban Society: The Management of Secondary Forest Resources in a Long-established Iban Community," *Borneo Review* 1(1): pp. 16–40.

____ (1996) "'All Threads are White': Iban Egalitarianism Reconsidered." In *Origins, Ancestry and Alliance: Explorations in Austronesian Ethnography*, James J. Fox, (ed.), pp. 73–112. Canberra: ANU E-Press.

____ (2002) "Sea Nomads and Rainforest Hunter-Gatherers: Foraging Adaptations in the Indo-Malaysian Archipelago." In *The Austronesians: Historical and Comparative Perspectives*, Peter Bellwood, James J. Fox and Darrell Tryon, (eds.), pp. 245–86. Canberra: ANU E-Press.

Shamsul A.B. (2004) "Anthropology, Identity and Nation Formation in Malaysia." In *The Making of Anthropology in East and Southeast Asia*, Shinji Yamashita, J.S. Eades and Joseph Bosco, (eds.), pp. 286–306. New York and Oxford: Berghanh Books.

Sinha, Vineeta (1997a) "Unpacking the Labels 'Hindu' & 'Hinduism' in Singapore," *Southeast Asian Journal of Social Science* 25(2): pp. 139–60.

____ (1997b) "Reconceptualising the Social Sciences in Non-Western Settings: Challenges and Dilemmas," *Southeast Asian Journal of Social Science* 25(1): pp. 167–81.

____ (2002) "Decentring Social Sciences in Practice through Individual Acts and Choices," *Current Sociology* 51(1): pp. 7–26.

____ (2006) *A New God in the Diaspora: Muneeswaran Worship in Contemporary Singapore*. Singapore and Denmark: Singapore University Press and NIAS.

____ (2010) *Religion and Commodification: Merchandising Diasporic Hinduism*. London and New York: Routledge.

Stephens, Jacintha (1982) *Catholic Vellala in Singapore*. Unpublished master's thesis, National University of Singapore.

Sun Chung-Hsing (1993) "Aspects of 'Sinicisation' and 'Globalisation'," *International Sociology* 8(1): pp. 121–22.

Tamney, Joseph (1992) *The Resilience of Christianity in the Modern World*. New York: State University of New York Press.

—— (1992) *The Resilience of Conservative Religion*. Cambridge: Cambridge University Press.

—— (1996) *The Struggle over Singapore's Soul: Western Modernization and Asian Culture*. Walter de Gruyter.

Thompson, Eric C. (2003) "Malay Male Migrants: Negotiating Contested Identities in Malaysia," *American Ethnologist* 30(3): pp. 418–38.

—— (2007) Unsettling Absences: Urbanism in Rural Malaysia. Singapore: NUS Press.

—— (2012) "Anthropology in Southeast Asia: National Traditions and Transnational Practices," *Asian Journal of Social Science* 40(6): pp. 664–89.

—— (2013) "In Defense of Southeast Asia: A Case for Methodological Regionalism," *TRaNS: Trans-National and -Regional Studies of Southeast Asia* 1(2): pp. 1–22.

—— (2014) "Immigration, Society, and Modalities of Citizenship in Singapore," *Citizenship Studies* 18(3/4): pp. 315–31.

Thompson, E.C., Pattana Kitiarsa, and Suriya Smutkupt (2016) "From Sex Tourist to Son-in-Law: Emergent Masculinities and Transient Subjectivities among Farang Men in Thailand," *Current Anthropology* 57(1): pp. 53–71.

Tong, Chee Kiong (1990) *Between Worlds: Studies of Sacred Elites*. Ohio State University Department of Anthropology.

—— (2004) *Chinese Death Rituals in Singapore*. London, New York: RoutledgeCurzon.

—— (2007) "Rationalizing Religion; Religious Conversion, Revivalism and Competition in Singapore Society," *Social Sciences in Asia*, no. 13, Monograph Series. Leiden: Brill.

—— (2007) *Religion, Nation State and Globalization in Southeast Asia*. Department of Sociology, Fu Jen Catholic University.

Tong Chee Kiong and Yong Pit Kee (1998) "Guanxi bses, xinyong and Chinese Business Networks," *British Journal of Sociology* 49(1): pp. 75–96.

Tong Chee Kiong and Chan Kwol Bun (2001) *Alternate Identities: The Chinese of Contemporary Thailand*. Leiden: Brill.

Walker, Anthony R. (1986) *The Toda of South India: A New Look*. New Delhi: Hindustan Publishing Corporation.

—— (2003) *Merit and the Millennium: Routine and Crisis in the Ritual Lives of the Lahu People*. New Delhi: Hindustan Publishing Corporation.

Walker, Anthony R., (ed.) (1994) *New Place, Old Ways: Essays on Indian Society and Culture in Modern Singapore*. Columbia, Missouri: South Asia Books.

Waterson, Roxanne (1995) "Houses and Hierarchies in Island Southeast Asia." In *About the House: Lévi-Strauss and Beyond*, Janet Carsten and Stephen Hugh-Jones, (eds.), pp. 47–68.

_____ (1995) "Houses, Graves and the Limits of Kinship Groupings among the Sa'dan Toraja," *Bijdragen tot de taal-, land-en volkenkunde*, (2de Afl), pp. 194–217.

_____ (2000) "House, Place, and Memory in Tana Toraja (Indonesia)," *RA Joyce, & SD Gillespie*, pp. 177–88.

_____ (2007) "Trajectories of Memory: Documentary Film and the Transmission of Testimony," *History and Anthropology* 18(1), pp. 51–73.

_____ (2011) *Paths and Rivers: Sa'dan Toraja Society in Transformation*. Leiden: Brill.

_____ (2012) *Living House: An Anthropology of Architecture in South-East Asia*. Clarendon (VT): Tuttle Publishing.

Wee, Vivienne (1988) *What Does "Chinese" Mean?: An Exploratory Essay*. Singapore: Department of Sociology, National University of Singapore.

_____ (1989) "Secular State, Multi-religious Society: The Patterning of Religion in Singapore." Paper for presentation at Conference on Communities in Question: Religion and Authority in East and Southeast Asia, May 2–10, 1989, Hua Hin, Thailand, 35 pages.

_____ (2002) "Ethno-nationalism in Process: Ethnicity, Atavism and Indigenism in Riau, Indonesia," *The Pacific Review* 15(4): pp. 497–516.

Wee, Vivienne and Kanishka Jayasuriya (2002) "New Geographies and Temporalities of Power: Exploring the New Fault-lines of Southeast Asia," *The Pacific Review* 15(4): pp. 475–95.

Wee, Vivenne and Cynthia Chou (1997) "Continuity and Discontinuity in the Multiple Realities of Riau, Bijdragen Tot De Taal-, Land- En Volkenkunde," *Journal of the Humanities and Social Sciences of Southeast Asia* 153(4): pp. 527–41.

Yeh Chi-jeng (1994) "A Sociological Analysis of Indigenization in Social Research," *Hong Kong Journal of Social Sciences* 3: pp. 52–78.

SECTION 3

TRENDS IN TRANSNATIONAL ANTHROPOLOGIES

CHAPTER 7

LOCAL AND TRANSNATIONAL ANTHROPOLOGIES OF BORNEO

Victor T. King and Zawawi Ibrahim

This chapter provides a chronological account of the development of anthropological traditions in four territories of Borneo, which cross three modern nation states: the two states of Malaysian Borneo (Sarawak and Sabah), the sultanate of Brunei Darussalam and the provinces of Indonesian Kalimantan.[1] Sarawak and to some extent Sabah took a leading role in setting research agendas and sponsoring field research. Until the 1970s, research was dominated by foreign male scholars, and these pioneering fieldworkers in the colonial environment set the research trajectories for others to follow. Some of the issues that dominated research up to the 1970s were guided by preoccupations of British social anthropology: social structure and organization, rights in land and other property, the operation of customary laws, local economic organization, agriculture and commercial production, and ethnic identities. Very little was done in Brunei for the three decades after World War II and the vast territories and complex mixes of populations and cultures to the south in Kalimantan also remained relatively remote to modern social scientific inquiry until the 1960s. From the 1970s, with the establishment of universities and research institutions in Borneo, local or locally based scholars increasingly took the lead in research, focusing initially and primarily on issues of socio-economic development. This focus has been sustained to the present, but there is also an emerging interest in reflexivity and the critique of colonial anthropology, with accompanying interests in agency, in the fluidity and flexibility of social and cultural processes, and especially in the construction, maintenance and transformation of identities. We can also identify a new, recent trend towards transnational rather than a national anthropology.

As other contributions to the present volume demonstrate, anthropology today is frequently dominated by a national frame of reference or what some refer to as methodological nationalism, organized in terms of the anthropologies of nation states in Southeast Asia (Canuday and Porio; Dang Anh; Nguyen; Sinha; Winarto and Pirous, all this volume). The island of Borneo, on the other hand, embraces three nation states: Malaysia, Indonesia and Brunei Darussalam. Moreover, contemporary Malaysian Borneo was formed from two British crown colonies created in 1946; the Brooke Raj in Sarawak and the Chartered Company in British North Borneo (now Sabah). These were previously British protectorates along with Brunei and were subject to quite different and rather distinctive European administrations. But the establishment of post-war crown colonies, and the financial and administrative support which this status afforded, gave these territories, particularly Sarawak, an early advantage in the development of social science research (King 1993). Early post-war research was dominated by anthropologists and sociologists from outside Borneo from the late 1940s through to the 1960s, but increasingly from the late 1970s locally based social scientists began to establish an agenda which focused on development-oriented research and on issues that were of interest to their respective governments. Subsequently, a growing interest in ethnic identities and cultural politics became apparent.

Brunei Darussalam, on the other hand, encouraged anthropological research in the late 1960s and 1970s (primarily undertaken by American anthropologists) when it was still a British protected territory, then directed social science studies in specific national ways. Following the foundation of an independent Malay Muslim monarchical state from 1984, and the establishment of Universiti Brunei Darussalam soon after in 1985, social science research increasingly conformed to government priorities. There were restrictions on foreign social scientists undertaking research, though local researchers and foreign scholars based in educational institutions in the country were, with some constraints, allowed access to field sites.

Research in the vast territories of Indonesian Kalimantan, in contrast to Malaysian Borneo and Brunei, proceeded in a more fitful, patchy way after full independence from the Dutch in 1949. The political and economic problems and instabilities experienced by the Republic of Indonesia under Sukarno and then in the early years of Suharto's military dictatorship made it difficult to develop and support a research infrastructure, especially in the remote terrains of the interior (Avé and King 1986a, 1986b). Only a handful of foreign anthropologists worked there up to the 1980s, after which more undertook work in Kalimantan. An important group of these foreign researchers, in collaboration with locally based scholars, produced important studies of environmental processes, ecology and local livelihoods in East Kalimantan. Another very significant local strand of work, was that based in Pontianak, West Kalimantan, pursued by mainly Catholic-educated indigenous researchers at the Institut Dayakologi (Dayakology Institute), who focused on matters of special concern to minority Dayak populations.

Emerging from a colonial and then a foreign-dominated social science legacy, all the territories of Borneo have experienced the increasing "indigenization" of social science research, particularly in Indonesian Kalimantan (Zawawi 20001, 2008a, 2008b, 2010, 2017). An overview of the establishment of anthropological traditions in Borneo must necessarily though briefly examine the colonial legacy and the contributions of anthropologists from outside the island. Such a historical context allows us to highlight and trace the shift toward the increasingly dominant voices, interests and perspectives of locally based scholars. In Borneo, moreover, we see an island of tremendous social-cultural diversity, divided across (at least) four territories and three nation states, and at the same time connected through locally grounded yet transnational research practices and perspectives.

Post-War Anthropology in Sarawak, Borneo and Beyond

Early post-war anthropology of Borneo was marked by the overwhelming importance of studies of Sarawak conducted primarily through the Sarawak Museum under Tom Harrisson's curatorship and under the auspices of the Colonial Social Science Research Council (CSSRC). Indeed, Borneo Studies in the 1950s, 1960s and even into the 1970s remained Sarawak-focused (see Appell 1977). The first substantial CSSRC anthropological studies in Sarawak comprised the Iban studies of J.D. (Derek) Freeman, W.R. Geddes' work on the Land Dayak (Bidayuh), H.S. Morris' coastal Melanau research and T'ien Ju-K'ang's study of the Chinese, presided over by Raymond Firth and guided by Edmund Leach on his research visit to Sarawak in 1947. The New Zealand connection was dominant in these studies (Freeman, Geddes and Firth were New Zealanders; and though Morris was born in England and spent his childhood in Rhodesia, his mother was from New Zealand). Although Leach briefly visited North Borneo in November 1947 and produced a report, the momentum that he achieved in Sarawak was not repeated in North Borneo, other than the study undertaken by Monica Glyn-Jones of the Penampang Dusun (1953). Given the brevity of his stay, Leach's report on his visit to North Borneo in November 1947, did not match his Sarawak report (1948, 1950).

The anthropological highlights of the 1950s and the early 1960s were undoubtedly Freeman's publications on Iban social structure (see 1957, 1960, 1961). The Sarawak Museum, under Harrisson, was preoccupied with the Niah Cave excavations, though Harrisson was also undertaking studies of the coastal Malays of Sarawak and the upriver Kelabit, and Rodney Needham was pursuing his research on the nomadic Penan of Sarawak in 1951–52 (1953). Harrisson and Needham were not part of the CSSRC studies. Most of the anthropological work in the first decade after 1945 was undertaken through or had a connection with Raymond Firth at the London School of Economics (LSE) and his close associates Maurice Freedman and Edmund Leach (before Leach went to Cambridge); the major exception was Needham at Oxford, who subsequently supervised Erik Jensen's work on Iban religion (1968, 1974). And Freeman, though he wrote his doctoral thesis at Cambridge under the supervision of Meyer Fortes (1953), had been trained at the LSE prior to leaving for Sarawak; even Fortes who spent most of his career at Cambridge from 1950 and between 1946–50 at Oxford had been a research student at the LSE in the 1930s, training with Bronislaw Malinowski and Firth. This was a period characterized by a sharp division between British social and American cultural anthropology. Freeman's early work showed the unmistakable influence of the British emphasis on social structure.

A significant feature of the anthropologists who carried out research in Borneo was that their work there was only part of their contribution to anthropological scholarship. They all undertook field research among other societies as well. Following his research among the Sarawak Chinese (1953) T'ien Ju-K'ang focused on mainland Chinese culture, society and history (1993, 1997). His pre-Sarawak doctoral thesis was on the Shan States of Yunnan-Burma (1948). William Geddes' doctoral work was on Fiji (1948). After Sarawak (1954, 1957), he then became involved in research in upland northern Thailand from 1959 to the early 1960s (1976). Stephen Morris had been trained originally in forestry, and then after his Melanau report (1953), he spent three years in Kampala on a doctoral study of East African Indians (1963, 1968). Leach had previously worked in Highland Burma, Firth in Polynesia and the Malayan Peninsula, and Needham did field research in the Malayan Peninsula and eastern Indonesia. Derek Freeman progressively left his Iban studies in the 1960s and moved on to Samoa (having been a school teacher there from 1940–43, before undertaking his Borneo research) and for the next three decades was engaged in a substantial critique of Margaret Mead's Samoan field research (1983, 1999).

The major legacy in early Borneo anthropology was left by Freeman. He returned to Borneo in 1961 where he was said to have suffered a nervous breakdown arising from the acrimonious encounters with Tom Harrisson. Freeman has indicated that this experience transformed his view of anthropology from a social structuralist perspective to an interactionist paradigm which aimed to discover the universal psychological and biological foundations of human behavior (1966, 1973; see Brown, 1991; and see Needham from a structuralist perspective, 1978a, 1978b, 1979, 1980). What the early colonial anthropology of Borneo, mainly social structuralist in inspiration, served to do was locate it within wider debates in anthropology. Freeman's legacy is especially noteworthy (see Murdock 1960a, 1960b). A landmark event was the publication of *Report on the Iban* (1970). Prior to this Freeman's *Iban Agriculture* and his *Report on the Iban of Sarawak* published in 1955, had been out of print and difficult to obtain. He also, for a time, supervised George Appell's doctoral research on the Rungus Dusun (1965). Appell undertook field research in British North Borneo (Sabah) as a research scholar at the Australian National University (ANU) from 1959 until 1964. Among Appell's legacies to Borneo studies was the founding of the Borneo Research Council and its *Bulletin*, the editing of two particularly important books on Borneo (1976a, 1976b) and co-editing a tribute to Derek

Freeman (Appell and Madan 1988). In support of the importance of Freeman's work and of the considerable corpus of anthropological material accumulated by him and other researchers on the Iban, Appell says:

> This uniqueness of [Iban] culture and optimistic vitality have brought researchers from around the world to study Ibanic society and culture, not only to make an ethnographic record for posterity but also to learn what contributions a study of their society and culture would make to social theory ... Furthermore, because of this extensive study, Iban society now provides the model, the background phenomena, on which all other ethnographic inquiries of Borneo societies can proceed. Iban research has informed the discussion of many theoretical issues in anthropological inquiry, particularly those dealing with the structure of cognatic societies, i.e., societies without any form of descent group. Thus, Iban culture forms the fundamental grounds against which other cultures are compared in order to elicit cultural information and to test hypotheses in social theory (2001: 741).

Appell also worked closely with such other anthropologists in Sabah as Clifford Sather (Bajau Laut kinship and domestic relations, 1971, 1997; see Morrison 1993) and Robert Harrison (socio-economic variation among rural Ranau Dusun, 1971) and was highly critical of the early studies of the Dusun by Thomas Rhys Williams (1965, 1969). There were other notable contributions to early anthropology in Sabah including by Fortier (cultural change among Chinese communities in rural areas, 1964); Crain (marriage and social exchange among the Lun Dayeh, 1970); and Han Sin Fong (occupational patterns and social interaction among the Chinese, 1971).

These early studies in Sarawak and Sabah can be perceived in various modes: colonial knowledge, socio-economic studies, social structural analyses, or applied anthropology. The context of the studies was the imperative of post-war socio-economic development under British colonialism, to gather detailed ethnographic material on major ethnic groups and to serve the practical aims of government (Appell 1977: 32). They are still models of ethnography which have continued to provide points of reference for subsequent research, even though there have been recent criticisms which draw attention to colonial and other preoccupations in their work (see Zawawi 2008a, 2008b, 2017). The scatter of studies undertaken in Kalimantan and Brunei from the 1960s, again primarily by foreign researchers, illustrated a continuing concern with social structure, though in some American work the concept of culture was also deployed; in Brunei, for example Brown (1969, 1970, 1976), Kimball (1975) and Maxwell (1980), and in Kalimantan, Conley (1976); Hudson (1967, 1972), King (1985), Miles (1976), Weinstock (1983), Herbert Whittier (1973), and Patricia Whittier (1981). However, the overwhelming dominance of studies of the Iban and Iban-related peoples continued.

From the late 1960s, the small number of early studies was followed by a burgeoning of research on Borneo, again mainly located in Sarawak, but with a consolidation of research on such groups as the Bidayuh and with a widening range of the ethnic groups covered. These studies, which continued to focus on social structure and social change, included Deegan on the Lun Bawang (1973), Peranio on Bisaya (1977), Metcalf on Berawan (1982), Rousseau on Kayan (1974), Grijpstra on Bidayuh (1976), Schneider on Selako (1974), Fidler (2010[1973]) on a Chinese upriver bazaar community, and Zainal Kling on the Saribas Malays (1973); and, among the Melanau-related upriver Kajang groups, Strickland on the Kejaman and Sekapan (1986, 1995); Nicolaisen on the Punan Bah (1976, 1977–78, 1983, 1986); and Alexander on the Lahanan (1987, 1989, 1990). Nevertheless, the dominance of studies of the Iban continued into the 1970s and embraced a range of social structural, cultural, historical, economic and practical policy issues; see Austin (1977), Chu (1978), Cobb (1988), Cramb (1987, 2007), Heppell (1975), Masing (1981, 1997), Uchibori (1978), Komanyi (1973), Padoch (1978), Pringle (1967, 1970), Schwenk (1975), Seymour (1972) and Sutlive (1972). This was further reinforced in the 1980s with studies of the Iban and Iban-related peoples of West Kalimantan, including the studies of the Kantu' (Dove 1981), Drake on Mualang (1982), and McKeown on the Merakai Iban (1989).

From the 1960s there was an increase in the number of women undertaking research in Borneo and most importantly an expansion of work by locally based social scientists. The rise of women's and local voices and perspectives within the research community paralleled a widening of the range of concepts and issues within research: an increasing concern with reflexivity, critiques of colonialism, postmodern concerns, and a shift toward an interest in agency, fluidity and flexibility and away from earlier social structuralist and corporatist frameworks (Armstrong 1991, 1992; Helliwell 1990, 2001).

We also see from the 1960s onward a focus on political ecology and environmental change. But more than any other trend, we see an all-consuming interest in identity and the construction thereof, as it relates to minorities and majorities within nation states, borders and boundaries, political party development, the media and globalization. An increase in research in hitherto unexplored ethnographic fields such as urban experience appear in more recent work. All of these trends, from the 1960s and 1970s onward, take place in a movement toward more applied, developmental and policy-related issues, and engineered agricultural transitions (resettlement, land development, sustainability). While these trends are clearly an "indigenization" of Borneo research with evermore locally grounded and locally driven research agendas, it is not a story of isolation from Western or global anthropologies, but rather one that sees an increasing reliance on transnational collaborative and team research. In the case of transnational studies in Borneo, this involves collaborations both across and beyond the island.

Indigenization and Shifting Concerns

From the late 1970s and onwards there was a significant shift in thematic interest and focus, prompted in no small part by the closer control which the three governments responsible for Borneo exercised over research undertaken by foreign researchers. This in turn coincided with the rapid increase in commercial logging in Sarawak, Sabah and Kalimantan and the obvious environmental, economic and social costs of the exploitation of the rainforests and the impacts on local communities.

For Sarawak, an important turning point towards a focus on socio-economic development from a local (Iban) perspective was Peter Kedit's research on issues of modernization and development primarily among the Iban (1980). It was probably Kedit's statement in the *Sarawak Museum Journal* that set the tone of subsequent research when he said that anthropology "should offer more studies of a practical nature ... [and also broaden] its empirical scope to understand and analyze, and to offer 'solutions' to the socio-cultural problems and processes that are taking place among the very subjects that anthropologists seek to study" (1975: 32). For a while the Sarawak government constrained but did not exclude foreign research, rather it promoted locally based fieldwork and a practical and policy oriented social science agenda.

Overwhelmingly, field research was dominated by local scholars. In Sarawak, there is a wide range of materials available, particularly from Universiti Malaysia Sarawak (UNIMAS), founded in 1992, and government institutions with a focus on rural development and agricultural transformations, changing gender issues, resettlement and land development, and environmental change. Much of this research appeared in the form of doctoral theses, primarily written at overseas institutions (see King 2017a; King 2017b: 91–93, 105–24 for a list of postgraduate theses). These included work by Abang Azhari Hadari, Abdul Majid Mat Salleh and Mohd Yusof Kasim, Abdul Rashid Abdullah, Aris, Bala (see 2002), Berma, Chan, Chin See Chung, Dimbab Ngidang, Hatta Solhee, Hew Cheng Sim (see 2003, 2007), Hong (see 1985, 1987), Kambrie, Jayl Langub, Jayum Jawan, Jegak Uli, Francis Jana Lian, Salfarina Abdul Gapor, Songan, and many others. Poline Bala has provided a valuable overview of the development of a social science tradition at UNIMAS, emphasizing the importance of moving from "colonial knowledge" to contemporary efforts of making social science relevant to the issues and concerns of the larger Malaysian society and "the use of applied research to national wealth creation" (Bala 2017: 287–88). In addition to rural development issues, these scholars have given particular attention to gender, disability, society and technology, heritage and critical perspectives on knowledge construction among other issues.

Overseas researchers also undertook work relevant to various practical development concerns, including Avé and King (1986a, 1986b), Brookfield, Potter and Byron (1995), Cleary and Eaton (1992), Janowski (1991), Persoon and Osseweijer (2008), Puri (2006), Sellato (1989, 1994), Sercombe and Sellato (2007), and Sutlive (1993). A similar account can also be given for Sabah where there has been a very prominent emphasis on applied work and policy issues through Universiti Malaysia Sabah founded in 1994, with such researchers as Cooke (1999, 2006) and Porodong (2010) among many others, and the Institute of Development Studies there. The advocacy of Appell and others (also see Doolittle 2005) also gave impetus to development-oriented concerns from the early years through to the present. In Sabah, too, there has been an emphasis on issues to do with tourism and development (see Goh 2007; Pianzin 1993; Ong 2008; Zainab Khalifah 1997). Pugh-Kitingan (2017) points to a rather more diverse set of interests in cultural knowledge in Sabah, including linguistic and ethnomusicological studies. The establishment of Universiti Malaysia

Sabah and the work of the Institute of Development Studies has also been at the center of an increasing focus on applied research in such fields as environmental anthropology, border studies, poverty issues, traditional medicine and legal anthropology (ibid.).

As King has argued previously, this more practically oriented work demonstrates "the crucial need to address the human dimensions of development, the complexity of development interventions and the need to listen to the voices of ordinary people who are the targets of centrally planned policies" (King 1999b: 28). By and large, this research has been primarily ethnographic, using "low level" (that is to say, locally rather than universally or theoretically oriented) concepts and focusing on practical issues. Whether specific research has made a difference to government policies, programs and projects is often difficult to establish. In some cases they have, but a thorough assessment would require even more detailed research to determine the precise lines of influence and the main contours of policy-oriented, local debates.

Turning to Kalimantan, and especially in the eastern province, much of the research has focused on such issues as rainforest clearance, changing systems of shifting cultivation, sustainable agricultural systems, responses to such hazards as fire, off-farm work and rural–urban linkages, poverty, resettlement and transmigration, health issues and rural development, and ethnobotanical knowledge and use of medicinal plants (see Colfer 2008; Colfer, Peluso and Chin 1997; Dahuri 1991; Dove 1981; Eghenter 1995; Eghenter, Sellato and Devung 2003; Fulcher 1983; Haug 2007, 2010; Knapen 2001; Kusuma 2005; Leaman 1996; Mackie 1986; Mayer 1996; Momberg 1993; Muhammad Yunus Rasyid 1982; Peluso 1983; Salafsky 1993; Syamsuni Arman 1987; Vargas 1985; Vayda 1981, 1983; Wadley 1997a, 2005; Wilistra 2000). Perhaps more than any other part of Borneo, the research here demonstrates the importance of transnational cooperation between locally based and foreign researchers.

Cultural Politics and Diverse Identity Studies

The applied, policy and practical concerns in Borneo research have continued within what we used to refer to as development studies. But during the past twenty years there have been other developments that have addressed issues in a much wider social science agenda and which have a resonance in Borneo itself. Most of them can be captured within the frame of cultural studies. It is in the cultural realm and the discourses that are generated in the interfaces between people and the nation state that have commanded attention (Metcalf 2010). In particular, diverse research intersects around the construction and contestation of identities and the relationship among identity formation, nation-building and globalization in what we (and others) would term "cultural politics." Cultural studies, in this sense, are not a movement away from, but rather into, a more politically informed anthropology, with concern for issues of power, empowerment and representation of local people and populations.

Cultural politics have been an important phenomenon across much of Southeast Asia in recent years (Kahn 1998). In the Borneo context this is due in no small part to dramatic events in Indonesian Kalimantan from late 1996 to 2001 with bloody conflicts between the Dayaks, Madurese and Malays in the provinces of West and Central Kalimantan. These were part of a wider series of ethnic conflicts in other parts of the Indonesian archipelago following the collapse of Suharto's New Order in 1998, the institution of decentralization policies and the politicization of ethnic identities (Colombijn and Lindblad 2002). Nevertheless, some of the conflicts predated these events; for example, evidence of Dayak–Madurese tensions and anti-Chinese actions can be traced back to the 1950s (Tanasaldy 2012).

Even from 1945 there was a politicization of ethnicity in the continuing struggle between the Indonesian nationalists and the Dutch colonialists, and before the introduction of Sukarno's Guided Democracy in 1959 and the implementation of the authoritarian policies of the New Order from 1966, the Dayaks of Kalimantan had already begun to organize themselves politically and to build a pan-Dayak identity (König 2012; Widen 2001, 2002). This occurred well before the non-Muslim indigenous populations of Sarawak and British North Borneo (Sabah) began to develop and express Dayak and sub-Dayak identities in the run-up to independence within Malaysia in 1963 (Leigh 1974). Dayak identities were also formed in relation and in opposition to the development of politically conscious movements among immigrant communities, particularly the Chinese, across the former territories of British and Dutch Borneo, and in what came to be the Federation of Malaysia. After 1963, the Malaysian Borneo territories were drawn into the model or template of ethnic difference that had been progressively rationalized in peninsular Malaysia. The sultanate of Brunei, too, has addressed the issue of ethnicity, language and culture that it has embedded in racial or ethnic categories in its 1959 Constitution (King 1994).

The wide-ranging contributions, intersecting with cultural politics and identity formation, can be placed under seven headings: (1) nation state, majorities and minorities; (2) religious conversion and identities; (3) media, identities and nation-building; (4) borderlands, margins and migrations; (5) interethnic relations and violence; (6) identity construction in tourism and museums; and finally (7) emerging middle classes, lifestyles and urban identities. In all of these cases, we see diverse developments of theoretically informed but locally grounded scholarship, quite in contrast to critiques of anthropology as "mere butterfly collecting" and local, non-Western scholarship as lacking a theoretical edge.

Nation state, majorities and minorities

The first category covers literature that moves from a focus on a local or defined population to one which analyzes a community or group within the context of the nation state; this involves engagement with political elites and associated dominant groups through which identities and resources have to be negotiated. Included here are, for example, Tsing's study of the Meratus Dayaks (1993), Kustanto's study of the Sungkung (2002), Heidhues' (2001, 2003) work on the Chinese in West Kalimantan, Winzeler on the relationship between the state and minorities (1997) and Widen's study of Ma'anyan Dayaks (2002) along with his recent historical analysis of the development of Dayak identity in Central Kalimantan (2017; see Kusni 1994, 2001). In a local research context, the work of the Institut Dayakologi in Pontianak has pioneered the study of Dayak culture in West Kalimantan with very specific applied issues in mind, including advocacy, networking, legal representation and facilitation programs. This work has focused on building cultural resilience, local consciousness and identity to better equip minority populations to fight for and secure their rights in their land, environment and livelihoods (Bamba 2017).

Religious conversion and identities

The literature on religious conversion and on transformations in religious ideas and practices has increased substantially in recent years and it points to a social and cultural process which has assumed much greater prominence in the context of nation-building in Borneo.

To provide a context for these changes we are fortunate to have major studies of "traditional" religions, which address issues of ritual performance, the language of ritual, cosmology, symbolism, and the transitions involved in birth, initiation, marriage and death, the architectural and material expressions of religion, the ways in which health and illness are conceptualized and dealt with in shamanism and spirit mediumship, and the interrelationships between religion and the mundane, everyday activities of securing a livelihood, particularly in the traditional pursuits of agriculture, and hunting and gathering. Included among these are Appleton's (2006) study of a range of ideas, values and ritual acts in relation to Melanau ontology; Bernstein's (1991) study of Taman shamanism; Kershaw's (2000) study of Brunei Dusun religion (also see Pudarno Binchin 2014); Masing's (1997) detailed examination of an Iban invocatory chant; Metcalf's (1982, 1989) work on Berawan religion and ritual; Morris' (1997) study of Oya Melanau religion; Rousseau's (1998; see 1990) major work on Kayan Religion; Sandin's (1980) study of Iban adat and augury; Sather's (2001) analysis of Iban shamanic chants; Schärer's (1963) earlier work on Ngaju religion; and Uchibori's (1978) on Iban mortuary rituals.

Following Conley's (1973) early study of Kenyah religious conversion, there has been a spate of studies, mainly examining processes of conversion and its social and cultural consequences, as well as the continuities and discontinuities that result from changes in religious belief and practice. Religious configurations, specific beliefs and practices, and the connections established between myth, cosmology and ethnic origins are important ingredients in the construction and maintenance of identities. Important among these many studies are those by Asiyah az-Zahra Ahmad Kumpoh (2011), Chua (2012), Connolly (2003), Fowler (1976), Annette Harris (1995), Fiona Harris (2002), Jay (1991), Lindell (2000), Schiller (1997), Tan Sooi Ling (2008), Thomson (2000), Westmacott (2002), and Zhu Feng (2004). The focus of this research on Borneo has been toward conversion to Christianity rather than to Islam, the impetus for which has come largely from American missionary activity, along with a more modest amount of activity originating from the United Kingdom and Germany.

Media, identities and nation-building

The third category of research on identities has taken the media route to nation-building and has posed the important question: How are communities and ethnic groups in Borneo responding and reacting to media-generated nation-building in Malaysia and Indonesia? This is an emerging area of research pioneered by Postill (2006), Barlocco (2008, 2013) and Bala (2008a), among others. It explores dimensions of identity formation and the ways in which minority populations respond to the opportunities and constraints presented within a nation-state structure. Postill and Bala take a more optimistic view of the state-local interface in Sarawak in relation to the Iban and Kelabit, in contrast to Barlocco in his study of the Kadazan Dusun in Sabah.

Borderlands, margins and migrations

Research within the fourth category has focused primarily on Indonesian border populations and the responses of these marginal communities in territorial terms to the pressures of what is perceived to be a remote central government. Moreover, a government dominated by culturally and ethnically different populations with different priorities. The work of Eilenberg (2012), focusing on the Indonesian side of the border, is important here. Research on the Sarawak side of the border has also focused on spatially marginal populations, cross-border relations and the ambiguous and shifting relations with the nation state (see Amster 1998; Bala 2002; Ishikawa 2010). This work also presents us with a range of case studies that complement and overlap with those on media-generated nation-building and the responses of minorities to the actions and ideologies of dominant political elites. It also demonstrates not only how borders are constructed but how they are perceived, traversed and transcended by populations living alongside them.

Interethnic relations and violence

This category of research has emerged in the necessary engagement with the violent interethnic conflicts in West and Central Kalimantan in the 1990s and the relationship between the construction, transformation and expression of ethnicity, the politicization of identity, the underlying reasons for ethnic conflict, and its cultural patterning and local interpretation. These are examined in the work of an increasing number of anthropologists as well as historians and political scientists influenced by ethnographic, anthropological approaches and qualitative research methods (see Davidson 2008; Harwell 2000; Heidhues 2001;

König 2012; Peluso 2003, 2006, 2008; Peluso and Harwell 2001; Sukandar 2007; Van Klinken 2004).

Identity construction in tourism and museums

Tourism began to be promoted vigorously in Borneo in the 1990s (King 1995; Zeppel 1994). Encouragingly, the research interest in tourism has continued in, for example, studies by researchers in Sabah (Goh 2007; Pianzin 1993; Ong 2008; Zainab 1997) and Sarawak (Kruse 2003). Prior to the establishment of universities in Borneo, museums were the major supporters and managers of research, the obvious examples being the Sarawak Museum and the Brunei Museum. From early on, their major influence has been in categorizing ethnic groups and presenting interpretations of culture and identity by attaching items of material culture to those groups. Their role in relation to the public and tourist visitors has become increasingly important as state governments have seen museums as significant government institutions in tourism promotion. It is clear from the work of Tillotson (1994) and Kreps (1994) that museums are important agents for constructing and presenting culture and identities, and, as departments responsible to government, they usually present a nation-state view of which ethnic groups are important and how they are defined. The recent Borneo-based, anthropological works cited above have approached such nationally framed identity construction with a critical eye.

Emerging middle classes, lifestyles and urban identities

Globalization is one of the current preoccupations of transnational anthropology generally and we might have anticipated that research on Borneo would have reflected this concern. Unfortunately, it has not to any significant degree. There is very little research available on urban societies in Borneo that documents what local people experience in relation to the most immediate manifestations of global processes, late modernity and social class formation, through encounters with the state and bureaucracy, nation-building symbols and actions, the media, technology and consumerism, international tourists, and representatives of other ethnic groups. There is nevertheless an emerging, though still rather modest, interest in identity construction in urban areas and the lifestyles of an expanding middle class (see Boulanger 2009).

New Trajectories of Locally Grounded Transnational Social Science

Although we have drawn attention to the divisions between Western scholars and local or locally based ones, and between colonial anthropology and indigenous scholarship, one of the noticeable more recent developments has been the "transnational" cooperation between Western and local researchers (Thompson 2012; Zawawi 2012, 2015). Our own book *Borneo Studies in History, Society and Culture* (2017) is evidence of this. It demonstrates transnational scholarship on Borneo, whilst at the same time utilizing the platform to highlight the contribution of local scholars and their research agendas. Certainly up to the 1990s, edited volumes were generally dominated by the contributions of Western scholars.

In 2008, based on Zawawi's six years of working at UNIMAS, an edited volume, *Representation, Identity and Multiculturalism in Sarawak* (2008b) was designed to encourage both established and younger Western anthropologists researching on Sarawak (Winzeler 2008; Boulanger 2008; Lindell 2008; Harris 2008; Postill 2008) to combine forces with a new generation of Asian anthropologists (Ishikawa 2008; Yongjin 2008) and young local scholars, drawn from anthropology, political science, law and social work including Welyne Jeffrey Jehom (Bidayuh, 2008), Voon Jan Cham (Sarawak Chinese, 2008), Poline Bala (Kelabit, 2008b), Ramy Bulan (Kelabit, 2008), Ling How Kee (Sarawak Chinese, 2008), Kelvin Egay (Kelabit-Iban, 2008), and Faisal Hazis (Sarawak Malay, 2008), many of whom are home-grown indigenous scholars based at UNIMAS. The book combines both multidisciplinary and transnational perspectives, expressing the simultaneous globalization and localization of knowledge production on Sarawak society and culture. It represents a foray into the forging of transnational anthropology with the knowledge production base being at the periphery rather than the center of what Zawawi calls the "social science knowledge scape."[2]

In this transnational interface, it is Western anthropologists such as Winzeler and Lindell who emerge with critical commentaries and critiques against some of the colonializing modes of approach and representation in the works of earlier Western anthropologists, such as Tom Harrisson and William Geddes. Fiona Harris delivers an equally vehement critique of the representation of gender in colonial writings; as has Hew Cheng Sim from a local perspective (2003, 2007,

2017). Postill is equally critical of the ethnicized "political shell" of the Malaysian state which marginalizes indigenous literary expression amongst Iban writers and intellectuals. Zawawi attempts to articulate the counter-narrations of Penan "development" against the grand narratives of Malaysian state "developmentalism," drawing inspiration from Maori anthropologist Linda Tuhiwai Smith's methodology of "storytelling" (Zawawi 2008c; Zawawi and NoorShah 2012; also see Smith 1999; Zawawi 2016). Other Asian and local scholars in the volume problematize the notion of identity of different ethnic communities in the context of so-called "Malaysian multiculturalism" and its notion of the nation. As reviewers of Zawawi's (2008b) book note, the transnational project represents an exercise in bringing to bear the perspective of cultural studies into anthropology (see Gabriel 2010; Bunnell 2010).

It also is a validation that the playing field and "knowledge-scape" of today's global anthropology has opened more opportunities for center-periphery transnational intellectual and scholar collaborative synergies than ever before, in which anthropologists from both worlds can interact on a more equal footing and even share similar counter-Eurocentric epistemologies. In this context, we suggest that the forging of a "national anthropology," should be more enriching if it were to be articulated not as a separate discourse, but rather as a part of a transnational discourse. We also recognize the problematical nature of national anthropology, particularly whether it becomes hegemonic or develops pluralist perspectives. Peter Kedit, in his early statement on the necessity for the redirection of research in response to Malaysian government policies of socio-economic restructuring, captures the transnational impulse. He states: "We in the Sarawak Museum feel responsible therefore to take whatever necessary steps towards streamlining research projects to this overall principle ... this does not imply that it is the beginning of the end of anthropological research. On the contrary, the implication is that research should continue with more vigour and purpose, than before. It is felt that there should be more encouragement among local and visiting researchers to work together" (1975: 31–32).

It is interesting to note the emphasis on transnational research, but equally important is the emphasis on the application of anthropology to address real-world problems. Pursuing this agenda, the emphasis was placed on the study of interethnic relations and national unity and integration and on minority groups; on "adat" or customary laws; on change and modernization; on government development policies; and finally, the restudying of the classics. In this Kedit emphasized that "there is a large scope for visiting scholars to play their role in this category of research" (1975: 33).

The vision spelt out by Kedit argued for the need for rigorous methodology and perhaps the exploration of "new social science theory." His emphasis on the study of minorities presaged what is now referred to as "identity politics." It also indirectly problematizes questions of national identity and national culture with regard to current issues that remain unresolved in Malaysia, including East Malaysia, and indeed in Kalimantan and Brunei. Borneo, in this light, is a particularly productive site not only to examine these local issues in global perspective but also to speak to global issues from a place that is at once peripheral, not just globally but within Malaysian and Indonesian nation states while simultaneously being an inherently transnational space crossing three nation-state boundaries.

Conclusion

In this chapter we have moved through trends spanning four generations: from first the traditional preoccupations of the early post-war colonial anthropologists, to a second generation that continued the legacy with modifications, to a third that became more localized, indigenized, practical and policy-directed in such areas as rural development and agricultural change, to a fourth that embraced post-modernism, reflexivity, and globalization paying increasing attention to identity, agency, and fluidity while critically deconstructing colonial anthropology and the early preoccupations with the identification of social structures, corporate social groups, and social functions. Finally, we pose the issue of a "national anthropology" and what this might look like in a Borneo context, particularly when Borneo studies has become increasingly transnational in bringing together the three nation states represented there.

There have obviously been different emphases on the ways in which social science research has developed in Malaysian Borneo, Kalimantan and Brunei Darussalam. But it is difficult to identify distinctive national traditions when the preoccupation with the application of research findings on practical and policy issues is clearly evident across Borneo. More particularly there has been an identifiable shift to concerns with identities and ethnicities in a range of dimensions. These find their roots in government policies of nation-building, in the relations between majorities and minorities, ethnic tensions, processes of cultural absorption, religious conversion, tourism development, increased movement across borders, and national educational and language policies.

We have also emphasized the transnational dimension in research on Borneo in regard to collaboration between local scholars and researchers from outside the region. There is substantial evidence of this trend across Borneo, expressed in collaborative programs of research supported by local universities and research institutions which have involved overseas researchers, and in such professional organizations as the Borneo Research Council which encourage transnational exchange. Nevertheless, the trend towards the indigenization of research will continue, and what was once seen as a periphery and an object of scholarly contemplation by Western outsiders has increasingly become a center for research but with the continued contribution of those from beyond the shores of Borneo. Borneo thus becomes a space for critical reflection, drawing strength from local grounding and practical concerns in which theoretically informed and practical research are not at odds but mutually reinforcing and enriching.

Notes

1. We draw some of the material for this paper in revised form from the recent, encyclopedic volume on *Borneo Studies in History, Society and Culture* (King et al. 2017); see in particular chapters by King (2017a, 2017b, 2017c) and Zawawi Ibrahim (2017).
2. See Zawawi's critique of Kuwayama's "world system" anthropology by utilizing Appadurai's "scape'" perspective, in Zawawi Ibrahim (2015); also see Kuwayama (2004, 2014).

References

Alexander, Jennifer (1987) *Uma Lahanan, Long Panggai: A Preliminary Report*, Macquarie University.

_____ (1989) "Culture and Identity: The Case of the Lahanan of Ulu Belaga," *The Sarawak Museum Journal*, special issue 40(4, pt 1): pp. 51–59.

_____ (1990) "Lahanan Social Structure: Some Preliminary Considerations," *The Sarawak Museum Journal* 41: pp. 189–212.

Amster, Matthew H. (1998) *Community, Ethnicity, and Modes of Association among the Kelabit of Sarawak, East Malaysia*, Unpublished PhD dissertation, Brandeis University, United States.

Appell, George N. (1965) *The Nature of Social Groupings among the Rungus Dusun of Sabah, Malaysia.* Unpublished PhD dissertation, Australian National University.

——— (ed.) (1976a) *The Societies of Borneo: Explorations in the Theory of Cognatic Social Structure.* Washington DC: American Anthropological Association.

——— (ed.) (1976b) *Studies in Borneo Societies: Social Process and Anthropological Explanation.* DeKalb: Northern Illinois University, Center for Southeast Asian Studies Special Report.

——— (1977) "The Status of Social Science Research in Sarawak and Its Relevance for Development." In *Sarawak: Research and Theory,* Mario D. Zamora, George N. Appell, Craig A. Lockard and Vinson H. Sutlive, (eds.). Williamsburg, Virginia: Boswell Printing and Publishing, Studies in Third World Societies, Issue no. 2: pp. 1–90.

——— (2001) "Iban Studies: Their Contribution to Social Theory and the Ethnography of Other Borneo Societies." In *The Encyclopedia of Iban Studies: Iban History, Society and Culture, Vol. 3,* Vincent H. Sutlive and Joanne Sutlive, (eds.), pp. 741–85. Kuching: The Tun Jugah Foundation.

Appell, George N. and Triloki N. Madan, (eds.) (1988) *Choice and Morality in Anthropological Perspective: Essays in Honor of Professor Derek Freeman.* Buffalo: State University of New York Press.

Appleton, Ann L. (2006) *Acts of Integration, Expressions of Faith: Madness, Death and Ritual in Melanau Ontology.* Phillips: Borneo Research Council, Monograph Series No. 9.

Armstrong, Rita (1991) *People of the Same Heart: The Social World of the Kenyah Badeng.* Unpublished PhD dissertation, University of Sydney, Australia.

——— (1992) "The Cultural Construction of Hierarchy among the Kenyah Badeng," *Oceania* 62: pp. 194–206.

Asiyah az-Zahra Ahmad Kumpoh (2011) *Conversion to Islam: The Case of the Dusun Ethnic Group in Brunei Darussalam.* Unpublished PhD dissertation, University of Leicester, United Kingdom.

Austin, Robert F. (1977) *Iban Migration: Patterns of Mobility and Employment in the 20th Century.* Unpublished PhD dissertation, University of Michigan, United States.

Avé, Jan B. and Victor T. King (1986a) *Borneo. People of the Weeping Forests: Tradition and Change in Borneo* (revised and expanded English edition). Leiden: Rijksmuseum voor Volkenkunde.

——— (1986b) *Borneo: Oerwoud in Ondergang, Culturen op Drift.* Leiden: Rijksmuseum voor Volkenkunde.

Bala, Poline (2002) *Changing Borders and Identities in the Kelabit Highlands: Anthropological Reflections on Growing Up Near an International Border.* Kota Samarahan: Universiti Sarawak Malaysia.

——— (2008a) *Desire for Progress: The Kelabit Experiences with Information Communication Technologies (ICTs) for Rural Development in Sarawak, East Malaysia.* Unpublished PhD dissertation, University of Cambridge, United Kingdom.

——— (2008b) "National Identity and Multiculturalism at the Margins: The Kelabit Experience in the Highlands of Central Borneo." In *Representation, Identity and Multiculturalism in Sarawak*, Zawawi Ibrahim, (ed.), pp. 139–53. Kajang: Persatuan Sains Sosial Malaysia; Kuching: Dayak Cultural Foundation Publication.

——— (2017) "An Overview of Anthropological and Sociological Research at the faculty of Social Sciences, Universiti Malaysia Sarawak." In *Borneo Studies in History, Society and Culture*, Victor T. King, Zawawi Ibrahim and Noor Hasharina Hassan, (eds.), pp. 283–302. Singapore: Springer.

Bamba, John (2017) "Institut Dayakologi: The Challenges of an Information and Advocacy Centre of Dayak Culture in Kalimantan." In *Borneo Studies in History, Society and Culture*, Victor T. King, Zawawi Ibrahim and Noor Hasharina Hassan, (eds.), pp. 313–40. Singapore: Springer.

Barlocco, Fausto (2013) *Identity and the State in Malaysia.* London and New York: Routledge.

Bernstein, Jay H. (1997) *Spirits Captured in Stone: Shamanism and Traditional Medicine among the Taman of Borneo.* Boulder: Lynne Rienner Publishers.

Boulanger, Clare L. (2008) "Repenting for the Sin of Headhunting: Modernity, Anxiety, and Time as Experienced by Urban Dayaks in Sarawak." In *Representation, Identity and Multiculturalism in Sarawak*, Zawawi Ibrahim, (ed.), pp. 229–37. Kajang: Persatuan Sains Sosial Malaysia; Kuching: Dayak Cultural Foundation Publication.

——— (2009) *A Sleeping Tiger: Ethnicity, Class and New Dayak Dreams in Urban Sarawak.* Lanham, Maryland and Plymouth: University Press of America.

Brookfield, Harold, Lesley Potter and Yvonne Byron (1995) *In Place of the Forest: Environmental and Socio-economic Transformation in Borneo and the Eastern Malay Peninsula.* Tokyo: United Nations University Press.

Brown, Donald E. (1969) *Socio-political History of Brunei: A Bornean Malay Sultanate.* Unpublished PhD dissertation, Cornell University, United States.

——— (1970) "Brunei: The Structure and History of a Bornean Malay Sultanate," *Brunei Museum Journal*, Monograph No. 2.

——— (1976) *Principles of Social Structure: Southeast Asia.* London: Duckworth.

——— (1991) *Human Universals.* New York: McGraw-Hill.

Bulan, Ramy (2008) "Resolution of Conflict and Disputes under Kelabit Customary Laws in Sarawak." In *Representation, Identity and Multiculturalism in Sarawak*, Zawawi Ibrahim, (ed.), pp. 155–74. Kajang:

Persatuan Sains Sosial Malaysia; Kuching: Dayak Cultural Foundation Publication.

Bunnell, Tim (2010) "Book Review of Zawawi Ibrahim's *Representation, Identity and Multiculturalism in Sarawak*," *Asian Journal of Social Science* 38(6): pp. 821–22.

Chu, Clayton Hsin (1978) *The Three Worlds of Iban Shamanism*. Unpublished PhD dissertation, Columbia University, United States.

Chua, Liana (2012) *The Christianity of Culture: Conversion, Ethnic Citizenship, and the Matter of Religion in Malaysian Borneo*. New York: Palgrave Macmillan.

Cleary, Mark and Peter Eaton (1992) *Borneo: Change and Development*. Oxford: Oxford University Press.

Cobb, Don David (1988) *Iban Shifting Cultivation: A Bioregional Perspective (Sarawak, Malaysia)*. Unpublished PhD dissertation, Arizona State University, United States.

Colfer, Carol Pierce (2008) *The Longhouse of the Tarsier: Changing Landscapes, Gender and Ways of Life in Borneo (1980–2007)*. Phillips: Borneo Research Council, UNESCO and CIFOR.

Colfer, Carol Pierce, Nancy Lee Peluso, and Chin See Chung, (eds.) (1997) *Beyond Slash and Burn: Building on Indigenous Management of Borneo's Tropical Rain Forests*. Bronx: New York Botanical Garden.

Colombijn, Freek and J. Thomas Lindblad, (eds.) (2002) *Roots of Violence in Indonesia: Contemporary Violence in Historical Perspective*. Leiden: KITLV Press.

Conley William W. (1976) *The Kalimantan Kenyah: A Study of Tribal Conversion in Terms of Dynamic Cultural Themes*. Nutley: Presbyterian and Reformed Publishing Co.

Connolly, Jennifer (2003) *Being Christian and Dayak: A Study of Christian Conversion among Dayaks in East Kalimantan, Indonesia*. Unpublished PhD dissertation, New School University, United States.

Cooke, Fadzilah Majid (1999) *The Challenge of Sustainable Forests: Forest Resource Policy in Malaysia 1970–1995*. Sydney: Allen & Unwin; Honolulu: University of Hawai'i Press.

—— (ed.) (2006) *State, Communities and Forests in Contemporary Borneo*. Canberra: Australian National University Press, Asia-Pacific Monograph 1.

Crain, Jay B. (1970) *The Lun Dayeh of Sabah, East Malaysia: Aspects of Marriage and Social Exchange*. Unpublished PhD dissertation, Cornell University, United States.

Cramb, Robert A. (1987) *The Evolution of Iban Land Tenure: A Study in Institutional Economics*. Unpublished PhD dissertation, Monash University, Australia.

—— (2007) *Land and Longhouse: Agrarian Transformations in the Uplands of Sarawak*. Copenhagen: NIAS Press.

Dahuri, Rokhmin (1991) *An Approach to Coastal Resource Utilization: The Nature and Role of Sustainable Development in East Kalimantan Coastal Zone, Indonesia*. Unpublished PhD dissertation, Dalhousie University, Canada.

Davidson, Jamie S. (2008) *From Rebellion to Riots: Collective Violence on Indonesian Borneo*. Madison, Wisconsin: University of Wisconsin Press.

Deegan, James L. (1973) *Change among the Lun Bawang: A Borneo People*. Unpublished PhD dissertation, University of Washington, United States.

Doolittle, Amity A. (2005) *Property and Politics in Sabah, Malaysia (North Borneo): A Century of Native Struggles over Land Rights, 1881–1996*. Seattle: University of Washington Press.

Dove, Michael R. (1981) *Subsistence Strategies in Rain Forest Swidden Agriculture: The Kantu' at Tikul Batu (Volumes I and II) (Indonesia)*. Unpublished PhD dissertation, Stanford University, United States.

Drake, Richard Allen (1982) *The Material Provisioning of Mualang Society in Hinterland Kalimantan Barat, Indonesia*. Unpublished PhD dissertation, Michigan State University, United States.

Egay, Kelvin (2008) "The Significance of Ethnic Identity among the Penan Belangan Community in the Sungai Asap Resettlement Scheme." In *Representation, Identity and Multiculturalism in Sarawak*, Zawawi Ibrahim, (ed.), pp. 239–55. Kajang: Persatuan Sains Sosial Malaysia; Kuching: Dayak Cultural Foundation Publication.

Eghenter, Cristina (1995) *Knowledge, Action and Planning: A Study of Long-distance Migrations among the Kayan and Kenyah of East Kalimantan, Indonesia*. Unpublished PhD dissertation, Rutgers University, United States.

Eghenter, Cristina, Bernard Sellato, and G. Simon Devung, (eds.) (2003) *Social Science Research and Conservation Management in the Interior of Borneo: Unravelling Past and Present Interactions of People and Forests*. Jakarta: Center for International Forestry Research.

Eilenberg, Michael (2012) *At the Edges of States: Dynamics of State Formation in the Indonesian Borderlands*. Leiden: KITLV Press, Verhandelingen van het Koninlijk Instituut voor Taal-Land en Volkenkunde, no. 275.

Faisal S. Hazis (2008) "Contesting Sarawak Malayness: Glimpses of the Life and Identity of the Malays in Southwest Sarawak." In *Representation, Identity and Multiculturalism in Sarawak*, Zawawi Ibrahim, (ed.), pp. 263–96. Kajang: Persatuan Sains Sosial Malaysia; Kuching: Dayak Cultural Foundation Publication.

Fidler, Richard C. (2010) *Kanowit: An Overseas Chinese Community in Borneo*. Sibu: Chinese Cultural Association.

Fortier, David H. (1964) *Culture Change among Chinese Agricultural Settlers in British North Borneo*. Unpublished PhD dissertation, Columbia University, United States.

Fowler, J.A. (1976) *Communicating the Gospel among the Iban*. Unpublished DMiss thesis, Southern Methodist University, United States.

Freeman, J.D. (Derek) (1953) *Family and Kin among the Iban of Sarawak*. Unpublished PhD dissertation, University of Cambridge, United Kingdom.

____ (1955a) *Iban Agriculture: A Report on the Shifting Cultivation of Hill Rice by the Iban of Sarawak*. London: HMSO, Colonial Office Research Study No. 19.

____ (1955b) *Report on the Iban of Sarawak*. Kuching: Government Printing Office.

____ (1957) "The Family System of the Iban of Borneo." In *The Developmental Cycle in Domestic Groups*, Jack Goody, (ed.), pp. 15–52. Cambridge: Cambridge University Press, Cambridge Papers in Social Anthropology, no. 1.

____ (1960) "The Iban of Western Borneo." In *Social Structure in Southeast Asia*, G.P. Murdock, (ed.), pp. 65–87. Chicago: Quadrangle Books.

____ (1961) "On the Concept of the Kindred," *The Journal of the Royal Anthropological Institute of Great Britain and Ireland* 91: pp. 192–220.

____ (1966) "Social Anthropology and the Scientific Study of Human Behaviour," *Man*, New Series 1: pp. 330–42.

____ (1970) *Report on the Iban*. London: The Athlone Press, LSE Monographs on Anthropology, no 41.

____ (1973) "Darwinian Psychological Anthropology: A Biosocial Approach [with Comments and Reply]," *Current Anthropology* 14: pp. 373–87.

____ (1983) *Margaret Mead and Samoa: The Making and Unmaking of an Anthropological Myth*. Cambridge: Harvard University Press.

____ (1999) *The Fateful Hoaxing of Margaret Mead: A Historical Analysis of her Samoan Research*. Boulder: Westview Press.

Fulcher, Mary Beth (1983) *Resettlement and Replacement: Social Dynamics in East Kalimantan*. Unpublished PhD dissertation, Northwestern University, United States.

Gabriel, Sharmani (2010) "Book Review of Zawawi Ibrahim's *Representation, Identity and Multiculturalism in Sarawak*," *Cultural Anthropology*, 21(1): pp. 169–73.

Geddes, W. (William) R. (1948) *An Analysis of Cultural Change in Fiji*. Unpublished PhD dissertation, University of London, United Kingdom.

____ (1954) *The Land Dayaks of Sarawak*. London: HMSO.

____ (1957) *Nine Dayak Nights*. London: Oxford University Press.

____ (1976) *Migrants of the Mountains: The Cultural Ecology of the Blue Miao (Hmong Njua) of Thailand*. Oxford: Clarendon Press.

Glyn-Jones, Monica (1953) *The Dusun of the Penampang Plains in North Borneo*. London: HMSO, Colonial Social Science Research Council.

Goh Hong Ching (2007) *Sustainable Tourism and the Influence of Privatization in Protected Area Management. A Case of Kinabalu Park, Malaysia*. Rheinischen Friedrich-Wilhelms-Universitat Bonn: PhD dissertation.

Grijpstra, B.G. (1976) *Common Efforts in the Development of Rural Sarawak, Malaysia*. Assen: van Gorcum.

Han Sin Fong (1971) *A Study of the Occupational Patterns and Social Interaction of Overseas Chinese in Sabah, Malaysia*. Unpublished PhD dissertation, University of Michigan, United States.

Harris, Annette Suzanne (1995) *The Impact of Christianity on Power Relationships and Social Exchanges: A Case Study of Change among the Tagal Murut, Sabah, Malaysia*. Unpublished PhD dissertation, Biola University, United States.

Harris, Fiona (2002) *Growing Gods: Bidayuh Processes of Religious Change in Sarawak, Malaysia*. Unpublished PhD dissertation, University of Edinburgh, United Kingdom.

——— (2008) "When Town and Kampong Collide: Representations of Gender in Sarawak." In *Representation, Identity and Multiculturalism in Sarawak*, Zawawi Ibrahim, (ed.), pp. 57–73. Kajang: Persatuan Sains Sosial Malaysia; Kuching: Dayak Cultural Foundation Publication.

Harrison, Robert (1971) *An Analysis of the Variation among Ranau Dusun Communities of Sabah, Malaysia*. Unpublished PhD dissertation, Columbia University, United States.

Harwell, Emily (2000) *The Un-natural History of Culture: Ethnicity, Tradition and Territorial Conflict in West Kalimantan, Indonesia, 1800–1997*. Unpublished PhD dissertation, Yale University, United States.

Haug, Michaela (2007) *Poverty and Decentralisation in Kutai Barat: The Impacts of Regional Autonomy on Dayak Benuaq Wellbeing. Making Local Government More Responsive to the Poor: Developing Inidcators and Tools to Support Sustainable Livelihood under Decentralisation. Research Report*. Bogor Barat: CIFOR.

——— (2010) *Poverty and Decentralisation in East Kalimantan: The Impact of Regional Autonomy on Dayak Benuaq Wellbeing*. Freiburg: Centaurus Verlag.

Heidhues, Mary F. Somers (2001) "Kalimantan Barat 1967–1999: Violence on the Periphery." In *Violence in Indonesia*, I. Wessel and G. Wimhofer, (eds.), pp. 139–51, Hamburg: Abera.

——— (2003) *Golddiggers, Farmers, and Traders in the "Chinese Districts" of West Kalimantan, Indonesia*. Ithaca: Cornell University Press.

Helliwell, Christine (1990) *The Ricefield and the Hearth: Social Relations in a Borneo Dayak Community*. Unpublished PhD dissertation, Australian National University.

——— (2001) *Never Stand Alone: A Study of Borneo Sociality*. Williamsburg: Borneo Research Council, Monograph Series No. 5.

Heppell, Michael (1975) *Iban Social Control: The Infant and the Adult*. Unpublished PhD dissertation, Australian National University.

Hew Cheng Sim (2003) *Women Workers, Migration and Family in Sarawak*. London and New York: RoutledgeCurzon.

____ (ed.) (2007) *Village Mothers, City Daughters: Women and Urbanisation in Sarawak*. Singapore: Institute of Southeast Asian Studies.

____ (2017) "Whither Gender Studies in Sarawak." In *Borneo Studies in History, Society and Culture*, Victor T. King, Zawawi Ibrahim, and Noor Hasharina Hassan, (eds.), pp. 261–82. Singapore: Springer.

Hong, Evelyne (1985) *See the Third World While it Lasts: The Social and Environmental Impact of Tourism with Particular Reference to Malaysia*. Penang: Consumers' Association of Penang.

____ (1987) *The Natives of Sarawak: Survival in Borneo's Vanishing Forests*. Penang: Institut Masyarakat.

Hudson, A.B. (1967) *Padju Epat: The Ethnography and Social Structure of a Ma'anjan Dayak Group in Southeastern Borneo*. Unpublished PhD dissertation, Cornell University, United States.

____ (1972) *Padju Epat: The Ma'anyan of Indonesian Borneo*. New York: Holt, Rinehart and Winston.

Ishikawa, Noburu (2008) "Cultural Geography of the Sarawak Malays: A View from the Margin of the National Terrain." In *Representation, Identity and Multiculturalism in Sarawak*, Zawawi Ibrahim, (ed.), pp. 257–61. Kajang: Persatuan Sains Sosial Malaysia; Kuching: Dayak Cultural Foundation Publication.

____ (2010) *Between Frontiers: Nation and Identity in a Southeast Asian Borderland*. Athens: Ohio University Press.

Jay, Sian Eira (1991) *Shamans, Priests and the Cosmology of the Ngaju Dayak of Central Kalimantan*. Unpublished DPhil thesis, University of Oxford, United Kingdom.

Jehom, Welyne Jeffrey (2008) "Ethnic Pluralism and Ethnic Relations in Sarawak." In *Representation, Identity and Multiculturalism in Sarawak*, Zawawi Ibrahim, (ed.), pp. 93–109. Kajang: Persatuan Sains Sosial Malaysia; Kuching: Dayak Cultural Foundation Publication.

Jensen, Erik (1968) *Iban Belief and Behaviour: A Study of the Sarawak Iban, Their Religion and Padi Cult*. Unpublished DPhil thesis, University of Oxford, United Kingdom.

____ (1974) *The Iban and their Religion*. Oxford: Clarendon Press.

Kahn, Joel S. (1998) *Southeast Asian Identities: Culture and the Politics of Representation in Indonesia, Malaysia, Singapore and Thailand*. London: I.B. Tauris Co. Ltd.

Kedit, Peter Mulok (1975) "Current Anthropological Research in Sarawak," *The Sarawak Museum Journal* 23: pp. 29–36.

____ (1980) *Modernization among the Iban of Sarawak*. Kuala Lumpur: Dewan Bahasa dan Pustaka.

Kershaw, Eva Maria (2000) *A Study of Brunei Dusun Religion: Ethnic Priesthood on a Frontier of Islam*. Williamsburg: Borneo Research Council, Monograph Series No. 4.

Kim Yongjin (2008) "Representing Ethnic Cultures in Sarawak, Malaysia: A Study of the Sarawak Cultural Village." In *Representation, Identity and Multiculturalism in Sarawak*, Zawawi Ibrahim, (ed.), pp. 111–18. Kajang: Persatuan Sains Sosial Malaysia; Kuching: Dayak Cultural Foundation Publication.

King, Victor T. (1985) *The Maloh of West Kalimantan: An Ethnographic Study of Social Inequality and Social Change in an Indonesian Borneo Society*. Dordrecht and Cinnaminson: Foris Publications, Verhandelingen van het Koninklijk Instituut voor Taal-, Land- en Volkenkunde, no. 108.

____ (1993) *The Peoples of Borneo*. Oxford: Blackwell.

____ (1994) "What is Brunei Society? Reflections on a Conceptual and Ethnographic Issue," *Southeast Asia Research* 2: pp. 176–98.

____ (ed.) (1995) *Tourism in Borneo*. Phillips: Borneo Research Council Proceedings Series, no. 4.

____ (ed.) (1999a) *Rural Development and Social Science Research: Case Studies from Borneo*. Phillips: Borneo Research Council Proceedings Series, no. 6.

____ (1999b) *Anthropology and Development in South-East Asia*. Kuala Lumpur: Oxford University Press.

____ (2017a) "Some Preliminary Thoughts on Early Anthropology in Borneo." In *Borneo Studies in History, Society and Culture*, Victor T. King, Zawawi Ibrahim, and Noor Hasharina Hassan, (eds.), pp. 15–34. Singapore: Springer.

____ (2017b) "Borneo and Beyond: Reflections on Borneo Studies, Anthropology and the Social Sciences." In *Borneo Studies in History, Society and Culture*, Victor T. King, Zawawi Ibrahim and Noor Hasharina Hassan, (eds.), pp. 79–124. Singapore: Springer.

____ (2017c) "Identities in Borneo: Constructions and Transformations." In *Borneo Studies in History, Society and Culture*, Victor T. King, Zawawi Ibrahim and Noor Hasharina Hassan, (eds.), pp. 179–207. Singapore: Springer.

King, Victor T., Zawawi Ibrahim, and Noor Hasharina Hassan (eds.) (2017) *Borneo Studies in History, Society and Culture*. Singapore: Springer.

Knapen, Han (2001) *Forests of Fortune? The Environmental History of Southeast Borneo, 1600–1880*. Leiden: KITLV Press.

Komanyi, Margit Ilona (1973) *Decision-making of Iban Women: A Study of a Longhouse Community in Sarawak, East Malaysia*. Unpublished PhD dissertation, New York University, United States.

König, Anika (2012) *The Cultural Face of Conflict: Dayak-Madurese Violence in 1996/97 in West Kalimantan, Indonesia*. Unpublished PhD dissertation, Australian National University.

Kreps, Christina Faye (1994) *On Becoming "Museum-minded": A Study of Museum Development and the Politics of Culture in Indonesia*. Unpublished PhD dissertation, University of Oregon, United States.

Kruse, William (2003) *Selling Wild Borneo: A Critical Examination of the Organised Iban Longhouse Tourism Industry in Sarawak, East Malaysia.* Unpublished PhD dissertation, Australian National University.

Kusni, J.J. (1994) *Dayak Membangun: Kasus Dayak Kalimantan Tengah* [*Dayak Development: The Case of Central Kalimantan Dayak*]. Jakarta: The Paragon.

——— (2001) *Negara Etnik: Beberapa Gagalan Pemberdayaan Suku Dayak* [*The Ethnic Nation: Several Failures to Empower the Dayak*]. Yogyakarta: Forum Studi Perubahan dan Perabadan.

Kustanto, Joannes Baptis Hari (2002) *The Politics of Ethnic Identity among the Sungkung of West Kalimantan, Indonesia.* Unpublished PhD dissertation, Yale University, United States.

Kusuma, Indah D. (2005) *Economic Valuation of Natural Resource Management: A Case Study of the Benuaq Dayak Tribe in Kalimantan, Indonesia.* Unpublished PhD dissertation, Louisiana State University, United States.

Kuwayama, Takami (2004) "The 'World-system' of Anthropology: Japan and Asia in the Global Community of Anthropologists." In *The Making of Anthropology in East and Southeast Asia*, Shinji Yamashita, Joseph Bosco and J.S. Eades, (eds.), pp. 35–56. New York: Berghahn Books.

——— (2014) "Bridging the Anthropology of Japan Outside Japan," *Japanese Review of Cultural Anthropology* 15: pp. 75–79.

Lake' Baling (2002) *The Old Kayan Religion and the Bungan Religious Reform.* UNIMAS: Institute of East Asian Studies.

Leach, E.R. (1947) *Visit to Kemabong, Labuan and Interior Residency, British North Borneo, 1–8 November 1947.* London: Colonial Social Science Research Council.

——— (1948) *Report on the Possibilities of a Social Economic Survey of Sarawak.* London: Colonial Social Science Research Council.

——— (1950) *Social Science Research in Sarawak: A Report on the Possibilities of a Social Economic Survey of Sarawak presented to the Colonial Social Science Research Council, London, March 1948–July 1949.* London: HMSO, Colonial Research Studies No. 1.

Leaman, Danna Jo. (1996) *The Medicinal Ethnobotany of the Kenyah of East Kalimantan (Indonesian Borneo).* Unpublished PhD dissertation, University of Ottawa, Canada.

Leigh, Michael B. (1974) *The Rising Moon: Political Change in Sarawak.* Sydney: Sydney University Press.

Linda, Amy (1975) *The Enculturation of Aggression in a Brunei Malay Village.* Unpublished PhD dissertation, Ohio University, United States.

Lindell, Pamela N. (2008) "A Critique of William Geddes' *The Land Dayaks of Sarawak.*" In *Representation, Identity and Multiculturalism in Sarawak*, Zawawi Ibrahim, (ed.), pp. 45–55. Kajang: Persatuan Sains Sosial Malaysia; Kuching: Dayak Cultural Foundation Publication.

——— (2000) *The Longhouse and the Legacy of History: Religion, Architecture and Change among the Bisingai of Sarawak (Malaysia).* Unpublished PhD dissertation, University of Nevada, Reno, United States.

Ling How Kee (2008) "Border Crossings: Towards Developing Multiculturalism in Social Research and Practice." In *Representation, Identity and Multiculturalism in Sarawak*, Zawawi Ibrahim, (ed.), pp. 175–91. Kajang: Persatuan Sains Sosial Malaysia; Kuching: Dayak Cultural Foundation Publication.

McKeown, Francis A. (1989) *The Merakai Iban: An Ethnographic Account with Especial Reference to Dispute Settlement.* Unpublished PhD dissertation, Monash University, Asutralia.

Mackie, Cynthia (1986) *Disturbance and Succession Resulting from Shifting Cultivation in an Upland Rainforest in Indonesian Borneo (Deforestation, Kenyah Dayak, Kalimantan).* Unpublished PhD dissertation, Rutgers University, United States.

Masing, James (1997) *The Coming of the Gods: An Invocatory Chant (Timang Gawai Amat) of the Iban of the Baleh River Region, Sarawak.* Canberra: Department of Anthropology, Research School of Pacific and Asian Studies, Australian National University, 2 vols.

Maxwell, Allen R. (1980) *Urang Darat: An Ethnographic Study of the Kadayan of the Labu Valley, Brunei.* Unpublished PhD dissertation, Yale University, United States.

Mayer, Judith Hannah (1996) *Trees vs Trees: Institutional Dynamics of Indigenous Agroforestry and Industrial Timber in West Kalimantan, Indonesia.* Unpublished PhD dissertation, University of California, Berkeley, United States.

Metcalf, Peter (1982) *A Borneo Journey into Death: Berawan Eschatology from its Rituals.* Philadelphia: University of Pennsylvania Press.

——— (1989) *Where are You, Spirits: Style and Theme in Berawan Prayer.* Washington DC: Smithsonian Institution Press, Smithsonian Series in Ethnographic Inquiry 13.

——— (2010) *The Life of the Longhouse: An Archaeology of Ethnicity.* Cambridge: Cambridge University Press.

Miles, Douglas (1976) *Cutlass and Crescent Moon: A Case Study of Social and Political Change in Outer Indonesia.* Sydney: Sydney University Press.

Momberg, Frank (1993) *Indigenous Knowledge Systems: Potentials for Social Forestry Development: Resource Management of Land-Dayaks in West Kalimantan.* Berlin: Technische Universität Berlin.

Morris, H.S. (1953) *A Report on a Melanau Sago Producing Community in Sarawak.* London: HMSO.

——— (1963) *Immigrant Indian Communities in East Africa.* Unpublished PhD dissertation, University of London, United Kingdom.

_____ (1991) *The Oya Melanau*. Kuching: Malaysian Historical Society (Sarawak Branch).

_____ (1997) *The Oya Melanau: Traditional Ritual and Belief with a Catalogue of Belum Carvings*. Kuching: The Sarawak Museum Journal, vol. 52, issue 73.

Morrison, Jean (1993) *Bajau Gender: A Study of the Effects of Socio-economic Change on Gender Relations in a Fishing Community of Sabah, East Malaysia*. Unpublished PhD dissertation, University of Hull, United Kingdom.

Muhammad Yunus Rasyid (1982) *Farmers' Participation in Rural Development Programs, Municipality of Samarinda, East Kalimantan, Indonesia*. Unpublished PhD dissertation, Louisiana State University, United States.

Murdock, George P., (ed.) (1960a) *Social Structure in Southeast Asia*. Chicago: Quadrangle Books.

_____ (1960b) "Cognatic forms of Social Organization." In *Social Structure in Southeast Asia*, George P. Murdock, (ed.), pp. 1–14. Chicago: Quadrangle Books.

Needham, Rodney (1953) *The Social Organisation of the Penan: A Southeast Asia People*. Unpublished DPhil thesis, Oxford University, United Kingdom.

_____ (1978a) *Primordial Characters*. Charlottesville: University of Virginia Press.

_____ (1978b) *Essential Perplexities*. Oxford: Clarendon Press.

_____ (1979) *Symbolic Classification*. Santa Monica: Goodyear Publishing Co.

_____ (1980) *Reconnaissances*. Toronto: University of Toronto Press.

Nicolaisen Ida (1976) "Form and Function of Punan Bah Ethno-historical Tradition," *The Sarawak Museum Journal* 24: pp. 63–95.

_____ (1977–78) "The Dynamics of Ethnic Classification: A Case Study of the Punan Bah in Sarawak," *Folk* 19–20: pp. 183–200.

_____ (1983) "Change without Development: The Transformation of Punan Bah Economy," *The Sarawak Museum Journal* 32: pp. 191–203.

_____ (1986) "Pride and Progress: Kajang Response to Economic Change," *The Sarawak Museum Journal* 36: pp. 75–116.

Ong Puay Liu (2008) *Packaging Myths for Tourism: The Rungus of Kudat*. Bangi: Penerbit Universiti Kebangsaan Malaysia.

Padoch, Christine (1978) *Migration and its Alternatives among the Iban of Sarawak*. Unpublished PhD dissertation, Columbia University, United States.

Padoch, Christine and Nancy Lee Peluso, (eds.) (1996) *Borneo in Transition: People, Forests, Conservation, and Development*. Kuala Lumpur and New York: Oxford University Press.

Peluso, Nancy Lee (1983) *Markets and Merchants: The Forest Products Trade of East Kalimantan in Historical Perspective*. Unpublished PhD dissertation, Cornell University, United States.

——— (2003) "Weapons of the Wild: Strategic Uses of Violence and Wildness in the Rain Forests of Indonesian Borneo." In *In Search of the Rain Forest*, C. Slater, (ed.), pp. 204–45. Durham: Duke University Press.

——— (2006) "Passing the Red Bowl: Creating Community Identity through Violence in West Kalimantan, 1967–1997." In *Violent Conflict in Indonesia: Analysis, Representation, Resolution*, C.A. Coppel, (ed.), pp. 106–28. London and New York: Routledge.

——— (2008) "A Political Ecology of Violence and Territory in West Kalimantan," *Asia Pacific Viewpoint* 49: pp. 48–67.

Peluso, Nancy Lee and Emily Harwell (2001) "Territory, Custom, and the Cultural Politics of Ethnic War in West Kalimantan, Indonesia." In *Violent Environments*, Nancy Lee Peluso and Michael Watts, (eds.), pp. 83–116. Ithaca: Cornell University Press.

Peranio, Roger D. (1977) *The Structure of Bisaya Society: A Ranked Cognatic Social System*. Unpublished PhD dissertation, Columbia University, United States.

Persoon, Gerard A. and Marion Osseweijer, (eds.) (2008) *Reflections on the Heart of Borneo*. Wageningen: Tropenbos International.

Pianzin, T.M. (1993) *Managing the Development of Tourism: A Case Study of Sabah, Malaysia*. Unpublished PhD dissertation, University of Strathclyde, United Kingdom.

Porodong, Paul (2010) *An Exploration of Changing Household Subsistence Strategies among Contemporary Rungus Farmers*. Unpublished PhD dissertation, University of Kent, United Kingdom.

Postill, John (2006) *Media and Nation-building: How the Iban became Malaysian*. Oxford and New York: Berghahn Books, Asia Pacific Studies No. 1.

——— (2008) "The Mediated Production of Ethnicity and Nationalism among the Iban of Sarawak, 1953–1976." In *Representation, Identity and Multiculturalism in Sarawak*, Zawawi Ibrahim, (ed.), pp. 195–228. Kajang: Persatuan Sains Sosial Malaysia; Kuching: Dayak Cultural Foundation Publication.

Pringle, Robert (1967) *The Ibans of Sarawak under Brooke Rule, 1841–1941*. Unpublished PhD dissertation, Cornell University, United States.

——— (1970) *Rajahs and Rebels: The Ibans of Sarawak under Brooke Rule 1841–1941*. London: Macmillan.

Pudarno, Binchin (2014) *Singing Siram Ditaan: Composition, Performance and Transmission of Epic Tales of Derato in Brunei Dusun Society*. Phillips: Borneo Research Council Inc. Monograph Series No. 14.

Pugh-Kitingan, Jacqueline (2017) "An Overview of Cultural Research in Sabah." In *Borneo Studies in History, Society and Culture*, Victor T. King, Zawawi Ibrahim and Noor Hasharina Hassan, (eds.), pp. 235–59. Singapore: Springer.

Puri, Rajindra K. (2006) *Deadly Dances in the Bornean Rainforest: Hunting Knowledge of the Penan Benalui*. Leiden: KITLV Press, Koninklijk Instituut voor Taal-, Land- en Volkenkunde, Verhandelingen 222.

Rousseau, Jérôme (1974) *The Social Organisation of the Baluy Kayan*. Unpublished PhD dissertation, Cambridge University, United Kingdom.

_____ (1990) *Central Borneo: Ethnic Identity and Social Life in a Stratified Society*. Oxford: Clarendon Press.

_____ (1998) *Kayan Religion: Ritual Life and Religious Reform in Central Borneo*. Leiden: KITLV Press.

Salafsky, Nick N. (1993) *The Forest Garden Project: an Ecological and Economic Study of a Locally Developed Land-use System in West Kalimantan, Indonesia*. Unpublished PhD dissertation, Duke University, United States.

Sandin, Benedict (1980) *Iban Adat and Augury*. Penang: Penerbit Universiti Sains Malaysia, for the School of Comparative Social Sciences.

Sather, Clifford A. (1971) *Kinship and Domestic Relations among Bajau Laut of Northern Borneo*. Unpublished PhD dissertation, Harvard University, United States.

_____ (1997) *The Bajau Laut: History: Adaptation, History and Fate in a Maritime Fishing Community in South-eastern Sabah*. Kuala Lumpur: Oxford University Press.

_____ (2001) *Seeds of Play, Words of Power: An Ethnographic Study of Iban Shamanic Chants*. Kuching: Tun Jugah Foundation; Williamsburg: The Borneo Research Council, Borneo Classics Series 5.

Schärer, Hans (1963) *Ngaju Religion: The Conception of God among a South Borneo People*. The Hague: Martinus Nijhoff, Koninklijk Instituut voor Taal-, Land- en Volkenkunde, Translation Series 6, translated by Rodney Needham from *Die Gottesidee der Ngadju Dajak in Sud-Borneo*, 1946, Leiden: E.J. Brill.

Schiller, Anne (1997) *Small Sacrifices: Religious Change and Cultural Identity among the Ngaju of Indonesia*. New York: Oxford University Press.

Schneider, William M. (1974) *The Social Organization of the Selako Dayak of Borneo*. Unpublished PhD dissertation, University of North Carolina, United States.

Schwenk, Richard Lloyd (1975) *Village and Regional Determinants of Family Innovativeness among the Rural Iban of Sarawak, Malaysia*. Unpublished PhD dissertation, Cornell University, United States.

Sellato, Bernard (1989) *Nomades et Sedentarisation à Borneo. Histoire Economique et Sociale* [*Nomads and Sedentarisation in Borneo. Economic and Social History*]. Paris: Éditions de l'École des Hautes Etudes en Sciences Sociales.

_____ (1994) *Nomads of the Borneo Rainforest: The Economics, Politics, and Ideology of Settling Down*. Honolulu: University of Hawai'i Press.

Sercombe, Peter G. and Bernard Sellato, (eds.) (2007) *Beyond the Green Myth: Hunters-Gatherers of Borneo in the Twenty-first Century*. Copenhagen: NIAS Press.

Seymour, James Madison (1972) *The Rural School and Rural Development among the Iban of Sarawak, Malaysia*. Unpublished PhD dissertation, Stanford University, United States.

Smith, Linda Tuhiwai (1999) *Decolonising Methdologies: Research and Indigenous Peoples*. Dunedin: Zed books and University of Otago Press.

Strickland, Simon S. (1986) "Long Term Development of Kejaman Subsistence: An Ecological Study," *Sarawak Museum Journal* 36: pp. 117–71.

_____ (1995) "Materials for the Study of Kejaman-Sekapan Oral Tradition," *The Sarawak Museum Journal*, special monograph 8, vol. 49.

Sukandar, Rudi (2007) *Negotiating Post-conflict Communication: A Case of Ethnic Conflict in Indonesia*. Unpublished PhD dissertation, Ohio University, United States.

Sutlive, Vincent H. Jr. (1972) *From Longhouse to Pasar: Urbanization in Sarawak, East Malaysia*. Unpublished PhD dissertation, University of Pittsburgh, United States.

_____ (1993) *Change and Development in Borneo*. Williamsburg: Borneo Research Council, Borneo Research Council Proceedings Series No. 1.

Syamsuni, Arman (1987) *Off-farm Work in Three Coastal Communities of West Kalimantan, Indonesia*. Unpublished PhD dissertation, Rutgers University, United States.

Tan Sooi Ling (2008) *Transformative Worship among the Selako in Sarawak, Malaysia*. Unpublished PhD dissertation, Fuller Theological Seminary, United States.

Tanasaldy, Taufiq (2012) *Regime Change and Ethnic Politics in Indonesia: Dayak Politics of West Kalimantan*. Leiden: KITLV Press.

Thompson, Eric C. (2012) "Anthropology in Southeast Asia: National and Transnational Practices," *Asian Journal of Social Science* 40: pp. 664–89.

Thomson, Larry Kenneth (2000) *The Effect of the Dayak Worldview, Customs, Traditions, and Customary Law (adat-istiadat) on the Interpretation of the Gospel in West Kalimantan, Indonesian Borneo*. Unpublished DMin thesis, Acadia Divinity College, Canada.

T'ien Ju-K'ang (1948) *Religious Cults and Social Structure of the Shan States of the Yunnan-Burma Frontier*. Unpublished PhD dissertation, University of London, United Kingdom.

_____ (1953) *The Chinese of Sarawak: A Study of Social Structure*. London: LSE, Monographs on Social Anthropology.

_____ (1993) *Peaks of Faith: Protestant Mission in Revolutionary China*. Leiden: E.J Brill.

_____ (1997) *Male Anxiety and Female Chastity: A Comparative Study of Ethical Values in Ming-Ching Times*. Leiden: Brill Academic Publishing.

Tillotson, Dianne M. (1994) *Who Invented the Dayaks? Historical Case Studies in Art, Material Culture and Ethnic Identity from Borneo*. Unpublished PhD dissertation, Australian National University.

Tsing, Anna Lowenhaupt (1993) *In the Realm of the Diamond Queen: Marginality in an Out-of-the-Way Place*. Princeton: Princeton University Press.

Uchibori, Motomitsu (1978) *The Leaving of the Transient World: A Study of Iban Eschatology and Mortuary Practices*. Unpublished PhD dissertation, Australian National University.

Van Klinken, Gerry (2004) "Ethnogenesis and Conservative Politics in Indonesia's Outer Islands." In *Indonesia in Transition: Rethinking "Civil Society", "Region" and "Crisis"*, Samuel Hanneman and Henk Schulte Nordholt, (eds.), pp. 107–28. Yogyakarta: Pustaka Pelajar.

Vargas, Donna Mayo (1985) *The Interface of Customary and National Land Law in East Kalimantan*. Unpublished PhD dissertation, Yale University, United States.

Vayda, Andrew P. (1981) Research in East Kalimantan on Interaction between People and Forests: A Preliminary Report, *Borneo Research Bulletin* 13: pp. 3–15.

——— (1983) "Progressive Contextualization: Methods for Research in Human Ecology," *Human Ecology* 11: pp. 265–81.

Voon Jan Cham (2008) "A Chinese Perspective on Sarawakian Multiculturalism." In *Representation, Identity and Multiculturalism in Sarawak*, Zawawi Ibrahim, (ed.), pp. 119–37. Kajang: Persatuan Sains Sosial Malaysia; Kuching: Dayak Cultural Foundation Publication.

Wadley, Reed L. (1997a) *Circular Labor Migration and Subsistence Agriculture: A Case of the Iban in West Kalimantan, Indonesia*. Unpublished PhD dissertation, Arizona State University, United States.

——— (ed.) (2005) *Histories of the Borneo Environment: Economic, Political and Social Dimensions of Change and Continuity*. Leiden: KITLV Press.

Weinstock, Joseph A. (1983) *Kaharingan and the Luangan Dayaks: Religion and Identity in Central-East Borneo*. Unpublished PhD dissertation, Cornell University, United States.

Westmacott, Karen (2002) *Christ is the Head of the House: Material Culture and New Modes of Consumption for the Kayan in the 1990s*. Unpublished PhD dissertation, Australian National University.

Whittier, Herbert L. (1973) *Social Organization and Symbols of Social Differentiation: An Ethnographic Study of the Kenyah Dayak of East Kalimantan (Borneo)*. Unpublished PhD dissertation, Michigan State University, United States.

Whittier, Patricia Ruth (1981) *Systems of Appellation among the Kenyah Dayak of Borneo*. Unpublished PhD dissertation, Michigan State University, United States.

Widen, Kumpiady (2002) *Dayak Identity: Impacts of Globalisation.* London: C. Hurst and Co Publishers.

____ (2017) "The Rise of Dayak Identities in Central Kalimantan." In *Borneo Studies in History, Society and Culture*, Victor T. King, Zawawi Ibrahim and Noor Hasharina Hassan, (eds.), pp. 273–82. Singapore: Springer.

Wilistra, Danny (2000) *Ecological and Socio-economic Interactions with Fire in the Forests of East Kalimantan Province, Indonesia.* Unpublished PhD dissertation, University of Wales, Bangor, United Kingdom.

Williams, T.R. (1965) *The Dusun: A North Borneo Society.* New York: Holt, Rinehart and Winston.

____ (1969) *A Borneo Childhood: Enculturation in Dusun Society.* New York: Holt, Rinehart and Winston.

Winzeler, Robert L., (ed.) (1997) *Indigenous Peoples and the State: Politics, Land, and Ethnicity in the Malayan Peninsula and Borneo.* New Haven: Yale University Press, Southeast Asia Studies.

____ (2008) "The Last Wildman of Borneo: Tom Harrisson and the Development of Anthropology in Sarawak." In *Representation, Identity and Multiculturalism in Sarawak*, Zawawi Ibrahim, (ed.), pp. 23–43. Kajang: Persatuan Sains Sosial Malaysia; Kuching: Dayak Cultural Foundation Publication.

Zainab Khalifah (1997) *Managing Tourism in National Parks: Case Studies of Taman Negara and Kinabalu Park, Malaysia.* Unpublished PhD dissertation, University of Strathclyde, United Kingdom.

Zainal, Kling (1973) *The Saribas Malays of Sarawak: their Social and Economic Organization and System of Values.* Unpublished PhD dissertation, University of Hull, United Kingdom.

Zawawi Ibrahim (2001) *Voices of the Crocker Range Indigenous Communities Sabah: Social Narratives of Transition in Tambunan and Its Neighbours.* Sarawak: Institute of East Asian Studies, Universiti Malaysia Sarawak.

____ (2008a) "Discoursing Representation, Identity and Multiculturalism in Sarawak." In *Representation, Identity and Multiculturalism in Sarawak*, Zawawi Ibrahim, (ed.), pp. 1–19. Kajang: Persatuan Sains Sosial Malaysia; Kuching: Dayak Cultural Foundation Publication.

____ (ed.) (2008b) *Representation, Identity and Multiculturalism in Sarawak.* Kuching: Persatuan Sains Sosial Malaysia and Dayak Cultural Foundation.

____ (2008c) "Development and Alternative Representations: Narrating a Deterritorialised Penan Landscape." In *Representation, Identity and Multiculturalism in Sarawak*, Zawawi Ibrahim, (ed.), pp. 75–89. Kajang: Persatuan Sains Sosial Malaysia; Kuching: Dayak Cultural Foundation Publication.

____ (ed.) (2012) *Social Science Knowledge in a Globalising World.* Kajang: Malaysian Social Science Association and Petaling Jaya: Strategic Information and Research Development Centre.

_____ (2015) "From a World System to a Social Science Knowledge 'Scape' Perspective: Anthropological Fieldworking and Transnationalizing Theory-making in the Periphery," *Journal of Glocal Studies* 2: pp. 45–68.

_____ (2016) "Anthropologising 'Human insecurities': Narrating the Subjugated Discourse of Indigenes on the Deterritorialised Landscapes of the Malaysian Nation State." In *Human Insecurities in Southeast Asia*, Paul Carnegie, Victor King and Zawawi Ibrahim, (eds.), pp. 21–51. Singapore: Springer.

_____ (2017) "Towards a Critical Alternative Scholarship on the Discourse of Representation, Identity and Multiculturalism in Sarawak." In *Borneo Studies in History, Society and Culture*, Victor T. King, Zawawi Ibrahim and Noor Hasharina Hassan, (eds.), pp. 35–55. Singapore: Springer.

Zawawi Ibrahim and NoorShah M.S., (eds.) (2012) *Masyarakat Penan dan Impian Pembangunan: Satu Himpunan Naratif Keterpinggiran dan Jatidiri* [*Penan Society and Dreams of Development: A Collection of Narratives of Marginalization and Identity*]. Petaling Jaya: SIRD.

Zeppel, Heather (1994) *Authenticity and the Iban: Cultural Tourism at Iban Longhouses in Sarawak, East Malaysia.* Unpublished PhD dissertation, James Cook University, North Queensland, Australia.

Zhu Feng (2004) *Christianity and Culture Accommodation of Chinese Overseas: The Case Study on Chinese Methodist Community in Sarawak (1901–1951).* Unpublished PhD dissertation, Chinese University of Hong Kong.

CHAPTER 8

BOUNDARIES AND AMBITIONS OF INDONESIAN ANTHROPOLOGY

Yunita T. Winarto and Iwan M. Pirous

"Why does a Balinese person study the Balinese?" asked a Japanese anthropologist who was studying the Leo people in Flores in the mid 1990s. We find this a compelling question. As Indonesian anthropologists, we observe that while Indonesia is fascinating to outsiders, it is also exceptionally so for Indonesians. Indeed, we notice that Indonesian anthropologists rarely study non-Indonesians. For some Indonesian anthropologists, this often entails studying their own ethnic group.

This fact prompts a related question, which is the central inquiry of this chapter: has Indonesian anthropology developed in the tradition of "auto-ethnography" (Buzard 2003), in which anthropologists study themselves or "represent" their own voices in their ethnographies? If we perceive Indonesia as a nation state, and the boundary of Indonesia's nation state as the "boundary" of Indonesian anthropology, the subject of inquiry for Indonesian anthropologists is overwhelmingly focused on the "self." Why is this so? Given the highly heterogeneous nature of Indonesian ethnicities, and linguistic and religious communities, Indonesian anthropologists can often be construed as "outsiders" of the groups they are examining.

Studying the "self" within the Indonesian nation-state boundary can hardly be categorized as conducting "auto-ethnography," except in particular cases where anthropologists conduct ethnography in their own "home" community of which they are members. Yet when examining the linkages Indonesian anthropology has built so far in Asia, the point of reference used by either Indonesian anthropologists or "others" is Indonesia within its nation-state boundary. For Indonesian anthropologists, Indonesia's cultural heterogeneity, complexity, and its immense sociocultural problems provide much opportunity for scholarly inquiry. The formation and growth of anthropology in Indonesia is intricately related to the history of Indonesia's independence, nation-building and development.

With its national focus, however, Indonesian anthropology has not completely neglected the need to engage with ethnographies beyond Indonesia's borders and the role Indonesian anthropologists can play in addressing the region's sociocultural problems. Anthropological moves toward the region beyond nation-state boundaries have taken diverse paths. This chapter examines the interrelationship between these two aspects of Indonesian anthropology: its foundations within development-oriented and ethnographically grounded research within the Indonesian nation-state framework, and its linkages beyond the nation, particularly in Asia. In reviewing this history, we also provide a genealogy of the discipline and its key players, a record that is little known outside of Indonesia.

Indonesian Anthropology: Locally Bounded, Nation-State Anthropology?

The development of Indonesian anthropology as a science has been deeply affected by the legacy of independence and the departure of Dutch academics, which was followed by the struggles of the newly formed multicultural nation striving for integration and prosperity (Prager 2005; Ramstedt 2005). Following the independence of Indonesia in 1949, Dutch involvement in Indonesian universities declined dramatically, as many important Dutch figures at Universitas Indonesia were sent home. During this period of decolonization Koentjaraningrat (1923–99), considered to be the founding father of Indonesian anthropology, strove to establish a strong basis for the growth of Indonesian anthropology so as to provide a significant contribution to the needs of the new nation (Koentjaraningrat 1969, 1974, 1981, 1982, 1985). These efforts cast a strong "applied" or practical dimension to the newly emergent, nationally oriented science. Less clear is how the theoretical questions posed by Dutch scholars shaped the kinds of research questions Indonesian anthropologists asked, even after independence.

Without a central theoretical paradigm in its early development, the most enduring legacy of Dutch anthropology was the analysis of adat, or customary law. Leiden professor Cornelis van Vollenhoven (1874–1933) studied and taught adat to Indonesian law students in the 1920s. In *The Adat-law of the Netherlands-Indies* (*Het adatrecht van Nederlandsch-Indië*), van Vollenhoven documented adat traditions of nineteen different regions, plus the adat traditions of foreign Orientals (*vreemde oosterlingen*, i.e. Arabs, Chinese and Indians). He strongly recommended that the colonial government recognize indigenous forms of adat law and refrain from imposing on the colony a system of common state and private law based on Western legal ideas. Although he was not trained as a professional ethnologist, his anthropological standpoint was clear: various forms of adat law cannot be studied alone without an understanding of the complexity of social, historical and cosmological contexts. Fox (2009: 10) argues that the *adat-recht* school, as developed by van Vollenhoven, "was the last, and possibly the only, comparative framework to attempt to embrace the whole of the Indonesian archipelago." However, from Fox's perspective, the comparison was more notable for its practical orientation to serve the colonial administration than for its theoretical contribution. It was based on a number of dubious assumptions about social life. The school thus largely disappeared as a way of considering Indonesia's social diversity (Fox 2009).

Even more committed to applied science was J.P.B. de Josselin de Jong, who argued that Indonesian anthropology could only come into existence with a deep understanding of the role of anthropology as a service to the home country. He tried to convince his "native" students that anthropology needed to provide answers to the problems of modernity (Prager 2005: 184). This clearly foreshadowed the role of anthropology in post-independence nation-building. Yet with respect to de Jong's influence, the question remains whether Indonesian anthropology has produced any lasting theoretical paradigm. If we take British structural functionalism as a successful anthropological school of thought for comparison, the answer is no. Dutch anthropology conducted in their colonies never generated a specific school of thought. The product of pragmatic colonial concerns, infused by nineteenth-century German academic traditions and practiced by academics who were *ambtenaren* (civil servants) rather than social scientists, anthropological approaches in Indonesia were more descriptive than analytical. Additionally, the disappearance of Dutch structuralism in Holland (in comparison to the rise of French and

British structuralism) may in part have been related to their difficult relations with Indonesia. Blok and Boissevain (1984: 387) argue that "an end had come to the triadic relationship which closely linked Leiden University with Indonesia studies, and both with structural anthropology."

In contrast to the ambitious project of van Vollenhoven, later indigenous predecessors (most notably Koentjaraningrat) seemingly followed their sentiments as "anti-Dutch nationalists," with which the future of Indonesian anthropology could only be portrayed through non-Dutch theoretical legacies. According to Koentjaraningrat, who had studied anthropology at Yale University, what was critically needed for Indonesian anthropology was "theoretical unity" with which anthropologists would produce "knowledge that can be used as a basis for political and economic analysis of the values that the bearers of different cultures adhere to" (Visser 1988: 752). As Ramstedt (2005) argues, Indonesian anthropology did gradually take its position as an applied science in Indonesia's nation-building project. Yet has Koentjaraningrat's vision of creating "theoretical unity" been accomplished?

During the same period, post-independence Indonesia came to be recognized as one of the world's great epicenters of social diversity (Fox 2009). Indonesia was the site for, and inspired, classic ethnographies and important theoretical models. Clifford Geertz's famous ethnographies were the product of fieldwork in Java and Bali. *Agricultural Involution* and *The Religion of Java*, were, according to Fox (2009), the basis of interpretative anthropology as a theoretical school and of "thick description" as an ethnographic writing technique, legacies which remain influential. Various other classic ethnographies emerged as the product of detailed meticulous fieldwork by foreign anthropologists. *The Javanese Family* by Hildred Geertz (1961); *Javanese Villagers* by Robert Jay (1969); *Harvest of the Palm* by James J. Fox (1977); and *Solo in the New Order* by James Siegel (1993) are only a few from a long list of classic ethnographies on Indonesia.

Given that Indonesia provides an immense diversity of settings for foreign scholars, it is not surprising that Indonesian anthropologists—the graduates of departments from eleven state universities—treat their home country and its diverse communities as their primary research focus. The formation and development of each department of anthropology spread across different locales in Indonesia were a key legacy of Koentjaraningrat's ambition to create a center of anthropological studies in each region of Indonesia. Such an endeavor was part of his effort to develop "non-Dutch theoretical legacies" with strong roots in Indonesian culture. The cultivation of local anthropologists was to strengthen the development of anthropology in the provinces.

The understanding of local cultures and sociocultural phenomena by local anthropologists would of course enrich the ethnographies of Indonesia. Doing anthropology "at home" has thus been common and expected. Examples of these are studies on the people and culture of Betawi (Shahab 1982, 1994, 2000); Bali (Pitana 1997); and Bugis (Idrus 2003a, 2016). As Ramstedt argues (2005: 210), "the focus of ethnographic study and research was on the cultures of Indonesia with fieldwork being carried out exclusively in the archipelago." The main reasons for this were not only the intention to represent their own people and culture, but also the need for anthropologists to study various problems emerging in Indonesia (Ramstedt 2005: 210).

As a result of doing anthropology at home, studying "others" outside their home communities or across ethnic group boundaries has often been out of the question for Indonesian anthropologists. For local anthropologists, examining "others" in a multicultural society has been quite challenging. Language and the archipelagic nature of Indonesia constitute barriers to moving beyond home communities. This focus on "self"-based studies of geographic or ethnic home communities by local Indonesian anthropologists may have formed the basis of sought-after, non-Dutch "theoretical unity", as articulated by Koentjaraningrat in his interview with Leontine Visser (1988: 752). Yet to make such a claim would require further examination of key questions. To what extent has there been intense knowledge production and sharing among the anthropological centers and scholars across Indonesia on the basis of local scholarly ethnographic research? Furthermore, what contribution does such knowledge make to the theoretical advancement of the anthropological approach to Indonesian studies, which has been largely descriptive and developmental thus far? Seeking answers to these questions would require greater historical analysis and synthesis of post-independence local anthropological work than has been done to date.

From Practicing Anthropology to Public and Engaged Anthropology

Koentjaraningrat's influence at Universitas Indonesia made anthropology a popular discipline, with the field considered an applied science with an important role to play in nation-building projects. In his popular book, *Kebudayaan, Mentalitet dan Pembangunan* [*Culture, Mentality and Development*] (1974), Koentjaraningrat argues for the need to understand existing cultures and Indonesian people's mentality and how to deal with diversity in a way that supports Indonesia's national development, as defined by the "New Order" regime (see Ramstedt 2005: 214). The Suharto regime's "New Order" (1965–98) vision of national development entailed managing local cultures to fit a capitalist and modernist model. Furthermore, state ideologists based their worldview on Western modernization theory; that is, on notions of "national security," "political stability" and "economic development." As argued by Ramstedt (2005: 214), "the function of anthropology in the 'New Order' Indonesia largely consisted of mediating between the tradition and an 'Asian'—that is Indonesian—variety of modernity." Academic critique was suppressed by the state in favor of a social science whose aim was to uphold state power. Nevertheless, despite bans on Marxism in academic discussions and texts, some anthropologists retained a critical stance toward the state-developmental model and promoted instead a more culture-based model of development.

The Indonesian state's regimes following the collapse of the New Order in 1998 led to the rise of turmoil related to ethnic-religious conflicts, regional autonomy and democracy. As such, Indonesian anthropologists developed their studies and engaged in a new range of issues—they were not only being challenged to provide in-depth understandings of the sociocultural roots of the nation's problems and their implications for people's livelihood, they were also called on to engage in solving these emerging problems. A shift in anthropological studies occurred, which saw the inclusion of these problems within their studies.

Over time, Indonesian anthropologists have not only practiced anthropology, they have participated in the development of "ethnographies of activism (Chari and Donner 2010), and/or public and engaged anthropology" (see Lassitter 2005a, 2005b, 2008; Borofsky 2007; Low and Merry 2010). The growth of such diverse kinds of engagement was the product of anthropologists' critical reactions and responses to the emerging unintended and unprecedented problems of various development programs, their humanitarian concerns, and the disciplinary perspectives and constraints after the collapse of the

New Order. Accordingly, as argued by Chari and Donner (2010: 1), a number of anthropologists are "transgressing disciplinary boundaries to address complexity and universality" and assume the role of "activist" (also see Low and Merry 2010 on activism as a form of engagement). By carrying out facilitative or collaborative ethnography with the subjects, and by not "emphasizing theory in one context and practice in another" as argued by Borofsky (2007: x), some anthropologists have initiated the growth of "public anthropology" and/or "engaged anthropology."

It is not easy, however, to delineate each of the various forms of engagement in the work of Indonesian anthropologists. Some conducted ethnographic studies as part of their graduate and post-doctoral research. Some published the results of their research following a single engagement or a combination of several forms of engagement. A number of anthropologists pursued engagement by producing practical solutions or combining both theoretical and practical significance. Table 1 presents examples of the fields of study, the anthropologists involved, and citations of their research, which further reflect the development of various fields of study within the field of anthropology in Indonesia.

Table 1. Field of Studies and Indonesian Anthropologists

No.	*Field of studies*	*Anthropologists*
1	Ethnic and religious conflicts, and multicultural issues: - Dayak and Madurese in Kalimantan - Maluku and Poso in Central Sulawesi	• Parsudi Suparlan and S. Boedhisantoso: recommendation and action to solve the conflicts. • Dedi S. Adhuri
2	Customary and cultural rights, agrarian issues and land grab	• Yando R. Zakaria (2012, 2014, 2015) • Suraya A. Affif (Afiff & Low 2007; Peluso, Afiff & Rakchman 2008; McCarthy, Vel & Afiff 2012; Afiff 2015)
3	Village affairs and the formation of the new Village Law (2014) with Y.R. Zakaria's significant role in the drafting stage of the law	• Yando R. Zakaria (2000, 2004; Zakaria & Simarmata 2015; Vel, Zakaria & Bedner 2017; Zakaria & Vel 2017) • Darmanto (Wardana & Darmanto 2017)

Table 1. Continued

No.	*Field of studies*	*Anthropologists*
4	Environmental change, degradation, natural resource management, conflict over tenure rights, conservation and community empowerment	• Iwan Tjitradjaja in his works on repositioning the local farmers as forest-conservers and no longer as forest-encroachers (mid to late 1990s) • Yunita T. Winarto on mangrove rehabilitation (Winarto et al. 1999), agricultural issues, farmers' empowerment, collaborative ethnography on climate change (Winarto 2004a, 2004b, 2005a, 2005b, 2006, 2011a, 2011b; Winarto & Stigter 2013, 2016, 2017; Winarto et al. 2011, 2013, 2017a, 2017b) • Suraya A. Afiff on conservation and environmental transformation (Afiff & Low 2008; Acciaioli & Afiff 2017; Großmann, Padmanabhan & Afiff 2017) • Semiarto A. Purwanto on urban farming (2009a, 2009b, 2011) and artisanal mining (2015a, 2015b, 2017) • Adi Prasetijo on deforestation, oil palm plantation and the livelihood transformation (2013, 2015) • Dedi S. Adhuri on fisheries, marine resource management and tenure conflicts (1998, 2003, 2009, 2013a, 2013b; Adhuri & Visser 2010; Adhuri & Satria 2010; Adhuri et al. 2015, 2016) • Zulkifli Lubis on forest fire (2017)
5	Tourism development, policy and implications	• I Gde Pitana (1997, 2000, 2013) • Jajang Gunawijaya (Gunawijaya & Pratiwi 2016)
6	Gender, sexuality and reproductive health	• Nurul I. Idrus on gender and violence (2001, 2002, 2003b, 2016; Idrus & Hardon 2015) • Irwan M. Hidayana on marital relations, reproduction, and gay identity and community (Hidayana 2012; Hidayana & Tenni 2015; McNally et al. 2015)

continued next page

Table 1. Continued

No.	*Field of studies*	*Anthropologists*
7	Medical and psychiatric issues, family planning, drugs and HIV-Aids	• Meutia F. Swasono (Swasono et al. 1997; Margono et al. 2006) • Sri Murni (Margono et al. 2006; Murni 2007) • Dian Sulistiawati on HIV-Aids therapeutic management (2013) • Irwan M. Hidayana (Hidayana & Tenni 2015)
8	Religious conversion and movement; religion in multicultural Indonesia	• A. Fedyani Saifuddin (2000, 2003, 2006, 2010, 2017) • Tony Rudyansjah (2012) • Imam Ardhianto (2012, 2015, 2017) • Dave Lumenta (2017)
9	Migration and human trafficking	• Dave Lumenta (2008; International Catholic Migrant Commission 2017) • Rhino Ariefiansyah (Azis et al. 2017; International Catholic Migrant Commission 2017) • Hestu Prahara (International Catholic Migrant Commission 2017)
10	Legal pluralism, gender, law and migrant women.	• Sulistyowati Irianto (2011, 2012, 2016; Irianto & Truong 2014)

In response to desperate problems, direct practical solutions were provided, as exemplified in the studies on solving ethnic conflicts by Dayak and Madurese in Kalimantan and in the study by Suparlan and Boedhisantoso. In his keynote speech at the national and international symposia of the journal, *Antropologi Indonesia*, Suparlan (1999a: 3) addressed the urgent need for Indonesian anthropology to contribute more significantly to the creation of Indonesia's civil society and democracy, as well as the formation of Indonesia's multicultural society through education (Suparlan 1999b, 2000a, 2000b, 2001, 2002). Some anthropologists voiced the need for counter-developmental discourse in response to state development programs, which have been insensitive to cultural rights and community lives, as raised by Yando R. Zakaria, a leading "anthropological activist." Zakaria (2004: 215) argues that developing community-based state management would alleviate the suppression of local communities by the state. He was further engaged in agrarian problems and contributed to the preparation of the new Village Law declared in 2014 by Joko Widodo, the current president (2014–19) (see Zakaria and Simarmata 2015; Vel, Zakaria and Bedner 2017; Zakaria and Vel 2017).

In the same vein, the late Iwan Tjitradjaja from Universitas Indonesia made community-based forest management a reality by converting the local forest community in Gunungbetung, Lampung, from "forest encroachers," as termed by the state, to "forest conservers." He was also successful in encouraging the Ministry of Forestry (in the early 2000s) to produce "community forest certificates" for farmers. Directly involving local farmers, as Tjitradjaja did, has become the "hallmark" of "collaborative transdisciplinary research and action," as well as a form of interdisciplinary collaboration between different disciplinary scientists. A group of anthropologists from Universitas Indonesia and Hasanuddin University, Makassar, developed a collaborative project with a biologist, geographer, and demographer, assisted by a local non-governmental organization (NGO) and farmers on mangrove rehabilitation and conservation in South Sulawesi (see Winarto et al. 1999). Anthropologists from Universitas Indonesia also developed a collaborative project with a group of farmer-plant-breeders in Indramayu, West Java, to produce a documentary film. The film had the objective of gaining the state's recognition and acknowledgment of the new skills, knowledge, and products of farmer-plant-breeders (Winarto 2011b; Ariefiansyah 2011; Winarto and Ardhianto 2011; Ardhianto 2011). Interdisciplinary and transdisciplinary collaboration became the underlying approach to further develop community engagement in response to global threats such as climate change.

The question remaining for Indonesian anthropologists is the extent to which their "activism" and "engaged anthropological work" have contributed to the development of anthropology as a science. Some academic events have been organized by the editors of *Antropologi Indonesia* to address the turmoil and various other problems that have emerged since the end of the New Order era (see *Jurnal Antropologi Indonesia* symposia proceedings from 2000, 2001, 2002a, 2002b, 2005). The themes of the journal's symposia strongly reflect the concerns of Indonesian anthropologists and their engagement with the ongoing sociocultural problems of the Indonesian state and society.

Yet to what extent have these important projects by Indonesian anthropologists generated new theoretical, conceptual or methodological issues? It is inevitable that most Indonesian scholars still use theoretical models developed by non-Indonesians, even as they have moved away from the legacy of Dutch scientific heritage. As more anthropologists—Koentjaraningrat's students—were sent to the United States, the Netherlands, Australia and Japan (see Prager 2005; Ramstedt 2005; Fox 2009), they cultivated the use of other anthropological theories, concepts and methods. Suparlan (1999a: 3) makes a strong claim for the need for Indonesian scholarship that is both theoretically novel, born of local world views, and yet remains relevant to the national need for an authentically Indonesian democratic and civil society. We share his concern, but we note that by considering the products of Indonesian anthropologists throughout the country, there is cause for optimism.

Studying "Others" Beyond the Indonesian Nation-State Boundary

Studying "others" has been integrated into the curricula of anthropology in various universities in Indonesia. The ethnography of Southeast Asia, Oceania/Melanesia, and Africa were taught in the Department of Anthropology at Universitas Indonesia in the 1960s and 1970s. The teaching was, however, mainly based on the available ethnographic literature. Koentjaraningrat played a significant role in paving the way for young Indonesian anthropologists to go abroad to pursue fieldwork and studies in the region as a means to advance global ethnographic teaching in Indonesia. He established collaborations with academic institutions and anthropologists in several countries in Asia (Ramstedt 2005). This marked the beginning of an era when linkages between Indonesia and the region were built upon ethnographic fieldwork carried out by Indonesian anthropologists in areas outside Indonesia. Research grants provided by international donor agencies opened up opportunities for more intense links between Indonesian anthropologists and Asian scholars within and beyond the borders of the nation state.

In the early 1970s, Koentjaraningrat sought cooperation with academic institutions in several countries (Japan, Malaysia, Thailand, Singapore and, at a later stage, Australia). Ramstedt (2005: 213) argues that the increasing attraction of investors from Japan and

Indonesia's neighbors was a motivating factor for Koentjaraningrat to establish his academic network with scholars in those countries (also see Dahsiar's [1976: 3] argument on Indonesian people's lack of understanding of Japanese culture).

To enable young anthropologists to pursue their studies and fieldwork abroad, Koentjaraningrat first focused on foreign language learning. Two scholars, Endang Partrijunianti and Jopie Wangania, were sent to Japan for non-degree studies after learning Japanese at the Faculty of Letters (now Faculty of Humanities), Universitas Indonesia. Other scholars that pursued foreign exchange programs were Siti Dahsiar (who studied at Tohoku University, Sendai after learning Japanese); Anrini Sofion (who carried out research in the southern part of Thailand after pursuing a master's degree at the Australian National University, where she studied Thai); and Amri Marzali (who was sent to Universiti Kebangsaan, Malaysia as a lecturer).

This program opened the gates for Indonesian anthropologists to conduct fieldwork in the region. The teaching of East Asian and Southeast Asian ethnography at Universitas Indonesia was enriched by these scholars' fieldwork and literature. In the early 1980s, an East Asian ethnography (*Etnografi Asia Timur*) program was first launched at Universitas Indonesia after the return of Endang Partrijunianti and Jopie Wangania. Their classes were also attended by students from the Department of Japanese at the Faculty of Letters at Universitas Indonesia. At a later stage, Chinese culture was also integrated into the syllabus and an invitation was extended to a Sinologist from the Faculty of Letters. After the return of Anrini Sofion from Thailand, Thai studies came to dominate the course on Southeast Asian ethnography (*Etnografi Asia Tenggara*) in the 1980s. At a later stage Amri Marzali taught Malay ethnography. More recently, Dave Lumenta and Yunita T. Winarto developed the course further. Such developments in the ethnographic syllabi were the concrete result of Koentjaraningrat's effort to establish linkages with scholars across Asia.

In addition to donor funding, academic institutions in the region have provided fellowships that have been essential for the development of research, collaboration and publications. As an example, with a research grant from the Southeast Asian Studies Regional Exchange Program (SEASREP), funded by the Toyota Foundation, Yunita T. Winarto carried out a comparative study among integrated pest management (IPM) farmers, and the alumni of IPM Farmer Field Schools (FFS) in Vietnam, Cambodia and Thailand from 2003 to 2005.

She focused on discovering the extent to which some similarities and differences were found in the evolutionary changes of rice farming culture among the alumni of IPM FFS in different countries and cultures. In one paper, Winarto argues for the use and advantages of examining the sociocultural changes the farmers experienced from a micro-evolutionary perspective in relation to agency and praxis, and how to study those changes using comparative analysis (Winarto 2005b). Winarto has developed her research from the more recent anti-essentialist perspective by emphasizing praxis, processes and variations in data collection and analyses.

Research grants provided by the Asian Public Intellectuals (API) Fellowship, sponsored by the Nippon Foundation for young and senior researchers in Asia, were also beneficial for Indonesian anthropologists to carry out their research in the region. One anthropologist, Yayan Indriatmoko, carried out his research among Orang Temuan in Tanjung Rambai, Selangor, Malaysia, and assessed their responses to the current development of Malays and the encroachment by the neighboring dominant Malay community onto their land (Indriatmoko 2004). Semiarto A. Purwanto did a comparative study on urban farming in Jakarta and the Philippines (Purwanto 2009a, 2009b, 2011). Recently, Iwan M. Pirous has conducted research on the activists of non-profit organizations in Thailand and the Philippines. In general, though scholars' issues, methods and perspectives vary, they share a similar perspective of looking "outward," following the pattern of their fellow foreign anthropologists studying in the region.

Studying Nation-State Borders and Mobile People

Globalization by means of global media flows, vast globalized financial transfers, overseas migration, and the enhancement of portable communication devices has been escalating since the 1990s and penetrates the daily life of Indonesians. However, in Indonesia, a shifting paradigm from nation-state based theories (including critical studies towards "developmentalism") to a more global and regional context was triggered by an economic crisis. The Asian financial crisis, beginning in July 1997, was a period of crisis that gripped much of Asia, and raised fears of a worldwide economic meltdown. Indonesian politics was heavily affected and changed after Suharto, the "father of development" for thirty-two years, stepped down from the presidency. This was the first time "globalization" reached universities as an axis to analyze sociocultural change, and consequently the nation-state based paradigm gradually declined in prominence. Transnationalism, as an alternative way to critically think about what was happening in contemporary Indonesian society, started to gain popularity among scholars in Indonesia. Through an International Symposium of *Jurnal Antropologi Indonesia*, this issue was first raised by a special panel focused on Malaysian border issues and migrant workers, coordinated by Johanis Haba and Riwanto Tirtosudarmo from the Indonesian Institute for Science and Research (Lembaga Ilmu Pengetahuan Indonesia) in 2001.

The issue of migrant workers has long been a key concern for Indonesian–Malaysian diplomatic relations. Over the past two decades in particular, this problem has caused tension between the two states. The intensity of the issue drastically increased during the Asian financial crisis of 1997. Anthropologists Dave Lumenta, Iwan M. Pirous, and Rhino Ariefiansyah, together with young scholars from the field of international relations, collaborated on research on regional migration. Their objective was to combine international relations theories of migration and anthropological studies of the construction of identities. This study (Hadi et al. 2005) argued that the causes and effects of migration and the presence of foreign migrant labor were by no means singularly economic. In recent years, the migration industry has developed significantly due to the privatization of migration infrastructure and the increasing involvement of migration brokers and agents. At the request of the International Catholic Migrant Commission of Malaysia (ICMC 2010), a number of anthropologists from the Center for Anthropological Studies at Universitas Indonesia produced a film and a document based on investigative research on human trafficking in Sabah as a basis for educating Malaysian police. In a conference on the migration industry held at the National University of Singapore (NUS) in 2017, Azis, Ariefiansyah and Utami presented the case of migration and brokerage in Indonesia (2017).

The effects of globalization on politics, economics, culture and identity are in fact more diverse than initially anticipated by neoclassical economists who were overtly influential in the initial formulation of migration theories. Moreover, methodologically, studies on migration, among others, have highlighted the problem associated with the world being described by ethnographers as having changed dramatically without a corresponding shift in disciplinary practices, since localized "fieldwork" has become hegemonic in anthropology.

As groups migrate, regroup in new locations, reconstruct their histories, and reconfigure their ethnic projects, the "ethno" in ethnography takes on a slippery, non-localized quality, to which the descriptive practices of anthropology will have to respond (Gupta and Ferguson 1996; also see Fox 2009).

Transnationalism as a paradigm poses new questions as migrant identities, and ethnic and national identities do not neatly intersect. In the case of migrants crossing Malaysian–Indonesian borders, for instance, such migrants are not necessarily ethnically, culturally or historically distinct from their host country's population. In addition, ambiguous "territoriality" has complicated or contradicted the processes of national identity formation throughout Southeast Asia. Contrary to the idea that nation states are able to unite the identities of their diverse populations into single, homogenous national identities, the Southeast Asian experience is plagued by the strengthening of minority identities. If the nation-state concept can be viewed as a product of early globalization (through colonialism), then transnational and migration research provides evidence that globalization in fact produces divergent, rather than homogenizing effects. Thus, in the context of Southeast Asia, migrant laborers are often placed in radically different situations and contexts, with different ramifications on migrant identities.

Dave Lumenta's 2008 doctoral thesis submitted to Kyoto University examines the relationship between states and mobile peoples in the processes of state-making. He covers not only wide geographical landscapes, but also historical trajectories of people's mobility over a long period of time (1900–2007). He questions whether mobile people are a consistent anathema to state projects; and in what ways mobile peoples relate to spatial approaches and the governing features of state-making. The study advances Indonesian anthropology both theoretically and methodologically, not only in its scope but also through the location of ethnographic fieldwork.

Studies on border regions carried out by Indonesian scholars have also been advanced by focusing on border zones other than those between Indonesia and Malaysia. Examples are studies on the border areas between Indonesia and Timor Leste by Johanis Haba (2005) and Yanuarius Koli Bau (2005); between Thailand and Burma (Ardhana 2005); and the border areas of Thailand (Maunati 2005). The results of their fieldwork were presented in the panel on "Cross-border Movements in Southeast Asia, Identity Politics and Citizenships" organized by Riwanto Tirtosudarmo and Johanis Haba for the Fourth International Symposium of *Jurnal Antropologi Indonesia* (2005).

Indonesian Anthropology in Regional Studies

In the last decade, collaborative regional projects between foreign scientists and Indonesian anthropologists have flourished. In many cases, though, Indonesian scientists were invited to be the foreign-partner investigators on studies carried out in Indonesia. This fact prompts a question on the place and role of Indonesian scholars. We find contradictory realities. On the one hand, Indonesian scholars continue to be positioned as experts on Indonesian societies, and less as experts on regional cultures outside Indonesia. On the other hand, knowledge of Indonesia continues to be generated largely by non-Indonesians. We find that although collaborative projects appear to be regional—in particular from the foreign scientists' point of view—the involvement of Indonesian collaborators suggests they were asked to largely conduct research on their own societies. Such unequal positioning makes Indonesian anthropology more auto-ethnographic than comparative, while researchers from elsewhere take the lead in their analysis across nation-state borders.

Examples of such comparative studies are the HIV projects in Indonesia and Vietnam (2005–2006); the concept of culture in Asia from the perspective of Southeast Asia (2006–2007); and the experience of migration in three countries in Southeast Asia (Indonesia, Thailand and Singapore in 2007). The first project was based on a network among three countries: the Netherlands (the Medische Committee Netherlands–Vietnam), Vietnam and Indonesia, where Irwan M. Hidayana was invited to study Indonesia's case (also see Hidayana 2012).

Another example is the comparative study of the concept of Southeast Asia as seen from students' perspectives or cognitive maps. The research project led by Eric C. Thompson from NUS, covered Indonesia, Thailand, Singapore and the Philippines. Again, Irwan M. Hidayana and Iwan M. Pirous represented Indonesia by carrying out the study on Indonesian students' perspectives (see Thompson et al. 2007). Pirous was also involved in a comparative study on the meaning of being a migrant. The study was carried out in Indonesia, Thailand and Singapore and was again led by Thompson. The research focused on the perceptions, knowledge and experience of Thai and Indonesian migrants.

A large number of so-called "Indonesianists" have also emerged from various academic institutions throughout the world from a diverse range of disciplinary backgrounds. The ethnographies based on their research in Indonesia have significantly influenced the understanding of Indonesia's problems and the development of Indonesian studies. These publications have generated a significant means of linking Indonesia to the world. We suggest that Indonesian scholars could benefit from studying this scholarship to enrich their understanding of their own nation and cultures. Prior to the advancement of the Internet, such important literature was not always accessible and available to Indonesian scholars. Organizing international academic events as a means to provide an opportunity for "Indonesianists" and Indonesian scholars to meet and establish linkages was a breakthrough.

An example is the international symposia from 2000 to 2017 organized by the editors of *Jurnal Antropologi Indonesia*. It was interesting to know the diverse range of issues and studies presented by both parties covering not only Indonesian sociocultural phenomena, but also the relationship of these phenomena to a globalizing world. The linkage between Indonesian anthropology and Asia was also examined in the Fourth International Symposium of *Jurnal Antropologi Indonesia* entitled, "Indonesia in the Changing Global Context: Building Cooperation and Partnership?" (2005). Knowledge generated from these symposia and transnational intellectual relationships have contributed significantly to the advancement of Indonesian anthropology.

Responding to Global Threats

As an archipelagic country along the equator surrounded by large oceans and nations, and as a religiously and ethnically heterogeneous society, challenges and threats to people's lives, nationhood and environment that come from elsewhere in the world have been increasing. Climate change and its consequences for agriculture, fisheries and forestry is one such challenge, as are terrorism and radicalism, which aim to replace the nation state's basic law and ideology of Negara Kesatuan Republik Indonesia and Pancasila with a globalized Islamic state. These global challenges and threats have prompted Indonesian anthropologists to contribute to the mitigation of these threats for the people and the nation state of Indonesia.

Recent global changes in climate have produced unprecedented consequences for agriculture and other means of natural resource management. Understanding the need for Indonesian farmers to adapt to uncommon risks, a Dutch agrometeorologist (Stigter) cooperated with Winarto to develop an inter- and transdisciplinary collaborative project to provide "climate services" to farmers. Through her work in the past decade, Winarto has contributed to the development of an anthropological role and methodology in line with the increasing engagement of anthropologists in Indonesia. Being engaged as both ethnographers—"cultural translators" between two domains of knowledge (scientific and local knowledge)—and facilitators, Winarto and Stigter have been able to establish an educational commitment for farmers using a new extension approach through the institutionalization of Science Field Shops in two regencies in West Java and West Nusa Tenggara (see Winarto and Stigter 2011, 2013, 2016, 2017; Winarto et al. 2011, 2013, 2015, 2017a, 2017b).

Fundamentalism, terrorism and radicalism have spread across the Indonesian state in the last decades. Whilst the Indonesian government has been preoccupied with tackling this movement all over the country, a number of anthropological scholars have been engaged not only as ethnographers, but also as part of the force combatting political violence through their research and publications. Among them is Al Chaidar from a university in Aceh and a doctoral candidate at Universitas Indonesia. He has examined terrorism movements in several countries in the world and produced a number of publications on political violence (see Chaidar and Sahrasad 2012, 2013; Sahrasad and Chaidar 2015; Chaidar et al. 2016). His work is an example of the significant role an anthropologist can play in providing thorough knowledge on, and sociocultural approaches to, alleviating the risks and consequences of such a movement.

The most prominent event in Indonesia following the spread of fundamentalism and radicalism was the series of mass demonstrations and movements in 2016 as an articulation of intolerance, reflected in the strong opposition to the non-Muslim ex-governor of Jakarta based on religious issues. These movements represented a serious violation of Indonesian state law and the basic philosophy of Pancasila and *Bhinneka Tunggal Ika* (Unity in Diversity). Seeing such a threat to the nationhood of Indonesia, in a surprisingly short period, Indonesian anthropologists from Aceh to Papua were able to consolidate themselves and unite in one voice and movement: *Darurat Keindonesiaan: Gerakan Antropologi untuk Indonesia yang Bineka dan Inklusif* (Indonesian Crisis: Anthropological Movement for Diversity and an Inclusive Indonesia). Through digital communication and socialization, up to 300 Indonesian anthropologists from all over the country joined the movement. In each place, local anthropologists communicated their declaration and campaign via press conferences and television or radio broadcasts on the same date—December 16, 2016 (see the declaration, *Antropologi untuk Indonesia* 2016). This was a monumental and surprising moment for the Indonesian government and society, and the first official declaration voiced by Indonesian scientists. This was followed by an event where anthropologists had a special audience with the president of Indonesia, Joko Widodo, to share their ideas on sustaining Indonesian diversity and an inclusive society (*Antropologi untuk Indonesia* 2017).

Working from within the Indonesian nation state to respond to, and solve threats originating from, the global sphere has now become a significant role for Indonesian anthropologists. It is proof that the activities of anthropologists in Indonesia are crucial to address emerging problems that could jeopardize the nation state and heterogeneous Indonesian society.

Indonesian Anthropology in Asia

As we have argued, the development of Indonesian anthropology was deeply affected by the history of Dutch colonialism, decolonization and the struggles of Indonesia as a new nation in the context of its heterogeneous society. The focus and orientation of Indonesian anthropologists on nation-building, development programs, diverse problems during and after the fall of Suharto and recent global threats, have led to the development of anthropological work in teaching, research and publishing which has been overwhelmingly framed within Indonesian nation-state boundaries. The founding father of Indonesian anthropology, Koentjaraningrat, fostered a strong applied dimension to Indonesian anthropology. Producing ethnographies for the needs of the Indonesian nation on the basis of the "self" studying "itself" (or "others" within the nation-state boundary) and using and adopting the theoretical and conceptual frameworks of "others"

(Western or in some cases Japanese), has been a particular characteristic of Indonesian anthropology. Since the 1990s, Indonesian anthropologists have expressed an urgent need to develop authentic, locally generated paradigms within Indonesian anthropology.

One step in this direction has been a new orientation towards ethnographic fieldwork in Asia beyond Indonesia. This was also based on a practical understanding of the need for Indonesians to better understand their neighbors in Southeast and East Asia. Despite its applied dimension, however, this fieldwork contributed to the advancement and teaching of regional ethnography in Indonesian universities. Moreover, such ethnographic fieldwork carried out by Indonesian anthropologists beyond the Indonesian nation state in Southeast and East Asia led to the development of a more serious link between Indonesian anthropology and the region through collaborative networks of Indonesian and non-Indonesian scholars.

In recent years, however, such traditional fieldwork in a "realist" mode based on "single-site mise en scène" ethnography has been critically questioned (Marcus 1998). Globalization, modernization and international threats have been intensifying everywhere and have penetrated Indonesian people's daily lives. A shifting paradigm from nation-state based ethnographies and theories to a more global and regional context has become more relevant. Mobility, migration and identity, weakening nation-state boundaries and transnationalism have become growing concerns for citizens, as well as important foci for Indonesian scholars and scholars of Southeast Asia. In addition to questions, a wide variety of other critical issues have become important among scholars, such as democracy, civil society, gender inequality, sustainable resource management and human rights, as well as inter-religious dialogues, media, health problems, financial and monetary crises, climate change, terrorism and radicalism, and many others. These issues provide a path for more intense links between Indonesia and the world, and in particular Asia, on the basis of scholars' similar interests and mutual concerns. A diverse range of comparative studies, collaborative exchange research programs, academic events and publications provide opportunities for enriched Indonesian ethnographies, the development of methods, and the broadening of conceptual and theoretical analyses, as well as enlarged academic networks and linkages.

Despite such a significant improvement in contemporary Indonesian anthropology, questions remain regarding the extent to which Indonesian anthropologists have been able to develop their own genuine conceptual, theoretical and methodological frameworks, so as to allow non-Indonesians to benefit from the contributions of Indonesian anthropologists and for Indonesian anthropologists to make a significant contribution to the development of anthropology as a global discipline.

Notes

* This chapter is a revised version of a paper presented at the conference on "The Asia Pacific and the Emerging World System" at Ritsumaikan Asia Pacific University, Beppu, Japan, December 13–14, 2008.

References

Acciaioli, G. and S.A. Afiff (2017) "Commodifying Conservation in Borneo," *Inside Indonesia* 127: Jan–Mar.

Adhuri, D.S. (1998) "Saat Sebuah Desa Dibakar Menjadi Abu: Hak Ulayat Laut dan Konflik Antar Kelompok di Pulau Kei Besar" ["When a Village was Burned to Ashes: Communal Marine Tenure and Social Conflict in Kei Besar Island"], *Antropologi Indonesia* 57: pp. 92–109.

_____ (2003) *Does the Sea Divide or Unite Indonesians? Ethnicity and Regionalism from a Maritime Perspective.* Working Paper No. 48. Resource Management in Asian Pacific Program (RMAP), Australian National University, Canberra.

_____ (2009) "Social Identity and Access to Natural Resources: Ethnicity and Regionalism from a Maritime Perspective." In *The Politics of the Periphery in Indonesia: Social and Geographical Perspectives*, M. Sakai, G. Banks and J.H. Walker, (eds.), pp. 134–52. Singapore: National University Press.

_____ (2013a) *Selling the Sea, Fishing for Power: A Study of Conflict Over Marine Tenure in the Kei Islands, Eastern Indonesia.* Canberra: ANU E-Press.

_____ (2013b) "Traditional and Modern: *Trepang* Fisheries on the Border of the Indonesian and Australian Fishing Zones." In *Macassan History and Heritage: Journeys, Encounters and Influences*, M. Clark and S.K. May, (eds.), pp. 183–203. Canberra: ANU E-Press.

Adhuri, D.S. and L. Visser (2010) "Territorialization Re-examined: Transborder Marine Resources Exploitation in Southeast Asia and Australia. In *Transborder Governance of Forests, Rivers and Seas*, W. de Jong, D. Snelder, and N. Ishikawa, (eds.), pp. 83–98. UK: Earthscan.

Adhuri, D.S. and A. Satria (2010) "Pre-existing Fisheries Management Systems in Lombok and Maluku, Indonesia." In *Managing Coastal and*

Inland Waters: Pre-existing Aquatic Management Systems in Southeast Asia, K. Ruddle and A. Satria, (eds.), pp. 31–55. Berlin: Springer Science.

Adhuri, D.S., D. Ferrol-Schulte, P. Gorris, W. Baitoningsih, and S. Ferse (2015) "Coastal Livelihood Vulnerability to Marine Resource Degradation: A Review of the Indonesian National Coastal and Marine Policy Framework," *Marine Policy* 52: pp. 163–71.

Adhuri, D.S., L. Laksmawati, H. Sofyanto, and N. Hamilton-Hart (2016) "Market for Small People: Markets and Opportunities for Upgrading Small Scale Fisheries in Indonesia," *Marine Policy* 63: pp. 198–205.

Afiff, S.A. (2015) "Learning from Green Enclosure Practice in Indonesia: Katingan REDD+ Case Study in Central Kalimantan." Paper presented at the International Academic Conference on "Land Grabbing, Conflict and Agrarian-Environmental Transformation: Perspectives from East and Southeast Asia" at Chiang Mai University, June 5–6.

Afiff, S.A. and C. Lowe (2007) "Claiming Indigenous Community: Political Discourse and Natural Resource Rights in Indonesia," *Alternatives: Global, Local, Political* 32(1): pp. 73–97.

_____ (2008) "Collaboration, Conservation, and Community: A Conversation between Suraya Afiff and Celia Lowe." In *Biodiversity and Human Livelihoods in Protected Areas: Case Studies from the Malay Archipelago*, N.S. Sodhi, G. Acciaioli, M. Erb and A. Khee-Jin Tan, (eds.), pp. 153–64. Cambridge: Cambridge University Press.

Antropologi untuk Indonesia (2016) "Gerakan Antropolog untuk Indonesia yang Bineka dan Inklusif: Pernyataan Sikap dan Seruan, Darurat Ke-Indonesia-an" ["The Movement of Anthropologists for the Diverse and Inclusive Indonesia"]. Statement and press conference, December 16.

_____ (2017). "Usulan Strategis Antropologi untuk Indonesia kepada Presiden Republik Indonesia dalam Merawat Indonesia yang Bineka dan Inklusif" ["The Strategic Suggestions of Anthropology for Indonesia to the President of the Republic of Indonesia in Nurturing the Diverse and Inclusive Indonesia"]. Strategic suggestions submitted to the president of the Republic of Indonesia, January 17.

Ardhana, I.K. (2005) "The Social and Economic Impacts on Development in the Cross-Border Areas between Thailand and Burma." In *Indonesia in the Changing Global Context: Building Cooperation and Partnership?* Proceedings of the 4th International Symposium of the Journal *Antropologi Indonesia* at the Faculty of Social and Political Sciences, Universitas Indonesia, Depok.

Ardhianto, I. (2011) "Benih Milik Saya, Kami, atau Mereka? Tumbuh Kembang Pranata Kepemilikan Benih Kultivar" ["My Seeds, Ours, or Theirs? The Development of Property Right Institutions for Cultivar Seeds"]. In *Bisa Dèwèk: Kisah Perjuangan Petani Pemulia Tanaman di Indramayu* [*We Can Do it Ourselves: The Story of the Struggles of*

Indramayu Farmer-Plant-Breeders], Y.T. Winarto, (ed.), pp. 307–25. Depok: P.T. Gramata Publishing.

——— (2012) "Hubungan Relasional dan Ontologi Moralitas: Meninjau Beberapa Tulisan Antropologi mengenai 'Ritus Kurban'" ["Relationality and the Ontology of Morality: Reviewing some Anthropological Writings on 'the Ritual of Sacrifice'"]. In *Antropologi Agama: Wacana-wacana Mutakhir dalam Kajian Religi dan Budaya* [*Anthropology of Religion: Contemporary Issues in the Study of Religion and Culture*], T. Rudyansjah, (ed.), pp. 109–34. Jakarta: UI Press.

——— (2015) "Publik Islam dalam Ruang Digital: Kontinuitas dan Transformasi Narasi Islam, Negara dan Kebangsaan di Indonesia" ["The Public of Islam in the Digital Space: Continuity and Transformation of Islamic Narratives, State and Nation in Indonesia"]. In *Etnohistori: Edisi Spesial Media Baru, Januari* [*Ethnohistory: New Special Edition, January*]. http://etnohistori.org/-edisi-media-baru-publik-islam-dalam-ruang-digital-kontinuitas-dan-transformasi-narasi-islam-negara-kebangsaan-di-indonesia-oleh-imam-ardhianto.html; accessed June 25, 2017.

——— (2017) "The Politics of Conversion: Religious Change, Materiality and Social Hierarchy in Central Upland Borneo," *The Asia Pacific Journal of Anthropology* 18(2): pp. 119–34.

Ariefiansyah, R. (2011) "Menuju Etnografi Visual Kolaboratif? Suatu Dinamika Hubungan Peneliti dan Subjek dalam Produksi dan Diseminasi Film Bisa Dèwèk" ["Towards the Collaborative Visual Ethnography? A Dynamics of the Relation between Researcher and Subjects in the Production and Dissemination of the Film on We Can Do it Ourselves"]. In *Bisa Dèwèk: Kisah Perjuangan Petani Pemulia Tanaman di Indramayu* [*We Can Do it Ourselves: The Story of the Struggles of Indramayu Farmer-Plant-Breeders*], Y.T. Winarto, (ed.), pp. 24–50. Depok: P.T. Gramata Publishing.

Azis, A., R. Ariefiansyah, and N.S. Utami (2017) "Precarity, Migration, and Brokerage in Indonesia: Insights from Ethnographic Research in Indramayu." Paper presented at the conference on The Migration Industry: Facilitators and Brokerage in Asia. Singapore: Asia Research Institute, National University of Singapore, June 1–2.

Bau, Y.K. (2005) "Pelintas Batas Tradisional RI-RDTL: Sebuah Perspektif Sosio-Antropologi" ["The RI-RDTL Traditional Transborder Trespassers: A Socio-Anthroplogical Perspective"]. In *Indonesia in the Changing Global Context: Building Cooperation and Partnership?* Proceedings of the 4th International Symposium of the *Jurnal Antropologi Indonesia* at the Faculty of Social and Political Sciences, Universitas Indonesia, Depok.

Blok, A. and J. Boissevain (1984) "Anthropology in the Netherlands: Puzzles and Paradoxes," *Annual Review of Anthropology* 13: pp. 333–44.

Borofsky, R. (2007) "Defining Public Anthropology: A Personal Perspective." Center for a Public Anthropology. http://www.publicanthropology.org/public-anthropology/; accessed April 28, 2008.

Buzard, J. (2003) "On Auto-Ethnographic Authority," *The Yale Journal of Criticism* 16(1): pp. 61–91.

Chaidar, A. and H. Sahrasad (2012) "Nasionalisme dan Islam di Indonesia: Beberapa Titik Temu Politik" ["Nationalism and Islam in Indonesia: Some Political Meeting Points"], *Jurnal Historia Vitae* 26(1): pp. 35–53. https://www.usd.ac.id/lembaga/lppm/jurnal.php?id=abstraksiandmodel=volumeandid_j=17andid_m=1048andid_k=767; accessed June 28, 2017.

_____ (2013) "Negara, Islam, dan Nasionalisme: Sebuah Perspektif" ["State, Islam, and Nationalism: A Perspective"], *Kawistara* 3(1): pp. 41–57.

Chaidar, A., B. Respini, and H. Sahrasad (2016) *From Shari'aism to Terrorism: Political Islam in Post-Authoritarian Indonesia.* Depok: LSAF, Freedom Foundation and Centre for Strategic Studies (CSS), Universitas Indonesia.

Chari, S. and H. Donner (2010) "Ethnographies of Activism: A Critical Introduction." *Cultural Dynamics* 22(2): pp. 1–11.

Dahsiar, A. S. (1976) "Shamanisme di Jepang ["Shamanism in Japan"], *Berita Antropologi* 8(25): pp. 3–10.

Fox, J.J. (1977) *Harvest of the Palm: Ecological Changes in Eastern Indonesia.* Cambridge: Harvard University Press.

_____ (2009) "A Complementarity of Methods: Ethnography and Comparative Analysis." Paper prepared for presentation at the International Conference and Summer School on Indonesian Studies, Faculty of Humanities, Universitas Indonesia, Depok, July 27–29.

Geertz, C. (1960) *The Religion of Java.* Glencoe: The Free Press.

Geertz, H. (1961) *The Javanese Family: A Study of Kinship and Socialization.* New York: The Free Press of Glencoe, Inc.

Großmann, K., N. Padmanabhan, and S.A. Afiff (2017) "Gender, Ethnicity, and Environmental Transformations in Indonesia and Beyond," *Austrian Journal of South-East Asian Studies* 10(1): pp. 1–10.

Gunawijaya, J. and A. Pratiwi (2016) "Destination Development for Rural Tourism Area in Wanayasa, Purwakarta, West Java, Indonesia," *E-Journal of Tourism* 3(2): pp. 105–13.

Gupta, A. and J. Ferguson. (1996) "Discipline and Practice: 'The Field' as Site, Method and Location in Anthropology." In *Anthropological Locations, Boundaries and Grounds of a Field Sciences*, A. Gupta and J. Ferguson, (eds.), pp. 1–46. Los Angeles: University of California Press.

Haba, J. (2005) "Community Development of People in the Border Areas between Indonesia and Democratic Republic of Timor Leste." In *Indonesia in the Changing Global Context: Building Cooperation and Partnership?* Proceedings of the 4th International Symposium of the

Jurnal Antropologi Indonesia at the Faculty of Social and Political Sciences, Universitas Indonesia, Depok.

Hadi, S., D. Lumenta, I.M. Pirous, R. Ariefiansyah, R.S. Jaslim and S. Fauzan R. (2005) "The Construction and Deconstruction of Migrant Identities in Contemporary Malaysia: Case Study of Indonesian Bugis Migrants in Sabah and Indonesian Kenyan Migrants in Sarawak." In *Indonesia in the Changing Global Context: Building Cooperation and Partnership?* Proceedings of the 4th International Symposium of the *Jurnal Antropologi Indonesia* at the Faculty of Social and Political Sciences, Universitas Indonesia, Depok.

Hidayana, I.M. (2012) *Life and Death with HIV/AIDS: Life Stories from Karawang, West Java.* Unpublished PhD dissertation. Amsterdam University, Netherlands.

Hidayana, I.M. and B. Tenni (2015) "Negotiating Risk: Indonesian Couples Navigating Marital Relationships, Reproduction and HIV." In *Sex and Sexualities in Contemporary Indonesia*, L.R. Bennett and S.G. Davies, (eds.), pp. 91–108. Oxon and New York: Routledge.

Idrus, N.I. (2001) "Marriage, Sex, and Violence." In *Love, Sex, and Power: Women in Southeast Asia*, S. Blackburn, (ed.), pp. 45–56. Melbourne: Monash Asia Institute.

——— (2002) "Women's Activism against Violence in South Sulawesi." In *Women in Indonesia: Gender, Equity and Development*, K. Roinson and S. Bessel, (eds.), pp. 198–208. Singapore: ISEAS.

——— (2003a) *To Take Each Other: Bugis Practices of Gender, Sexuality and Marriage.* Unpublished PhD dissertation, Australian National University.

——— (2003b) "Presumed Consent: Marital Violence in Bugis Society." In *Violence Against Women in Asia*, L. Manderson and L.R. Bennett, (eds.), pp. 41–60. London: RoutledgeCurzon.

Idrus, N.I. and A. Hardon (2015) "Chemicals, Biocapital and the Everyday Lives of Sex Workers and Waitresses in South Sulawesi." In *Sex and Sexualities in Contemporary Indonesia*, L.R. Bennett and S.G. Davies, (eds.), pp. 129–47. Oxon and New York: Routledge.

Idrus, N.I. (2016) *Gender Relations in an Indonesian Society: Bugis Practices of Sexuality and Marriage.* Leiden: Brill.

Indriatmoko, Y. (2004) "*Orang Asli*, Land Security and Response to the Dominant Society: Case Study of Tanjung Rambai *Temuan*, at Ulu Langat District, Selangor." In *Nippon Foundation-Asian Public Intellectuals Program*, pp. 52–67. Tokyo.

International Catholic Migration Commission (2017) *Bondaged Souls: Migration and Situation of Trafficking in Sabah, Malaysia.* Sabah: International Catholic Migration Commission.

Irianto, S. (2011) *Access to Justice and Global Migration: Study on Indonesian Women Domestic Migrant Workers in the United Arab Emirates.* Jakarta: Yayasan Obor Indonesia.

_____ (2012) "The Changing Socio-legal Position of Women in Inheritance: A Case Study of Batak Women in Indonesia." In *The Family in Flux in Southeast Asia: Institution, Ideology, Practice*, Y. Hayami, J. Koizumi, and C.S.R. Tosakul, (eds.), pp. 105–28. Kyoto: Kyoto University and Silkworm Books.

_____ (2016) *Inheritance Legal Pluralism and Gender Justice*. Jakarta: Yayasan Obor Indonesia.

Irianto, S. and T.D. Truong (2014) "From Breaking the Silence to Breaking the Chain of Social Injustice: Indonesian Women Domestic Migrant Workers in the United Arab Emirate." In *Migration, Gender and Social Justice: Perspectives on Human Insecurity and Environmental Security and Peace 9*, DOI 10.1007/978-3-642-28012-2_2.

Jay, R.R. (1969) *Javanese Villagers: Social Relations in Rural Modjokuto*. Cambridge: The Massachusetts Institute of Technology.

Jurnal Antropologi Indonesia (2000) *The Beginning of the 21st Century: Endorsing Regional Autonomy, Understanding Local Cultures, and Developing National Integration*. Proceedings of the 1st International Symposium of the *Jurnal Antropologi Indonesia* held at Hasanuddin University, Makassar.

_____ (2001) *Globalization and Local Culture: A Dialectic towards the New Indonesia*. Proceedings of the 2nd International Symposium of the *Jurnal Antropologi Indonesia* held at Andalas University, Padang.

_____ (2002a) *Rebuilding Indonesia, a Nation of "Unity in Diversity": Towards a Multicultural Society*. Proceedings of the 3rd International Symposium of the *Jurnal Antropologi Indonesia* held at Udayana University, Denpasar.

_____ (2002b) *Dinamika Sosial-Budaya di Daerah Perbatasan Indonesia Malaysia* [*Socio-Cultural Dynamics in the Border Region of Indonesia Malaysia*] 26(67). http://journal.ui.ac.id/index.php/jai/issue/view/492/showToc.

_____ (2005) *Indonesia in the Changing Global Context: Building Cooperation and Partnership?* Proceedings of the 4th International Symposium of the *Jurnal Antropologi Indonesia* held at the Faculty of Social and Political Sciences, Universitas Indonesia, Depok.

Koentjaraningrat (1969) *Arti Antropologi untuk Indonesia Masa Ini* [*The Meaning of Anthropology for Contemporary Indonesia*]. Unpublished manuscript. Lembaga Research Kebudayaan Nasional LIPI Series 1(1). Jakarta: Lembaga Ilmu Pengetahuan Indonesia.

_____ (1974) *Kebudayaan, Mentalitet dan Pembangunan* [*Culture, Mentality and Development*]. Jakarta: Gramedia.

_____ (1981) "Orientasi Nilai Budaya terhadap Kebudayaan Nasional" ["Cultural Value Orientation towards National Culture"], *Analisis Kebudayaan* 2(2): pp. 8–14.

_____ (1982) "Arti Antropologi Terapan dalam Pembangunan Nasional" ["The Meaning of Applied Anthropology in National Development"]. In *Masalah-masalah Pembangunan: Bunga Rampai Antropologi Terapan* [*Problems of Development: Applied Anthropological Volume*], Koentjaraningrat, (ed.), pp. 5–10. Jakarta: LP3ES.

_____ (1985) "*Persepsi Masyarakat terhadap Kebudayaan Nasional*" ["The Perception of Society towards National Culture"]. In *Persepsi Masyarakat terhadap Kebudayaan* [*The Perception of Society towards National Culture*], Alfian (ed.), pp. 99–140. Jakarta: Gramedia.

Lassitter, L.E. (2005a) *The Chicago Guide to Collaborative Ethnography*. Chicago: University of Chicago Press.

_____ (2005b) "Collaborative Ethnography and Public Anthropology," *Current Anthropology* 46: pp. 83–106.

_____ (2008) "Moving Past Public Anthropology and Doing Collaborative Research," *NAPA Bulletin* 46: pp. 83–106.

Low, S.M. and S.E. Merry (2010) "Engaged Anthropology: Diversity and Dilemmas: An Introduction to Supplement 2," *Current Anthropology* 51(Supplement 2): pp. 5203–26.

Lubis, Z. (2017) *Menggantang Asa di Kabut Asap: Fenomena Environmentaliti Friksi dalam Penanggulangan Kebakaran Lahan Gambut* [*Expecting Hopes under the Haze: A Phenomenon of 'Frictional Environmentality' in Controlling Peatland Fires*]. Unpublished PhD dissertation, Universitas Indonesia.

Lumenta, D. (2008) "The Making of a Transnational Continuum: State Partitions and Mobility of the Apau Kayan Kenyah in Central Borneo, 1900–2007." Unpublished PhD dissertation, ASAFAS Kyoto University, Japan.

_____ (2017) "The Political Economy of Ending Headhunting in Central Borneo: Inter-colonial and Kenyah Perspectives on the 1924 Kapit Peacemaking Agreement and its Aftermath," *Modern Asian Studies*, in press. DOI 10.1017/Soo26749X16000056.

Marcus, G. (1998) *Ethnography through Thick and Thin*. Princeton: Princeton University Press.

Margono, S.S., T. Wandrab, M.F. Swasono, S. Murni, P.S. Craig, and I. Akira (2006) "Taeniasis/cysticercosis in Papua (Irian Jaya), Indonesia." *Parasitology International* 55(Supplement): pp. 5143–48.

Maunati, Y. (2005) "Living in the Border Areas of Thailand: Ethnic Minorities and their Identities." In *Indonesia in the Changing Global Context: Building Cooperation and Partnership?* Proceedings of the 4th International Symposium of the *Jurnal Antropologi Indonesia* at the Faculty of Social and Political Sciences, Universitas Indonesia, Depok.

McCarthy, J.F., J. Vel, and S.A. Afiff (2012) "Trajectories of Land Acquisition and Enclosure: Development Schemes, Virtual Land Grabs, and Green Acquisitions in Indonesia's Outer Islands," *Journal of Peasant Studies* 39(2): pp. 521–49.

McNally, S., J. Grierson, and I.M. Hidayana (2015) "Belonging, Community and Identity: Gay Men in Indonesia." In *Sex and Sexualities in Contemporary Indonesia*, L.R. Bennett and S. Davies, (eds.), pp. 203–17. Oxon and New York: Routledge.

Murni, S. (2007) "Beliatnt Sentiyu: Pengubatan Tradisional Orang Dayak Benuaq, Kalimantan Timur, Indonesia" ["Beliatnt Sentiyu: Traditional Healing of Orang Dayak Benuaq, East Kalimantan, Indonesia"]. Paper presented at the International Seminar on Innovating Approaches Looking Beyond Conventionalities, Bangi-Selangor, March 13.

Peluso, N.L., S.A. Afiff, and N.F. Rackhman (2008) "Claiming the Grounds of Reform: Agrarian and Environmental Movements in Indonesia," *Journal of Agrarian Change* 8(2/3): pp. 377–407.

Pitana, I Gde (1997) *In Search of Difference: Origin Groups, Status and Identity in Contemporary Bali.* Unpublished thesis, Australian National University.

——— (2000) *Cultural Tourism in Bali: A Critical Appreciation.* Denpasar: Research Center for Culture and Tourism, Udayana University.

——— (ed.) (2013) *Ekonomi Hijau dalam Pariwisata* [*Green Economy in Tourism*]. Jakarta: Pusat Penelitian dan Pengembangan Kebijakan Kepariwisataan, Badan Pengembangan Sumber Daya, Kementerian Pariwisata dan Ekonomi Kreatif.

Prager, M. (2005) "From *Volkenkunde* to *Djurusan Antropologi*: The Emergence of Indonesian Anthropology in Postwar Indonesia." In *Asian Anthropology*, J. van Bremen, E. Ben-Ari, and S.F. Alatas, (eds.), pp. 179–200. London and New York: Routledge.

Prasetijo, A. (2013) "Behind the Forest: The Ethnic Identity of Orang Kubu (Orang Rimba), Jambi - Indonesia." Conference paper presented at the 10th International Conference on Hunting and Gathering Societies. Liverpool: Liverpool School of Archaeology, Classics and Egyptology, University of Liverpool, June 25–28.

——— (2015) *Orang Rimba: True Custodian of the Forest: Alternative Strategies and Actions in Social Movement against Hegemony.* Jakarta: KKI Warsi and ICSD Publishing.

Purwanto, S.A. (2009a) "Urban Agriculture in a Developing Country: The Experience of the Philippines' Urban Agriculture." *Confluence and Challenges in Building the Asian Community in the Early 21st Century.* The Work of the 2008/2009 API Fellows. Tokyo: The Nippon Foundation.

——— (2009b) "Rural-Urban Linkage in Jakarta's Urban Agriculture: The Case of Karawang of West Java Migrants." Paper presented at the international symposium on Status and Tendency of Suburban Agriculture in South and Southeast Asia Countries. College of Bioresource Science, Nihon University.

——— (2011) "Bertani di Dua Kota Asia: Menarik Pelajaran dari Jakarta dan Manila" ["Farming in Two Cities in Asia: Gaining Lessons from Jakarta and Manila"]. Paper presented at the Seminar on Membangun City Branding Kota Semarang, August 9.

____ (2015a) "The Dynamic of Artisanal Mining in Kalimantan, Indonesia." Paper presented at the workshop on Environmental Transformation, Ethnicity and Gender in Kalimantan, Indonesia. Passau: University of Passau, June 10–12.

____ (2015b) "The Golden Way: Institutionalizing Illegal Activities in Indonesia." Paper presented at the workshop on Mining in Indonesia: Local, National and Global Frameworks. Canberra: Australian National University, September 20–21.

____ (2017) "Positioning Illegal Gold Mining in the Current Indonesian Development." Paper presented at the Roundtable Workshop on Mining Politics and Justice in Indonesia. Singapore: National University of Singapore, May 4.

Ramstedt, M. (2005) "Anthropology and the Nation State: Applied Anthropology in Indonesia." In *Asian Anthropology*, J. van Bremen, E. Ben-Ari, and S.F. Alatas, (eds.), pp. 200–23. London and New York: Routledge.

Rudyansjah, T. (2012) "*Going Native* sebagai Tabu dan Identitas Tempatan sebagai Titik Pijakan Etnografis" ["*Going Native* as Taboo and Local Identity as an Ethnographic Standpoint"]. In *Antropologi Agama: Wacana-wacana Mutakhir dalam Kajian Religi dan Budaya* [*Anthropology of Religion: Contemporary Issues in the Study of Religion and Culture*], T. Rudyansjah, (ed.), pp. 1–30. Jakarta: UI Press.

Sahrasad, H. and A. Chaidar (2015) "Islam, Fundamentalism and Democracy: A Perspective from Indonesia," *Jurnal Ilmu Ushuluddin* 2(4): pp. 307–28.

Saifuddin, A.F. (2000) *Agama dalam Politik Keseragaman: Kebijakan Keagamaan di Indonesia pada Masa Orde Baru* [*Religion in the Politics of Uniformity: The Policy to Religions in the New Order of Indonesia*]. Jakarta: Ministry of Religious Affairs.

____ (2003) "Muhammadiyah Multikultural: (Re)konstruksi Muhammadiyah pada Abad ke Dua Puluh Satu" ["The Multicultural Muhammadiyah: (Re)construction of Muhammadiyah in the Twenty First Century"], *Jurnal Tanwir* 2(1): pp. 45–62.

____ (2006) "Integrasi, Konflik, dan Resistensi: Suatu Pendekatan Antropologi mengenai Agama" ["Integration, Conflict, and Resistance: An Anthropological Approach to Religion"], *Harmoni: Jurnal Multikultural dan Multireligi* 5(19): pp. 21–34.

____ (2010) "Agama dalam Pendekatan Sosial Budaya: Dari Positivisme Hingga Konstruktivisme" ["Religion in Sociocultural Approach: From Positivism to Constructivism"]. In *Agama dalam Perbincangan Sosiologi* [*Religion in Sociology Conversation*], R. Lubis, (ed.), pp. 1–12. Jakarta: Ciptapustaka.

____ (2017) "Five Letters that Hurt: Multicultural Indonesia in Current Faster Change Era," *Asia Pacific Journal of Advanced Business and Social Studies* 3(2): pp. 168–75.

Shahab, Y.Z. (1982) *The Position of Betawi Women*. Unpublished Master's thesis, Australian National University.

____ (1994) *The Creation of Ethnic Tradition: The Betawi of Jakarta*. Unpublished PhD thesis, University of London, United Kingdom.

____ (2000) "Aristocratic Betawi: A Challenge to Oustiders' Perspectives." In *Jakarta-Batavia: Socio-Cultural Essays*, P. Nas, (ed.), pp. 199–228. Leiden: KITLV Press.

Siegel, J.T. (1993). *Solo in the New Order: Language and Hierarchy in an Indonesian City*. Princeton: Princeton University Press.

Sofion, A. (1975) "Agama Buda di Muangthai" ["Budhism Religion in Muangthai"], *Berita Antropologi* 7(20): pp. 8–30.

____ (1989). "Beberapa Aspek Kehidupan Desa Thai Islam Hua Sai di Propinsi Nakhon Srithammarat, Thailand Selatan" ["Several Aspects of Islamic Thai Village Life of Hua Sai in the Province of Nakhon Srithammarat, South Thailand"], *Berita Antropologi* 13(46): pp. 110–59.

Sulistiawati, D. (2013) *Living with HIV-AIDS: Dari Memahami Virus hingga Menormalkan Kembali Kehidupan Pribadi* [*Living with HIV-AIDS: From Understanding Virus to Re-normalizing Private Life*]. Unpublished PhD dissertation. Universitas Indonesia.

Suparlan, P. (1999a) "Antropologi Indonesia dalam Memasuki Abad ke-21" ["Indonesian Anthropology Entering the 21st Century"], *Antropologi Indonesia* 23(58): pp. 1–4.

____ (1999b) "Kemajemukan, Hipotesis Kebudayaan Dominan dan Kesukubangsaan" ["Plurality, the Hypothesis of Dominant Culture and Ethnicity"], *Antropologi Indonesia* 23(58): pp. 13–20.

____ (2000a) "Bhinneka Tunggal Ika, Masih Mungkinkah: Wawancara Wimar Witoelar dengan Parsudi Suparlan" ["Unity in Diversity, Is It still Possible: Wimar Witoelar's interview with Parsudi Suparlan"], *Antropologi Indonesia* 24(62): pp. 129–34.

____ (2000b) "Masyarakat Majemuk dan Perawatannya" ["Plural Society and its Nurturance"], *Antropologi Indonesia* 24(63): 1–14.

____ (2001) "Kesetaraan Warga dan Hak Budaya Komuniti" ["The Equality of Citizens and the Cultural Right of Community"], *Antropologi Indonesia* 25(66): pp. 1–12.

____ (2002) "Menuju Masyarakat Indonesia yang Multikultural" ["Towards a Multicultural Indonesian Society"], *Antropologi Indonesia* 26(69): pp. 98–105.

Swasono, M.F., M.J. Melalatoa, S. Murni, and U.R. Kosasih (1997) "*Masyarakat Dani di Irian Jaya: Adat Istiadat dan Kesehatan*" ["Dani Society in

Irian Jaya: Traditional Customs and Health"], *Berita Antropologi* 53: pp. 1–27.

Thompson, E.C., C. Thianthai and I.M. Hidayana (2007) "Culture and International Imagination in Southeast Asia," *Political Geography* 26(3): pp. 268–88.

Vel, J., Y. Zakaria, and A. Bedner (2017) "Creating Indonesia's Village Law," *Inside Indonesia* 128: Apr–Jun. http://www.insideindonesia.org/creating-indonesia-village-law; accessed June 24, 2017.

Visser, L. (1988) "Interview with Koentjaraningrat," *Current Anthropology* 29(5): pp. 749–53.

Wardana, A. and Darmanto (2017) "Traditional Village Institutions and the Village Law," *Inside Indonesia* 128: Apr–Jun. http://www.insideindonesia.org/traditional-village-institutions-and-the-village-law; accessed June 24, 2017.

Winarto, Y.T. (2004a) "Farmer Field School, Farmer Life School, and Farmers Club for Enriching Knowledge and Empowering Farmers: A Case Study from Cambodia." In *Small-scale Livelihoods and Natural Resources Management in Marginal Areas: Case Studies in Monsoon Asia*, K.G. Saxena, L. Liang, Y. Kono, and S. Miyata, (eds.), pp. 221–31. Tokyo: United Nations University.

_____ (2004b) "The Evolutionary Changes in Rice-crop Farming: Integrated Pest Management in Indonesia, Cambodia and Vietnam," *Southeast Asian Studies Journal (Tonan Ajia Kenkyu)* 42(3): pp. 241–72.

_____ (2005a) "Empowering Farmers, Improving Techniques? The Integrated Pest Management in Cambodia and Thailand." *ARI Working Paper* no. 54, November. www.ari.nus.edu.sg/pub/wps.htm; accessed March 15, 2006.

_____ (2005b) "Examining Evolutionary Changes in a Comparative Perspective: The Cambodian and Thai Cases of Rice Farming Culture." Paper presented in the panel on "Land, Farming and the Transformation of Agricultural Communities" in the Southeast Asian Studies Regional Exchange Program (SEASREP) 10th Anniversary Conference: "Southeast Asia: A Global Crossroads," Chiang Mai, December 8–9.

_____ (2006). "Self-governance and Conflicting Interests in Farm Resource Management," *Masyarakat Indonesia: Majalah Ilmu-ilmu Sosial Indonesia* 32(1): pp. 22–37.

_____ (2011a). "Integrated Pest Management in Indonesia." In *Complicating Conservation in Southeast Asia: Beyond the Sacred Forest*, M.R. Dove, P.C. Sajise, and A. Doolittle, (eds.), pp. 276–301. Durham and London: Duke University Press.

_____ (ed.) (2011b) *Bisa Dèwèk: Kisah Perjuangan Petani Pemulia Tanaman di Indramayu* [*We Can Do it Ourselves: The Story of the Struggles of Indramayu Farmer-Plant-Breeders*]. Depok: P.T. Gramata Publishing.

Winarto, Y.T. and I. Ardhianto (2011) "Mencatat Jejak Pengetahuan, Mendokumentasikan Praktik dan Produk Pemuliaan Tanaman" ["Writing the Foot Paths of Knowledge, Documenting the Practice and Products of Plant Breeding"]. In *Bisa Dèwèk: Kisah Perjuangan Petani Pemulia Tanaman di Indramayu* [*We Can Do it Ourselves: The Story of the Struggles of Indramayu Farmer-Plant-Breeders*], Y.T. Winarto, (ed.), pp. 230–76. Depok: P.T. Gramata Publishing.

Winarto, Y.T. and K. Stigter, (eds.) (2011) *Agrometeorological Learning: Coping Better with Climate Change.* Saarbrűcken: LAP LAMBERT Academic Publishing GmbH & Co. KG.

——— (2013) "Science Field Shops to Reduce Climate Vulnerabilities: An Inter- and Transdisciplinary Educational Commitment," *Collaborative Anthropologies* 6: pp. 419–41.

——— (2016) "Incremental Learning and Gradual Changes: 'Science Field Shops' as an Educational Approach to Coping Better with Climate Change in Agriculture." In *Promoting Climate Change Awareness through Environmental Education*, L. Wylson and C. Stevenson, (eds.), pp. 60–95. Hershey (PA): IGI Global Publisher.

——— (2017) "Anthropology Teaming up with Agrometeorology: Getting University Science to Assist Farmers with Climate Resilience," *Asian Politics and Policy* 9(3): pp. 479–92.

Winarto, Y.T., H. Arifin, Y. Purwanto, Y.E.M. Prioharjono, A. Qasim, B. Gala, and M. Lampe (1999) "Abrasion, Mangrove Conservation, Coral Reef Degradation: Cases from the Coastal of South Sulawesi and the Offshore of Pulau-pulau Sembilan." Jakarta: Department of Anthropology, FISIP Universitas Indonesia in collaboration with UNESCO and MAB. Translation into English by E.M. Choesin.

Winarto, Y.T., K. Stiger, H. Prahara, E. Anantasari, and Kristiyanto (2011) "Collaborating on Establishing an Agro-meteorological Learning Situation among Farmers in Java," *Anthropological Forum* 21(2): pp. 175–98.

Winarto, Y.T., K. Stigter, B. Dwisatrio, M. Nurhaga, and A. Bowolaksono (2013) "Agrometeorological Learning Increasing Farmers' Knowledge in Coping with Climate Change and Unusual Risks," *Southeast Asian Studies* 2(2): pp. 323–49.

Winarto Y.T., K. Stigter, and R. Ariefiansyah (2015) "Interpreting the Present, Anticipating the Future: Continuous Learning in Ongoing Climate Change," *Environmental Education in Indonesia Workshop, Depok, 13–14 December 2015.* Depok: University of Western Australia (Australia Research Council) and the Centre for Anthropological Studies, Faculty of Social and Political Sciences, Universitas Indonesia.

——— (2017a) "Anticipating the Future," *Inside Indonesia* 127: Jan–March 2017. http://www.insideindonesia.org/anticipating-the-future; accessed April 18, 2017.

Winarto, Y.T., K. Stigter, and M.T. Wicaksono (2017b) "Transdisciplinary Responses to Climate Change: Institutionalizing Agrometeorological Learning through Science Field Shops in Indonesia," *Austrian Journal of South-East Asian Studies* 10(1): pp. 65–82.

Zakaria, Y. (2000) *Abeh Tandeh: Masyarakat Desa di Bawah Rezim Orde Baru* [*Abeh Tandeh: Village Society under the New Order Regime*]. Jakarta: Lembaga Studi dan Advokasi Hak-hak Masyarakat (ELSAM).

——— (2004) *Merebut Negara, Beberapa Catatan Reflektif tentang Upaya-upaya Pengakuan, Pengembalian, dan Pemulihan Otonomi Desa* [*Seizing the State, Some Reflective Notes of the Efforts of Recognizing, Returning, and Recovering Village Autonomy*]. Yogyakarta: Lingkar Pembaruan Desa dan Agraria (KARSA).

——— (2012) "Makna Amandemen Pasal 18: Undang-Undang Dasar 1945 bagi Pengakuan dan Perlindungan Masyarakat Adat di Indonesia" ["The Meaning of Amandment of Chapter 18: 1945 Constitution for Recognizing and Securing Customary Societies in Indonesia"]. Paper presented at the conference on Dialog Nasional dalam rangka Satu Dasawarsa Amandemen UUD 1945: "Negara Hukum ke mana akan Melangkah?" Jakarta, October 9–10.

——— (2014) "Konstitutionalitas Kriteria Masyarakat (Hukum) Adat dan Potensi Implikasinya terhadap Perebutan Sumberdaya Hutan Pasca Putusan Mahkamah Konstitusi Nomor 35/PUU-X/2012: Studi Kasus Kabupaten Kutai Barat, Kalimatan Timur" [The Constitutionality of the Criteria of (Legal) Customary Societies and the Potentials of its Implication on the Grabbing of Forest Resources in the Post Period of Constitutional Court's Decision No.35/PUU-X/2012: A Case Study of Kutai Barat Regency, East Kalimantan], *WACANA: Jurnal Transformasi Sosial* 33(16): pp. 99–135.

——— (2015) *Etnografi Tanah Adat: Konsep-konsep Dasar dan Pedoman Kajian Lapangan* [*The Ethnography of Customary Land: Basic Concepts and Guidance for Field Examination.*] Report submitted to Lingkar Pembaruan Desa dan Agraria (KARSA): The Forest Trust, Yogyakarta.

Zakaria, Y. and R. Simarmata (2015) *Mempromosikan Program Inklusi Sosial dan Pembangunan yang Inklusif melalui Upaya Optimalisasi Undang-Undang Nomor 6 Tahun 2014 tentang Desa* [*Promoting the Social Inclusion Programme and the Inclusive Development through the Efforts of Optimalizing Law No. 6, 2014 on Village*]. Report submitted as short time consultant to KOMPAK, a bilateral agreement between Indonesia and Australia, Jakarta.

Zakaria, Y. and J. Vel (2017) "New Law, Old Bureaucracy," *Inside Indonesia* 128: Apr–Jun. http://www.insideindonesia.org/new-law-old-bureaucracy; accessed June 2, 2017.

CHAPTER 9

ASSESSING DOI MOI (RENOVATION) ANTHROPOLOGY IN VIETNAM

Dang Nguyen Anh

The establishment or at least the institutionalization of Vietnamese anthropology (see Nguyen, this volume) dates back to 1959 when its disciplinary predecessor, ethnology, began to be taught in the Department of History at the National University of Hanoi. This coincided with the general arrival of the social sciences in Vietnamese universities and research institutes. Anthropology was further institutionalized with the founding of the Department of Ethnology at the National University of Hanoi in 1967 and the Institute of Ethnology (under the Vietnam Academy of Social Sciences) in 1968. Over the last five decades, anthropology in Vietnam has undergone many drastic changes as it has grown and developed (Vuong Xuan Tinh 2013).

This chapter examines how Vietnamese anthropology has responded to Doi Moi or "renovation," a series of market-oriented policy reforms officially introduced in 1986 that have accelerated since the 1990s. These changes are rooted in the administrative and training structure of postcolonial ethnology in Vietnam. Although anthropology has emerged from ethnology, the latter still influences the role of anthropological research in post-reform governance and social transformations. The chapter begins with a brief discussion of Vietnamese anthropology prior to renovation (see Nguyen, this volume). It then turns to the changes in organization, training and methods that emerged in the Doi Moi era, followed by a discussion the key concerns of Doi Moi anthropology. During this era, anthropology has focused on national priorities, including economic development and especially updated issues of ethnic minority culture and ethno-national sentiments. Having traced the main trends of Doi Moi anthropology, I conclude with suggestions for the continued "post-" or "later-Doi Moi" renovation of the structure, mandates and practice of anthropology to meet the visions of Vietnam's future.

Vietnamese Anthropology before Renovation

Prior to the country's Doi Moi period, anthropology was mostly housed under departments of history that were typically founded in the 1950s in Vietnam. At the Hanoi University of Social Sciences and Humanities, Ho Chi Minh University of Social Sciences and Humanities, and Hue University of Sciences, anthropology departments belonged to the Faculty of History. This association of anthropology with history was also seen at research institutions. For example, in 1968, ten years after its establishment, the Department of Anthropology of the Institute of History in Hanoi was separated from its parent organization to serve as the core of the Institute of Anthropology.

However, it would not be until the beginning of the twenty-first century that anthropology would undergo its most dramatic transformations. The Institute of Ethnology, in combination with the Vietnam Association of Ethnology and the Department of Ethnology at the Hanoi University of Social Sciences and Humanities, presided over three national conferences in Hanoi, Ho Chi Minh City and Hue on reforming research, teaching, and archival materials. Most significantly, these meetings focused on the conversion from ethnology to anthropology. In 2001, a national conference on "Enhancing the quality of researching and teaching ethnology/anthropology within the context of the country's modernization" convened in Hanoi to address two key issues related to the renovation of ethnology: the separation of ethnology from departments of history to become an independent discipline and the renaming of the Institute of Ethnology as the Institute of Anthropology (Khong Dien 2001).

The association of anthropology with history is also reflected in the training for the former in Vietnam. Prior to 2005, in accordance with regulations at the Ministry of Education and Training, the doctoral training code of the Institute of Anthropology fell under "history." Between 2004 and 2012, the bachelor, master's, and doctoral training codes in the Department of Anthropology at the Ho Chi Minh University of Social Sciences and Humanities, and the Department of Anthropology under Hanoi University of Social Sciences and Humanities were converted from displaying anthropology as a major within history to an independent discipline. Although this is only a branch code arranged by the Ministry of Education and Training, it reflects the bureaucratic organization of professional sciences in Vietnam. Furthermore, the structure of anthropological curricula usually consisted of two or three courses from history with the rest allocated to anthropology.

Well into the 1990s, the content of knowledge and training mainly complied with a Soviet model largely focused on comparative ethnological studies. This limited the scope of anthropology to the study of ethnic minorities in relation to national policies. Research methods were almost always qualitative, with little interest in quantitative and interdisciplinary methods in the broader social sciences. Training occurred both domestically and internationally, mainly in the former Soviet Union and Eastern European countries. Since the break up of the Soviet Union and Eastern European bloc, the relationship between Vietnamese academic anthropology and the academies of former Soviet countries dwindled, as reflected in the lack of updates to teaching syllabi, methodological innovation, teaching practicums, translation projects and so on.

The objective of pre-Doi Moi anthropological research was usually to describe the characteristics of ethnic minorities or contribute to the explanation of historical developments within Vietnam (see Be Viet Dang 1988). In general, anthropology research was scarce and focused on rural areas. There were a handful of studies on urban populations, but they mostly dealt with relatively remote highland towns and urban centers rather than Vietnam's major, lowland cities (Nguyen Van Huy 1982).

The desire to improve on or even replace the Soviet ethnological model eventually led to the renovation of anthropology in Vietnam. At the same time, the political, economic, and social conditions in Vietnam led to a slow integration of Vietnamese anthropology with its counterparts in America and Europe. Historically, anthropology has been heavily influenced by intellectual traditions coming from Britain and France. For an extended period prior to the Doi Moi era, well-known foreign anthropological scholars from many countries and continents visited Vietnam (e.g. Catherin Gough from Canada, Yogesh Atal from India, Chester Goffman from the United States). During their visits, these scholars mainly looked for the emergence of anthropological research in Vietnam. However, because of a lack of development in local anthropology, the main contacts between Vietnam and international scholars came from related disciplines including archeology, sociology, ethnology and religious studies.

Anthropology under Renovation

In the current Doi Moi era, Vietnamese anthropology has come into contact, had exchanges with, and inquired into Western anthropological approaches and trends. The renovation of Vietnamese anthropology can be traced to the beginning of the twenty-first century, when the discipline was required to comprehensively renovate its research, teaching and information, documentation and libraries. These reforms have encompassed a broad set of interrelated aspects of anthropological practice in Vietnam. First is the interconnected concern of how anthropology is institutionally organized, with teaching and research divided between universities and research institutes, and the impact this has on postgraduate training. Second, the past two decades have seen reform in the primary methods that anthropologists use in field research. During the 1980s and 1990s, the Vietnamese anthropologists conducted their fieldwork based on "participant observation," spending a long period living as closely as possible with the community being studied; sharing the activities of daily life; participating in the texture of daily social interactions; and identifying underlying patterns. They analyzed this experience and exchanged ideas with members of the study community. Over the last twenty years, the anthropologists have applied more survey-oriented, quantitative interviews to supplement if not substitute for participant-observatory methods. And finally, we see a trend in the later Doi Moi period toward greater interdisciplinary work, as anthropology recently became more firmly established as an independent discipline apart from both history and ethnology. These changes in the conduct of fieldwork and methods continue to grow as the knowledge reveals more information for investigation.

During the first decade of the current century, activities related to the institutionalization of a renovated Vietnamese anthropology ramped up. In 2004, the Department of Anthropology at the Ho Chi Minh City University of Social Sciences and Humanities was created out of the Department of Ethnology to become the first Department of Anthropology in Southern Vietnam. A year later, the training code for a doctorate in social and cultural anthropology at the Institute of Ethnology was recognized by the Ministry of Education and Training. In 2005, the Institute of Ethnology was also officially renamed the Institute of Anthropology, and the Vietnam Association of Ethnology was renamed the Vietnam Association of Ethnology and Anthropology. Continuing this trend, the Department of Anthropology under the Faculty of History at the Hanoi University of Social Sciences and Humanities became an independent department in March 2010. To this day, the department provides degrees from a bachelor to a doctorate in anthropology. In the same year, the Institute of Sociology, under the Vietnam Academy of Social Sciences, founded a Department of Anthropology with the purpose of training postgraduates in ethnology and anthropology.

Along with the development of anthropology as an independent discipline, the Ministry of Education and Training has allowed for the training of anthropology at three levels: bachelor, master's, and doctorate. In the past decade, besides domestic training, there have been several dozen individuals from research institutes and universities in Vietnam going abroad for postgraduate studies in anthropology. A number of younger Vietnamese anthropologists have also gone abroad to study in other countries, including the United Kingdom, Canada, Denmark, Germany, Holland, the United States, Australia, Thailand, China, Japan and South Korea. These training programs have contributed to enhancing both the quantity and the quality of human resources in the field of anthropology while at the same time influencing current research topics in the discipline in Vietnam. The number of students has reached several dozen. Upon their return to home institutions, the newly trained anthropologists were very eager to set up and pursue projects in line with the anthropological training they had received abroad.

However, the reforms have in certain times and places resulted in asynchronous outcomes or relationships. For example, the post-graduate training program at the Faculty of Anthropology under the Vietnam Graduate Academy of Social Sciences grants doctorates in anthropology, but the master's program is in ethnology. Furthermore, it is still under the purview of the history department and faculty to approve "professor" and "associate professor" titles in anthropology. These are inadequacies in administration and organization that need to be overcome for anthropology to become a truly independent discipline.

Any nation that wants its social science research to be effective and of high quality needs to have institutions of international standing for research, training and the teaching of these disciplines. Anthropology is a good example for this viewpoint. Since Doi Moi, research, training and teaching in anthropology have improved considerably but the three are still not adequately integrated. For example, regulations on the responsibilities of research staff on their teaching duties in universities and institutions, especially for anthropology postgraduates, remain unclear. In particular, teaching and research are institutionally segregated. Yet research combined with teaching has long been recognized as an effective training method for social scientists in general and anthropologists in particular. Enabling such a combination would facilitate increased international integration.

The renewal of anthropology is also evident in developments in anthropological methodology in Vietnam. Until recent years, these methods remained mainly qualitative, including participatory observation, in-depth interviews, and research on material culture. In parallel with the conversion from ethnology to anthropology, Vietnam anthropologists have also started applying new research methods and techniques. One noticeable difference is that quantitative research has an increasingly important role in anthropology in Vietnam, especially through the use of survey and statistical data. For example, the North American trained graduates are able to employ survey data and quantitative analysis in their research. In practice, by the end of the 1980s, such methods were used when conducting interdisciplinary research with sociology or poverty assessment at the Institute of Anthropology. However, these methods were not encouraged at that time. Questionnaires became more popular among anthropologists after Doi Moi, not only applied in socio-economic survey programs but also in a broad array of varied research topics. They have become the principal research method preferred by post-graduate anthropology students. Broadly speaking, interdisciplinary training courses in social sciences have been introduced in order to understand social problems and generate comprehensive knowledge.

Besides sociological survey methods and techniques of data collection in field research, anthropologists also apply methods related to development projects such as Rural Rapid Assessment (RRA) and Participatory Rural Assessment (PRA), with tools like group discussions, focus group interviews, participatory mapping, and ordering community priorities. The use of such research tools is evidenced in published work during this time, with authors utilizing available quantitative and statistical data in their works (Vuong Xuan Tinh 2007; Tran Van Ha and Dang Thi Hoa 2009). The relationship between the anthropologists and those they study has also changed radically in recent years, moving from one of privileged observer to the "other" being observed, towards something closer to dialogue and exchange.

Another new development in Vietnamese anthropology is in interdisciplinary studies. Besides the application of the above-mentioned tools and methods, interdisciplinary studies also involve the participation from scientists of other disciplines such as economics, sociology, linguistics and development studies. One strong example is a research program concerning food security at the Institute of Anthropology that was conducted from 2006 to 2008. In that project, anthropologists, economists, agriculturalists, and health and gender experts were all significantly involved. The *Journal of Anthropology* (the official publication of the Institute of Anthropology) also publishes many articles by social scientists from other disciplines. In fact, over 30 percent of the total research articles published use interdisciplinary methods (Vuong Xuan Tinh 2013).

Key Concerns of Renovation Anthropology

From its initial appearance up until the renovation period, Vietnamese anthropology made many important contributions. For example, the list of components of ethnic groups in Vietnam, developed and announced in 1979, contributed significantly towards enriching the scientific base for the research of Vietnamese ethnic groups. Furthermore, anthropology contributed in the development of national policies and their implementation, especially in preserving national unity and the cultural values of ethnic groups in Vietnam.

During the renovation period, anthropology continued to contribute to the country's industrialization and modernization in both research and development consultancy to meet the practical needs of the country's economic and social development. Anthropologists combined basic research with applied research, revealing the socio-economic and cultural characteristics of each region. These studies have contributed to policy recommendations on various issues such as land reform, religion, hunger and poverty, emigration, resettlement, education, and health among ethnic minority populations. On that basis, anthropology has contributed by serving as the scientific basis for solving the pressing issues of our time (Pham Quang Hoan 2009).

In addition to policy recommendations through research, many anthropologists work as consultants for development programs and projects. Anthropologists participate in consulting with the main aim of providing an academic perspective to such programs and projects. They serve as experts, resource persons or consultants for a wide range of projects, including hunger eradication and poverty alleviation, forest allocation, irrigation, rural credit, rural to urban migration, education, health and forestry extension (Doan Viet 2012; Tran Quy Long 2015; Hess và To Thi Thu Huong 2012). Many investment decisions and policy interventions are heavily influenced by research findings produced by anthropologists.

The dual approach of both basic and applied research in Vietnam has led to anthropological contributions in both policy and practice in achieving the country's sustainable development goals. This is in evidence through multiple studies: land use in provinces of the Central Highlands; migration of ethnic minorities; resettlement; food security of ethnic minorities in highland regions; the sustainable development of border areas; and cross-border relations. It can also be seen through the socio-economic and environmental impact assessments of hydroelectric and irrigation projects, resettlement, education and health development projects in ethnic areas in the Mekong, as well as impact assessments for policy programs in education, health, and poverty alleviation in ethnic and mountainous areas (Vi Van An and Bui Minh Thuan 2012; Nguyen Van Toan 2011; Nguyen Van Suu 2010; Tran Quy Long 2015; Tran Hong Hanh 2009; Nguyen Thi Thanh Binh and Nguyen Thu Quynh 2017). Such research findings have made important contributions in recognizing and evaluating the economic, social and cultural development of ethnic groups as well as in analyzing important factors that serve as the scientific basis for proposal and recommendations on state policy. The above-mentioned results show the active role and contribution of anthropological research during Vietnam's renovation, integration and development.

From the end of World War II until the present day, it appears that we are living in a period when nationalist and ethnic sentiments are at their highest. Protests among ethnic minorities indicate an increased desire for equality. There is also a strong relationship between ethnic groups and the nation. Furthermore, attempts at the preservation of cultural characteristics among ethnic groups themselves can be observed. For example, Khmer ethnic minority has requested and sent petitions to the government for renaming itself (Phan 2015). Raising awareness of ethnic minority rights has contributed to efforts in preserving and protecting the different cultures of ethnic minorities against the onslaught of assimilation and globalization. As Nguyen (this volume) notes, the tendency to see ethnic minorities as "traditional" is not without its own pitfalls. Nevertheless, an awareness of the importance of cultural preservation has manifested through avenues such as development policies, programs and projects in Vietnam (as it has in many other countries; Winarto and Pirous, this volume). In turn, these policies and practices require input from anthropological research in the coming stages of national and social development.

The trend of international exchange and integration that has arrived with globalization has created conditions for numerous ethnic groups to mutually learn from and share with one another, leading to new developments in economic, social and cultural life. Still, besides these positives, there are also negative impacts under globalization, especially from the vantage point of nationalism. Due to the impact of historical, political, economic and social factors around the world, national and ethnic inter-group relationships have sparked burning conflicts in many areas of the world, especially in the Balkan Peninsula, Caucasus, Russia-Ukraine, Syria and the Middle East, and the Korean Peninsula.

In these areas, conflict and civil wars concerning nationalism combined with religion, separatism and extremism have proliferated. Political actors often take advantage of fault lines to incite distrust and conflict that can even lead to war. International terrorist organizations depend on national and religious matters to gain publicity and grow in number. As such, we can predict that national and religious conflict in many areas in the world, including Southeast Asia, will continue in the coming decades. The future of ethnic groups will be increasingly linked to the fate of their nation state. In Vietnam, from now to 2020 and beyond, nationalism and the nation state will find themselves in a new context with new conditions, bringing challenges and opportunities for the further development and relevance of renovation (and post-renovation) anthropology as a discipline.

Due to globalization, industrialization and modernization, ethnic groups in Vietnam will undoubtedly continue to develop and change profoundly. The large difference between the highlands and the lowlands as well as between the ethnic majority Kinh and ethnic minorities are likely to gradually decrease. Socio-economic development can be expected to promote a more singular national Vietnamese identity, especially in the relationship between the ethnic majority and ethnic minorities. If positive gains in social inclusion and economic prosperity are shared by ethnic minorities within Vietnam, increasingly positive affiliation with Vietnam as a national identity may be expected. Conversely, if these conditions are not met and, to some extent, even if they are, tensions between (Vietnamese) nationalism and (minority group) ethno-nationalism in Vietnam are likely to continue to be a significant issue. In particular regions, including provinces in the Northwest, Central Highlands, and Southwest, tensions and conflicts between ethnic minorities, the state, and ethnic majorities continue to take place. Anthropology should take an active role in addressing these issues.

With the repeated calls for equality, unity and mutual assistance for common development between ethnic groups, policies need to be developed and implemented that consciously take into account regional and international changes. These include policies on hunger eradication and poverty alleviation in areas with a high density of ethnic minorities. The focus of these policies should be aimed at implementing programs and projects to continue building infrastructure, developing the economy, and enhancing education, health care, and the quality of life of all Vietnamese, regardless of ethnicity. The role of anthropology will be to provide detailed information on the intersection between local, regional and global conditions.

Despite much effort and considerable achievement, there remain significant challenges over the coming decades. These include continued hunger and poverty for some ethnic groups, especially in the highlands and remote areas; differences in development between the lowland and highland areas; and the ever-present risk of resource depletion and environmental regression. Furthermore, the relationships between ethnic majorities and minorities as well as cross-border relations need to continue to be studied and handled with care as they constantly evolve. Anthropology should be well suited to provide context-sensitive information through which positive policies can be formulated.

Post-Doi Moi, New Directions

Vietnam has experienced thirty years of Doi Moi (1986–2015) and is entering a "post-Doi Moi" era which focuses on intensive reforms and integration. The approaches to, and concerns of, anthropology under Doi Moi have now become part of anthropology's institutional and intellectual structure in Vietnam. Thus, before concluding, this section sketches out emergent areas of concern for anthropology built on the reforms of the thirty years of Doi Moi, moreover in the broader international context of "globalization." In light of both these international and domestic developments, the tasks ahead for the Institute of Anthropology and anthropology as a discipline in Vietnam are as follows, in terms of research priorities, continuing to improve on teaching and methods, and further institutionalization, first, it is necessary to research, evaluate and monitor nationalism around the world, especially within Southeast Asia and those countries that border Vietnam. It is also critical to forecast what will happen in these nation states over the coming decades. Accordingly, it is important to point out how events that occur around the world, in other words the ongoing impacts of globalization, influence the development and stabilization of ethnic groups in Vietnam, especially with groups that have cross-border relations.

Second, it is necessary to research, evaluate and understand nationalism and ethno-national sentiments in Vietnam as they continue to evolve. We must seek to understand new trends amongst ethnic groups especially in their development and evolution; the relationship between ethnic groups and the state; between ethnic minorities and ethnic majorities; and in cross-border relations. Therefore, the key issue is in determining the development of the Vietnamese nation state in its current and future context.

Third, it is necessary to develop a strong anthropological research community that has the competence and qualifications to conduct new research. Anthropologists need the requisite training and experience in effectively connecting with regional and international anthropologists through multiple networks, in order to help Vietnamese anthropology integrate better with global anthropology. Training a community of experts is a costly process and requires considerable investment.

Fourth, in parallel with building and developing a team of anthropological researchers in terms of both quantity and quality of scholarship, it is necessary to publish and publicize research that affirms the role and influence of anthropology with regard to policy formation. This is especially so in subjects that revolve around the state, community, enterprises and ethnic groups. One aspect of this is to focus on the development of a Vietnamese anthropology database based on work done during the Doi Moi period. This database system needs to be compiled and modernized to encourage domestic and foreign usage. Through international integration, we are increasingly finding opportunities to enrich the database of Vietnamese social sciences, especially in historical matters concerning sensitive and complex issues such as national sovereignty in the East or the so-called "South China" Sea.

Fifth, linking research to training, allowing continued renovation and updating of new knowledge in interactive, professional and modern directions, is another critical step. The separation of research institutes from universities for an extended period has led to anthropological research not being tested for quality via feedback from students. The discipline of anthropology in Vietnam will be strengthened if those regularly teaching anthropology are continually involved in research projects and vice versa.

Sixth, it is necessary to continue promoting cooperation with domestic and international research and training organizations, especially with the anthropological research community in Southeast Asia as it shares many similarities with Vietnam. Cooperation must be based on the principle of mutual benefit, and in the form of participating in common research projects, exchanging scholars, and holding conferences and workshops on topics of mutual interest. To integrate Vietnamese anthropology into global anthropology, it would be necessary to attract and create conditions for foreign scholars to come and work in Vietnam, making the best use of international anthropology scholars. The ability of Vietnamese anthropologists to propose good ideas, search for partners, and to engage in serious implementation of signed contracts to complete significant research work have important implications in drawing the world's attention and support for the ongoing renovation of anthropology in Vietnam.

Conclusion

To meet new demands for development and international integration, Vietnamese anthropology has gradually evolved as an independent discipline. However, this conversion cannot dismiss the dominant influences of history and ethnology as the predecessors of today's anthropology. Along with a general trend in international anthropological research, contemporary Vietnamese anthropology has updated itself with state-of-the-art research topics and methods, especially in the move toward interdisciplinary approaches.

To achieve international integration, Vietnamese anthropology needs to continue its renovation synchronically, from organizational change to improving training and research (Vuong Xuan Tinh 2013). Ideally, Vietnamese anthropologists will have further opportunities to contact, exchange and share their experiences with international scholars. Hands-on training and on-the-job guidance from international scholars are greatly effective for young anthropologists. Research and methodological training has to be in line with international standards while also allowing for consideration for the Vietnamese political and academic context and concerns. English has to be the main language for research and training in anthropology, and researchers need to be fluent in the language, using it in international workshops and in scholarly discussions and exchanges. Additionally, the clarification of regulations on integrating research with training and sending staff overseas for research and pedagogical purposes is required.

Still, the renovation of Vietnamese anthropology has to be based on Vietnam's particular characteristics, insofar as it is a nation with diverse ethnic groups and distinctive regions, attention to which are required for sustainable development. Anthropologists must prioritize the needs of Vietnam's ongoing development as an integrated nation and there are numerous important points which researchers will need to pay attention to in the future. Enhancing the relationship between researchers and policymakers will create favorable conditions for using anthropological research. This will also serve as an important base for the international integration of Vietnamese social sciences and create more opportunities for advancing social scientific knowledge in the world. This will require a significant investment in developing anthropology to achieve international integration. It then becomes necessary to find international resources that can finance anthropological research and training projects as well as encourage further cooperation and synergy between domestic and international anthropologists.

To achieve that objective, it is necessary to have an open political system that welcomes rationalism; a community of researchers devoted to basic research matters in particular and national development strategies in general; solid channels that popularize research results; socially critical messages; and a regular dialogue channel between academics and decision makers. This will lead to a dynamic combination between research, policy, and decision-making processes based on proper scientific evidence.

References

Bế Viết Đẳng (1988) "Nhìn lại 20 năm nghiên cứu của Viện Dân tộc học" ["Looking back 20 Years of Research of the Institute of Ethology"], *Tạp chí Dân tộc học* [*Journal of Ethnology*] 1: pp. 9–13.

Đậu Tuấn Nam (2009) "Đặc điểm di dân tự do của người Hmông ở miền Tây Thanh hóa, Nghệ An" ["Characteristics of the Spontaneity of the Hmong People in the Western Part of Thanh Hoa Province], *Tạp chí Dân tộc học* [*Journal of Ethnology*] 3: pp. 15–23.

Đoàn Việt (2012) "Biến đổi về vốn xã hội của người Chăm Hồi giáo từ việc đi làm ăn qua biên giới" ["Change in social capital of Cham Islamic people as resulted from cross-border migration"], *Tạp chí Dân tộc học* [*Journal of Ethnology*] 5&6: pp. 56–65.

Hess, Juergen và Tô Thị Thu Hương (2012) "Chi trả dịch vụ môi trường rừng tại Việt nam kết nối chủ rừng và người sử dụng dịch vụ môi trường rừng" ["Payment for Forest Environmental Services in Vietnam, Linking Forest Owners and Users of Forest Environment Services"], *Tạp chí Dân tộc học* [*Journal of Ethnology*] 1: pp. 48–55.

Khổng Diễn (2001) "Dân tộc học Việt Nam trong xu thế hội nhập và phát triển" ["Vietnam's Ethnology in the Trend of Integration and Development"], *Tạp chí Dân tộc học* [*Journal of Ethnology*] 4: pp. 4–11.

_____ (2003) "35 năm Viện Dân tộc học (1968–2013)" ["35 Years of the Institute of Ethnology 1968–2013"], *Tạp chí Dân tộc học* [*Journal of Ethnology*] 6: pp. 5–10.

Nguyễn Thị Thanh Bình và Nguyễn Thu Quỳnh (2017) "Chuyển đổi sinh kế dưới tác động của quá trình đô thị hóa ở một xã người Tày khu vực miền núi Đông bắc Việt Nam" ["Livelihood Transformations under the Impact of Urbanization in a Commune of Tay People in the Northeast Region of Vietnam"], *Tạp chí* Xã hội học [*Journal of Sociology*] 5: pp. 26–39.

Nguyễn Văn Chính (2007) "Một thế kỷ Dân tộc học Việt Nam và những thách thức trên con đường đổi mới và hội nhập" ["One Century of Vietnamese Ethnology and Challenges on the Way of Renovation and Integration"], *Tạp chí Văn hóa dân gian* [*Journal of Folklore*] 5 (113): pp. 47–67.

Nguyễn Văn Huy (1982) "Một số vấn đề nghiên cứu cư dân thành thị ở miền núi" ["Some Research Issues on Urban Residents in the Mountainous Areas"], *Tạp chí Dân tộc học* [*Journal of Ethnology*] 1: pp. 5–13.

——— (1983) "Nhìn lại 15 năm nghiên cứu sự phát triển các quan hệ dân tộc ở nước ta" ["Looking back at 15 Years of Research on Ethnic Relations in Our Country"], *Tạp chí Dân tộc học* [*Journal of Ethology*] 4: pp. 38–51.

Nguyễn Văn Sửu (2010) "Khung sinh kế bền vững: Một cách phân tích toàn diện về phát triển và giảm nghèo" ["Sustainable Livelihood Framework: A Comprehensive Analysis of Development and Poverty Reduction"], *Tạp chí Dân tộc học* [*Journal of Ethnology*] 2: pp. 3–12.

Nguyễn Văn Toàn (2011) "Tổng quan nghiên cứu về định canh định cư" ["An Overview of Research on Resettlement"], *Tạp chí Dân tộc học* [*Journal of Ethnology*] 5: pp. 15–24.

Phạm Quang Hoan (2009) "Viện Dân tộc học – Thành tựu 40 năm xây dựng và phát triển (1968–2008)" ["Institute of Ethnology – Achievement of 40 Years of Construction and Development 1968–2008"], *Tạp chí Dân tộc học* [*Journal of Ethnology*] 1/2: pp. 6–9.

Phan Văn Hùng (2015) *Một số vấn đề dân tộc ở nước ta trong giai đoạn phát triển mới* [*Some Issues on Ethnicity in Our Country in the New Phase of Development*]. Hà Nội: Nhà xuất bản Sự thật [Truth Publisher].

Trần Hồng Hạnh (2009) "Những biến đổi kinh tế – xã hội ở vùng cao Việt Nam" ["Socio-economic Changes in the Hightlands of Vietnam], *Tạp chí Dân tộc học* [*Journal of Ethnology*] 1&2: pp. 13–135.

Trần Qúy Long (2015) "Di cư lao động xuyên biên giới ở một số khu vực biên giới phía Bắc" ["Cross-border Labour Migration in Some Border Areas of the North], *Tạp chí Gia đình và Giới* [*Journal of Gender*] 5: pp. 130–42.

Trần Văn Hà và Đặng Thị Hoa (2009) "Ảnh hưởng của các yếu tố xã hội và văn hóa đến cơ chế ứng phó với tình trạng thiếu lương thực của người Khơ-mú" ["Influences of Social and Cultural Factors on the Coping Mechanism for Food Shortages among Khmu People], *Tạp chí Dân tộc học* [*Journal of Ethnology*] 1&2: pp. 74–89.

Trường Đại học Khoa học Xã hội và Nhân văn, Đại học Quốc gia Thành phố Hồ Chí Minh [University of Social Sciences and Humanities, National University of Ho Chi Minh City] (2012) *Ngành Dân tộc học 10 năm xây dựng và phát triển (2002–2012)* [*Ethnological Discipline over 10 Years of Development (2002–2012)*]. Ho Chi Minh City: Thành phố Hồ Chí Mi.

Vi Văn An và Bùi Minh Thuận (2012) "Tái định cư và sự thay đổi sinh kế của người Thái ở bản Mà, xã Thanh Hương, huyện Thanh Chương, tỉnh Nghệ An" ["Resettlement and Changing Livelihood of Thai People in Ma Village, Thanh Huong Commune, Thanh Chuong District, Nghe An Province"], *Tạp chí Dân tộc học* [*Journal of Ethnology*] 2: pp. 33–42.

Vương Xuân Tình (2013) "Định hướng phát triển của Viện Dân tộc học giai đoạn 2013–2020 và tầm nhìn đến năm 2030" ["Direction of Development of the Institute of Sociology for the Period of 2013–2020], *Tạp chí Dân tộc học* [*Journal of Ethnology*] 5: pp. 4–13.

_____ (2007) *Các nhóm dân tộc ở Việt Nam. Tập 1: Nhóm ngôn ngữ Việt-Mường. Nhà xuất bản Đại học Quốc gia, Hà Nội* [*Ethnic Groups in Vietnam. Volume 1: Viet-Muong Linguistic Group*]. Hanoi: National University Publisher.

CHAPTER 10

THE TRANSNATIONAL ANTHROPOLOGY OF THAILAND

Ratana Tosakul

From the 1950s to the present, Thailand has been at the center of shifting approaches to ethnographic and anthropological transnational studies. The "transnational anthropology of Thailand" refers to ethnographic studies of transnational processes conducted by Thai anthropologists or Thai scholars in other disciplines who have adopted anthropological research methodologies. In this chapter, I outline the development of ethnographic accounts pertaining to Thai transnational anthropology with reference to the theoretical approaches utilized by anthropologists as well as the different substantive aspects of transnational studies. Taken as a whole, important historical continuities mark Thai scholars' ongoing interest in diasporic or transnational Tai/Thai communities. Nevertheless, Thai transnational anthropology has also undergone an important paradigm shift: from early historical perspectives rooted in essentialist views of Tai/Thai peoples to contemporary studies of transnational processes, building on theoretical advances of postmodernism and globalization studies. By examining the economic, political, or cultural dimensions of transnational processes from diverse perspectives, contemporary transnational Thai anthropology is finding new ways to explore the dynamic and complex work of cultural construction amid the multiple, fluid and often over-determined conditions of transnational and diasporic lived experience.

Although anthropology in the West, since its inception, has had an orientation toward studying non-European societies, most Thai anthropologists have been inclined towards studying their own Tai/Thai people. Even when they study societies outside Thailand, they tend to focus on Thais residing in other countries. Consequently, I begin with an analysis of transnational Thai anthropology's initial interest in the broad dispersion and historical mobility of Tai/Thai peoples. Many Thai scholars, especially in the twentieth century, tended to look to the distant past and to Tai groups residing outside Thailand to find the cultural roots of Tai/Thai people. From the 1950s to 1990s, such ethnic studies from an essentialist viewpoint were common. Thai scholars tended to look at cultural attributes as fixed and passed on from one generation to the next. Transnational processes were seen through the medium of language and other shared cultural attributes, emphasizing persistence and stability rather than change.

By the twenty-first century, newer diasporic and transnational studies began to blossom. Diverse contemporary issues reflecting different forms of movement and dislocation (from travel to involuntary mobility) have inspired a move away from essentialist studies and toward scholarly interest in dynamic transnational processes: such as cross-border flows of ideas and practices; international mobility and exchange; the social and cultural constitution of cross-border dynamics; their localization in specific institutional settings; and the constitution of meanings and subjectivities in transnational contexts (Brah 1996; Gupta and Ferguson 1997; Hannerz 1997; Appadurai 2008 [1991]). In the second half of the chapter I document how transnational Thai anthropologists have applied these new research orientations to the study of Tai/Thai peoples and review the resulting theoretical and substantive innovations. I conclude with a look at some of the ways in which an emerging generation of scholars trained in postmodernism and globalization theory is forging new directions for transnational Thai anthropology.

Tai Ethnic Studies: 1950s to 1980s

Thai transnational anthropology began with studies of ethnic Tai outside Thailand. These studies generally assumed that Tai/Dai people outside Thailand share a common origin and cultural roots with Thais in Thailand. The problem of how to interpret the past has long troubled anthropologists and scholars from other disciplines in Thailand. Two main questions—who are the Tai and where did their ancestors come from?[1]—have concerned many Thai scholars and the state agencies that funded this research. In studying Tai outside Thailand, most ethnographic accounts from the 1950s to 1980s searched for shared Tai/Thai cultural roots, attempting to find similarities and differences among ethnic Tai within and outside Thailand. Two pioneering and influential scholars in this vein were Banchob Bandhumedha, an etymologist worked on comparative linguistics of Tai groups in Asia, and Bunchai Srisawadi, a local politician from Chiang Rai province in northern Thailand, who studied hill tribes of northern Thailand and China.[2] In contrast to Banchob and Bunchuai, a third pioneering scholar of transnationalism, Suthep Soonthornpaesuch did not focus on Tai/Thai outside Thailand, but rather on diasporic Muslim communities in northern Thailand during the 1970s.[3]

Banchob Bandhumedha (1920–92) trained as an etymologist at Chulalongkorn University, under Phya Anumarn Rajadhon, the guru of Thai cultural studies from the 1940s to 1960s. After completing her MA thesis entitled "Pali and Sanskrit in Thai Language" in 1944, she received her PhD from Banaras Hindu University of India in 1952, studying with Suniti Kumar Chatterji, a renowned etymologist of India. Suniti helped connect Banchob with the Tai Ahoms in Assam, Arunachal Pradesh in India, and she went on to make a comparative study of their language with that of Thai in Thailand. From 1955 to 1985, Banchob conducted research in Assam, India, and in the Kachin, Shan and Mon states of Myanmar, which contributed to her pioneering work in linguistic transnational anthropology (Suddan 2002; Kanya 2001). She was not only interested in Tai-Thai language, but also Mon-Khmer, Melayu, Chinese, Hindi and Tibetan languages (Suddan Wisudthiluck 2002: 95–96). Although she focused on language studies as a window onto the origin of the Tai/Thai ethnic group, she also made notes on the different aspects of social life of the Tai ethnic groups, some of which were subsequently published. Her travel accounts (1983) provide descriptions that remain important for contemporary Tai studies in a variety of disciplines including linguistic anthropology, history, political economy, archeology and etymology.[4]

A second pioneering scholar, Bunchuai Srisawadi, published a two volume ethnographic account of the Tai Lue in Xishuangbanna, China, during 1954–55 (2004a, b). Bunchuai was the Minister of Parliament for Chiang Rai province in northern Thailand. Similar to Banchob, he did not receive training in anthropology, but studied and wrote prolifically on the life, society and culture of Tai outside Thailand and the hill people in northern Thailand.[5] Like Banchob,

Banchuai drew on essentialist models of cultural origins in searching for similarities and differences among ethnic Tai within and outside Thailand. Both Banchob and Bunchuai's ethnographic accounts contain a strong sentiment of pan-Tai/Thaism, which received considerable social recognition from the Thai government of General Plaek Phibunsongkram. This perspective encoded assumptions about ethnic hierarchies that can pose problems for present-day readers. For example, Bunchuai's analysis of Akha sexuality in a northern province of Thailand was fiercely contested in 2011 by the Akha themselves as being a misrepresentation creating an image of uncivilized hill peoples with loose and immoral sexual behaviors.[6]

In contrast to Banchob and Bunchai, Suthep Soonthornpaesuch was the second Thai anthropologist to receive professional anthropological training overseas (Scupin 1996). He studied anthropology at the School of Oriental and African Studies (SOAS) in England for his master's and at the University of California-Berkeley in the United States for his PhD. Upon graduation, he returned to teach anthropology at Chulalongkorn University and subsequently moved to Chiang Mai University in northern Thailand. He was among the forerunners of Thai anthropology who trained numerous graduate students. His unpublished PhD dissertation entitled "Islamic Identity in Chiang Mai City: A Historical and Structural Composition of Two Communities" (1977) is a pioneering work in diaspora and Muslim studies of Thailand.

Pan-Thai Projects: 1980s to 1990s

Studies of Tai culture continued to thrive into the 1990s through the work of professionally trained Thai anthropologists and historians. Their studies were primarily focused on Tai/Thai outside Thailand. In particular, three major research projects were conducted between the late 1980s and the 1990s under the leadership of Shalardchai Ramitanondh (Chiang Mai University), Chattip Nartsupha (Chulalongkorn University), and Sumitr Pitiphat (Thammasat University). While each of these projects had its roots in earlier understandings of a fixed and stable Tai/Thai culture, the resulting publications pointed to a growing recognition of cultural dynamism and processes of identity construction within transnational Thai anthropology.

In the first of these projects, Shalardchai headed up long-term study (1986–92), which resulted in a voluminous publication entitled

ไต (*Tai*) (1998). The project was a joint effort of scholars from Thailand, Burma and India, aimed at a cross-country comparative study of the culture and societies of Tai-speaking peoples in northern Thailand, the Shan state of Burma and the Assam state in India (Shalardchai et al. 1998: 4). In addition, it sought to understand processes of adaptation by diverse Tai ethnic groups for peaceful coexistence with other ethnic groups locally and internationally. The project concluded that the core of Tai culture consists of peasant-based societies with Buddhist and animistic beliefs and therefore is inherently anti-state. Nevertheless, beyond identifying common roots of Tai/Thai culture, the project's main contribution was to undermine idealized notions of Thai-ness and Thai nationalism by highlighting the cultural and linguistic diversity of different Tai groups.

From 1993 to 1999, a second long-term project in Tai studies flourished at Thammasat University under the leadership of Sumitr Pitiphat. While director at the Institute of Thai Studies at Thammasat, Sumitr showed great interest in Tai studies, particularly the origin and sociocultural evolution of ethnic Tai outside Thailand.[7] He brought together graduate students, researchers and faculty members to conduct anthropological fieldwork in Laos, Vietnam, China and India. Most accounts produced by the project during this period can be classified as a general survey of Tai peoples outside Thailand.

In 1995, a third large-scale research project entitled Social and Cultural History of Tai Peoples was started by Chattip Nartsupha, a political economist and former dean of the Faculty of Economics, Chulalongkorn University. A graduate from Tufts University in the United States, Chattip promoted the "community culture" concept of Thai village life as foundational to the social development of modern Thai society. Like the projects directed by Shaladchai and Sumitr, Chattip's Tai Peoples research aimed to assist in discovering common roots of Tai/Thai culture and in documenting diverse cultural histories of Tai peoples in Asia. The project was multidisciplinary, including history, anthropology, linguistics, archeology and economics. One of the most fascinating ethnographic records produced in the project was *Lak Chang* by Yos Santasombat (2001). A renowned Thai anthropologist, currently affiliated with Chiang Mai University, Yos conducted fieldwork with the Tai/Dai ethnic group in Daikong, in rural southwestern China, between 1997 and 1998, publishing his ethnography in Thai in 2000 and in English the following year. *Lak Chang* contributed to understanding the dynamics of social change among the Tai ethnic minority in rural China. Yos noted that processes of Tai ethnic identity construction were fluid and flexible as members of ethnic Tai minorities attempted to negotiate and defend their interests within the structural constraints of the more powerful Chinese state society.

With these large-scale research projects, by the 1990s Tai studies reached its peak led by Thai scholars affiliated with various universities in Thailand. Thai government agencies such as the Office of National Culture Commission financially supported The Study of Tai Culture project, drawing more than 800 people to its conference in Bangkok in 1995 (Keyes 1995). Nonetheless, these Tai projects were not state-led but academic and intellectual endeavors in search of Tai/Thai cultural roots transnationally and trans-locally. Still, researchers inevitably brought their own perspectives to data theorization. Initially these perspectives and political positions were heavily influenced by Thai nationalism and a discourse of Thai-ness, with scholars being both products and agents of the Thai social structure (Bourdieu 1977). Such ethnographic works have been criticized as primarily reflecting a nostalgia for Tai/Thai-ness from a distant past. They also reflect a sentiment of Pan-Tai/Thaism (Charnvit Kasetsiri 1999; Nidhi Eawsiwong 2001). However, as with Yos' (2001) *Lak Chang*, more recent linguistic and anthropological studies of Tai groups by Thai anthropologists have moved away from such positivistic and essentialist tendencies in studying Tai culture and identity politics. This shift reflects important theoretical and substantive changes within transnational Thai anthropology, especially since the 2000s.

Issue-Oriented Studies: 2000s to the Present

In recent years, transnational Thai anthropology has shifted its focus from interpretations of a Tai/Thai historical and cultural past, to the exploration of contemporary issues, especially highlighting rural-urban relations but also ranging across different disciplines including population demography, sociology, anthropology, political science and economics. These shifting research interests are themselves a reflection of changes in Thai society and political economy beginning several decades earlier.

From the 1960s to 1970s, Thai society witnessed a movement of dislocated and displaced people locally and internationally. In Thailand, scholars have observed migration and transmigration of its rural populations from the countryside to urban areas, primarily due to rural poverty. These rural migrants have moved to global cities, particularly to metropolitan Bangkok and overseas, seeking both employment and the modernity of urban life (Mills 1997). Simultaneously, war and its aftermath in Laos, Vietnam and Cambodia led to an influx of people crossing the Thai national border in search of refuge. In response, a number of universities in Thailand established academic institutions to conduct research into these developments. For instance, the Institute of Asian Studies (IAS) at Chulalongkorn University was established in 1967 and the Institute for Population Studies and Social Research (IPSR) at Mahidol University in 1971, producing numerous population and migration studies.

Thai transnational anthropology has also responded to significant changes taking place in anthropology as a whole, in particular a growing attention to cultural processes associated with "globalization" (Welz 2008). Diaspora, migration, the mobility of people, things, and ideas, and other transnational processes have become central to the contemporary research agenda of anthropology worldwide, calling into question classical paradigms of cultural and ethnic identities bounded by village communities or nation states. Thai anthropology was not immune to these trends. Many Thai anthropologists began to ponder questions pertaining to transnational anthropological studies. For instance, what do we mean by transnational anthropology? How does it connect with ideas of diaspora, nationalism and transnationalism? In thinking through the category of diaspora and its link to geopolitical entities such as nation states, how can we understand the concept of nationhood and nationalism versus local ethnic community and individual identities? Many Thai scholars now seek to explain these and other contemporary transnational cultural processes whether they involve Tai/Thai groups or others.

Newer Studies of Tai and Non-Tai Groups

Since the start of the twenty-first century, Tai studies by Thai anthropologists began to discard the nostalgic sentiment and chauvinism associated with being ethnic Tai/Thai. There has also been a gradual inclination to include non-Tai ethnic groups in their studies. For example, Niti Pawakapan, currently affiliated with Chulalongkorn University, has focused his studies on the fluidity of ethnic identity of Burmese-Shan peoples currently residing on the northwestern Thailand border with Burma (2009). Also, in his earlier work, Niti examined processes of social integration of Chinese migrants in New Zealand (2005). Similarly, Prasert Raengkla (2013) conducted his fieldwork with Karen refugees residing along the Thailand–Myanmar border and inside Myanmar. Tassana Nualsomsri (2013) did fieldwork with Yogya people in Indonesia. And Ratana Boonmathya (2002) worked with Kachin people in upper Burma. Such recent trends in Tai/Thai studies depart from earlier research by including non-ethnic Tai/Thai as research subjects. Newer studies are also much more engaged with the postmodern conditions and shifting cultures under globalization. They address experiences of people who encounter dynamism, fluidity and blurred genres of social and political life in their everyday lives.

Since the 1990s, anthropology at Chiang Mai and Thammasat universities has contributed significantly to transnational studies with the use of modern anthropological approaches. At Chiang Mai, the Regional Center for Social Science and Sustainable Development (RCSD) was established in 1998 at the Faculty of Social Sciences in response to the need for the integration of natural and social sciences to understand sustainable development issues in mainland Southeast Asia. The faculty started a regular publication called *Social Science Journal* (**วารสารสังคมศาสตร์**) as a forum for ethnographic and related research. Furthermore, many leading anthropologists have produced ethnographic accounts pertinent to contemporary Thai transnational anthropology including Yos Santasombat (2001), Prasit Leepreecha (2002), Kwanchewan Buadaeng (2007), Aranya Siriphon (2007, 2010), Wasan Panyagaew (2005, 2007, 2008, 2010) and Pinkaew Luangaramsri (2011, 2013).

At Thammasat, the Tai studies project begun by Sumitr Pitiphat in the 1990s has continued to prepare and re-orient young graduate students in anthropology to conduct transnational studies in Southeast Asia. For example, in 1999, Silapakit Tikantikul participated as a graduate student in Sumitr's research team in Vietnam. Subsequently, he became interested in Vietnamese culture and society, studying Vietnamese in Hanoi. Eventually, for his MA thesis (2003), he wrote an innovative ethnographic account of the Vietnamese water puppet performances. Another graduate student on Sumitr's project, Pichet Saipan, received his PhD in cultural anthropology from the University of Social Sciences and Humanities, Hanoi (Vietnam National University) and is currently a faculty member at Thammasat. Pichet's work with ethnic Tai in Vietnam and the Lao People's Democratic Republic

(Laos) employed Tambiah's (2000) concept of transnational movements to analyze transethnic identities in northwestern Vietnam (Pichet 2004). A third student of Sumitr, Samerchai Poolsuwan, obtained his MA and PhD in physical anthropology from the University of Michigan. Samerchai has published numerous studies in transnational anthropology including Tai studies in China and Myanmar and comparative symbolic interpretations of Buddhist mural paintings of temples in Thailand and Myanmar (Samerchai 1996).

By the early 2000s, a "new wave" of Thai anthropologists had completed their higher education overseas. The majority returned to teach at Thailand's universities and colleges. Graduating in 2007 from the University of Wisconsin-Madison, Yukti Mukdawijitra has produced numerous essays in Thai and English, adopting critical theory to explore notions of linguistic cosmopolitanism. In one article, Yukti seeks to "understand how the Vietnamese state and its Tai minority negotiate policies toward writing systems" (2012: 207). Contending that the politics of Tai script is an example of cosmopolitanism, Yukti argues that, "in the processual politics of orthography and spatial-political formation, the case of the Tai in Vietnam demonstrates that the hinterland of Southeast Asia is also an area where cosmopolitanism plays a significant role" (ibid.). Through this piece, Yukti adopts a concept of cosmopolitanism to theorize the development of proto-imagined communities among Tai in the hinterland of Southeast Asia.

Similarly innovative work comes from Pinkaew Luangaramsri and Prasit Leepreehca, who received their PhDs from the University of Washington in 2000 and 2001 respectively. Pinkaew was a pioneering Thai anthropologist during the early 2000s, introducing border studies to graduate students at Chiang Mai University. Her research has contributed to understanding transnational processes of rural transformations and socio-economic impacts on local communities in southern Laos through the penetration of Asian regional capital, primarily from Vietnam and China (2001). Prasit specialized in ethnic studies, especially the ethnic Hmong in a transnational and globalized world (2002). Along this same line, Kwanchewan Buadaeng, who obtained her PhD from the University of Sydney in 2001, has produced numerous studies of cross-border culture of ethnic Karen in Thailand and Myanmar (2007).

Yet other examples of the new innovative generation are Wasan Panyagaew and Atchariya Nate-Chei. Wasan received his PhD in anthropology from the Australian National University in 2006. His doctoral thesis adopts a cross-border culture approach to examine the transnational migration and movements of Dai/Tai, especially the Tai Lue people in the upper Mekong (2005). His research includes Lampun in northern Thailand, as well as Muang Yong in the Shan State of Burma and Xishuangbanna in Yunnan Province, China (Wasan Panyagaew et al. 2010). Atchariya, an anthropologist affiliated with Naresuan University, did her doctoral fieldwork between 2007 and 2011 with White Tai in Vietnam and studied under leading anthropologists at Chiang Mai University. Challenging earlier ideas about "commodification" and "minority politics," Atchariya (2011) explores touristic space as the contextual setting for close interactions between hosts and guests in the White Tai villages in Mai Chau district in the northwest uplands of Vietnam.

Border and Cross-Border Cultures

Beyond continued interest in Tai/Thai ethic studies, recent work in border and cross-border studies by Thai anthropologists and other Thai scholars who have employed ethnographic research methodology has been on the rise. For example Pitch Pongsawat, a social scientist currently affiliated with Faculty of Political Science, Chulalongkorn University, obtained his PhD in 2007 from Department of City and Regional Planning, University of California at Berkeley. His PhD dissertation (2007) employed critical historical analysis and ethnographic fieldwork to understand both particular and general dynamics of functions and formations of Thailand–Myanmar border towns. He argues that both political economy and geopolitics of Thailand and Myanmar have intensified not only due to uneven economic development but also uneven regulations between the bordering spaces of the two nations. This unevenness produces a specific form of cross-border economy and urban development at the core area of the cross-border region.

Recent work in transnational Thai anthropology also highlights a range of specific, contemporary issues including marriage migration (Ratana Boonmathya 2005; Panitee Suksomboon 2008, 2009; Chantanee Charoensri 2014), Mekong cross-border cultures (Ratana Tosakul et al. 2010; Pichet Saiphan and Khamphaeng Thipmountaly 2011), Thai diaspora (Ratana Tosakul 2013), displaced Karen refugees (Prasert Raengkla 2013), and Tai cosmopolitanism (Yukti Mukdawijitra 2012). The work of these scholars has been influenced not only by postmodernism but also by other Western perspectives including political economy, geopolitics, urban and regional politics and policies, class-based analysis, gender studies, cross-border marriage, village cosmopolitanism, ethnic studies, identity construction and the role of religious institutions in relation to migration. While drawing on Western and global theoretical trends, Thai anthropologists have made their own substantial contributions to each of these fields.

The Mekong region—including China, Vietnam, Laos, Thailand, Myanmar and Cambodia—has become a crossroads for transnational studies by many Thai anthropologists. As one example, the Mekong Ethnography of Cross-Border Cultures (MECC) project brought together scholars in the different fields of anthropology, sociology, political science, cultural studies and cultural heritage to explore the dynamism and complexity of the region.[8] The MECC was a three-year collaborative anthropological research project starting in 2007 and involving scholars from China, Thailand, Laos, Vietnam, Myanmar and Cambodia. It has become a model of research collaboration among scholars from different Mekong countries towards developing shared knowledge, theoretical perspectives, and methodologies. In order to promote such cooperation, MECC research teams were composed of researchers from two or more Mekong countries. Each team was required to collaborate on research proposal development, ethnographic field research, and the write up of findings. There were a total of eight collaborative research teams with projects covering a broad range of topics from family and marriage across borders to ethnic identity and cross-border trade with the main approach being to study transnational cultural processes.

Similar to MECC, two research centers in northeastern Thailand promote studies pertaining to multiculturalism and transnationalism of people in the Mekong countries. The first is the Center for Research on Plurality in the Mekong (CERP), established in 2003 at Khon Kaen University. The center publishes the *Journal of Mekong Societies*, showcasing contemporary ethnographies by scholars interested in cultural pluralism in the Mekong region. The second center is the Mekong Sub-Region Social Research Centre (MSSRC), established in 2000 at Ubon Ratchathani University. MSSRC has constantly supported studies and seminars pertaining to changing regional sociocultural phenomena.

Suchada Thaweesit from the MSSRC (PhD, University of Washington) is currently affiliated with Mahidol University. Working with displaced Laotians in Northeastern Thailand, Suchada (2013) notes how policies and practices of inclusion and exclusion by the Thai state impact ethnic minorities along the Thai–Lao border. The Laotians she studies, although they have lived in Thailand for over thirty years, have not been granted Thai citizenship. Many of them also lack evidence to establish citizenship with the Lao state. This problematic legal status puts them at risk of living in a cycle of poverty and discrimination. It has also led to limited rights for legal employment, education and other state welfare.

In another MSSRC project, Natedao Taotawin, currently a faculty member at Ubon Ratchathani University, conducted fieldwork on the temporary and seasonal cross-border migration of young Lao women into Thailand. Natedao notes that representations of female migrants as "the other" and "victims" not only ignore self-perceptions and the fluidity of identities of female migrants, but also prevent them from participating in the resolution of their own problems, leading to increased marginalization and vulnerability. They are perceived as inferior and powerless and thus easily subject to strict state control and other forms of domination (2008: 146). Pruk Taotawin (2007) also studies the Thai–Lao border utilizing the concept of glocalization and Foucauldian analysis to understand the relationship between farm producers in Lao PDR and layers of farm product distributors in a cross-border trade network.

Jakkrit Sangkhamanee's border research is also of interest. Jakkrit received his PhD in anthropology from the Australian National University and is currently affiliated with Chulalongkorn University. His research interests explore nature and culture as well as border studies. His survey of the anthropology of border studies (2009) argues for the need to develop conceptual frameworks and methodologies in Thai social sciences to deal with the complex dynamics that characterize borders. In another piece, Jakkrit (2012) reviews several academic works pertaining to cross-border trade, exploring how spaces of trade offer insight into anthropological understandings of territorialization within transnational processes; his work highlights the demarcation of formal and informal trading practices as well as the intricate relationship between locality, nation state, regional economy and the transformation of trading practices at international borders.

Cross-border scholarship from regional universities in the South of Thailand including Walailak, Songkhla and Thaksin universities tend to focus on the Malays in Southern Thailand. This includes work by local and international scholars investigating violence in the three most southern provinces of Thailand—Yala, Pattani and Narathiwat. Researchers also study how the different parts of Malay culture are expressed in everyday practice. A good example of the latter is the work of Sutthiporn Bunmak (2011b), currently affiliated with Thaksin University who emphasizes cross-border culture in his study of southern Thai tom yam food businesses in Malaysia. Sutthiporn (2011a) adopts social network theory to analyze the diverse social networks of Nayu migrants from southern Thailand who are often unauthorized workers in the nearly 5,000 tom yam restaurants across Malaysia. Complex cross-border networks connect Nayu migrants currently working in Malaysia, and former migrants and non-migrants in Thailand. Nayu migrants have depended on these multiple networks and personal contacts to seek employment and business investment opportunities in Malaysia.

Pornpan Khemkunasai (2012) from Thaksin offers another example of recent cross-border studies in Thai anthropology. Her work examines the history of informal networks and the social relationships involved in cross-border rice trading along the Thai–Malaysian border. Through ethnographic fieldwork in a village situated on the Go Lok riverbank opposite the Malaysian border, Pornpan confirmed that cross-border rice trade networks operate on the basis of participants' shared cultural characteristics including language, ethnicity, religious beliefs and locality. These common traits strengthen relationships within their networks and are an important strategy to avoid tight control by local authorities.

Marriage Migration

Anthropologists began noting the migration of Thai villagers from rural areas to the urban metropolis to seek better employment in the 1960s and 1970s but it was only from the 1990s that Thailand witnessed a growing transnational movement of village women, particularly from northeastern and northern Thailand, who were marrying Western men and moving to reside with them overseas. In recent years, this phenomenon has attracted growing interest from Thai anthropologists and sociologists. Research on marriage migration has flourished in Thai transnational anthropology as scholars adopt approaches and methodologies influenced by Western models but redefine and reinterpret these through local knowledge and practice.

Ratana Tosakul's ethnographic account, published both in Thai (Ratana Boonmathya 2005) and English (Ratana Tosakul 2010), offers a pioneering analysis of marriage migration following fieldwork in 2004 in a northeastern Thai–Lao village. The research adopts an agent-oriented approach, focusing on how village women adopted marriage migration as a strategy for poor rural households in northeastern Thailand. The argument utilizes the concept of local/global synergy and gender analysis to study how marriage migrants create a transnational space that links the local-traditional with the global-modern for upward social mobility. Importantly, the project laid the ground for subsequent studies surrounding marriage migration.

Panitee Suksomboon's work is one such example. Panitee completed her PhD in sociology from Leiden University and is currently with Thammasat University. In her dissertation (2009), she adopts a feminist approach to analyze Thai women's transnational marriages in the Netherlands. She also uses social remittances as the medium to analyze the traditional role of Thai wives as dutiful daughters in supporting their rural parental home. Chantanee Charoensri (2014), currently a lecturer in sociology at Thammasat University, has also published on Thai marriage migration. Her work explores how women struggle to live up to traditional norms and obligations amid the social structural constraints of poverty in the Thai countryside. Under such circumstances, some poor women choose sex work and marriage migration as a strategy to fulfill their roles as dutiful daughters or/and good mothers. Through studying their life-course trajectories, Chantanee aims to dismantle the negative social stereotypes attached to Thai women who marry foreign men.

Similar to Chantanee, Angeles and Sirijit Sunanta (2009) note that the transnational marriages of village women in northeastern Thailand are reconfiguring gendered familial obligation especially regarding daughterly duties. Their paper discusses how the economic and social remittances of Thai wives create new local-global connections, bypassing the Thai state's institutions and agencies and highlighting the latter's failure to sufficiently address the plight of poor villagers in the rural countryside. Village women's upward economic mobility and adherence to traditional filial roles contribute to their communities' favorable acceptance of their ties to foreign husbands, encouraging more women to enter transnational marriages. Sirijit and Angeles (2013) also argue that Thai marriage migration represents an intimate link between the global political economy and an individual's desires, aspirations and imagination in the realm of personal and marital relationships. Transnational marriage relationships are embedded in a context of spatial and economic inequalities at the local, national and global level, and exhibit class and gendered strategies by which marginalized subjects attempt to surpass otherwise limited opportunities for upward social mobility.

At Khon Kaen University, Patcharin Lapanun, a cultural anthropologist, also studies Thai marriage migration. Her PhD dissertation (2013) examines how marriages between rural women in northeastern Thailand (Isan) and Western (*farang*) men have reshaped the characteristics of Isan families and communities. Focusing on a village in Udorn province, where 159 village women have become *mia farang* (wives of Westerners), Patcharin's work combines detailed ethnography with theoretical and methodological insights concluding that such marriages serve as a channel for women's natal families and rural residents to interact with global processes. Following the arguments of Keyes (2010) and Pattana Kitiarsa (2006, 2014), Patcharin's research contributes to a growing appreciation of "cosmopolitan villagers" of northeastern Thailand. In other work, Patcharin (2012a) goes further to deconstruct the classic binary opposition between romantic love and material incentives. She notes that the "logics of desire" that compel people to get married comprise a complex set of multiple motivations that cannot be attributed wholly to either material incentives or emotional ties (2012a: 3). More recently, Patcharin (2014) argues that *mia farang* constitute a distinct social category, a "class" on their own with implications for village social and economic hierarchies. Employing Bourdieu's notion of class distinction, she notes how the tastes and consumption patterns of *mia farang* are mutually convertible to a cultural and symbolic marker for differentiation.

Thai Diaspora and Other Displaced Peoples

Thailand both imports and exports migrant labor. The country currently hosts a large number of migrant laborers from Myanmar, Laos, Cambodia and occasionally Vietnam who provide a cheap labor supply for the nation's industrial, service and domestic sectors. Simultaneously, laborers from the Thai countryside regularly migrate to seek employment overseas in places such as the Middle East, Japan, Korea, Taiwan and Singapore. Both these directions of transnational labor mobility have been the focus of research by Thai anthropologists, although studies by scholars residing and working overseas are rare. A notable exception is the work of Pattana Kitiarsa, the late Thai anthropologist affiliated with the National University of Singapore (NUS). His research with Thai-Isan migrants in Singapore (2006, 2014) employs the concept of local/global interface to understand the dynamism of social life and of identity construction among male village migrants from northeastern Thailand working in Singapore. Pattana notes that transnational labor migration often starts with the desire to acquire a safe and prosperous future. The temptation of "global cities" as a place to attain that desire looms large within the context of rural-urban migration flows. His book (2014) reveals the complex processes that uncover the bare lives and desires of male migrant workers, who face overwhelming stress and diminished gender roles while living under Singapore's strict foreign labor regulations. Pattana's in-depth analysis of migrant social life and gendered identity provides an invaluable contribution to our understanding of labor transnationalism in Southeast Asia.

Ratana Tosakul's research has investigated related cultural processes of individual and community identity formation in the Thai diaspora. While serving as a visiting professor at Seijo University in Tokyo from April 2013 to March 2014, she conducted ethnographic fieldwork with Thai diasporic people there and in Ibaraki prefecture. She discovered that the revival of Buddhist beliefs and practices in the host society was a cultural source of reference and identity formation for Thai migrants living in Japan with their Japanese spouses, similar to Prasert's (2013) research discussed below.

Transnational migration into Thailand has attracted more sustained research attention among a "new wave" of Thai scholars. Prasert Raengkla obtained his PhD in anthropology from the Australian National University and is currently based at Thammasat University. His ethnographic work with the Karen in Myanmar and on the Thai–Myanmar border (2013) offers a fascinating analysis of how Karen refugees seek to rebuild their lives in the context of forced dislocation, including efforts to revive their traditional Buddhist beliefs and practices. In other work, Raya Muttarak (2004), an Oxford PhD and research scholar with the World Population Program, reflects on the unequal relationships and conflicts that arise between foreign domestic service workers and their Thai employers. Exploring the public and private dimensions of domestic work and workers in Thai middle-class households, Raya argues that relationships between employers and domestic workers develop at a close proximity and domestic service becomes a highly contestable and personalized arena revealing complex inequalities of gender, race, ethnicity and class.

As Prasert's and Raya's research reflects, since the 1990s Thailand has witnessed a rising number of migrant workers from Myanmar into Thailand, many seeking both refuge from civil war in their homeland and better employment. In a recent example of collaboration between local and international anthropologists, Thai PhD student Nobpaon Rabibhadhana from the Graduate School of Asian and African Area Studies, Kyoto University and Professor Yoko Hayami of Kyoto University examine migrant workers' social networks in their paper "Seeking Haven and Seeking Jobs: Migrant Workers' Networks in Two Thai Locales" (2013). They note that previous studies tend to focus on state policies and economies or more journalistic accounts of individual migrant experiences. Little has been done to analyze micro processes through which migrants' networks form across the border and within the country. By examining two locales—one on the border at Mae Sot and another further inland in Samut Songkham province—the authors argue that transnational migrant workers formulate and define their space through adaptive networks influenced by geopolitical factors and local socio-economic and historical-cultural dynamics. The interplay between macro policies, micro-level migrant agency, and meso-level networks define each locale.

Additional ethnographies of the lived experiences of migrants from Myanmar in Thailand include two MA theses completed at Thammasat University. Adisorn Kerdmongkol's (2011) master's thesis employed de Certeau's concept of an everyday practice of power and resistance in his analysis of Pa-O migrants from Myanmar working in Bangkok. Similarly, Worachet Khiewchan (2011) conducted fieldwork at a Thai border school where students from Myanmar cross the border daily for their education. His analysis applies Agamben's notion of the practice of sovereign power in the exception to explore this process of cross-border schooling. Meanwhile, a recent PhD dissertation (Nattchawal Pocapanishwong 2014), also completed at Thammasat University, examines transnational migration from Myanmar, using anthropological methods to understand the dynamism of "locality" and "trans-locality" in the multi-ethnic community of Ranong—a border town in Thailand near Myanmar. Her study found that recent migrant workers from Myanmar, usually perceived by the locals of Ranong as "alienated others," have been adapting themselves to the cultural milieu of the area by establishing their own imagined trans-local community through their religious practices. These include organizing Buddhist ceremonies and festivals, erecting Burmese-style pagodas, promoting Burmese cultural education and other schooling for their children through a religious network, and providing social welfare for funerals. While providing migrants with adaptive resources, migrants' Buddhist religious practices retained symbolic associations with "Burma-ness," thereby maintaining social hierarchy between locals and migrants.

Future Directions

Many new transnational ethnographies are being produced by Thai anthropologists and graduate students in Thailand. Compared to prior decades, there has been a marked increase in theoretically sophisticated work. Many of these anthropologists have adopted postmodern theoretical models in combination with a local/global interface in their analyses. They have also redefined and reformulated concepts developed in the West to take account of local knowledge, perspectives and practices. In this regard, research into Thai women's transnational marriage migration has been particularly productive and is likely to continue to attract scholarly attention as seen in recent ethnographies by Ratana Boonmathya (2005), Panitee Suksomboon (2009), Ratana Tosakul (2010, 2012), Sirijit Sunanta (2013, 2014), Patcharin Lapanun (2013, 2014), and Chantanee Charoensri (2014). Valuable topics within marriage migration studies have included cross-border marriage, "dutiful daughters," social remittances, local/global synergy, structure versus the agency of the subject, and village cosmopolitanism. The transnationalism of labor migration, both to and from Thailand, has also been a growing focus of anthropological research. Nevertheless, ethnographies that analyse the lived experiences of such migrants in relation to transnationalism and postcolonialism in the global economy are still limited and deserve further attention.

Most recently, there has been rising interest among young Thai anthropologists to undertake transnational projects that involve the study of "others" outside Thailand. In this vein, there is a growing tendency among Thai anthropologists, especially at Thammasat, Chiang Mai, Khon Kaen and Ubon universities, as well as other regional universities in northeastern and southern Thailand, to conduct ethnographic fieldwork internationally, albeit not exclusively doing transnational studies. For example, Saipin Suputtamongkol (2007), who earned her PhD from Harvard University, did dissertation fieldwork in Capur, a small town in southern Italy. Boonlert Visetpricha (2015) conducted anthropological fieldwork with homeless people in Manila, the Philippines, and recently completed his PhD dissertation in 2015 at the University of Wisconsin-Madison.[9] Oradi Inkhong is currently pursuing her PhD at Cornell and plans to conduct comparative ethnographic research of ethnomusicology with the Thai Lanna and Shan in Burma.

It is important to recognize that projects such as these and, in fact, all substantive work in transnational Thai anthropology, both past and present, would not have been possible without access to funding. Historically transnational Tai studies projects have consistently received financial support from major Thai government institutions including the Thai Khadi Institute of Thammasat University and Thailand Research Fund. The Thai government still remains the major source of funding for research in the social sciences, humanities and natural sciences. However, there has been an increase in access to international research funds, from sources such as SEASREP, Ford Foundation, Rockefeller Foundation, Japan International Cooperation Agency, Nippon Foundation, and the National University of Singapore. Usually, these transnational studies are intellectual endeavors and not state-led projects. Private and government research funding institutions have a broad range of agendas for policy-relevant research and specific guidelines for research grantees to comply with, but this does not appear to have a negative effect on the content or findings of scholarship, especially in data collection and theorization. There is also a tendency to divide tasks based on regional specialization and geographical specificity. For example, Khon Kaen and Ubon Ratchathani universities are well known for their Mekong region cross-border studies whereas Chiang Mai and other northern universities specialize in Myanmar and China transnational studies. Likewise, most universities in the southern provinces focus on transnational Muslim/Malay studies. Generally, research collaboration and exchange is done through individual researchers and academic institutions, as shown in the case of MECC.

As illustrated throughout this chapter, recent decades have witnessed important theoretical shifts that have transformed Thai transnational anthropology in particular and Thai anthropology as a whole. The search for Tai/Thai linguistic and cultural roots dominated the field in the twentieth century, but these concerns have now given way to research informed by theories of postmodernism and globalization. In relation to postmodernism, many native Thai anthropologists are learning to study their own societies and cultures in a postmodern world of transnational cultural processes. Postmodernism rearranges power away from individuals, classes and state bureaucracies, embedding it in the frames of discourse and knowledge. This is especially pertinent to how one interprets and represents culture in the postmodern era. New, globally trained anthropologists from countries in the previously so-called "Third World" are becoming cultural brokers able to redefine received Western models of social science by drawing on relevant local knowledge, perspectives and practices.

In similar ways, globalization has provided Thai anthropology with a critical counterpoint to conventional, essentialist concepts of culture. One distinctive development is the redefining of the relationship between culture, power and place, challenging the way anthropology locally and internationally perceives the world as "a series of discrete, territorialized cultures" (Gupta and Ferguson 1997: 3). Upon deeper questioning, this conventional approach in anthropology dissolves into a series of challenging issues about the contested relations between difference, identity, and place issues that have had a significant impact on Thai transnational anthropology through studies of marriage migration, the local/global interface, and diasporic subjects.

Consequently in the twenty-first century, Thai anthropology has developed a focus on diasporic and transnational scholarship that is in line—both epistemologically and methodologically—with contemporary global anthropology. As Thompson has noted "the shifting center of gravity within the anthropology of Southeast Asia from European and American centers toward the region is increasingly perceptible across Southeast Asia" (2012: 664). The shift remains fragile in many respects. Nevertheless, starting in the 1960s, we now have three or four generations of Thai anthropologists who have been trained in modern anthropology. They have been largely, though by no means exclusively, influenced by the modern American anthropology tradition and other Western perspectives. Still, I agree with Thompson (2012) that similar to other Southeast Asian anthropologists, Thai scholars have sought to develop an autonomous local anthropology. The work reviewed in this chapter clearly demonstrates that Thai anthropologists are succeeding in this task.

Notes

1. Thai people in Thailand today are linguistically related to Tai ethnic groups in Southeast Asia. Based on historical and linguistic research, Tai people are believed to have migrated from southern and southwestern Mainland China to Vietnam, Thailand, Laos, Myanmar and even the Assam state of India. Recent genetic studies suggest that Thais in Thailand are genetically more related to the Mon-Khmer people in Southeast Asia than those in southern China (Samerchai Poolsuwan 2001: 9–11).
2. Banchob Bandhumedha and Bunchaui Srisawadi did not have professional educational training in anthropology but both employed ethnographic methods to collect field data for analysis. Their travel accounts and ethnographies are considered pioneering examples of Tai studies, inspiring many subsequent professionally trained Thai anthropologists to carry out their studies with Tai groups in Asia.
3. I found only the works of these three pioneering scholars reflecting transnational studies from the 1950s to 1980s. By the late 1960s, anthropology was officially established in major universities of Thailand including Chulalongkorn University in 1963, Chiang Mai University in 1964 and Thammasat University in 1965. Thai anthropology during this period was influenced by classical paradigms bounded by village communities and the Thai nation state (see Keyes 1978).
4. This is the most distinctive travel account by Banchob Bandhumedha, recording her journeys during 1956 to the Tai in the Shan State of Myanmar. Her account was published in 1958/59 as a series in the Thai women's magazine titled *สตรีสาร* [*Satrisan*]. It was subsequently compiled and published as a book by the Thai National Identity Commission in 1983.
5. Bunchuai's more well-known publications include *Thirty Ethnic Groups in Chiangrai Province* [30 ชาติในเชียงราย] (2004c), *Tai in Sip Song Panna* (ไทสิบสองปันนา) (2004a,b), *The Royal Kingdom of Laos* [ราชอาณาจักรลาว] (2004d), and Hilltribes in Thailand [ชาวเขาในไทย] (2002), which received an award from the United Nations.
6. Source: www.oknation.net (accessed on April 19, 2014).
7. Abstracts of the projects of Sumitr Pitiphat and his research associates can be found in the Thai Khadi Research database at http://tkri.tu.ac.th/. The Princess Maha Chakri Sirindhorn Anthropology Centre www.sac.or.th, (accessed on April 24, 2014) maintains a detailed list of Sumitr Pitiphat's publications in relation to Tai ethnicity, community studies and archeology.
8. The MECC was funded by the Princess Maha Chakri Sirindhorn Anthropology Centre (SAC), which was established in 1992 as an initiative of Silapakorn University.

9. Both Saipin Suputtamongkol and Boonlert Visetpricha are currently affiliated with Thammasat University. Their ethnographies are not strictly transnational in focus; however, both are pioneering examples of Thai anthropologists working on non-Thai communities outside of Thailand.

References

English Language

Angeles, L. and Sirijit Sunanta (2009) "Demanding Daughter Duty: Gender, Community, Village Transformation and Transnational Marriages in Northeast Thailand," *Critical Asian Studies* 40(4): pp. 549–74.

Appadurai, Arjun (2008[1991]) "Global Ethnoscapes: Notes and Queries for a Transnational Anthropology." In *The Transnational Studies Reader*, Sanjeev Khagram and Peggy Levitt, (eds.), pp. 50–63. New York and London: Routledge.

Aranya Siriphon (2007) "Dress and Cultural Strategy: Tai Peddlers in Transnational Trade along the Burma–Yunnan Frontier," *Asian Ethnicity* 8(3): pp. 219–34.

_____ (2010) "Thai Traditional Dress Knowledge, Cultural Transfer and Alternative Modernities along the Burmese–Yunnan Border." In *Cultural Resource Studies Asian Linkage Building Seminar 2010*, Working Paper, pp. 84–99. Kanazawa: Graduate School of Human and Socio-Environmental Studies, Kanazawa University.

Atchariya Nate-Chei (2011) "Beyond Commodification and Politicisation: Production and Consumption Practices of Authenticity in the White Tai Tourist Market in the Uplands of Vietnam," *ASEAS-Austrian Journal of South-East Asian Studies* 4(1): pp. 30–50.

Banchob Bandhumetha (1952) *Observations on Indo-Siamese Glossary: The Indo-Arayan Element in the Siamese Language, a Linguistic and Cultural Study*. Unpublished PhD dissertation, Banaras Hindu University, Varanasi, India.

Boonlert Visetpricha (2015) *Structural Violence and Homelessness: Searching for Happiness on the Streets of Manila, the Philippines*. Unpublished PhD dissertation, University of Wisconsin-Madison, Uniyed States.

Bourdieu, Pierre (1977) *Outline of a Theory of Practice*, Richard Nice (trans.). Cambridge: Cambridge University Press.

Brah, Avtar (1996) *Cartographies of Diaspora: Contesting Identities*. London and New York: Routledge.

Chantanee Charoensri (2014) "Thai Daughters, English Wives: A Critical Ethnography of Transnational Lives." In *Contemporary Socio-Cultural and Political Perspectives in Thailand*, Pranee Liamputtong, (ed.), pp. 299–310. Dordrect: Springer.

Charnvit Kasetsiri (1999) "Is 'Thai' Studies Still Possible?" Keynote address at the 7th International Conference on Thai Studies, Amsterdam, July 4–8.

Gupta, Akhil and James Ferguson, (eds.) (1997) *Culture, Power and Place: Explorations in Critical Anthropology*. Durham: Duke University Press.

Hannerz, Ulf (1997) "Flows, Boundaries and Hybrids: Keywords in Transnational Anthropology," Working Paper 2K-02, Department of Social Anthropology, Stockholm University.

Keyes, Charles F. (1978) "Ethnography and Anthropological Interpretation in the Study of Thailand," *The Study of Thailand: Analyses of Knowledge, Approaches, and Prospects in Anthropology, Art History, Economics, History and Political Science* 54: pp. 1–60.

——— (1995) "Who are the Tai? Reflections on the Invention of Identities." In *Ethnic Identity: Creation, Conflict, and Accommodation*, 3rd edition, Lola Romanucci-Ross and George De Vos, (eds.), pp. 136–60. London: Alta Mira Press.

——— (2010) "From Peasant to Cosmopolitan Villagers: Refiguring the 'Rural' in Northeastern Thailand." Presentation at Department of Anthropology, University of Copenhagen, September 1.

Kwanchewan Buadaeng (2007) "Ethnic Identities of the Karen Peoples in Burma and Thailand." In *Identity Matters: Ethnic and Sectarian Conflict*, James L. Peacock, Thornton, Patricia M. and Inman, Patrick. B., (eds.), pp. 73–97. New York, Oxford: Berghahn Books.

Mills, Mary Beth (1997) "Contesting the Margins of Modernity: Women, Migration, and Consumption in Thailand," *American Ethnologist* 24(1): pp. 37–61.

Natedao Taotawin (2008) "Cross-border Mobility, Sexual Violence and Otherness in the Thai–Lao Border Zone." In *Transborder Issues in the Greater Mekong Sub-Region*, Suchada Thaweesit, Peter Vail, and Rosalia Sciortino, (eds.), pp. 145–64. Ubon Ratchathani: MSSRC, Ubon Ratchathani University.

Niti Pawakapan (2005 [2003]) "No Longer Migrants: Southern New Zealand Chinese in the Twentieth Century." In *Chinese Migrants Abroad: Cultural, Educational, and Social Dimensions of the Chinese Diaspora*, Michael W. Charney, Brenda S.A Yeoh, Tong Chee Kiong, (eds.), pp. 204–28. Singapore: Singapore University Press.

——— (2009 [2006]) "'Once Were Burmese Shans': Reinventing Ethnic Identity in Northwestern Thailand." In *Centering the Margin: Agency and Narrative in Southeast Asian Borderlands*, Alexander Horstmann and Reed L. Wadley, (eds.), pp. 27–52. New York and Oxford: Berghahn Books.

Nobpaon Rabibhadana and Yoko Hayami (2013) "Seeking Haven and Seeking Jobs: Migrant Workers' Networks in Two Thai Locales," *Southeast Asian Studies* 2(2): pp. 243–83.

Panitee Suksomboon (2008) "Remittances and 'Social Remittances': Their Impact on Livelihoods of Thai Women in the Netherlands and Non-migrants in Thailand," *Journal of Gender, Technology and Development* 12: pp. 461–82.

_____ (2009) *Thai Migrant Women in the Netherlands: Cross-Cultural Marriages and Families*. Unpublished PhD dissertation, Leiden University, Netherlands.

Patcharin Lapanun (2010a.) "Becoming a Bride: Negotiating Material Desire, Sexuality, and One's Fate." Presentation at ANRC Workshop 'Human Security and Religious Certainty in Southeast Asia', Chiang Mai, January 15–17.

_____ (2010b) "Transnational Marriages of Rural Isan Women and the Local Influences." Presentation at the RCSD International Conference "Revisiting Agrarian Transformations in Southeast Asia: Empirical, Theoretical and Applied Perspectives", Chiang Mai, May 13–15.

_____ (2012a.) "It's Not Just About Money: Transnational Marriages of Isan Women," *Journal of Mekong Societies* 8(3): pp. 1–28.

_____ (2012b) "Social Relations and Tensions in Transnational Marriage for Rural Women in Isan Thailand." In *The Family in Flux in Southeast Asia: Institution, Ideology, Practice*, Yoko Hayami, Junko Koizumi, Chalidaporn Songsamphan, and Ratana Tosakul, (eds.), pp. 483–504. Kyoto: Kyoto University Press.

_____ (2013) *Logics of Desire and Transnational Marriage Practices in a Northeastern Thai Village*. Unpublished PhD dissertation, Vrije Universiteit of Amsterdam, Netherlands.

_____ (2014) "*Mia Farang*: An Emerging Social Category in Thai Society." Presented at the Asian Pacific Sociological Association (APSA) Conference 'Transforming Societies: Contestations and Convergences in Asia and the Pacific", Faculty of Social Sciences, Chiang Mai University, February 15–16.

Pattana Kitiarsa (2006) "Village Transnationalism: Transborder Identities among Thai-Isan Migrant Workers in Singapore." Working Paper 71, Asia Research Institute, National University of Singapore.

_____ (2014) *The "Bare Life" of Thai Migrants in Singapore*. Chiang Mai: Silkworm Books.

Pichet Saiphan and Khamphaeng Thipmountaly (2011) *Shaping Identity of the Tai Groups in Northern Border Area of Laos–Vietnam*. MECC research project. Bangkok: Princess Maha Chakri Sirindhorn Anthropology Centre.

Pitch Pongsawat (2007) *Border Partial Citizenship, Border Towns, and Thai–Myanmar Cross-Border Development: Case Studies of Two Thai Border Towns*. PhD dissertation, Department of City and Regional Planning, University of California at Berkeley.

Prasert Raengkla (2013) "Refuge and Emplacement through Buddhism: Karen Refugees and Religious Practices in a Northwestern Border Town of Thailand," *The Asia Pacific Journal of Anthropology* 14(1): pp. 8–22.

Ratana Tosakul (2010) "Cross-Border Marriage: Experiences of Village Women from Northeastern Thailand with Western Men." In *Asian Cross-border Marriage Migration: Demographic Patterns and Social Issues*, Melody Chia-Wen Lu and Wen-Shan Yang, (eds.), pp. 179–99. Amsterdam: Amsterdam University Press.

—— (2012) "Transnational Families: My Family Is Here and There." In *The Family in Flux in Southeast Asia: Institution, Ideology and Practice*, Yoko Hayami, Junko Koizumi, Chalidaporn Songsampan, and Ratana Tosakul, (eds.), pp. 505–26. Chiang Mai: Silkworm Books.

—— (2013) "Thai Diaspora in Japan." Presentation for a public lecture at the Graduate School of Arts and Literature, Seijo University, Tokyo, December 12.

Ratana Tosakul, Chintana Khouangvichit and Chandavane Sisoulath (2010) "Romances across Borders: Experiences from Laos." MECC research project. Bangkok: Princess Maha Chakri Sirindhorn Anthropology Centre.

Raya Muttarak (2004) "Domestic Services in Thailand: Reflection of Conflicts in Gender, Class and Ethnicity," *Journal of Southeast Asian Studies* 35(3): pp. 503–29.

Saipin Suputtamongkol (2007) *Technicians of the Soul: Insanity, Psychiatric Practice, and "Culture-Making" in Southern Italy.* Unpublished PhD dissertation, Department of Anthropology, Harvard University,.

Scupin, Raymond (1996) "The Emergence of Anthropology in Thailand: The Role of Suthep Soonthornpaesuch," *Crossroads: An Interdisciplinary Journal of Southeast Asian Studies*, 10(1): pp. 113–28.

Sirijit, Sunanta (2013) "Gendered Nation and Classed Modernity: Perceptions of *Mia Farang* (Foreigners' Wives) in Thailand." In *Cleavage, Connection and Conflict: Rural, Urban in Contemporary Asia*, T. Bunnell, D. Parthasarathy, and Eric C. Thompson, (eds.), pp. 183–200. Dordrecht: Springer.

—— (2014) "Thailand and the Global Intimate: Transnational Marriages, Health Tourism, and Retirement Migration." Working Paper 14-02, Max Planck Institute for the Study of Religious and Ethnic Diversity, Germany.

Sirijit, Sunanta and L. Angeles (2013) "From Rural Life to Transnational Wife: Agrarian Transition, Gender Mobility and Intimate Globalization in Transnational Marriages in Northeast Thailand," *Gender, Place, and Culture* 20(6): pp. 699–717.

Suchada Thaweesit (2013) "Integration of Contemporary Displaced Laotians in Northeastern Thailand." Presentation at the 4th Lao Studies Conference, Center for Southeast Asian Studies, University of Wisconsin, April 22.

Suthep Soonthornpaesuch (1977) *Islamic Identity in Chiang Mai City: A Historical and Structural Composition of Two Communities*. Unpublished PhD dissertation, University of California Berkeley, United States.

Sutthiporn Bunmak (2011a) "Migrant Networks of Irregular Nayu Workers in Malaysia: The Case of the Tom Yum Restaurants in Kuala Lumpur," *Malaysian Journal of Society and Space* 7(2): pp. 37–44.

_____ (2011b) "The Position and Meaning of Tom Yam Restaurants in Malaysia." Presentation at the 11th International Conference on Thai Studies, Bangkok, July 26–28.

Tambiah, Stanley J. (2000) "Transnational Movements, Diaspora and Multiple Modernities," *DAEDALUS* 129(1): pp. 163–94.

Thompson, Eric C. (2012) "Anthropology in Southeast Asia: National Traditions and Transnational Practices," *Asian Journal of Social Science* 40: pp. 664–89.

Wasan Panyagaew (2005) *Moving Dai: Towards an Anthropology of People "Living in Place" in the Borderlands of the Upper Mekong*. Unpublished PhD dissertation, Australian National University.

_____ (2007) "Re-Emplacing Homeland: Mobility, Locality, a Returned Exile, and a Thai Restaurant in Southwest China," *The Asia-Pacific Journal of Anthropology* 8(2): pp. 117–35.

_____ (2008) "Moving Dai: The Stories of a Minority Band from the Upper Mekong." In *Challenging the Limits: Indigenous Peoples of the Mekong Region*, Prasit Leepreecha, Don McCaskill, and Kwanchewan Buadaeng, (eds.), pp. 307–29. Chiang Mai: Mekong Press.

_____ (2010) "Cross-Border Journeys and Minority Monks: The Making of Buddhist Place in Southwest China," *Asian Ethnicity* 11(1): pp. 43–59.

_____ (2011) "Modern Road, Mobility and Changes in Community Life: A Study in Xishuangbanna, Yunnan Province in the People's Republic of China." Research Report 6, Regional Center for Social Sciences and Sustainable Development (RCSD), Chiang Mai University.

_____ (2013) "Remembering with Respect: History, Social Memory and the Cross-Border Journeys of a Charistic Lue Monk," *The Asia Pacific Journal of Anthropology* 14(1): pp. 23–40.

Wasan Panyagaew and Phra Sanpawut Apisit (2010) "Transporting Cultures across Borders: The Lue from Muang Lamphun to Muang Yong in 'Sipsong Panna'." MECC research project. Bangkok: Princess Maha Chakri Sirindhorn Anthropology Centre.

Welz, Gisela (2008) "Multiple Modernities: The Transnationalization of Cultures." In *Transcultural English Studies: Theories, Fictions, Realities*, Frank Schulze-Engler and Sissy Helff, (eds.), pp. 37–58. New York: Rodopi.

Yos Santasombat (2001) *Lak Chang: A Reconstruction of Tai Identity in Daikong*. The Thai-Yunnan Project, Canberra: Australian National University Press.

Yukti Mukdawijitra (2011) "Language Ideologies of Ethnic Orthography in a Multilingual State: The case of Ethnic Thai Orthographies in Vietnam," *Journal of the Southeast Asian Linguistics Society* 4(2): pp. 92–119.

—— (2012) "Contesting Imagined Communities: Politics of Script and Tai Cosmopolitanism in Upland Vietnam," *Cultural Dynamics* 24(2–3): pp. 207–25.

Thai Language

Adisorn Kerdmongkol (2011) "แรงงานข้ามชาติชาวปะโอ: ชีวิตข้ามพรมแดนบนพื้นที่ของอำนาจและการต่อรอง" ["Pa-O Migrant Workers from Myanmar in Bangkok Thailand: Power and Resistance"]. Unpublished Master's thesis, Faculty of Sociology and Anthropology, Thammasat University, Thailand.

Anan Ganjanapan (2003) "การทะลุกรอบคิดของทฤษฎีและวิธีวิทยาของการทะลุกรอบคิด" ["Surpassing Theoretical Constraints and Methodology for Surpassing"]. In *ทะลุกรอบคิดทางทฤษฎี* [*Breaking Through Theoretical Frameworks*], Anan Ganjanapan, (ed.), pp. 7–78. Bangkok: Princess Maha Chakri Sinrindhorn Anthropology Centre.

Banchob Bandhumedha (1944) "คำบาลีสันสกฤตที่ใช้ในภาษาไทย" ["Pali-Sanskrit in Thai Language"]. Unpublished Master's thesis, Faculty of Arts, Chulalongkorn University, Thailand.

—— (1983) *กาแลหม่านไตในรัฐฉาน* [*A Journey with the Tai in Shan State*]. Bangkok: The National Identity Commission

Bunchuai Srisawadi (2002) *ชาวเขาในไทย* [*Hilltribes in Thailand*]. 2nd edition. Bangkok: Matichon Publishing House.

—— (2004a) *ไทสิบสองปันนา* [*Tai Xishuangbanna*]. Book 1, 3rd edition. Bangkok: Siam Press.

—— (2004b) *ไทสิบสองปันนา* [*Tai Xishuangbanna*]. Book 2, 2nd edition. Bangkok: Siam Press.

—— (2004c) *๓๐ชาติในเชียงราย* [*Thirty Ethnic Groups in Chiang Rai Province*]. 3rd edition. Bangkok: Siam Press.

—— (2004d) *ราชอาณาจักรลาว* [*The Royal Kingdom of Laos*]. Bangkok: Siam Press.

Chattip Nartsupha (2000) "Foreword." In *หลักช้าง: การสร้างใหม่ของอัตลักษณ์ไตในใต้คง* [*Lak Chang: A Reconstruction of Tai Identity in Daikong*], Yos Santasombat, pp. 17–19. Bangkok: Amarin Printing and Publishing.

Jakkrit Sangkamanee (2009) "พรมแดนศึกษาและมานุษยวิทยาชายแดน: การเปิดพื้นที่สร้างเขตแดนและการข้ามพรมแดนของความรู้" ["Border Studies and Anthropology of Border Studies: The Making of Space, Territory, and Transboundary of Border Knowledge"], *Social Science Journal* 20: pp. 208–26.

—— (2012) "ชุมทางการค้ากับการสร้างสลายเส้นแบ่งพรมแดน: มานุษยวิทยาปริทัศน์" ["Trading at Crossroads and the De/re-territorialization of Borders: An Anthropological Review"], *Social Science Journal* 25(2): pp. 17–61.

Kanya Leelalai (2001) *ประวัติศาสตร์ชนชาติไต* [*The History of Ethnic Tai*]. Bangkok: Amarin Printing and Publishing.

Nattchawal Pocapanishwong (2014) "การเชื่อม (ข้าม) ถิ่นที่: ปฏิสัมพันธ์ของผู้คนบนเมืองชายแดนกับการต่อรองความหมายผ่านพื้นที่/ชุมชนทางศาสนาของผู้อพยพข้ามพรมแดนชาวพม่าในจังหวัดระนอง" ["Translocality: The Interaction of Peoples in Borderland and the Negotiation in Religious Sphere of the Transnational Burmese Migrant in Ranong Province]. Unpublished PhD dissertation, College of Interdisciplinary Studies, Thammasat University, Thailand.

Nidhi Eawsiwong (2001) "Introduction." In *ประวัติศาสตร์ชนชาติไต* [*The History of Ethnic Tai*], Kanya Leelalai, pp. 18–26. Bangkok: Thailand Research Fund.

Office of the National Culture Commission, Ministry of Education, Thailand (1995) *การศึกษาวัฒนธรรมชนชาติไต* [*A Study of Tai Culture*]. Bangkok: Kuru Sapha Lardpao Press.

Pattana Kitiarsa (2003) "Introduction." In *หุ่นน้ำเวียดนาม* [*The Vietnamese Water Puppet*], Silapakit Tikantikul, pp. 9–25. Chiang Mai: In-Som Fund for Anthropological Research.

Pichet Saiphan (2004) "การแปลงผ่านอัตลักษณ์ชาติพันธุ์ในภาคตะวันตกเฉียงเหนือของเวียดนาม" ["Transforming Ethnic Identity in Northwestern Vietnam"]. In *ความเป็นไทย, ชาติและชาติพันธุ์ : วิถีชีวิตและความหลากหลายในโลกปัจจุบัน* [*Thai-ness, Nation and Ethnicity: Ways of Life and Diversity in Contemporary World*], Vipas Patchayaporn, (ed.), pp. 95–136. Paper Series Number 38. Bangkok: Princess Maha Chakri Sirindhorn Anthropology Centre.

Pinkaew Luangaramsri (2011) *ทุนนิยมชายแดน นิคมอุตสาหกรรม และการเปลี่ยนแปลงของสังคม: เกษตรกรรมในภาคใต้ของลาว.* [*Border Capitalism, Industrial Estate and Social Transformations: Agriculture in Southern Laos*]. Chiang Mai: Faculty of Social Sciences, Chiang Mai University.

_____ (2013) *รายงานฉบับสมบูรณ์โครงการย้อนพินิจคุณภาพการศึกษาด้านสังคมวิทยาและมานุษยวิทยา* [*Final Report of Reassessing Educational Quality of Thai Sociology and Anthropology*]. Bangkok: Thailand Research Fund.

Prasit Leeprecha (2002) "เครือญาติข้ามพรมแดนรัฐชาติ: กรณีกลุ่มชาติพันธุ์ม้ง" ["Transnational Kinship: A Case of Ethnic Hmong"], *Warasan Sangkhomsat* 15(1): pp. 167–86.

Pornpan Khemkunasai (2012) *ความสัมพันธ์บริเวณพื้นที่ชายแดนผ่านเครือข่ายการค้าข้าวระหว่างรัฐ : กรณีศึกษาหมู่บ้านนูโร อำเภอเวียง จ. นราธิวาส* [*Borderlands Relations Through the Network of Rice Trade across States: Nuro Community, Wiang District of Narathiwat Province*]. Bangkok: Thailand National Research Fund.

Pruk Taotawin (2007) "การค้าข้ามพรมแดนในฐานะปฏิบัติการเชื่อมต่อโลกกับท้องถิ่น" ["Cross-border Trade as a Practice Linking Global to Local"], *Social Science Journal* 19(2): pp. 156–91.

Ratana Boonmathya (2002) "พิธีมะเนากับตัวตนคนกะฉิ่น" ["The Manau Ritual Dance and the Kachin Identity"]. In *อัตลักษณ์, ชาติพันธุ์ และความเป็นชายขอบ* [*Identity, Ethnicity and Marginality*], Pinkaew Luangaramsri, (ed.), pp. 118–71. Bangkok: Princess Maha Chakri Sirindhorn Anthropology Centre.

_____ (2005) "ภรรยาฝรั่ง: ผู้หญิงอีสานกับการแต่งงานข้ามวัฒนธรรม" ["Farang's Wives: Village Women from Northeastern Thailand and Cross-cultural Marriages"], *Journal of Mekong Societies* 1(2): pp. 1–52.

Shalardchai Ramitanondh, Ranoo Wichasilp, and Virada Somsavadi, (eds.) (1998) *ไต* [*Tai*]. Chiang Mai: Women's Studies Center, Chiang Mai University.

Silapakit Tikantikul (2003) *หุ่นน้ำเวียดนาม* [*The Vietnamese Water Puppet*]. Chiang Mai: In-Som Fund for Anthropological Research.

Samerchai Poolsuwan (1996) *สัญลักษณ์ในงานจิตรกรรมไทยระหว่างพุทธศตวรรษที่ 19 ถึง 24* [*Symbols in Thai Fine Arts from 19 to 24 B.E.*]. Bangkok: Thammasat University Press.

_____ (2001) *วิทยาศาสตร์กับความจริงในวัฒนธรรมไทย* [*Natural Science and Truth in Thai Culture*]. Bangkok: Kob Fai Publishing House.

Suddan Wisudthirak (2002) *ชีวิต ความคิด และการเดินทางของศาสตาจารย์ ดร. บรรจบ พันธุเมธา* [*Life, Thoughts and Journeys of Professor Dr. Banchob Bandhumedha*]. Bangkok: Thai Khadi Research Institute, Thammasat University.

Sumitr Pitiphat (1999) *คนไทและเครือญาติในมณฑลไหหลำและกุ้ยโจวประเทศจีน* [*Tai and their Kin Groups in Hainan and Kui Chow, China*]. Bangkok: Thai Khadi Research Institute, Thammasat University.

_____ (2000) *คนไทเมืองกว่า ไทแถงและไทเมืองในประเทศเวียดนาม* [*Tai of Qua, Tai of Thaeng and Tai Muang in Vietnam*]. Bangkok: Thai Khadi Research Institute, Thammasat University.

_____ (2003a) *คนไทแดงในแขวงหัวพัน สาธารณรัฐประชาธิปไตยประชาชนลาว* [*Tai Daeng in Hua Phan, Lao PDR*]. Bangkok: Thai Khadi Research Institute, Thammasat University.

_____ (2003b) *ศาสนาและความเชื่อไทดำในสิบสองจุไท สาธารณรัฐสังคมนิยมเวียดนาม* [*Religion and Beliefs of the Black Tai in Sipsong Chu Tai, Vietnam*]. Bangkok: Thai Khadi Research Institute, Thammasat University.

Sumitr Pitiphat and Damrongphol Inchan (2003) *ขบวนการฟื้นฟูภาษาความเชื่อและพิธีกรรมของไทยอาหมในรัฐอัสสัมประเทศอินเดีย* [*Movements for the Revival of Linguistics, Religious Beliefs and Rituals of Tai Ahom in Assam, India*]. Bangkok: Thai Khadi Research Institute, Thammasat University.

Sumitr Pitiphat, Paritta Koanantakul, Samerchai Poolsuwan, and Wilaiwan Kanittanan (2002) *ชุมชนไทในพม่าตอนเหนือ : รัฐฉานตอนใต้ ภาคมัณฑะเลย์ และคำตี่หลวง* [*Tai Communities in the Shan State and Khamti Luong of Upper Burma*]. Bangkok: Thai Khadi Research Institute, Thammasat University.

Sumitr Pitiphat, Pichet Saiphan, Narisa Detsupa, and Tiamjit Puangsomjit (2003) *ใย้ ไต และเกาลาน:กลุ่มชาติพันธุ์ไทในเวียดนามเหนือ* [*Tai Ethnic Groups in Vietnam: Tay, Giay and Cao Lan*]. Bangkok: Thai Khadi Research Institute, Thammasat University.

Sumitr Pitiphat and Samerchai Poolsuwan (2000) "ไท" และ "จ้วง" ในมณฑลยูนนาน สาธารณรัฐประชาชนจีน บทวิเคราะห์จากข้อมูลภาคสนาม ["Tai" and "Chung" in Yunnan Province,

China: An Analysis from Fieldwork]. Bangkok: Thai Khadi Research Institute, Thammasat University.

Sumitr Pitiphat, Tiamjit Phuangsomjit, and Pichet Saipan (2003) *ไทแดงที่อำเภอบาเทื้อก จังหวัดแทงหัว ประเทศเวียดนาม: สภาพชีวิตและการเปลี่ยนแปลงทางวัฒนธรรม* [*Tai Daeng in Ba Teuk District of Hua Theang in Vietnam: Living Conditions and Cultural Change*]. Bangkok: Thai Khadi Research Institute, Thammasat University.

Sumitr Pitiphat and Samerchai Poolsuwan (2001) *คนไตและลาจีในภาคเหนือของเวียดนาม* [*The Tai and Lachi in Northern Vietnam*]. Bangkok: Thai Khadi Research Institute, Thammasat University.

_____ (2003) *คนไตในซือเหมา มณฑลยูนนาน สาธารณรัฐประชาชนจีน ประวัติศาสตร์การเมือง สังคมและวัฒนธรรม* [*Tai in Si Mao, Yunnan Province: Political History, Society, and Culture*]. Bangkok: Thai Khadi Research Institute, Thammasat University.

Tassana Nualsomsri (2013) "ขบวนการเคลื่อนไหวเพื่อคงสถานะพิเศษเมืองยอกยาการ์ต้าและสุลต่านในประเทศอินโดนีเซีย" ["'Yogya Tetap Istimewa': A Movement on Maintaining Yogya's and Sultan's Specialty in Indonesia"]. Unpublished Master's thesis, Faculty of Sociology and Anthropology, Thammasat University, Thailand.

Wasan Panyagaew (2009) "เณรพระข้ามชาติ: ขบวนการรื้อฟื้นและสืบสานพระศาสนาของชาวลื้อสิบสองปันนา" ["Transnational Novices and Monks: Movement for Revival and Sustenance of Buddhism of Lue Xishaungbanna"], *Wasasan Silpasat*, Special Issue: pp. 129–59.

_____ (2011) "บทบรรณาธิการ: วัยรุ่นกับวัฒนธรรมสมัยนิยม" ["Editorial: Youth and Popular Culture"], *Warasan Sangkhomsat* 22(1): pp. 7–22. Chiang Mai University.

_____ (2012) *ลื้อข้ามแดน: การเดินทางของคนหนุ่มสาวชาวลื้อเมืองยองรัฐฉานประเทศพม่า* [*Moving across Borders: A Journey of Young Lue from Moung Yong, Shan State, Myanmar*]. Chiang Mai: Center for Research and Academic Service, Chiang Mai University.

_____ (2015) "ชีวิตและงานของ ผศ. สุเทพ สุนทรเภสัช : นักมานุษยวิทยารุ่นบุกเบิกของประเทศไทย." ["Life and Work of Assistant Professor Suthep Soonthornpaesuch: A Pioneering Thai Anthropologist"]. Faculty of Social Sciences, Chiang Mai University.

Worachet Khiewchan (2011) "โรงเรียนชายแดน: ปฏิบัติการของอำนาจอธิปัตย์ในสภาวะยกเว้น" ["The Border School: Sovereign Power in the State of Exception"]. Unpublished Master's thesis, Faculty of Sociology and Anthropology, Thammasat University, Thailand.

Websites and TV Series

OkNation. www.oknation.net, accessed on April 19, 2014.

Princess Maha Chakri Sirindhorn Anthropology Centre. www.sac.or.th; accessed on April 24, 2014.

Voice TV, IASEAN Program Series, accessed on May 3, 2014.

About the Contributors

Jose Jowel Canuday is Assistant Professor and Chair of the Department of Sociology and Anthropology at the Ateneo de Manila University. He was a journalist based in Mindanao in the Southern Philippines before earning a master's in anthropology from Xavier University and a doctorate in social and cultural anthropology from the University of Oxford.

Dang Nguyen Anh is Professor and Vice President of the Vietnam Academy of Social Sciences (VASS). He participates in and coordinates a range of research activities on social development, human migration and population in Southeast Asia and the Mekong subregion. Prof. Anh is also a guest lecturer at the National University of Hanoi, the National Economic University, University of Jakarta, Tshinghua University and Kyoto University. He is the author of numerous monographs and academic papers, including several articles that appeared in *Asian and Pacific Migration Journal*, *Population Research and Policy Review*, *International Migration Review*, *Asia-Pacific Population Journal*, *International Journal for Family Planning* and *World Development*. He holds a PhD in sociology from Brown University.

Victor T. King is Professor of Borneo Studies, Institute of Asian Studies, Universiti Brunei Darussalam; Emeritus Professor, University of Leeds; and Professorial Research Associate, School of Oriental and African Studies, London. He was formerly Executive Director of the White Rose East Asia Centre, Universities of Leeds and Sheffield (2006–2012). He has long-standing interests in the sociology-anthropology of Southeast Asia, covering social and cultural change, development, tourism and heritage, ethnicity and identity, area studies, as well as museum and photographic studies. He has edited or co-edited eight books in these fields since 2013.

Maria F. Mangahas is Associate Professor in the Department of Anthropology at the University of the Philippine Diliman. She received her PhD in social anthropology from the University of Cambridge in 2001. Her field research has been among fishing communities in the Philippines and she has published or presented papers on indigenous coastal resources management, collective fishing technology, fisher knowledges, systems of sharing and sharing-out, gear conflicts and social change, as well as notions of "luck" and leadership. She also did research into the phenomenon of "digitized scandal" including its role as a form of alternative media. She was President of the Ugnayang Pang-Aghamtao, Inc. (Anthropological Association of the Philippines) from 2014–2017.

Nguyen Van Chinh is Associate Professor and Head of the Department of Development Anthropology at the University of Social Sciences and Humanities, VNU Hanoi. He received a PhD in anthropology from the University of Amsterdam. As a specialist in the fields of anthropology of development, his academic concerns and publications concentrate on ethnicity, cross-border mobility, migration and development in Vietnam and the Mekong region.

Chivoin Peou is Lecturer at the Royal University of Phnom Penh. He holds a PhD in sociology from the University of Melbourne. His research and teaching covers the life course, young people, social change and uncertainty, and media studies. His work has appeared in the *Journal of Youth Studies*, *Journal of Education and Work*, *Journal of Rural Studies* and *International Journal of Emerging Technologies and Society*, among others.

Iwan Pirous completed his master's degree at Nottingham Trent University. His research and writing has focused on Iban borderland identities in Borneo and the meaning of modernity for Indonesian artists. His work has appeared in the *Indonesian Journal of Social and Cultural Anthropology* among other publications.

Emma E. Porio is Professor and Chair (1996–2002; 2008–2014) in the Department of Sociology and Anthropology at the School of

Social Sciences, Ateneo de Manila University. She holds an AB in anthropology from the University of San Carlos, an MA (Population Studies) and a PhD (Sociology), both from the University of Hawaii (Manoa). Her research and teaching cover sociology, quantitative and qualitative methods, theories of development, gender, class and ethnicity in the Philippines and Southeast Asia, as well as risk and resilience to climate disasters. Her work has appeared in the *Asian Journal of Social Science, Current Sociology, Philippine Sociological Review* and *Nature*, among others. Her most recent work is *Ecological Liberation Theology: Faith-Based Approaches to Poverty and Climate Change in the Philippines* (with W. Holden and K. Nadeau), Springer Publications (2017).

Suzanna R. Roldan is Lecturer at the Department of Sociology and Anthropology, Ateneo de Manila University. Her areas of interest are in anthropology of health and maritime anthropology, economic anthropology, applied anthropology and qualitative research methods. She did ethnographic research in Bicol, Pangasinan, and La Union as well as supported social development organizations' (government and non-government) livelihood development initiatives nationwide. She received her Master of Arts in anthropology from the University of the Philippines.

Vineeta Sinha is Professor and Head of the Department of Sociology at the National University of Singapore. She holds a PhD in anthropology from Johns Hopkins University. Her research areas include Hindu religiosity in the Diaspora, religion-state encounters, critique of sociological theory, and women in academia and leadership. She is author of numerous books including *A New God in the Diaspora* (NUS Press, 2005), *Religion and Commodification* (Routledge, 2010), *Religion-State Encounters in Hindu Domains* (Springer, 2011) and *Sociological Theory beyond the Canon*, with Syed Farid Alatas (Palgrave Macmillan, 2017).

Eric C. Thompson is Associate Professor in the Department of Sociology at the National University of Singapore. He holds a PhD in sociocultural anthropology from the University of Washington. His research and teaching covers anthropology, gender studies, Southeast Asian studies, and research methods. His work has appeared in the journals *American Ethnologist, Current Anthropology, Jurnal*

Antropologi Indonesia and *Journal of Sociology and Anthropology* (Thammasat University), among others. He is author of *Unsettling Absences: Urbanism in Rural Malaysia* (NUS Press, 2007).

Ratana Tosakul is a Visiting Professor at the Center for Global Language and Society in Higher Education, Tokyo University of Foreign Studies. She holds a PhD in sociocultural anthropology from the University of Washington. Her research focuses on transnational anthropology with gender sensitivity and is based in Thailand and Japan. She has published in both Thai and English on topics of rural development, gender relations and transnational marriage.

Yunita T. Winarto is Professor in the Department of Anthropology, Faculty of Social and Political Sciences at Universitas Indonesia. She holds a PhD in anthropology from the Australian National University. Her research and community engagement focus on the dialectics of scientific and local knowledge, natural resource management in agriculture, and response farming to climate change. Her works have been published in several journals and edited volumes. She is the author of *Seeds of Knowledge: The Beginning of Integrated Pest Management in Java* (Yale Southeast Asia Council, 2004).

Yeoh Seng-Guan is Associate Professor of Social Anthropology at the School of Arts & Social Sciences, Monash University Malaysia. He holds a PhD from the University of Edinburgh. He is an urban anthropologist who has done fieldwork in Malaysia, the Philippines, and Indonesia. Besides academic publications, he also produces ethnographic documentaries.

Zawawi Ibrahim is Professor of Anthropology in the Faculty of Arts and Social Sciences and Institute of Asian Studies at Universiti Brunei Darussalam. He holds a PhD in social anthropology from Monash Universty, Melbourne. His work has appeared in *Journal of Contemporary Asia*, *Critical Asian Studies*, *Modern Asian Studies* and *Asian Journal of Social Science*, among others. He is author of *The Malay Labourer: By the Window of Capitalism* (ISEAS, 1998) and editor of *Representation, Identity and Multiculturalism in Sarawak* (Malaysian Social Science Association, 2008) and *Social Science and Knowledge in a Globalising World* (PSSM, 2012) among other works.

Index